POPULATION

POPULATION
A BASIC
ORIENTATION

second edition

Charles B. Nam
Florida State University

Susan G. Philliber
Columbia University

PRENTICE-HALL, INC., Englewood Cliffs, New Jersey 07632

Library of Congress Cataloging in Publication Data

NAM, CHARLES B.
   Population : a basic orientation.

   Bibliography:
   Includes index.
   1. Population. 2. Demography. I. Philliber, Susan
Gustavus,   II. Title.
HB871.N25 1984   304.6'2   83-4478
ISBN 0-13-687210-7

Editorial supervision and
  interior design: Serena Hoffman
Cover design: Ben Santora
Manufacturing buyer: John Hall

The first edition of this book was published under the title
Population: The Dynamics of Demographic Change.

PRINTED IN THE UNITED STATES OF AMERICA

10 9 8 7 6 5 4 3 2 1

ISBN 0-13-687210-7

PRENTICE-HALL INTERNATIONAL, INC., *London*
PRENTICE-HALL OF AUSTRALIA PTY. LIMITED, *Sydney*
EDITORA PRENTICE-HALL DO BRASIL, LTDA., *Rio de Janiero*
PRENTICE-HALL CANADA, INC., *Toronto*
PRENTICE-HALL OF INDIA PRIVATE LIMITED, *New Delhi*
PRENTICE-HALL OF JAPAN, INC., *Tokyo*
PRENTICE-HALL OF SOUTHEAST ASIA PTE. LTD., *Singapore*
WHITEHALL BOOKS LIMITED, *Wellington, New Zealand*

To Marjorie and Bill Wesley

CONTENTS

PREFACE

In recent years, public attention has increasingly been focused on the rapid changes in population taking place throughout the world and the impact that these changes have on ways of human life. The call for greater concern about population developments has come from many quarters—government officials, lay leaders, environmentalists, and social scientists. Their approaches to the population question are varied. Some sound an alarm of impending doom, while others express complete faith in the human race to conquer its major problems; still others reserve normative judgment about the course of population and attempt instead to study the causes and consequences of population change. The latter approach is that of the scientist and, especially, of the *demographer*—the specialist in population studies. It is the approach taken in this volume.

Every textbook is written with certain objectives in mind. Ours can be stated explicitly at the outset:

First, the book is written primarily for undergraduate college students taking a first course in population or demography. The book can be used in departments of sociology, economics, political science, geography, or urban planning. This is not to say that it will not be of interest to others, for we have attempted to write it in such a way that a wide audience will find it both readable and informative. We have adopted a nontechnical approach in the main body of the text, and reserved more technical discussion for supplements at the end of each chapter.

Second, in contrast both with lengthy volumes, which often contain more information than the reader wants or has time for, and with exceedingly short books, which do not leave the reader with an adequate understanding of the subject matter, this treatise is designed to deal with the fundamentals of population study in an economical but complete manner. It should be possible for the student to cover the whole book in a reasonable amount of time, say in an academic term. If further information is desired, suggested readings are listed at the end of each chapter.

Third, the book gives a basic social orientation to demography. Any study of population must necessarily touch upon several academic fields, since the subject has medical, biological, geographical, psychological, and economic, as well as sociological, aspects. But given our own limited training and our belief that a general social approach is the single most useful one to studying population, we have tried to stress it. This means that we will be looking at population change mainly from the perspective of the sociologist, but we will not ignore other perspectives where they seem to be particularly relevant in order to comprehend population trends.

Fourth, the book perceives population in a dynamic framework. Too often the student of population is made to see it as a static phenomenon, with people as almost lifeless objects making up a society or community and identified as statistics in a tabular presentation. Statistics are valuable as a tool for studying populations mainly because they enable us to give a needed quantitative dimension to demography; censuses and vital records are critical to demographic analysis mainly because we can use them to provide a snapshot of the continuing process of population change. However, understanding the demographic process means not only counting and classifying people, but also fully comprehending the mechanics of the process—what generates it, how it takes place, what conditions modify it.

Finally, we want to inform readers about both the determinants and consequences of demographic change. Population factors and social factors can be viewed as in continuous interaction, the second set affecting the first, and vice versa. If population change is to be understood by key decision-makers as well as by the public, its social determinants must be analyzed and those that are most critical identified. Once this is achieved, intelligent decisions can be made about how, if at all, the population process might be altered. At the same time, if an understanding of population change is needed to assess its impact on the quality of life, then the alternative ways demographic change affects social institutions and the behavior of individuals and groups in society must be traced. At the close of each chapter, we have introduced issues for discussion that enable teacher and student alike to explore determinants and consequences of population change more fully.

Achieving these objectives is a large order that cannot be solely the work of two persons. While some of the research reported here, the particular approach used, the organization of materials, and the form of expression are our own, the book is the result of the efforts of many people. We are particularly grateful to our fellow social scientists who, over the years, have published the results of their studies and thus enabled us to integrate them into a more comprehensive framework. Phillips Cutright of Indiana University read drafts of this second edition, as he did of the first, and offered valuable suggestions for revision. We are also grateful to the following reviewers for their helpful suggestions: Paul Tschetter, East Carolina University; George F. Stine, Millersville State College; Wilfred G. Marston, University of Michigan; and Mark La Gory, University of Alabama at Birmingham. Secretarial assistance was provided by Marie Burkel and Chris Reams. Finally, thanks are due to Ed Stanford and Susan Taylor for their interest in seeing that a book of this type remained available for academic use and in an attractive format.

CHARLES B. NAM
SUSAN PHILLIBER

CHAPTER ONE
THE POPULATION OUTLOOK

"Boy, did I have an afternoon! The census man was here."

Drawing by George Price; © 1940, 1968 *The New Yorker* Magazine, Inc.

Our introduction to the study of population focuses on three areas: a general conceptual orientation, a review of demographic data sources, and an examination of world population trends. These topics will provide us with the basic tools for a more intensive analysis of the dynamics of population change.

PERSPECTIVES ON POPULATION

The term *population* conjures up varying images. To some, population means a set of numbers in a census report or a statistical abstract. To others, it is an aggregate of people who are found in a given location. To still others, it is a target group for whom the government, business, or other organization attempts to provide services, sell products, or plan the future.

Population can be all of these things, but these views of it are only static ones; people appear as if objects in a snapshot. To a demographer, the term *population* indeed represents the same phenomena, but it also has a dynamic aspect. Populations never remain the same from one time period to the next. There may be additions to the population or subtractions from it, the ages of its members advance, and other characteristics of members are altered as time goes by.

Population Behavior

In order to understand the various dimensions of population, we must first examine information about its past and present situation and we must explore the dynamic factors that produce and change it. We are thus dealing with the what, when, how, and why of population processes.

In a very real sense, population is the result of behavior. A variety of behavioral conditions determine whether or not a baby is born, a person lives or dies, someone moves or does not, or some population characteristics change. Social processes are forever shaping the demographic world in which we live.

When social scientists speak of behavior, they refer to ways of thinking and acting. Population change can be looked at as the result of thinking and acting with regard to population matters; hence, the notion of population as behavior. Moreover, behavior can be analyzed at different levels of thinking and acting. That is, elements of population change are the outcomes of behavior on the part of individuals, couples, families, kinship networks, associational groups, reference groups, neighborhoods, communities, societies, and other social groupings.

Levels of Population Analysis

For the sake of convenience, we may identify three categories to describe these levels of behavior:

The first we are calling *micro*, because it focuses on individuals (or couples) who are ultimate decision-makers concerning population actions.

The second is identified as *medial*, and refers to families, church groups, work groups, neighborhoods, and other groups of which individuals are members or with which they identify. These units mediate between the larger social forms and the individual.

The larger forms are specified as *macro*, and include regions, societies, and the world itself.

Population processes may be examined at any of these levels. For example, we may want to compare the population growth rates of nations, and how groups within the nation change in size may not be of special interest. Or we might consider religious-group differences in fertility, and how individuals pattern their fertility may be of lesser consequence. Or perhaps it is the variation among individuals in chances of survival that captures our attention, and death rates at macro and medial levels are not particularly relevant.

Alternatively, the three categories will sometimes represent levels of influence or sets of factors that impinge upon population outcomes. For example, a macro influence on fertility might be a nation's level of economic development, which has an inverse relationship to the birthrate. Federal health laws will have an impact on mortality. Climatic factors will induce some people to change their residence.

Medial influences are generally normative influences that operate through institutions of the community or group attachments of the individual. They are the mores or folkways that set standards of behavior for persons. Parents or other family members approve or disapprove of population-related behaviors. The local church pastor gives sermons on those topics. One's social-class grouping defines the life-style to be maintained and the world views that provide an outlook on demographic behavior.

Finally, the micro influences appear in the form of unique characteristics of the individual and his or her idiosyncratic ways of thinking and acting. As individuals live in society and within groups, they learn and internalize some norms and not others. They develop tastes for particular values and goods. In addition, there is the personal biological makeup of each individual. A man or woman may be physiologically unable to produce children. An invalid may be incapable of migration, and a person with a genetic deficiency may be subject to the risk of early mortality. Any complete explanation of population change would have to take into account the interaction of these individual factors with those at the group and societal levels.

In the parts of this book that follow, we will utilize these alternative perspectives and draw upon them where appropriate. It is not our intention to force all forms of population analysis into a rigid mold. The concepts already mentioned, as well as others referred to throughout this volume, are useful only to the extent that they help us comprehend the determinants and consequences of population structures and processes.

INFORMATION ON POPULATION

Demographers and other social and behavioral scientists have conducted different types of research that provide a knowledge base for learning about population structure and change. Their ability to produce such knowledge is highly dependent upon the availability of sources of data that include various items of population interest.

Availability of useful data is a prerequisite for analysis of population trends. Satisfactory demographic information is likewise necessary for an accurate appraisal of how population interrelates with other aspects of society. It is appropriate, therefore, to ask the following questions:

1. What types of population data are we usually interested in?
2. What are the various sources of population data?
3. Which sources provide which types of data?
4. What can we say about the quality of population data?

Types of Population Data

The range of items of population information that analysts might want is enormous, but all of this information can be conveniently encompassed in seven categories: population size, mortality, fertility, geographic mobility, population composition, population distribution, and population characteristics.

Population size refers to the sheer numbers of people, but these numbers may be of interest as of the distant past, the recent past, the present, or the future; and we may want to know what these head counts are in the world, a country, a city, or our immediate neighborhood. Studying basic population change means analyzing shifts in numbers of people over time.

Mortality is concerned with deaths that occur in a population, and there may be interest in knowing their causes, their distribution across demographic categories such as age and sex, and their timing. When we try to account for changes in population size over time, mortality change is one of three essential components of that overall growth or decline.

Fertility is a second component of population change; it deals with the reproductive behavior of women and men, their efforts and relative success at fertility control, and their actual childbearing performance. We often focus our attention on fertility of particular groups, such as teenagers or Roman Catholics, in an effort to see if, and why, they behave differently from other groups in their fertility-related activity.

Geographic mobility is the third component of population change and encompasses many types of movements, including local, interregional, and international changes of residence, as well as moves of a more temporary nature, such as commuting and establishing part-time second residences.

Population composition conventionally refers to the age, sex, and racial or ethnic attributes of people, those largely ascribed features of basic demographic structure.

Population distribution has to do with geographic location of people or their attributes, generally classified by particular places or types of areas, ranging from a given city, town, county, or country to constructs such as urban or metropolitan areas.

Population characteristics, finally, include all other identifiers of people, such as their family status, education, occupation, income, and additional social and economic characteristics.

This sevenfold classification of types of data is somewhat arbitrary, but the importance of each category is reflected in the substantial treatment of all of them in the remaining chapters of this book. In their totality, they constitute the fundamental aspects of all inquiries into the dynamics of population change.

Sources of Population Data

Demographic information can be obtained from a variety of sources, among which are censuses, vital registration systems, population registers, sample household surveys, governmental and private records, and estimation techniques. Sources such as the census and vital registration are traditional, going back to early periods of history. Other sources, such as the sample survey, many governmental records, and estimation techniques, are fairly modern developments. Moreover, the latter are increasingly being used in population research.

Censuses are familiar to most people, since they are taken in all parts of the world and are administered by countries that include nearly all of the population of the globe. Even if individuals have not themselves been interviewed by census takers or completed census forms, they are generally aware that census information about them was obtained from adult members of their households or from neighbors. Some may deny that they were counted in a census, because they were unaware that a census taker called or a form was delivered by the post office, but the chances are exceedingly high that they were included, because censuses are known to be substantially complete, particularly in modern nations. Some people are missed, of course, and some are counted more than once.

A population census is a costly and time-consuming operation. The total process involves collecting, compiling, editing, and publishing demographic, economic, and social data for a specified date covering all persons in a delimited territory. Reports of the population of the United States from the 1980 census refer to the census date of April 1, 1980. What is probably scarcely known is that preparatory work on that census began shortly after the 1970 census was taken, and work relative to the products of that census may still be going on in 1987 or later. Decisions had to be made very early about how the census was to be carried out, what questions were to be asked, what segments of the population different questions would refer to, how the reported information was to be coded and tabulated, and how the resulting data would be disseminated to the public. Procedures were developed that were tested, revised, and retested in locations throughout the country. Census materials were subsequently prepared, the census field staff hired, and the count taken. A variety of publications, computer data tapes, and other unpublished tabulations are being provided for public use.

Since the United Nations now provides recommendations for the conduct and content of censuses, it is not surprising that there is some similarity in the censuses of different countries. Still, each nation's government must decide which items of information should be collected and what resources are available to take the census. Consequently, there are some differences in the content of the data forms that are used. Table 1.1 shows comparisons of census items for the United States in 1980, Canada in 1981, and Indonesia in 1981. The first two are highly developed countries; the third is a developing nation.

TABLE 1.1 Population items on census schedules

Item	United States 1980	Canada 1981	Indonesia 1981
Sex	E	E	E
Age/date of birth	E	E	E
Household relationship	E	E	E
Marital status	E	E	E
First marriage date or age	S	S	S
Number of children ever born	S	S	S
Number of children still living			S
Last child born			S
Contraceptive knowledge and use			S
Place of birth	S	S	S
Residence 5 years ago	S	S	S
Last place of residence			S
Current place of residence	E	E	E
Duration of residence in current province			S
Citizenship	S	S	
Year of immigration	S	S	
Ancestry/nationality	S	S	E
Race	E		
Spanish/Hispanic origin or descent	E		
Current language	S	S	S
Language first learned		E	
Speak English	S	S	
Speak French		S	
Religion		S	E
Veteran status	S		
Disability or handicap	S		E
Sickness during the past week			S
Activity during the past week	S	S	S
Hours worked last week	S	S	S
Occupation	S	S	S
Industry	S	S	S
Class of worker	S	S	
Place of work	S	S	
Travel time to work	S		
Means of transportation to work	S		
Weeks worked in previous year	S	S	
Activity 5 years ago	S		
School enrollment	S	S	
Educational attainment	S	S	S
Nonregular schooling completed		S	
Degrees, certificates, or diplomas		S	
Amount of income by source in previous year	S	S	

E = *asked of everyone*
S = *asked of sample*

Certain questions are asked of everyone in all three censuses and might be regarded as universal items of information. These include sex, age, relationship among household members, marital status, and current place of residence. They define family composition and habitat. Other questions are asked of samples of persons in all three censuses and can, therefore, be considered of common importance but not as essential as the first group. These include time of marriage and child-bearing, residence at birth and five years earlier, ancestry or nationality and language, economic activity, and educational attainment. They are measures of two of the components of population change—fertility and mobility—and of three crucial societal conditions—ethnicity, education, and the economy. The ethnicity questions, however, are basic enough to be asked of everyone in Indonesia but only of samples in Canada and the United States.

The disparities in census content are intriguing. Among the ethnic questions, religion is an item in Canada and Indonesia but not in the United States, while race and Hispanic origin are unique to the United States, and speaking the French, as well as English, language is unique to Canada. Items related to fertility are most detailed in Indonesia, citizenship and time of immigration are peculiar to the United States and Canada, veteran status is found only in the United States census, as is elaboration of travel-to-work patterns, and monetary income is absent only from the Indonesian census. These variations reflect the circumstances that are important in each culture. Each has its own ethnic concerns, and the birthrate is a more pressing problem in Indonesia, whereas immigration, home-to-work travel, and monetary income are much less relevant in that country.

Vital registration entails systematically collecting and organizing records of critical or vital life events; namely, those relating to births, stillbirths, adoptions, marriages, annulments, separations, divorces, and deaths. The records provide a validation of these events that are frequently useful for personal reasons. For example, proof of one's age can be established from a birth certificate. For demographic purposes, vital registration is an important adjunct to a census. Censuses are usually taken every five or ten years. Vital statistics, especially on births and deaths, permit an assessment of how the population is changing between censuses and what are the components of population change.

Although data from vital registrations are published periodically, usually annually or biennially, the collection and processing of the data is a continuous operation. After the event occurs, a certificate is completed that describes the circumstances of the event, such as the names of the involved person or persons; their residence and characteristics; and the date, time, and place of occurrence of the event. The certificates are filed with a local agency, and copies or summaries of them are reported to successively higher administrative echelons, such as from county to state to national government.

Vital registration is virtually complete in its coverage in all modern countries, but it is absent or incomplete in many developing nations. In a country such as the United States, which has a complete system of recording births and deaths and nearly complete area coverage of marriages and divorces, each state designs its own forms and determines the content of the forms. The U.S. government, in order to achieve some level of national comparability for statistical purposes, provides model certificates, which most states essentially copy. The Certificate of Live Birth for the State of Florida (see Figure 1.1) is typical of such a form. The top half of the certificate concerns basic infor-

FIGURE 1.1   A sample birth certificate

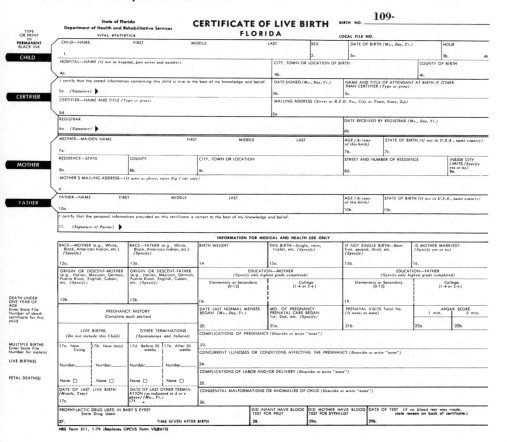

mation about the baby and the parents. The lower half of the certificate, which is restricted to research uses, includes more detailed health and socioeconomic data.

Population registers are systems of continuous population accounting whereby local communities keep track of the population, recording additions to, and subtractions from, that population. The register has features of both a census and vital registration. Like a census, total population coverage is attempted, and some characteristics of the people are identified. Like vital registration, births, deaths, and other vital events are recorded. Additionally, data are gathered on the movement of people into and out of the area.

In practice, population registers ordinarily consist of a personal card for each inhabitant or a book in which entries of critical events are made. When an infant is born in a community, a record is made of it, and the household's records are changed accordingly. When someone in the household dies, that person's record is removed from the register. When a person changes residence, the record is removed from the collection and transferred to the community of destination. It would appear that population registers duplicate the functions of censuses and/or vital registration, but countries that maintain registers find them independently useful for administrative and research purposes. They update censuses, and they go beyond vital statistics in the recording of events such as residential moves. Still, population registers are to be found in only a minority of countries (for example, the Netherlands, Denmark), principally those whose systems of social services require frequent determination of eligible populations.

A *sample household survey,* as a recurrent demographic data source, is found in an increasing number of countries. The idea of drawing a sample of a population from which to gather information that will be representative of the whole population is relatively new, having grown out of advances in statistical sampling techniques in the 1930s. Most censuses now employ this principle by asking some basic questions of everyone and other questions of only a sample, as indicated before. The typical sample household survey is much like the sample part of a census, but it usually covers a smaller sample, is conducted much more frequently (annually, quarterly, or monthly), and has greater flexibility in terms of varying the content from period to period and experimenting with questions that may not be appropriate for, or difficult to collect in, a census.

The monthly Current Population Survey of the United States is a government-derived source of labor-force data (employment and unemployment) for the nation and large areas within it, as well as for describing other characteristics of the population during intercensal years. This survey, begun in the mid-1940s, covers approximately 1 out of every 1,200 households in the country. The World Fertility Survey is a standardized data-collection instrument for measuring fertility trends and patterns in a large number of countries. Population-based sample surveys are also conducted by private agencies: for instance, Gallup, Roper, Harris, Yankelovich, and university-based organizations, for example, the National Opinion Research Center (NORC) at the University of Chicago and the Institute for Survey Research (ISR) at the University of Michigan. These surveys include items of demographic relevance but typically have a wider scope of subject matter, focusing especially on public-opinion issues.

A number of *public and private records* other than those completed in vital registration are used to supplement the population sources already described. These include such diverse records as those related to baptisms and burials, immigration and naturalization, social security, unemployment insurance, hospitals and health agencies, life insurance, armed forces, and military conscription. Frequently, genealogies and city directories serve as the basis for developing family or community demographic measures.

It is sometimes the case that none of the aforementioned sources offers the kind of data needed for population analysis, or that the available data are of extremely poor quality, out of date, or not specific to the groups or areas of interest. Here, the methodological ingenuity of demographers has led to a number of *estimation techniques,* which enable one to approximate the needed data. For example, where there is no birth certification in an area, estimates have been made of fertility levels by linking census age and sex patterns and other demographic indicators of that area to those of other areas that do have the reported information. Also, different models of estimating population size and characteristics for past, present, and future dates have been constructed from partial information and assumptions about the behavior of variables for which data are lacking.

Relating Data Sources and Needs

Given the demand for certain types of demographic data, where can they be found? The student of population will find that some kinds of information are much more readily accessible than others. Recalling our categories of population information, we can now list sources of data for each:

1. *Total population figures* for areas can be obtained from a census count, by a count of persons listed in population registers, or by some estimation technique. Vital registration and other administrative records deal only with certain events or with limited

populations, and sample surveys, while they may be fairly representative of total populations, do not provide reliable figures on the size of the populations themselves.

2. *Mortality data* are obtained principally from death-registration statistics, but when these are lacking, they can be gotten from population registers, from retrospective questions in censuses and surveys, and from life-insurance records, although the latter do not permit complete coverage. When all other sources are devoid of mortality data, of course, the information can be estimated.

3. *Fertility information* is obtained from birth records in the vital-registration system, from population registers, and from censuses and surveys. In the first two sources, births are counted one at a time, as they occur; in the latter sources, a woman can be asked about all the children she has had up to the time of the inquiry. Fertility data can, likewise, be generated by estimation.

4. *Data on mobility* are complete only in population registers. Since censuses and surveys are taken at particular points in time and are usually limited in scope, questions on mobility in these sources deal with whether or not a person resides at the same place as at an earlier point in time (for example, five years ago). Clearly, such an approach does not permit specification of all the moves in that period. Although all residential mobility is not generally recorded, as are births and deaths, except in population registers, statistics on *immigration* and *emigration* (movement into and out of a country) are usually compiled by governments. Since direct data on mobility are not often available, such data are frequently calculated indirectly, through estimation techniques. For instance, if one knows how much the total population of an area has changed over a period of time, as well as the births and deaths that occurred in that area during the interim, then it is possible to deduce the net mobility of the area (that is, the balance of movement in and out).

5. The items encompassed by *population composition, distribution,* and *characteristics* are traditionally covered in censuses and surveys and, to some extent, in registers. Some population characteristics are also recorded in various administrative sources. For example, education data can be drawn from school records, income data from tax records, and health data from medical records.

The Quality of Population Data

Some time ago, a book was published entitled *How to Lie with Statistics*.[1] Despite the provocative title, the author did not intend to lead people down illegal or unethical paths; rather, his point was that we should not accept statistics at their face value. For some reason, people question the spoken or written word more than they do spoken or written numbers. There seems to be a magical quality and definitiveness about statistics that encourages their acceptability. Throughout the book, the author gave examples of how statistics could be unrepresentative, misleading, or downright untrue, and he cautioned users of statistical information of the need to evaluate information before using it.

The users of population data should be guided by the same caveat. Some data are so bad as to be unusable; others are so good that analyzing them without attention to their quality would do no great harm. But most data are in that middle region, which necessitates that we examine the extent and nature of data errors; that is to say, most data are usable, but *data quality* has to be looked at in the context of the precision we require to make decisions. A statement that the People's Republic of China is the country with the world's largest population can hardly be challenged, since that country's estimated population of over one billion people is almost double the size of the population of India, the obvious runner-up. We would have to accept an enormous amount of error in the population figures for those two countries before questioning the generalization. On the other hand, in order to say that survey results that show the unemployment rate to be 6.7 percent one month and 6.8 percent in the next month indicate an upward trend, we would have to demonstrate extraordinarily high reliability in the data.

When we speak about quality of data, we refer to several dimensions. One has to do with *unit coverage*; that is, whether people or events are undercounted or overcounted. A second has to do with *item coverage*, the completeness of information for people and events that were covered. For example, some requested items on a birth certificate may not be filled in. A third quality of data concern is with *validity of response*, or the degree to which the respondent gave the desired information. A fourth deals with *coding* or *classification error*, or the accuracy with which responses were placed in the appropriate analytical categories. A fifth relates to *sampling reliability*, in cases where the information was collected or tabulated on a sample basis. Even though samples are drawn randomly, they may not be truly representative of a population. A sixth concern of data quality has to do with *processing error*, or the mistakes that may have been introduced by humans, mechanical, or electronic machines in converting recorded data into tabulated data. And a seventh concern is with *publication errors*, which creep in as a result of typographical or proofreading mistakes. Of course, some of these errors can never be made known to us, and some may be compensating or random, so that their effects on the products may be minimal. At times, we can measure some of the separate components of error, but mostly we settle for a net error figure.

Censuses vary greatly in their quality. Nigerian censuses were taken in 1952–53, 1962, 1963, and 1973, but demographic experts deemed none of them adequate for making a population estimate. Such an estimate was derived through indirect means. The United States Census of 1970 was evaluated as having a net undercount of 2.5 percent (about 7.5 percent for blacks). Analysis of reports on selected items showed relatively small net errors and somewhat larger gross errors. An item such as age was reasonably well reported, whereas socioeconomic items were subject to more misreporting but within a tolerable level for most uses. As a result of great expenditures of time, effort, and money, the net undercount in 1980 was reduced to a fraction of 1 percent (about 4 percent for blacks, and it was especially high for young black males).

Vital registration in developing countries tends to be highly deficient. Even where such systems exist, the registration may be so inadequate that it cannot measure accurately levels of fertility and mortality or trends in these components. Such factors as inadequate public information about the system, illiteracy and lack of motivation among the masses, and also lack of motivation among local registrars contribute to this condition.

In developed countries, vital-registration systems are stronger as a result of greater investments in their conduct and popular acceptability. In the United States, over 99 percent of births and deaths are registered, according to evaluation studies.

A well-designed survey based on a probability sample is subject to a known level of *random sampling* (or chance) variability as well as biases derived from the other sources previously mentioned. The U.S. Current Population Survey reports include tables of sampling errors and occasional discussions of other types of error, which allow the user to estimate the limitations of the data for use in analysis. A postenumeration evaluation of the World Fertility Survey in Fiji revealed that knowledge questions were likely to have the greatest error, questions on factual items for current and recent periods the least error. Because of the careful way the original survey was undertaken, the measured variances and biases were relatively small. Less-carefully designed and executed surveys could be replete with errors.

WORLD POPULATION TRENDS

Now that we have adopted a perspective on population and some notions about the nature and sources of demographic data, we can turn our attention to population conditions throughout the world—past, present, and probable future. This type of descriptive information will give us a sense of the magnitude of population change and better equip us to consider its dynamics.

Population Trends in Prehistory

Estimates of when *homo sapiens* (thinking person) first roamed the earth range up to about 400,000 years ago, and *homo sapiens sapiens* (modern person) has been dated back to approximately 30,000 to 40,000 years ago. These figures are based on recent archaeological expeditions that led to the reconstruction of skeletons and artifacts from fragmentary findings. Determination of population levels through demographic techniques is limited to a still more recent period, but one can reach logical conclusions about relative population size in prehistory by relating different sources of information.

From time immemorial until the modern era, world population was obviously maintained at a precariously low level. It is likely that, in those early periods, people were congregated in a limited number of locations. Those in some locations were periodically decimated by waves of excess mortality, and those groups that survived withstood extinction by a combination of high fertility, development of natural immunity to certain diseases, and wandering to escape natural disasters. Increasing ability to cope with the environment enabled some settlements to increase their numbers and provide the base for further population gains.

Figure 1.2 depicts the general course of population growth from 8000 B.C. to the present and projected to the turn of the century. Clearly, we live in a period that might be labeled demographically deviant. What processes kept growth relatively low until recent times, and what has caused the abrupt upturn?

Although the curve shown outlines a gradual and relatively smooth growth pattern until about the seventeenth or eighteenth century, Deevey proposed that an evolution of population took place in three stages.[2] In the nearly one million years prior to 8000 B.C., the number of hominids (humanlike primates, including homo sapiens) was barely sufficient to guarantee survival of the species. The intellectual superiority of homo sapiens, claimed Deevey, enabled them to maintain their numbers and compete favorably in a hunting and food-gathering era. A second population surge about ten thousand years ago heralded the agricultural revolution in which humans became plowers and herders, and the population grew sharply. The third surge came with the scientific-industrial revolution, about two hundred to three hundred years ago, and once again, the number of humans was increased significantly.

FIGURE 1.2   Long-range trend of world population growth

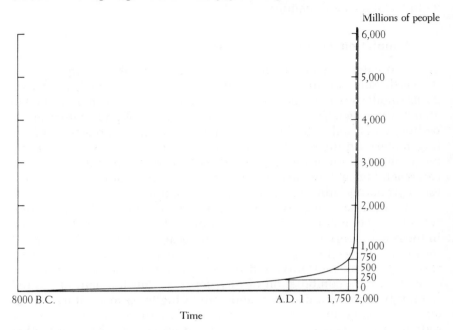

Source: John Durand, "The Modern Expansion of World Population," *Proceedings of the American Philosophical Society,* Philadelphia, June 1967, p. 139.

Population Trends from 8000 B.C. to the Eighteenth Century

The next era of demographic history was of long duration, from the New Stone Age through the Bronze and Iron periods, the Dark Ages, the Renaissance, and the Reformation. During this era, the population of the earth grew from roughly five million to well over a half billion. Instead of relying on consumption of food in its naturally available forms, people began to develop other sources of food, through agriculture and domestication of animals. This critical change in people's relation to the land enabled them to harness better the earth's resources. In order to maximize the gains to be made by these new economic modes, they also changed their residential modes. Wandering gave way to settlement, and isolation of family and kinship groups was replaced by formation of communities, commercial towns, and then cities. Great empires and cultures developed, and the major contemporary religions came into being.

By about 4000 B.C. the number of people on the globe may well have reached 86 million. At the birth of Christ, it is believed that the figure stood between 270 and 330 million. It must be understood, however, that no enumerations of population took place and that these estimates are the result of a piecing together of human history by anthropologists, paleontologists, demographers, and other scientists. The figures are approximate, but they do indicate very broad differences in order of magnitude between large epochs in past eras of history.

At the beginning of the Christian era, population size stabilized and in some periods even declined as devastating disease took a heavy toll of the populace. By the year 1000, the growth rate recovered, and from then until the middle of the fourteenth century, population increase was rapid, especially in northern Europe. The bubonic plague, the Black Death of Europe, occurred in 1348 and thwarted population growth for several decades. In fact, by the year 1400, the numbers on earth, and especially in Europe, were below what they had been fifty years earlier. Before another hundred years had passed, however, social, economic, and intellectual revolutions set the stage for the modern period of population expansion. By 1500, probably 440 million to 540 million people dotted the sphere, and the pace of demographic growth was augmented.

Population Trends Since the Eighteenth Century

What has come to be referred to as the world *population explosion* was a more or less gradual process, which picked up momentum sometime during the late seventeenth and early eighteenth centuries. It is not possible to establish an exact date when the rate of population growth of the world began to accelerate markedly. For the sake of convenience, we have taken as the starting point of this modern period the year 1750. Estimates of the population of the world and its major areas are shown in Table 1.2 for various dates back to the birth of Christ and up to the present. Average annual rates of population increase are shown in Table 1.3 for five time periods going back to 1750.

World population in the mid-eighteenth century had attained a level close to 800 million. The mark of 1 billion was first reached shortly after 1800, and one and two-thirds billion was topped by 1900. The 1982 population level of 4.6 billion thus was more than five and one-half times that in 1750 and nearly three times that at the turn of the present century. In terms of growth rates, the population increased

TABLE 1.2   Population estimates in millions for world regions since the time of Christ

Area	YEAR					
	0	1000	1500	1750	1900	1982
World total	270–330	275–345	440–540	735–805	1,650–1,710	4,585
China	70–90	50–80	100–150	190–225	400–450	1,000
India-Bangladesh- Pakistan	50–100	50–100	75–150	160–200	285–295	900
Southwestern Asia	25–45	20–30	20–30	25–35	40–45	106
Japan	1–2	3–8	15–20	29–30	44–45	119
Remainder of Asia (excl. USSR)	8–20	10–25	15–30	35–55	110–125	546
Europe (excl. USSR)	30–40	30–40	60–70	120–135	295–300	488
USSR	5–10	6–15	10–18	30–40	130–135	270
North Africa	10–15	5–10	6–12	10–15	53–55	117
Remainder of Africa	15–30	20–40	30–60	50–80	90–120	381
North America	1–2	2–3	2–3	2–3	82–83	256
Middle and South America	6–15	20–50	30–60	13–18	71–78	378
Oceania	1–2	1–2	1–2	2	6	24

Sources: Data through 1900 are from John Durand, "Historical Estimates of World Population: An Evaluation," *Population and Development Review* 3:3 (September 1977), 259; data
for 1982 are derived from Population Reference Bureau, *1982 World Population Data Sheet.*
*Durand's figures are often shown as ranges, due to the uncertainty of the estimates. These
ranges define limits within which there is little preference for figures. It is possible that the
true figure lies outside the range, but a figure within the range is more likely to be correct.
See Durand, "Historical Estimates," p. 260.*

roughly 0.5 percent per year from 1750 to 1900, close to 1 percent per
year in the first half of the twentieth century, and nearly 2 percent per
year since 1950. On a relative basis, the real population explosion first
occurred in the twentieth century; in fact, in the second half of this
century.

Since the upsurge in population during the modern period is
associated with the Industrial Revolution and the related social and
economic development of the Western world, it has been commonly
assumed that the contemporary population expansion began its rapid
pace in Europe. Durand has demonstrated that, while European or Eu-
ropean-origin peoples contributed more than their proportionate share
to the expansion of world population during the nineteenth century,
accelerating population growth was common to many widely spaced
parts of the earth throughout the modern period. Since the Industrial
Revolution did not occur in many of these places, this raises questions
about its role as a major source of the population upsurge.

TABLE 1.3 **Trends in average annual rate of population increase for the world and major areas**

Area	YEAR				
	1750–1800	1800–1850	1850–1900	1900–1950	1950–1981
World Total	0.4	0.5	0.5	0.8	1.9
Asia (excl. USSR)	0.5	0.5	0.3	0.8	2.0
China (mainland)	1.0	0.6	0.0	0.5	1.8
India, Bangladesh, and Pakistan	0.1	0.3	0.4	0.8	2.2
Japan	0.0	0.1	0.7	1.3	1.1
Indonesia	0.2	1.2	1.2	1.2	2.1
Remainder of Asia (excl. USSR)	0.1	0.5	0.7	1.3	2.5
Africa	0.0	0.1	0.4	1.0	2.5
North Africa	0.2	0.5	1.2	1.4	2.5
Remainder of Africa	0.0	0.0	0.2	0.9	2.6
Europe (excl. USSR)	0.4	0.6	0.7	0.6	0.7
USSR	0.6	0.6	1.1	0.6	1.3
America	1.1	1.5	1.8	1.5	2.0
North America	2.5	2.7	2.3	1.4	1.4
Middle and South America	0.8	0.9	1.3	1.6	2.6
Oceania	0.0	0.0	0.0	1.6	1.8

Source: John Durand, "The Modern Expansion of World Population," *Proceedings of the American Philosophical Society,* Philadelphia, June 1967, p. 137; and data derived from Population Reference Bureau, *1981 World Population Data Sheet.*

It has been pointed out that if one views total human existence on earth as lasting one day, then the modern era of population growth covers less than a minute. Yet probably a fourth of all human beings ever born have lived during this brief time span. Estimates of all the persons who have ever lived on earth range from seventy to eighty billion.[3] On this basis, about one out of eighteen persons ever on earth is now living. These numbers are, of course, only illustrative. An estimate of the number ever living on earth depends on a number of factors, including when the human race is assumed to have begun.

The conclusion to be reached from this overview of world population trends is that demographic growth in recent times has been more rapid than at any earlier period of human existence on earth. Furthermore, a continuation of these trends for an indefinite period of time will result in immensely larger numbers of humans on the globe.

Considering that there are roughly 45.8 million square kilometers of arable land area in the world, the population density of the earth can be placed at about one hundred persons per square kilometer. This can hardly be regarded as overcrowding, but two factors must be considered. First, while much of the area on earth is technically arable, conditions for developing the soil and enhancing crop productivity are extremely costly, so that some arable land cannot reasonably be made very fertile. Second, even if there is more land than needed presently or in the near future to accommodate the population, the desire of most people for an adequate level of living and a gregarious social life leads them to congregate in a limited number of places. If a given square kilometer of arable land contained one hundred persons, the chances are that all or nearly all of the people within it would be living together on a few acres rather than residing randomly throughout the area.

In 1982, the 4.6 billion people of the world were distributed unevenly over the surface of the globe, as seen in Table 1.2 and Appendix A. A majority (58 percent) were to be found on the Asian continent, with over one-fifth (22 percent) in the People's Republic of (Mainland) China and another one-sixth (16 percent) in India alone. Europe (excluding the USSR) contained 11 percent, Africa a like 11 percent, and Latin America 8 percent. The USSR and the United States, the "superpowers," together had only 11 percent of the world's population, and Canada and Oceania (central and south Pacific region) contained a mere 1 percent of the total. The United States, with 232 million people in 1982, had a population about ten times the size of Canada's; more than three times that of Mexico; roughly four times that of either West Germany, France, or the United Kingdom; slightly smaller than that of the USSR; one-third that of India; and less than one-fourth that of China.

Variations in Population Change

Clearly, although the world's population in 1982 was growing at the rate of 1.7 percent per year, the population in some parts was growing more rapidly and in other parts less rapidly. The rate of natural increase (balance of births over deaths without consideration of international migration) is shown for each area in Appendix A. Africa's annual rate of natural increase was 2.9 percent, while the rate was 2.3 in Latin America, 1.9 in Asia, and 1.3 in Oceania. Below-average rates were found in North America (0.7), the USSR (0.8), and Europe (0.4). Within each of these broad regions, rates of natural increase differed considerably. For example, within Africa, it was as high as 3.9 in Kenya and as low as 1.2 in Gabon; within Latin America, the range was from 3.5 in Honduras to 0.8 in Cuba, Barbados, and Uruguay; within Asia, it varied from 3.8 in Syria to 0.8 in Japan and within Europe, the rate was 2.2 in Albania but −0.2 (a decline) in West Germany.

Of course, some countries experienced greater or lesser total population growth, due to an imbalance of immigration and emigration. This has been especially true for the United States, Mexico, and selected other countries of the world. In later chapters, we will examine that phenomenon in some detail.

At current rates of natural increase, a nation such as West Germany would continue to lose population and several nations would remain stable in size. It would take eighty-eight to ninety-six years for the USSR and the U.S. to double their size based on natural increase, China would require about forty-eight years to reach twice its present size, while India would double its population in thirty-five years, and Kenya in a mere eighteen. None of these rates is fixed, however, and it is reasonable to expect that most of them will be modified in years to come.

While it is evident that all parts of the world have participated in the modern population expansion, the course of population development in individual countries has differed considerably. A description of the trends in a few countries (Table 1.4) will give some idea of the variations and further insight into some of the underlying factors, which will be analyzed in subsequent sections of this volume.

POPULATION TRENDS FOR SELECTED COUNTRIES

United States

For a century and a half prior to the establishment of this nation, it is estimated that the total population growth rate was erratic but averaged about 3 percent per year. At the time of the first census, in 1790, shortly after the country was founded, the population stood at 3.9 million. The 3 percent growth rate was maintained until about the Civil War period. Beginning in the 1860s, the rate began a progressive decline, falling below 2 percent per year at about the turn of the century. A low point was reached during the Depression years of the 1930s. With the advent of World War II, population growth recovered, and the rate moved back up close to the 2 percent level by the mid-1950s. The course of population shifted again, and the growth rate resumed its low level of less than 1 percent by 1972. This general level has persisted to the present. The population pattern in the United States can thus be described as one of high growth in the early years, with the rate declining generally until the 1930s, rising again to a moderately high level by the 1950s, and then declining to the current stable low level.

TABLE 1.4 Historical population trends for the United States, Ireland, Japan, India, Brazil, and Kenya

UNITED STATES			IRELAND			JAPAN		
Date	Population (000)	Average Annual Growth Rate	Date	Population (000)	Average Annual Growth Rate	Date	Population (000)	Average Annual Growth Rate
1790	3,929	—	1687	2,167	—	1250	9,750	—
1800	5,308	3.01	1726	3,031	0.86	1575	18,000	0.19
1810	7,240	3.10	1777	3,740	0.41	1726	26,549	0.26
1820	9,638	2.86	1821	5,421	0.84	1792	24,891	−0.10
1830	12,866	2.89	1831	6,193	1.33	1852	27,201	0.15
1840	17,069	2.83	1841	6,529	0.53	1872	32,634	0.91
1850	23,192	3.07	1851	5,112	−2.45	1885	37,502	1.07
1860	31,443	3.04	1861	4,402	−1.50	1920	55,391	1.11
1870	39,818	2.36	1871	4,053	−0.83	1925	59,179	1.32
1880	50,156	2.31	1881	3,870	−0.46	1930	63,872	1.53
1890	62,948	2.27	1891	3,469	−1.09	1935	68,662	1.45
1900	75,995	1.88	1901	3,222	−0.74	1940	72,539	1.10
1910	91,972	1.91	1911	3,140	−0.26	1955	89,300	1.39
1920	105,711	1.39	1926	2,972	−0.37	1960	93,200	0.85
1930	122,775	1.50	1936	2,968	−0.01	1970	104,665	1.16
1940	131,669	0.70	1946	2,955	−0.04	1981	117,800	1.07
1950	151,326	1.39	1951	2,961	0.04			
1960	179,323	1.70	1956	2,898	−0.43			
1970	203,212	1.25	1961	2,818	−0.56			
1981	229,800	1.11	1966	2,884	0.46			
			1971	2,978	0.64			
			1981	3,400	1.32			

Sources: For the United States, U.S. Bureau of the Census, *Statistical Abstract of the United States,* Washington: U.S. Government Printing Office, 1973, p. 5. For Ireland, Robert E. Kennedy, Jr., *The Irish: Emigration, Marriage, and Fertility,* Berkeley: University of California Press, 1973, p. 212; United Nations, *Demographic Yearbook,* New York, 1972; and K. H. Connell, *The Population of Ireland, 1750–1845,* Oxford: Clarendon Press, 1950, p. 25. For Japan, Irene B. Taeuber, *The Population of Japan,* Princeton, N.J.: Princeton University

Ireland

A number of European countries experienced population-growth patterns not unlike those of the United States, although the trend toward stabilization of the growth rate began at an earlier period of history and developed over a longer period of time. Ireland is an example of a European country in which the growth pattern has been radically different. Table 1.4 indicates that the Irish people numbered just over two million in 1687. Despite erratic growth and some short periods of decline, the population grew steadily for the next one hundred years at

INDIA[a]			BRAZIL			KENYA		
Date	Population (000)	Average Annual Growth Rate	Date	Population (000)	Average Annual Growth Rate	Date	Population (000)	Average Annual Growth Rate
1600	100,000	—	1808	2,419	—	1950	6,121	—
1800	120,000	0.60	1823	3,961	2.82	1955	7,034	2.8
1834	130,000	0.24	1830	5,340	4.27	1960	8,157	3.0
1845	130,000	0.00	1854	7,678	1.51	1965	9,549	3.2
1855	175,000	2.97	1872	9,930	1.43	1970	11,256	3.3
1867	194,000	0.86	1890	14,334	2.04	1975	13,481	3.6
1871	255,166	6.85	1900	17,319	1.89	1981	16,500	3.4
1881	257,380	0.09	1920	30,636	5.70			
1891	236,700	−0.80	1940	41,565	1.53			
1901	236,300	−0.02	1950	51,944	2.23			
1911	252,100	0.65	1960	70,967	3.12			
1921	251,400	−0.03	1970	93,204	2.73			
1931	279,000	1.04	1981	121,400	2.40			
1941	316,700	1.27						
1951	361,100	1.31						
1961	439,200	1.96						
1971	547,950	2.21						
1981	688,600	2.28						

Press, 1958, pp. 20, 22, 46, 60, and 61; United Nations, *Demographic Yearbook,* New York, 1960, 1972. For India, Kingsley Davis, *The Population of India and Pakistan,* Princeton, N.J.: Princeton University Press, 1951, pp. 25 and 27; S. Chandrasekhar, *India's Population,* Meerut: Meenakshi Prakashan, 1967, p. 4; and United Nations, *Demographic Yearbook,* New York, 1972. For Brazil, T. Lynn Smith, *Brazil: People and Institutions,* Baton Rouge: Louisiana State University Press, 1972, p. 44. For Kenya, U.S. Bureau of the Census, *World Population 1979,* Washington, 1980, p. 92. All 1981 figures are from Population Reference Bureau, *1981 World Population Data Sheet.*

[a]*From 1891 onward, figures are adjusted to the present area of the country.*

an average of close to 1 percent per year. During the next half of the century, the rate of growth quickened, with an annual average of over 1 percent reached by the 1830s. By the mid-1800s, the pattern reversed itself and the population of Ireland began to decline. Even though it had risen from 3.7 million in 1777 to 6.5 million in 1841, by 1961 the population size had fallen to far below its 1777 level. Most of the decrease took place during the last half of the nineteenth century, as a result of heavy emigration. The numbers stabilized after 1910, at nearly three million. Throughout the first half of the twentieth century, the growth rate hovered close to zero, but after 1950 the population again declined and this change was sustained until the late 1960s, when a modest increase in the rate of growth was recorded. By 1982, Ireland enjoyed a growth rate of 1.2, which raised its population to 3.5 million. This country can thus be described as one whose population showed early moderate growth tendencies but assumed a pattern of sharp decline after the middle of the nineteenth century, until it returned to slow growth in the twentieth century.

Japan

Population records in Japan cover more than a thousand years. Estimates suggest a population of less than four million in the early tenth century, with an increase to nine or ten million by the thirteenth century. The population of the country seems to have grown at an irregular rate from the thirteenth to the sixteenth century. It is believed to have increased rapidly in the seventeenth century and to have changed little from the early eighteenth century until 1852. Steady growth at a rate fluctuating narrowly at about 1 percent per year characterized the Japanese demographic picture between 1852 and 1920. For several decades after 1920, the population grew at about 1.5 percent annually, and in recent years the rate has stayed closer to 1 percent. Although demographic growth in Japan took place at a moderate rate through most of its modern history, the smallness of the land area created heavy population densities. In 1981, there were 2,145 persons per square kilometer of arable land in the country, making it one of the more densely settled areas of the world.

India

More typical than Japan of Asian population development is India. During the 2,000 or so years prior to the modern period, India's population must have remained virtually stationary. The probable course was gradual growth for a short period, followed by an abrupt decline, the long-term trend being one of virtually fixed numbers. From 1600 until 1845, India's numbers may have increased from about 100 million to roughly 130 million. The average annual percentage growth during that time was minute. From 1845 to 1871, the date when the first Indian census was taken, there is reason to believe that the growth rate accelerated, but the data are of insufficient quality to document the trend. Beginning with 1871, however, ten-year censuses have been conducted, which provide a reasonable basis for reckoning demographic change. The average annual increase from the time of the first census until the eighth census, in 1941, is calculated to be about 0.6 percent, close to the increase for the world as a whole. During the last two decades of that time span, though, the annual increase rose to 1.2 percent, and in subsequent years the rate has continued upward, until it presently stands at 2.0 percent. What is particularly critical in the case of India is that such a growth rate will double its population in thirty-five years, which in 1982 numbered well over 700 million, more than North America and Latin America combined. One can therefore describe the trend of India's demographic growth as one of general stability with a small margin of increase for a long sweep of its history, followed by rapidly rising rates of growth during the past half century. Allowing for variations in tempo and in population size, the Indian pattern is one shared by many countries in Asia, Africa, and Latin America.

Brazil

As is the case with many Latin American countries, reliable demographic data for Brazil are available only from about 1872, when the first census was taken. From that time until 1950, the growth of population in Brazil has been one of the most rapid in the larger countries of the world, with the annual rate of increase averaging about 2 percent. Since 1950 the growth rate has risen sharply and approaches 2.5 percent a year at the present time. Although Brazil's population size is only one-sixth that of India's, a continuation of its annual growth rate will double its population in twenty-nine years.

Kenya

As a continent, Africa is experiencing the highest rate of population growth. Presently, Kenya is the nation with the highest growth rate among all countries of the world. Sound information is lacking for a very long historical perspective of that area, however. The first Kenyan Census, in 1948, revealed that the population size would soon be 6 million people. From 1950 to 1975, the number more than doubled and the growth rate increased steadily. By 1982, that rate stood at 3.9 percent per year.

VARIATIONS IN GROWTH

The population-growth profiles of the countries illustrated do not adequately define the variability of trend patterns among nations throughout the world. Almost every country has some unique aspect to its population development. Many countries can be grouped, however, on the basis of general similarities in their population trends. There are countries that have never experienced rapid population expansion, others that are in the midst of such expansion, and still others that have encountered rapid expansion at some time in the past but now have more moderate rates of demographic growth. Even within these types, there are differences in the regularity with which growth patterns evolved. In some nations, the transitions from slow to rapid increase and back again have been relatively smooth and gradual; in others, the changes have been irregular and sometimes quite dramatic. Moreover, population trends vary by areas within countries, just as national patterns vary within regions and the world.

Forecasting Future Population

The history of population growth gives us a framework for anticipating future levels of population. Yet the course of population change in the years ahead is a function of many variables, some of which can be measured reasonably well but others of which usually elude us. Fifty years ago, there were few persons who had a valid expectation of where the world would stand demographically half a century later. Even ten years ago, it was difficult to determine the status of population in many parts of the world a decade later. At least, the disagreement among experts was substantial.

When demographers want to estimate numbers of people in the future, they do not gaze into a crystal ball. Rather, they devise a model or scheme that will enable them to take account of factors related to population in the past, make assumptions about the behavior of those factors in the future, extend those conditions to a later period of time, and calculate what future population will be under those circumstances. Some of these models are highly simplistic, while others are more refined.

One might assume, for instance, that the current rate of population growth will continue unabated into the future. Such an assumption for the world as a whole would lead to a situation whereby, in a few thousand years, so many people would be covering the earth that human bodies would be piling on top of one another at a rate exceeding the velocity of light! This startling projection leads to two points: first, that we have the inherent potential for very rapid population increase in the world, and second, that it is inconceivable that population on earth can grow to such dimensions. Some forces must operate ultimately to reduce the population growth rate.

Choosing reasonable assumptions about future demographic conditions is basic to plausible calculations of projections. That is why trying to determine the population of an area in years to come is at once a science and an art. It is a science in the sense that the analyst can use a systematic and carefully detailed procedure for estimating the population in subsequent years. It is an art to the degree that the analyst must exercise sensitivity and sound judgment in deciding what the possible alternative assumptions are, which ones seem most reasonable, and which combinations of assumptions are most realistic.

The most fashionable projection model at present is one that disaggregates areas and components of population change into the smallest units for which data are available, assumes trends for each that reflect ongoing and foreseen processes, projects these, and then reaggregates the elements into a total future estimate.

Such an approach was employed for arriving at the population projections shown in Appendix A. The results show that, by the year 2000, there will be over 6 billion people on earth. Even allowing for moderation in fertility levels in many parts of the world, the momentum of demographic growth will carry the human stock to where it will include 33 percent more of us in less than twenty years' time. The population of Asia at the turn of the century will exceed 3.5 billion (one-third of it being in China), the population of Latin America (over half a billion) will exceed that of Europe, and the people of the African continent will number close to 1 billion.

According to the latest United Nations estimate, the global population could stabilize itself at 10.5 billion by the year 2110.[4] This assumes, of course, that the present tempo of population programs and policies is sustained. The pace of fertility decline is critical in reaching stabilization. A more rapid decrease in fertility could allow population to level off at 8 billion by the year 2070, while a slower decrease could mean a plateau of over 14 million by 2130.

How accurate these forecasts will be depends on the scientific and artful skills of the demographers involved. One can find specialists whose predictions lead to higher figures and others who suggest lower ones. Whether larger or smaller numbers signify optimism or pessimism hinges on one's set of values concerning the probable consequences of those numbers. In the ensuing chapters, our discussion will provide some basis for evaluating such consequences.

NOTES

1. Darrell Huff, *How to Lie with Statistics* (New York: W. W. Norton & Co., Inc., 1954).

2. Edward S. Deevey, Jr., "The Human Population," *Scientific American,* 203 (September 1960), 194–204.

3. Annabelle Desmond, "How Many People Have Ever Lived on Earth?" *Population Bulletin,* 18 (February 1962), 1–19; and Nathan Keyfitz, "How Many People Have Lived on Earth?" *Demography,* 3, no. 2. (1966), 581–582.

4. Rafael M. Salas, "State of the World Population," *Populi*, 8, no. 2 (1981), 3–11.

SUGGESTED ADDITIONAL READINGS

The most useful references on world population data are:

UNITED NATIONS, *Demographic Yearbook*. New York: United Nations, annual (a compilation of population statistics). The volume for 1979 is *Special Issue: Historical Supplement*.

U.S. BUREAU OF THE CENSUS, *World Population 1979—Recent Demographic Estimates for the Countries and Regions of the World*. Washington: U.S. Government Printing Office, 1980.

International standards for demographic data are presented in:

UNITED NATIONS, *Principles and Recommendations for Population and Housing Censuses*, Statistical Papers, Series M, No. 67. New York: United Nations, 1980.

_____, *Principles and Recommendations for a Vital Statistics System*, Statistical Papers, Series M, No. 19, Rev. 1. New York: United Nations, 1973.

_____, *Methodology of Demographic Sample Surveys*, Statistical Papers, Series M, No. 51. New York: United Nations, 1971.

_____, *Methodology and Evaluation of Population Registers and Similar Systems*, Studies in Methods, Series F, No. 15. New York: United Nations, 1969.

Volumes dealing with sources, types, and quality of population data are numerous, but the standard reference is:

SHRYOCK, HENRY S., JACOB S. SIEGEL, AND ASSOCIATES. *The Methods and Materials of Demography*. 2 vols. Washington, D.C.: U.S. Government Printing Office, 1971. A condensed version, edited by Edward Stockwell in 1976, is available through the Academic Press.

The best initial approach for surveying the existing literature on a population topic is to consult:

Population Index (a quarterly bibliographic source issued by the Office of Population Research, Princeton University).

For current research and writings, examine especially the following journals in the population field:

Demography (issued quarterly by the Population Association of America).

Population Studies (issued three times a year by the Population Investigating Committee in London).

Population (Issued six times a year by Institut National d'Etudes Démographiques in Paris).

Population and Development Review (issued quarterly by the Population Council, a private group in New York).

Social Biology (issued quarterly by the Society for the Study of Social Biology).

Population and Environment (issued quarterly by the Division of Population and Environmental Psychology of the American Psychological Association).

Population Bulletin (a journal of the Population Reference Bureau).

Family Planning Perspectives and *International Family Planning Perspectives* (journals of World Population Planned Parenthood).

Studies in Family Planning (another journal of the Population Council).

American Demographics (a journal for public and business use published by a private group in Ithaca, New York).

Population Research and Policy Review (published three times a year by Elsevier Scientific Publishing Company).

TECHNICAL SUPPLEMENT NO. 1

Measuring Population Change

Several measures of population change are referred to in this chapter. There are figures that show absolute numbers of population increase or decrease and percentage shifts between two points in time. These simple calculations are made by taking the difference between the two numbers being compared and subtracting the number at the earlier date from the number at the later date (the *absolute change*) and dividing that result by the number at the earlier date (the *percentage change*).

Doubling time and average annual *rates of population change* were also discussed. Both of these measures are elements of a more general formula, which can take the form of:

$$r = \frac{1}{n} \log_e \frac{p^{t + n}}{p^t}$$

where r = average annual rate of change
   n = number of years in the time period
   $\log_e$ = natural logarithm
   $p^{t + n}$ = population at the end of the period
   p^t = population at the beginning of the period

If two population figures and the time period between them are known, one can derive the rate of change. If one accepts a given rate of change and sets the population at the later date to double the amount at the earlier date, then the doubling time (or value of n) can be deduced for that rate of change. If one knows the current population and assumes a given rate of change over a certain number of years, the resulting population at the end of that time (p^{t+n}) can be estimated. In each case, there is one unknown value in the equation.

The formula cited is referred to as an exponential one, and is basically the same as that used in calculating compound interest on bank accounts. Here the rate is compounded annually, meaning, for example, that the base for the implied annual rates is larger each year in the case of a growing population.

We can illustrate the use of the formula by reference to data for the world in Appendix A. If the growth rate were to continue at 1.7 percent per year, how long would it take for the population size of 4,585 million to double (that is, reach 9,170 million)? The formula can then be expressed as:

$$.017 = \frac{1}{n} \log_e \frac{9,170}{4,585}$$

$$\text{or} \quad n = \frac{1}{.017} \log_e 2.00$$

$$= \frac{.6932}{.017}$$

$$= 40.78 \text{ or } 41 \text{ years}$$

ISSUES SUPPLEMENT NO. 1

Is World Population Growth Too Rapid?

Although readers have not yet been exposed to some of the arguments on the advantages and disadvantages of population growth, and particularly on present rates of population growth, they may very well have adopted a position on the topic based on earlier readings and general values. Presented below are two contrasting positions on the future course of population growth. Which argument seems to be stronger? Is there a middle ground?

> *Mankind itself may stand on the brink of extinction; in its death throes it could take with it most of the other passengers of Spaceship Earth. No geological event in a billion years—not the emergence of mighty mountain ranges, nor the submergence of entire subcontinents, nor the occurrence of periodic glacial ages—has posed a threat to terrestrial life comparable to that of human overpopulation.* (Paul R. Ehrlich and Anne H. Ehrlich, *Population, Resources, Environment.* San Francisco: W. H. Freeman & Company, Publishers, 1970, p. 1.)

> *The usual argument that population will grow to a doomsday point is based on the crudest sort of curve-fitting, a kind of hypnotism by mathematics. Starkly, the argument is that population will grow in the future because it has always grown in the past. Certainly this proposition is not even true historically; population has been stationary or gotten smaller in large parts of the world for long periods of time . . . it is assumed that if society's birth rate is high now, it will continue to be high later. But one need* not *believe that if people decide to have more children now, they will also continue indefinitely to have them at the same rate . . . when people judge the negative consequences of children to be greater than the positive consequences—personally and collectively—they will then reduce the rate at which they have babies.* (Julian L. Simon, *The Economics of Population Growth.* Princeton: Princeton University Press, 1977, pp. 493–495.)

CHAPTER TWO
UNDERSTANDING
POPULATION CHANGE

"But demographic projections indicate that within twenty years, this town will be big enough for both of us."

Every area of science requires frameworks for comprehending and organizing its subject matter. Demography, as the science of population analysis, incorporates a variety of frameworks for understanding population status and dynamics. These frameworks help describe and explain both demographic structures and processes as well as the determinants and consequences of population change.

THEORY AS A SYSTEM OF UNDERSTANDING

We frequently attach the term *theory* to frameworks for comprehending a scientific area. What do we mean by theory? In common parlance, we often use the word when we have in mind a hunch or speculation. "I have a theory about that" may signify that the speaker has some notion concerning one factor affecting a situation, a notion that may be based on a casual observation, recall of some past event, or a report by someone else. Possibly, that theory may have a sturdier foundation, but more than likely it will not.

Scientists generally use the term *theory* to refer to a rigorous, systematic approach to developing knowledge about an area. Theory in this sense can serve three functions:

1. It can provide a basis for integrating the elements of knowledge that already exist about a subject.
2. It permits location of gaps in the body of knowledge that need to be filled in order to improve explanation and prediction of behavior and events.
3. It enables students of the subject to develop generalizations about trends and relationships involving the subject matter.

All sciences have theories, but not all science is purely theoretical. Scientific research can lead to three types of products. The first is simple *description*, or the identification of items of research interest and their distribution and form, such as the level of a birthrate or the number of persons in each income category. The second is *relational patterns*, or the way in which different items empirically relate to one another, such as the relationship of the birthrate to income level and, perhaps further, how that linkage varies between cities and suburbs. The third is *theory*, or systems of explanation, such as a model that helps us specify which variables are important and generally have the greatest direct effect on the birthrate, and which influence the birthrate indirectly or are only spuriously related. Theories lead us to causal interpretations.

The classical approach to theory in the social sciences is one that implies experimentation and has essentially been borrowed from the natural sciences. This approach requires that we define concepts or terms carefully, hypothesize the nature of relationships among these concepts or terms, acquire data that are adequate for testing the hypotheses, perform the hypothetical tests, and conclude whether or not the hypotheses are supported. In the social sciences, we attempt to use this natural-science model of theory; but frequently we cannot control the experimental situation in the same way that natural scientists can in their laboratories. It becomes necessary, therefore, that we construct tests of theory that may not be so rigorous in most instances but allow us to determine if the weight of evidence lies on one side or another. The ultimate objective of providing an integrated body of knowledge, identifying gaps in that body, and generalizing about the relationships of variables within the body can still be achieved.

A sound theoretical orientation in population studies will distinguish between categories of subject matter, levels of influence or analysis, and products of scientific research, which have already been discussed, but also of three other dimensions—objectives of studying subject matter, levels of complexity, and levels of generalization. The *objective of studying the subject matter* refers to whether the focal subject is of interest in terms of its own status, as a determinant of other conditions, or as a consequence of other conditions. By *levels of complexity*, we refer to the number and linkages of variables involved. These levels can be described as comprehensive, middle range, or ele-

TABLE 2.1 Dimensions of population understanding

Categories of Subject Matter	*Objective of Studying Subject Matter*
1. Size	1. Interest in status of subject matter
2. Mortality	2. Determinants of other conditions
3. Fertility	3. Consequences of other conditions
4. Mobility	
5. Composition	*Levels of Complexity*
6. Distribution	1. Comprehensive
7. Characteristics	2. Middle range
	3. Elemental
Levels of Influence or Analysis	
1. Macro	*Levels of Generalization*
2. Medial	1. To population being studied
3. Micro	2. To populations of that type
	3. To broader classes of populations
Products of Scientific Research	
1. Description	
2. Relational patterns	
3. Theory	

mental. Finally, any results or findings based on research can take one of three *levels of generalization*—limited to the population being studied, generalizable to populations of that type, or generalizable to broader classes of populations. These various dimensions are summarized in Table 2.1.

As we examine each development of population understanding throughout this chapter, we will suggest how it fits into this taxonomy. Aspects of understanding are relevant to all sections of this volume. In the remainder of this chapter, however, we will deal with an overview of population understanding as it has evolved over time.

HISTORICAL STAGES OF POPULATION UNDERSTANDING

We have separated those ideas that various writers have expressed about population into stages that are basically chronological but also focus on major figures whose remarks have captured particular attention.

Population Understanding from Antiquity[1]

One can search the writings of past centuries and discover numerous references to population or its change components. The Bible abounds with "begats" to signify the fertility of Biblical characters, and the injunction to "be fruitful and multiply" is indicative of encouragement of high fertility. Descriptions of migrations of Biblical peoples are widespread. These demographic concerns were not examined in a theoretical manner, however. At best, they were descriptional in nature, elemental in complexity, and they did not imply generalization to other groups.

The ancient Chinese philosophers combined their values about population with aspects of analytical demography. Confucius and his followers advanced the idea that population growth may reduce output per worker, depress levels of living for the masses, and engender strife. They also recognized the notion of optimum population distribution by holding government responsible for maintaining an ideal relation between land and population, through moving people from overpopulated to underpopulated areas. The ancient Chinese were also cognizant of certain checks to population growth, such as increasing mortality when food supplies were limited, infant mortality being related to early marriage, and the demographic effects of wars. By and large, these writers were supportive of population increase through marriage and procreation.

Throughout the early Greek and Roman periods, expressions about population were more likely to reflect the values of the writers and be prescriptive in nature rather than to attempt explanations. Both Plato and Aristotle considered population size and distribution to be critical elements of their ideal city-states. They believed it was necessary to optimize the population and land so that defense and security could be maximized, the resources would be adequate for the people, and government could manage efficiently. Plato specified that the city-state have 5,040 citizens, and measures were proposed to compensate for underpopulation (such as incentives to higher fertility and immigration) and overpopulation (birth control and colonization). The Romans were more inclined to look at demographic conditions over the whole empire instead of each city-state. Population increase was favored for its military potential. The Roman laws facilitated marriage and child-bearing in support of large populations.

Hebrew, Christian, and Moslem religious leaders and writers of the medieval period largely encouraged population expansion and discouraged limitations on population growth. Christian authors, in particular, took positions in defense of Church teachings. They condemned polygamy, divorce, abortion, infanticide, and child exposure; however, they also glorified virginity and continence and frowned upon remarriage. On balance, they advocated conditions favorable to population growth. This position was based not only on theology but on the realities of high mortality levels as well. While most Moslem writers voiced similar concerns and mainly took value stances, the prolific author Ibn Khaldun expounded theoretical notions in the fourteenth century about population that seemed to have anticipated the formulations of recent times. He maintained that a densely settled population was conducive to higher levels of living, since it permitted a greater division of labor, a more effective use of resources, and military and political security. Also, he recognized that periods of prosperity alternate with periods of decline and that population and economic cycles moved together. These cyclical variations generated positive and negative impacts on the society and its social institutions.

Pre-Malthusian Perspectives

It is apparent that population perspectives are heavily influenced by societal conditions. The social evolution that brought the Renaissance, the Industrial Revolution, and new governmental forms created circumstances that led many to view population in different terms than formerly. The rise of mercantilism, which accorded power and wealth to the state and stressed the accumulation of money and precious metals, favored expansion of foreign trade and the development of manufacturing. Botero, a spokesman for the mercantile view, regarded the strength of the state as in its population size and the predominance of industry over agriculture. Mercantilist writers discussed many factors that were determinants or consequences of demographic change, but they were not systematic in their treatment of these factors in the manner of today's analysts.

The subsequent period of physiocratic thought provided a reaction to mercantilist thinking. Physiocrats believed in the strategic importance of the agricultural areas in developing the economy. While not urging population increase, they saw population growth as stimulating agricultural production and, hence, the economy. Quesnay, a leading physiocrat writer, felt that population growth must be limited by the means of subsistence and therefore should not be too rapid.

Throughout the few centuries of conflicting philosophical thought related to population, there occurred the development of what later was known as political arithmetic, a forerunner of today's social statistics. In the mid-seventeenth century, John Graunt published his "bills of mortality" of the City of London, in which he observed the regularity of various vital statistics, especially the sex ratio at birth, fertility and mortality rates, and the relation between burials and christenings in the city as compared with a rural area, and constructed a schematic life-table design. His collaborator, William Petty, applied Graunt's statistical techniques to linking population change with social and economic conditions. These descriptive and rational analyses found their way into later theoretical expositions of other writers.

The continuing dialogue about population growth and the means of subsistence was heightened during the eighteenth century. The debate was often confused by the entanglements of arguments concerning the causes of population growth and those regarding the social philosophies of the debaters. The two basic camps have been labeled the *optimists* and the *pessimists*. The former were led by an Englishman, William Godwin, and a Frenchman, Marquis de Condorcet. They believed in human perfectibility, in scientific advances as being able to provide the necessary means of subsistence, and in the rationality of people to regulate their reproduction. The plight of the poor, they said, could be eliminated by changes in social institutions that would erase class barriers and redistribute wealth.

Malthus on Population

Thomas Malthus became the standard-bearer for the pessimists. His social philosophy was in stark contrast to that of Godwin and Condorcet. He stated that "the principal and most permanent cause of poverty has little or no direct relation to forms of government, or the unequal distribution of property."[2] Further, the poor were poverty-stricken due to their own behavior, particularly their high fertility and consequent burdensome family size. Overpopulation brought with it certain necessary evils, and the poor acquired their proportional share of them. Programs to subsidize the underprivileged, known in England as the "Poor Laws," were not a solution, since they only placed a tax on the classes above them and would not alter the behavior of the poor.

Malthus's political views were based on his social ideology and his analysis of population-food relationships. It is the latter that established his reputation in history. In fact, neither his philosophical nor scientific views were novel. But his writings on population were presented in an organized way, with clearly stated principles and a fair amount of documentation. He may have been the first person of his time to have effectively combined political commentary and statistical reasoning, a merger of the enlightenment philosophies and political arithmetic. Whether his population understanding was wholly independent of his values is debatable. Nevertheless, his writings on population have had a strong influence on subsequent theorizing in this field.

The basic arguments of Malthus were laid out in his *Essay on Population,* published anonymously in 1798. In the second and later editions, in which he was recognized as the author, he altered some of his positions in response to the criticisms of the first edition and his admittedly more thorough research. However, he included in the published volumes both his understanding of population principles and his views of their consequences for the society.[3] Our further attention will be directed to his population analysis as expounded in the later editions.

Malthus began with the notion of "the constant tendency in all animated life to increase beyond the nourishment prepared for it."[4] He assumed that "population, when unchecked, goes on doubling itself every twenty-five years, or increases in a geometrical ratio."[5] Moreover, "considering the present average state of the earth, the means of subsistence, under circumstances the most favourable to human industry, could not possibly be made to increase faster than in an arithmetical ratio."[6] These assumptions were supported by all known evidence about demographic and agricultural growth he could determine. Hence, "the increase of the human species can only be kept down to the level of the means of subsistence by the constant operation of the strong law of necessity, acting as a check upon the greater power."[7]

What, then, are the ways in which population growth can be checked? They fall under two general headings—the preventive and the positive checks. The *preventive check* arises from reasoning "about distant consequences"[8] and leads to prevention or delay of marriage.

The *positive checks* include every cause "which in any degree contributes to shorten the natural duration of human life."[9] These include "all unwholesome occupations, severe labour and exposure to the seasons, extreme poverty, bad nursing of children, great towns, excesses of all kinds, the whole train of common diseases and epidemics, wars, plague, and famine."[10] All of these checks are resolvable into moral restraint (the restraint from marriage), vice, and misery.

Malthus recognized the various means that result in death (the positive checks), but he restricted his definition of the preventive checks to that of postponement of marriage. Since delaying marriage itself would cause hardships of all kinds, population growth would be basically controlled by a variable death rate.

Clearly, two major considerations were not entertained adequately by Malthus's formulations. First, he was shortsighted where agriculture was concerned. He failed to see the revolutions in agriculture that increased immeasurably the amount of food per acre of land that could be produced. Second, although implicitly considering birth prevention a vice, he underestimated the degree to which the "passion between the sexes"[11] would likely be vented without the risk of conception. Religiously opposed to birth control, he did not anticipate either the technological advances in fertility regulations or the desire of the vast proportion of people to make use of it.

Malthus's ideas about population, as opposed to his political perspectives, differed from those of most of his predecessors in terms of their scientific orientation. Reverting to the dimensions of population understanding cited earlier, we can say that he had developed a theoretical framework that focused on population size but incorporated concerns about fertility and mortality. His theory had the broad objective of being oriented to the determinants and consequences of demographic change. It was a macro-level framework with a middle-range level of complexity and generalization intended for all classes of populations.

In the period following Malthus's *Essay*, his views on population were supported by some and challenged by others. The critics pointed to indications of more extensive use of preventive checks, social and economic progress that changed life-styles, and reduced *fecundity* (the physiological ability to reproduce). Economists argued about the ties between demographic change and economic productivity, with economic theory heavily influenced by Malthus's thinking.

Socialist Population Thought

The belief that society's ills would largely disappear if the social class system of the capitalist nations were to be eliminated has roots that go well back into pre-Malthusian debates. This notion became more widespread in the late nineteenth century and was solidified with the writings of Marx and Engels.[12] Marx stated that there was no universal law of population, as Malthus had argued, but rather that population conditions were related to social and economic situations in each society. Overpopulation only existed in a capitalist society; in a socialist one, the economy would always find places for available labor. Moreover, class differences in fertility and mortality were determined by variations in levels of living. These would be diminished as wealth was distributed more equally among the people.

Engels elaborated Marxian thinking by pointing out that, in a planned socialist society, fertility could be controlled. He added that the productive power of mankind was unlimited and, hence, population growth need not be alarming. Contemporary socialists have advocated Marxian principles of reorganizing society with needed fertility regulation as the means for optimizing population size.

Population was not a central concern of traditional socialist writers. To the extent that it was discussed, it had a more ideological bent. Freed from the political contexts, particularly in the more modern era, socialists have examined population in ways not very different from those who have espoused other ideologies.

The Balancing Equation of Population

Scientific analysis of demographic change prospered most when it was realized that population should not be viewed as a unitary phenomenon but instead as the net result of several demographic processes. These processes may not all move in the same direction or with the same magnitude. A feature of Malthus's theory was his separation of fertility and mortality as elements of population change. A singular contribution of his work was recognition of the need for disaggregating change into its components.

This principle of component analysis leads us to identify three elements through which all population change in an area must take place: births, deaths, and geographic movement. It is the balance of these three variables that results in demographic shifts (see Technical Supplement No. 2).

Early Modern Model Builders

The continuing debate engendered by Malthusian theory focused on limits of fertility and mortality (preventive and positive checks) and consequently on natural increase (the excess of births over deaths). The more systematic analysts of this issue attempted to develop models or frameworks for studying relationships between fertility and mortality as they changed over time.

One approach emphasized the universality of the processes by postulating that their trends were basically determined by biological causes. Pearl and Reed proposed that all populations tend to grow in the form of a mathematical logistic (or S-shaped) curve.[13] That is, a population at first increases in a geometric progression but is later hindered in its growth, so that it attains a level where it remains in stationary equilibrium. They tested this model by examining fruit flies in a closed, restricted living space. The small initial population of flies multiplied rapidly until available space was confining, and then, through limitations on reproduction, their numbers leveled off. This formula was later applied to an analysis of U.S. population trends. The "logistic" argument supported the Malthusian principle, but its critics suggested that the explanations for the phenomenon were mainly social, economic, and cultural. Other biologically based models have been developed that describe cycles of population change and resort largely to assumptions about changing fecundity.

Another category of models based on patterns of fertility and mortality is that referred to as *formal, pure,* or *stable-population* theories. These ignore the external causes or consequences of demographic change and instead focus on the internal structure of populations and relationships of fertility and mortality. Lotka was able to demonstrate mathematically that, in a closed population (one with no effect of migration), if age-specific fertility and mortality remain constant over time, the population will assume a fixed age structure as well as constant birth and death rates.[14] Others have since shown that even some departures from these assumptions will not invalidate the nature of the interrelationships. Consequently, it has been possible to use this model to estimate either fertility or mortality or age composition where reasonable assumptions can be made about the other two. This procedure has been especially valuable for studying the population of countries with inadequate data sources.

In the early 1900s, Landry, and later Thompson and Notestein,[15] compared the fertility and mortality trends of countries at different stages of economic development and generalized about a sequence of changes that they attributed to urbanization and industrialization. This formulation became known as the theory of the *demographic transition.* Basically, the demographic-transition idea posits three types of populations or three stages (see Figure 2.1). In the first stage, the population has both high fertility and high mortality. Since growth is perceived as determined solely by the balance between fertility and mortality, such a population has a low rate of growth and possibly occasional periods of numerical decline. This has been called the Malthusian stage, because the positive checks on population are generally

FIGURE 2.1   The demographic transition

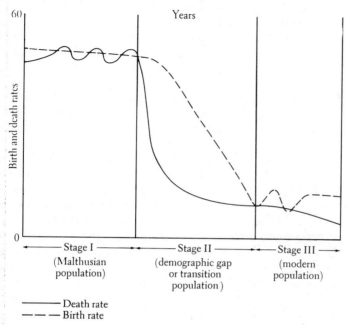

    Death rate
- - - Birth rate

severe and not controllable. Small societies may have vanished under such conditions. Societies under such a regime can be characterized as having a preindustrial economy and a nonurban environment.

The second stage of the demographic transition is one that continues to have high fertility but declining mortality. This is sometimes referred to as the *demographic gap*, since the levels of birth and death rates are quite different. The imbalance results in a very high growth rate. The economy in such a society is typically a developing one, so that some control over death has been achieved but little regulation of births is yet occurring.

The third stage is one with generally low fertility and mortality. This type of population is generally characteristic of industrialized countries where the population growth is low. In contrast with the Malthusian stage, when a variable death rate largely determined the direction and degree of population change, in this modern stage, a variable but reduced birthrate governs population growth or decline.

Over the long term, the sequence of the three stages of transition from high birth and death rates to low birth and death rates happen to result in a logistic rate of population growth. This model of the transition is a very crude picture of actual demographic change in certain societies, however, and its generality has been questioned in several ways. It is basically a description of historical developments in births and deaths occurring in Europe and the United States. Many analysts used the formulation to extrapolate that experience to other parts of the world, on the assumption that the sequence of transition stages was an inevitable one.

One set of challengers doubted that, even in Western societies, the process unfolded as described. Some argued that the demographic gap, or the period of rapid growth, was caused not only by a falling death rate but by a rising birthrate as well. It appears that the nuclear family became more widespread as industrialization took place. When more people who were normally tied to the land and to the extended family were free to marry, the birthrate went up somewhat, helping to increase the imbalance between births and deaths.[16] According to others, improvements in health resulting from mortality declines had the effect of increasing fecundity of women, who could then bear more children. Thus, it is false to postulate that all the growth in the gap period was caused by falling death rates.

Another serious criticism of the demographic-transition idea is that, while the transition framework may offer a partial picture of what happened to some countries during the last few centuries, it does not qualify as a true theory, because the complexity of explanation was low and it outlined relational patterns that could not be generalized to all countries undergoing development. Thompson himself pointed out that the time required for lowering birthrates could be subject to great variability between nations. He suggested that this time depends on some weighted combination of the rate of spread of birth control and the rurality of the population, a time that he was unable to predict.

Other variables may also enter in. It has long been apparent that the initial levels of fertility and mortality in a country will affect the time it takes the vital rates to come down. The variability in the means available for reduction of these rates is a further complication in determining just how long transition takes. Some have been skeptical of the ability of transition theory to predict future population-growth patterns.

> A reappraisal of the Western demographic transition in terms of its resource base and its economic, social, and intellectual aspects indicates that its precise repetition anywhere in the world is so improbable as to approach the inconceivable.[17]

It has been noted by many demographers that even the time required for the decline in the death rate, which has been occurring in many nations of the world, is subject to great variability.[18] While the countries of Western Europe had to wait for the slow development of medical technology in order to bring death rates down, the countries of Asia, Latin America, and Africa today can "borrow" death-control technology from more developed countries and greatly speed the reduction of their death rates. The desire to control death is, after all, a cultural universal, whereas the desire to control birth is not. A country may eagerly adopt methods of saving lives but hesitate or refuse to control births. The period of the demographic gap may thus be lengthened, making for high and sustained population growth. Will the death rate go back up in such countries before births are controlled?

This possibility has led some writers, Cowgill notable among them, to suggest that demographic transition, while useful, does not cover all the possible ways in which natural increase or decrease may occur.[19] Cowgill assumed that populations change in such a way as to ultimately produce an S-curve of growth. Exploring the logical possibilities that such an assumption would produce, Cowgill came up with four cycles of growth. These are illustrated in Figure 2.2.

Cycle I is called the *primitive cycle* and is typical of under-

FIGURE 2.2 Cowgill's population growth cycles

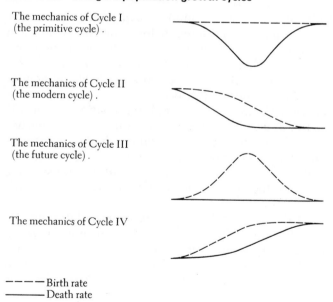

The mechanics of Cycle I
(the primitive cycle).

The mechanics of Cycle II
(the modern cycle).

The mechanics of Cycle III
(the future cycle).

The mechanics of Cycle IV

– – – – Birth rate
———— Death rate

Source: Reprinted by permission of the University of Chicago Press from Donald Olen Cowgill, "The Theory of Population Growth Cycles," *American Journal of Sociology,* 55, no. 2 (September 1949). Figures 2–5, pp. 165–170, redrawn as one figure. Copyright © 1949 University of Chicago.

developed areas. In these areas, the birthrate remains stationary, while the death rate declines. The death rate then eventually rises again to terminate the cycle. This pattern is reminiscent of the Malthusian or first-stage transition population.

Cycle II is the *modern cycle* and is characterized by falling birth and death rates, with the death rate falling more rapidly than the birthrate. The cycle is closed when the birthrate again approaches the death rate. This is much like the traditional model of the demographic transition.

Cycle III, which Cowgill called the *future cycle,* is characterized by a rising birthrate, while the death rate remains constant. To close the cycle, the birthrate falls. Such a pattern occurs for short periods of time in countries that have completed the transition and may have occurred for short periods of time in nations in the first stage of the transition. This cycle is known to us because of the post-World War II *baby boom.*

Finally, Cycle IV opens with a rising birthrate and closes with the death rate also rising to reach the birthrate. While this cycle has no precedent in history, it does constitute another mathematical possibility of an S-shaped growth curve. It is also consistent with the Malthusian notion of "positive checks" being a solution to a rapidly growing population.

Birth and death rates may also combine to produce natural decrease. In some countries, fertility has fallen below mortality, leading to fewer persons in the population. Notestein used the term *incipient decline* to herald that possibility. In modern societies, there have usually been conscious demographic responses to such a phenomenon, rendering natural decrease a short-run process.

The most obvious criticism of demographic transition as general population theory is that it was incomplete demographically. In particular, it neglected the third component of population change, geographic or residential mobility. Even though most societies in the earlier stages of transition did not experience much migration across their borders, when it did occur, the population balance could be very significantly influenced.

For example, in 1955 the growth-per-thousand population for Israel was 39. The natural increase per 1,000 in Israel during this same time period was only 23.1. In Puerto Rico, the growth rate was 10 per 1,000 during 1955, while the natural increase was 27.2 per 1,000—a difference accounted for by a net *out-migration* of 17.2 persons per 1,000.

Other examples of migration as an important variable in population growth or decline are readily available. Certainly in early times, when many cultures were based on a hunting and/or gathering economy, the wanderings of people made a difference in the population size of an area they abandoned or invaded. Irish history shows a steady loss in population in that country for many years, in spite of a high birthrate and a lower death rate. This loss in population was entirely due to emigration from Ireland (as discussed in Chapter 1).

Modern examples of the importance of migration in explaining patterns of population growth or decline include the large-scale movement of people during times of war. Refugees and displaced persons, as well as temporary movements of armies and citizens evacuating cities, cannot be ignored in calculations of population growth and decline. Further, in countries where natural increase or decrease is zero—that is, births and deaths are equal—migration accounts for 100 percent of the change in population size.

Internal migrations are also relevant for certain types of population growth and decline.[20] The westward movement in the United States accounted for the tremendous growth of the West Coast population in this country. This growth could not have been predicted by looking at the natural increase of this area alone.

Another way in which mobility can be important is in its effect on natural increase or decrease. It has been posited, for example, that the rate of natural increase in a community may be directly related to the ease with which the number of excess persons can be reduced by out-migration. In recent years, much more attention has been given to population mobility by demographic model-builders, even if largely outside the transition framework.

Despite its shortcomings, the demographic-transition framework has remained popular, since it seems to capture in outline form what is apparently the general historical course of fertility and mortality. Attempts to strengthen it have thus been more frequent than attempts to bury it. Migration has been added to the birth and death relationships to expand the variations in potential stages that might develop and to cover all of the basic components. Others have identified critical variables that, when added to the basic model, fortify its predictive power. For example, age at marriage, the availability of contraception, and perception of its use are variables that help explain the earlier European pattern.[21] Similarly, land availability, the economic expansion rate, and cultural factors are items that increase our comprehension of the transition process.[22] Cowgill also proposed improving the theory by including variables such as environmental resources and the economic structure of the society.[23] His test of the utility of the transition framework was based on generation of some logical demographic and social outcomes, such as shifts in age and marital composition, which he found to be tenable.

Just as Malthus had paved the way for an analytical approach to population thinking, so the architects of demographic-transition theory had adopted a scheme that had the fundamental underpinnings of a macro framework for understanding population change over the long haul.

EXPANDING POPULATION PERSPECTIVES

To say that population change is caused by changes in fertility, mortality, and population mobility is, however, only the beginning of an explanatory scheme. Certainly, analyzing change in terms of components of population has been a considerable improvement over viewing population as a unitary phenomenon. To indicate that some other variables are involved in the process in a facilitative way is likewise helpful in conceptualizing the relationships more thoroughly.

But many questions about population change are still left unanswered. What specifically causes fertility to increase or decrease? Why do some societies have higher mortality than others? What motivates people to migrate? These are the kinds of questions a complete theory of population change must answer in order to be most useful in explaining population growth and decline. The transition and other models discussed above are therefore weak, since they consider in only a limited way what factors cause the components of population to change.

In the remainder of this chapter, we will deal briefly with some of the broader theoretical approaches employed by population specialists today. These approaches may focus on either the macro, medial, or micro levels of influence or they may span two or three of these. They can also be seen as general approaches within which different categories of population subject matter might be treated. These approaches will be referred to as *ecological, sociocultural, modernization, institutional, normative, socialization, economic decision-making,* and *psychological decision-making.*

Ecological Approach

This is a macro perspective of demographic structure and change that is based on the biological notion of organisms adapting to their environment. Those who espouse the human-ecological point of view typically use four referential concepts: population, environment, technology, and organization.[24] The unit of ecological analysis is the human population located in a particular area. The environment of the area provides resources that are used to maintain life, but the environ- ment can have negative as well as positive features. Moreover, just as the environment influences the population, so does the population modify the environment. Technology involves both a "complex of art and artifact whose patterns are invented, diffused, and accumulated" and "a set of techniques employed by a population to gain sustenance from its environment and to facilitate the organization of sustenance- producing activity."[25] Ecologists are interested in social organization for the way in which it functions to order and integrate ecological processes. Each of the four categories in this ecological complex in- teracts with the other three in a dynamic system.

Actually, the four categories are broad ones, which encompass a number of different variables. Thus, population can be separated into all of the elements listed under our subject-matter classification. It has been suggested, for example, that fertility, mortality, and migration can be defined as "a set of alternative means available to populations which seek an equilibrium between their size and sustenance organiza- tion."[26] In this way, Southern black migration can be seen as generated by environmental and technological factors interacting with a reorga- nization of agriculture and rural societal institutions.

The ecological perspective enables us to make generalizations at the macro level, but it is not effective in dealing with medial- or micro- level phenomena. For those, we must turn to other approaches.

Sociocultural Approach

Some analysts choose to stress the general features of a society that influence population processes. Anthropologists have placed great emphasis on cultural patterns, economists on the type of economy, and some sociologists on the broader social institutional network. Fre- quently, these are combined into one perspective operating at the mac- ro level.

Davis and Blake tried to account for gross differences in fertility between the developed and developing countries of the world by iden- tifying *intermediate variables* (factors affecting exposure to inter- course, to conception, and to gestation and successful parturition) through which other social forces influencing fertility must operate.[27] Moreover, they indicated the way the particular type of social organiza- tion found in a society acts through the intermediate variables to change fertility. Davis has also utilized this general orientation in de- veloping an understanding of how societies bring fertility under con- trol after mortality has declined appreciably (as in the demographic transition).[28] One cannot, he argues, point to a single type of response (such as abortion in Japan and delayed marriage in Ireland). Rather every society has employed a *multiphasic response* that uses every demographic means possible to adjust to the situation. The social system as a whole reacts to the situation and calls forth those aspects that can be most effective socially and culturally in responding to the circumstances.

This type of approach has some similarities to the ecological perspective, in that it suggests ways in which parts of the societal complex interact with one another. Ecologists, however, tend to shun the cultural and behavioral aspects and highlight the more formal structural relationships.

Modernization Approach

A third macro perspective that views social factors in a somewhat different way is one stressing "a persistent, inclusive process of change, a dynamic social force that has transformed and reshaped human societies."[29] Modernization encompasses social, economic, political, and cultural changes in societies. It involves "increased division of labor, specialization, differentiation of institutions and structures, and social expansion."[30] As societies modernize, they alter the value of, and means for regulating, population processes.

The mortality transition is described as resulting from revolutions in agriculture and industry that brought about new public-health and medical technologies and enabled increased survival.[31] However, some countries benefited from these social revolutions through technological diffusion from developed to developing nations without themselves undergoing modernization to any great extent. Nevertheless, modernization may be necessary for modified population processes to be sustained. Spraying insecticides on lands and water infected with malaria-carrying flies may arrest the disease quickly, but poor nutrition, inadequate education, low income, and other characteristics of premodern societies may subject people to renewed risks at later times when the carriers of that or other diseases become rampant again.

Institutional Approach

Some analysts have chosen to focus their attention on particular institutional forms as they affect demographic processes. Each process and each cultural setting might call forth a different set of crucial institutions. This differs from the approaches cited earlier in that a bridge is made between the macro and medial levels. The more abstract societal processes are made more real by reducing them to segments of society that directly influence individual behavior.

Transformations in economic, educational, political, administrative, and familial institutional forms can be related to changes in fertility in various societies and communities.[32] Furthermore, changes in family structure and consequent shifts in wealth flows between parents and children during economic development have an impact on fertility.[33] In both instances, analysis proceeds from the country to the community and deals with variables that are real to the persons involved in the demographic process.

Normative Approach

Sociologists and anthropologists have long stressed the role of *norms* (guides to behavior) that emanate from institutional settings in shaping attitudes and actions of people. Norms have been referred to in some writings as the basis for understanding variations in population-related behavior. They also provide a linkage among the macro, medial, and micro levels.

It is through norms that broad institutional mechanisms are elaborated and specified for the individual.[34] For instance, controls on fertility are available in all societies, but cultural prescriptions (what to do) and proscriptions (what not to do) regarding sexual practices and conception are indicated by the consensus of each group and imposed or taught to the group's members. Frequently the norms, and values on which they are founded, are focused on certain themes. In premodern societies, having many children can be justified as a means of compensating for the high mortality among infants and children and as a force for maintaining strong kinship ties in a community.

Socialization Approach

Reference to norms suggests a process whereby guides for behavior are mediated from those who support them to those who do not or have not yet adopted such guides (for instance, children). Population socialization has been developed as an area of study that looks at the *agents* involved (who does the socializing), the *content* and *form* of the process (what, and when, and where it occurs), and the *consequences* (extent of changes in values, attitudes, behaviors) in the demographic sphere.[35]

While socialization can occur at any point in the life cycle, its heaviest influence is among young people who are trying to learn how to become adults. Hence, most research using this approach is concerned with children and youth and how they acquire the basis for becoming *population actors*. The socialization approach serves as a linkage between the medial and micro levels, thereby facilitating the comprehension of how factors at the group and individual levels are translated from one to another.

Economic Decision-Making

The ultimate population actors are individuals who make choices about what they do or do not do. Each person, to the extent that he or she is a unique human being, has a set of factors on which to operate that is peculiar to that individual. The most influential of these factors may be common for large numbers of people, and it may seem that those factors are the only ones of importance. Researchers from different disciplines may look at this social-psychological process and extract those variables that are most meaningful to students of that discipline.

In this context, economists have advanced several specific micro-level approaches to population understanding that fall into the realm of economic decision-making. Two dominant examples are the *household-demand approach* and the *relative-income approach*. In the first case, it is postulated that "what people do with their time can be understood in terms of the value of the time of each family member, the family's endowment, and the relative prices of the family's market inputs and outputs."[36] Within this framework, people decide the value of their investments, including the time and expenditure involved in having and rearing children and the worth of making a residential move. In the second case, the mechanism that is seen as determining a cyclical pattern of demographic behavior of an aggregate (for example, the baby boom followed by a *baby bust*) is the view that those approaching reproductive ages compare the economic opportunities available to them (which varies because of their relative numbers) and adopt a family size consistent with the kinds of opportunities their children might expect. Thus, the baby-boom cohort became discouraged by competition for places in preferred schools and in desirable jobs and scaled down the number of children they would have relative to the number their parents had.

Psychological Decision-Making

It has been stated that the decision models in population psychology "share the general assumption that individuals' choices are at least partly determined by their beliefs about the consequences that could result from making any given choice."[37] Three specific micro models most widespread in the treatment of population by psychologists are those related to *subjective-expected utility, cognitive-affective consistency,* and *value-x expectancy.*

In the subjective-expected utility model, individuals compare probable outcomes of various alternatives and choose the one they expect will lead to the highest utility. (This cost-benefit calculus framework is one shared by economists.) The cognitive-affective consistency model indicates that attitudes about a phenomenon depend upon the perceived relationship of that phenomenon to particular values and the importance to the person of these values. For example, women favoring birth control are likely to stress the positive aspects over the negative consequences. The value-x expectancy model argues for seeing behavioral intention, which predicts actual behavior, as a function of attitude toward performing the act in question and a normative component.

These eight conceptual approaches summarized here are not comprehensive population theories. Nevertheless, they sensitize us to critical variables and relationships and help sharpen our thinking in trying to understand aspects of population change. More generally, they span the range of macro, medial, and micro levels of analysis necessary to picture population status and dynamics in all of their manifestations. In subsequent chapters of this book, there will be occasion to refer to them again.

NOTES

1.   This summary and later references to population writings in earlier times are based on parts of Chapter III of U.N. Department of Economic and Social Affairs, *The Determinants and Consequences of Population Trends*, Vol. 1 (New York: United Nations, 1973).

2.   T. R. Malthus, *An Essay on Population*, Everyman's Library, Vol. 1 (New York: Dutton, 1952).

3.   Ibid.

4.   Ibid., p. 5.

5.   Ibid., p. 8.

6.   Ibid., p. 10.

7.   Ibid., p. 11.

8.   Ibid., p. 12.

9.   Ibid., p. 14.

10.   Ibid., p. 14.

11.   Ibid., p. 312.

12.   These are neatly quoted and summarized in Ronald L. Meek, *Marx and Engels on Malthus* (London: Lawrence and Wishart, 1953).

13.   Raymond Pearl and Lowell Reed, "On the Rate of Growth of Population of the United States Since 1790 and Its Mathematical Representation," *Proceed-*

ings of the National Academy of Science, 6 (1920), 275–288. The logistic growth principle had been advanced earlier by P. F. Verhulst in "Recherches mathematiques sur la loi d'accroissement de la population," *Nouveaux Memoires de l'Academie Royale des Sciences et Belles-Lettres de Bruxielles,* 18, no. 1 (1845).

14.   A. J. Lotka, "Population Analysis," in *Population Theory and Policy,* ed. J. J. Spengler and O. D. Duncan (New York: Free Press, 1956).

15.   Adolphe Landry, *Traite de démographie,* (Paris: Payot, 1945); Warren S. Thompson, "Population," *American Journal of Sociology,* 34 (May 1929), 959–975; Frank W. Notestein, "Population—The Long View," in *Food for the World,* ed. Theodore W. Schultz (Chicago: University of Chicago Press, 1945), pp. 36–57.

16.   William Petersen, "The Demographic Transition in the Netherlands," *American Sociological Review,* 25 (June 1960), 334–347.

17.   Irene B. Taeuber, "The Future of Transitional Areas," in *World Population and Future Resources,* ed. Paul K. Hatt (New York: American Book Company, 1952), pp. 25–38. See also Irene B. Taeuber, "Japan's Demographic Transition Re-examined," *Population Studies,* 14 (July 1960), 28–39; and Ronald Freedman, "Theories of Fertility Decline: A Reappraisal," *Social Forces,* 58, no. 1 (September 1979), 1–17.

18.   George J. Stolnitz, "The Demographic Transition: From High to Low Birth Rates and Death Rates," in *Population: The Vital Revolution,* ed. Ronald Freedman (New York: Doubleday, 1964), pp. 30–46.

19.   Donald O. Cowgill, "The Theory of Population Growth Cycles," *American Journal of Sociology,* 55, no. 2 (September 1949), 163–170.

20.   Dov Friedlander, "Demographic Responses and Population Change," *Demography* 6, no. 4 (November 1969), 359–381; George L. Wilber, "Demographic Transition: An Analytical Framework" (Paper presented to the Population Association of America annual meeting, Cincinnati, Ohio, April 1967).

21.   A. J. Coale, "The Demographic Transition Reconsidered," *Proceedings of the International Population Conference,* Liege, 1973, 53–57.

22.   Steven E. Beaver, *Demographic Transition Theory Reinterpreted* (Lexington, Mass: Heath, 1975).

23.   Donald O. Cowgill, "Transition Theory as General Population Theory," *Social Forces,* 41 (March 1963), 270–274.

24.   See Otis Dudley Duncan, "Human Ecology and Population Studies," in *The Study of Population,* ed. P. M. Hauser and O. D. Duncan (Chicago: University of Chicago Press, 1959), pp. 681–684. The foundation of this approach was set down by Amos H. Hawley, *Human Ecology* (New York: Ronald Press, 1950).

25.   Duncan, "Human Ecology," 682.

26.   David F. Sly, "Migration and the Ecological Complex," *American Sociological Review,* 37, no. 5 (October 1972), 615–628. For an extension of those ideas, see David F. Sly and Jeff Tayman, "Ecological Approach to Migration Reexamined," *American Sociological Review,* 42, no. 5 (October 1977), 783–794.

27.   Kingsley Davis and Judith Blake, "Social Structure and Fertility: An Ana-

lytic Framework," *Economic Development and Cultural Change,* 4 (April 1956), 211–235.

28. Kingsley Davis, "The Theory of Change and Response in Modern Demographic History," *Population Index,* 29, no. 4 (October 1963), 345–366.

29. Calvin Goldscheider, *Population, Modernization, and Social Structure* (Boston: Little, Brown, 1971), p. 79.

30. Ibid., p. 93.

31. Ibid., pp. 102–124.

32. Geoffrey McNicoll, "Institutional Determinants of Fertility Change," *Population and Development Review,* 6, no. 3 (September 1960), 441–462.

33. J. C. Caldwell, "The Mechanisms of Demographic Change in Historical Perspective," *Population Studies,* 35 (March 1981), 5–27.

34. Ronald Freedman, "Norms for Family Size in Underdeveloped Areas," *Proceedings of the Royal Society,* 159 (1963), 220–234.

35. See Susan Philliber and Charles Nam, special editors and contributors to a forum on population socialization in *Population and Environment,* 3, no. 1 (Spring 1980).

36. T. Paul Schultz, *Economics of Population* (Reading, Mass: Addison-Wesley, 1981), pp. 2–3.

37. Nancy E. Adler, "Decision Models in Population Research," *Journal of Population,* 2, no. 3 (Fall 1979), 187–202.

SUGGESTED ADDITIONAL READINGS

Useful summaries of population thought in history include:

BONAR, JAMES, *Theories of Population from Raleigh to Arthur Young.* New York: A. M. Kelley, 1966.

GLASS, D. V., AND D. E. C. EVERSLEY, EDS., *Population in History.* London: E. Arnold, 1965.

HUTCHINSON, E. P., *The Population Debate.* Boston: Houghton Mifflin, 1967.

OVERBEEK, J., *History of Population Theories.* Rotterdam: Rotterdam University Press, 1974.

UNITED NATIONS DEPARTMENT OF ECONOMIC AND SOCIAL AFFAIRS, *The Determinants and Consequences of Population Trends,* vol. 1, Chap. III, "Population Theory." New York: United Nations, 1973.

Discussions of the general role of demographic theory are contained in:

ROBINSON, WARREN C., "The Development of Modern Population Theory," *American Journal of Economics and Sociology,* 23 (October 1964), 375–392.

VANCE, RUPERT, "Is Theory for Demographers?" *Social Forces,* 31 (October 1952), 9–13.

Useful classical writings on demographic theory and evaluations of them include:

MALTHUS, T. R., *An Essay on Population*, Everyman's Library, Vol. 1. New York: Dutton, 1952.

MEEK, RONALD L., ED., *Marx and Engels on The Population Bomb*. Berkeley: Ramparts Press: 1971.

PETERSEN, WILLIAM, *Malthus*. Cambridge, Mass.: Harvard University Press, 1979.

TECHNICAL SUPPLEMENT NO. 2

The Balancing Equation of Population

All population change operates through the basic components of population—fertility, mortality, and mobility. The formula that depicts this relationship is called the *balancing equation of population.*

Consider population change between two points in time. The population at the second point in time is equal to the population at the first point in time, plus the births occurring during the time interval, minus the deaths occurring during the time interval, plus the residential movement of persons into the area during the time interval, minus the residential movement of persons out of the area during the time interval. The effects of these last two variables are generally combined into a positive or negative net effect. In symbolic form, this equation appears as follows:

$$P_2 = P_1 + B - D \pm M$$

For example, if we use data (expressed in thousands) for the United States between 1970 and 1979, the equation becomes:

$$\underset{220,099}{\underbrace{\underset{\text{population}}{1979}}} = \underset{203,302}{\underbrace{\underset{\text{population}}{1970}}} + \underset{30,567}{\underbrace{\underset{\text{births}}{1970\text{--}79}}} - \underset{17,800}{\underbrace{\underset{\text{deaths}}{1970\text{--}79}}} + \underset{4,030}{\underbrace{\underset{\text{net immigration}}{1970\text{--}79}}}$$

This equation assumes a constant land area under consideration, although population in a given political unit (for instance, a city) may also increase or decrease due to boundary changes resulting from annexation or cession of territory.

The net effect of the first two components of the balancing equation (births and deaths) is referred to as *natural increase* (if births are greater) or *natural decrease* (if deaths are greater). These terms arise from the observation that birth and death are "natural" phenomena and are the boundary points in the human life cycle.

ISSUES SUPPLEMENT NO. 2

The influence of Thomas Malthus on population thinking has been profound. His name and ideas seem always to be with us. Yet students of the field are in some disagreement on just how relevant Malthus's theory is today. Consider the following three perceptions, and then analyze the issue and make your own judgment.

> *Malthus has the faults of a pioneer, but his* Essay on the Principle of Population *is more directly relevant today than the works of any predecessor, and even of many successors. He saw the potential for the rapid growth that has indeed taken place since he wrote, and for the deterioration in human welfare that this increase in numbers can affect. He saw also how control over such multiplication could be established—by the gradual inculcation in each person of a higher aspiration, which would induce him to forego a numerous progeny in exchange for other values.* (William Petersen, *Population,* 3rd ed. New York: Macmillan, 1975, p. 144.)

> *Malthus believed that the positive checks were more powerful than the preventive, and that, among the preventive checks, only the postponement of marriage was of practical significance . . . he defined postponement of marriage as "moral restraint" and all other preventive checks as "vice." He then unconsciously made the assumption, very common in human reasoning, that what one feels is ethically bad cannot be empirically predominant. Postponement of marriage thereby became for him the only check which could lower fertility enough to escape the direct pressure of lack of subsistence . . . thus one of Malthus' great empirical mistakes is traceable to a weakness of his conceptual framework, the confusion of moral evaluation with scientific analysis.* (Kingsley Davis, "Malthus and the Theory of Population," in Paul F. Lazarsfeld and Morris Rosenberg, *The Language of Social Research.* New York: Free Press, 1955, pp. 552–553.)

> *Malthus's great contribution to social thought was to call attention to population pressure as a major source of human suffering. Yet Malthus's view of human nature was that of a biological determinist. Even in overcrowded societies living close to the bare subsistence level there are . . . social and cultural restrictions on fertility unrelated to population pressure. Conced-*

ing the rigor of Malthus's thought, the correctness of his insistence that human numbers cannot go on increasing indefinitely, and the relevance of population pressure to the social and economic plight of contemporary underdeveloped nations, the conception of an unchanging, biologically fixed human nature from which he derived his law has long since been rejected by social scientists. (Dennis H. Wrong, *Population and Society,* 4th ed. New York: Random House, 1977, p. 123.)

CHAPTER THREE
MORTALITY: TRENDS AND DETERMINANTS

"The survival rate of married or remarried women in a sample of 52 women with an average age of 75 was higher than that of the never-married, the separated, the unremarried divorced, or the unremarried newly widowed..."

Drawing by Lou Myers; © 1976 *The New Yorker* Magazine, Inc.

It is clear from the preceding chapter that mortality is not only one of the basic components of population change but also one of the most critical in terms of the history of modern population expansion. Declines in the death rate preceding any major declines in the birthrate account for a considerable part of the population explosion that has occurred in many countries. At the same time, the trend of mortality has not always been downward, nor has it ordinarily been smooth. Death rates have risen in different parts of the world at different points in time, and there have typically been annual and seasonal fluctuations in mortality patterns.

The aim of this chapter is to analyze mortality as a component of population change. In so doing, we shall first examine long-term trends of mortality in the world and its major regions, subsequently look at short-term variations in the death rate, and then consider the way mortality is related to age. Using the explanatory framework outlined in Chapters 1 and 2, attention is given to macro, medial, and micro factors that influence mortality. Finally, the future trend of mortality is assessed.

LONG-TERM MORTALITY TRENDS

Three measures of mortality are cited in order to describe death patterns. (These are each shown in the World Population Data Sheet in Appendix A). The *crude death rate* (number of deaths per thousand population per year) is the most frequently available statistic. It is called crude because the people in the denominator (the population at risk) have unequal risks of survival, largely because of their age. When the crude death rate of two or more populations is compared, the population with the oldest age composition will tend to have the highest crude death rate, because more of its people are in higher-risk age categories. This can mislead us if we are interested in comparing the underlying force of mortality (the risks relative to given ages) among the populations. Similarly, other compositional factors such as sex or race can also confound comparison of mortality rates.

A second measure is the *infant mortality rate* (deaths of babies prior to the first birthday per thousand live births per year). This measure is regarded as a particularly important one, since a substantial part of the total death rate in countries with high mortality is due to the death of infants.

Still a third measure, *life expectancy at birth* (the average number of years of life to be lived by a group of babies born at the same time), provides us with a different kind of picture of survival prospects, since it shifts our attention from mortality in a given time period (such as in a calendar year) to mortality probabilities over the lifetimes of people (or of a cohort).

Data to develop these measures of the mortality of a population have been available only in comparatively recent times. Yet some information has been developed that shows the mortality experience of people in early history. There is no evidence that *life-span* (the ultimate age to which people can live) has changed at all over time. Some humans are believed to live to about 120 today, and no reliable record suggests a greater life-span in previous eras. There are occasional reports of those who are celebrating their 150th birthday or whose parents lived to that age, but one might suspect such reports, since it has been shown that a high proportion of people assumed to be even centenarians have misreported their age and are, in fact, somewhat short of a hundred years old.[1] At least, such longevity would be exceedingly rare.

One may be confident, however, that life expectancy has been changing over time (see Technical Supplement No. 3). Even though life-span has remained constant, the greater survival of infants and reductions in mortality at middle and older ages mean that more persons today live beyond infancy and to more advanced ages than previously. Archaeologists have determined that Neanderthals (approximately 110,000 to 35,000 years ago) lived, on the average, to age twenty-nine, with a rather small chance of surviving to forty years of age. The average length of life increased slightly during the Upper Paleolithic and Mesolithic periods (about 35,000 to 8,000 years ago), reaching approximately thirty-two years.[2] Slow but continued increases are estimated to have occurred during the Neolithic and Bronze Age eras (approximately 8,000 to 3,000 years ago), but more reliable records for classical Greece and Rome (the centuries around the time of Christ) put life expectancy in the thirty-two to thirty-five-year age range.[3]

While these early estimates of life expectancy are questionable, the evidence indicates that no ancient or medieval population boasted an average longevity greater than about thirty-five years. Moreover, no sharp changes in average length of life took place until about the eighteenth or nineteenth century. Prior to that time, mortality rates were variable, reflecting vulnerability to crop failures, epidemics, and the like. Even today, after various means of death control have produced profound alterations in mortality patterns, life expectancy for some of the least-developed countries is not much above that in medieval times (see Figure 3.1).

FIGURE 3.1 Life expectancy

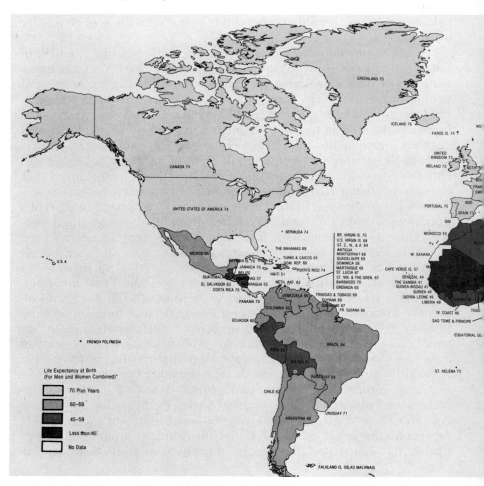

Prepared by the Population Reference Bureau, Inc., Washington, D.C., with the support of the Demography Division of the Office of Population, U.S. Agency for International Development, April 1981.

Developed Regions of the World

Although the mortality levels of the developed countries were already moderately low when death statistics were first compiled, substantial gains in survival were made in the ensuing years. It is impossible, without the benefit of adequate data, to trace the long course of

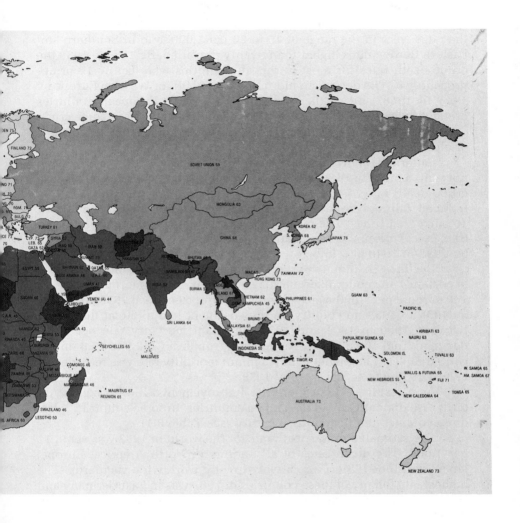

mortality in these nations as they underwent the demographic transition. It is reasonable to expect, however, that death rates were considerably higher before than after death records became available, and that the long-term history of mortality in developed countries was one of a slow but continual transition from high to low death rates.

It is only within the past few decades that this uniformly low level of mortality has been attained in modernized nations. In Europe, for example, the only countries between 1906 and 1910 with crude death rates below 15 per 1,000 were Denmark, England and Wales, the Netherlands, Norway, and Sweden.[4] In other parts of Western Europe the rates were in the range of 15 to 20 per 1,000, and in Southern and Eastern Europe rates higher than twenty prevailed. By 1935 to 1938 the crude death rates for most European countries were below 15 or approaching it. The decline in mortality leveled off for Western Europe by 1955 to 1958, and further reductions for other European countries brought them all to a comparably low level. In recent years, some crude death rates may have risen as a consequence of increasing proportions of older persons in the populations.

Patterns of mortality decline in North America and Oceania were not unlike those in Western Europe. In the United States, for instance, a crude death rate of 16.2 per 1,000 in 1900 to 1904 was progressively reduced, falling below 10 in about 1950 and stabilizing between 9 and 10 since that time.[5] The downward trend was even more profound in the Soviet Union, where a death rate of 32.4 in 1896 to 1897 fell to 17.6 by 1938 to 1940 and to below 10 by 1950 to 1954.[6]

Declines in infant mortality played a major role in raising life expectancy in modernized nations. Whereas infant mortality rates of 100 or more per 1,000 were common in Europe between 1935 and 1938, by 1955 to 1958 no country on the continent had a rate at that level. Between 1900 to 1904 and 1973 the infant mortality rate per 1,000 declined from 100.8 to 17.3 for Australia and from 142.9 to 17.6 for the United States. The Soviet Union's infant mortality rate was recorded as 273 in 1913 and fell to 22.6 by 1973.[7]

As a result of these mortality improvements, life expectancy at birth rose dramatically in developed countries. In some countries it has doubled since the turn of the century (see Table 3.1).

The estimated crude death rate for the world in 1982 was about 11 per 1,000. The death rates of all nations in North America, Europe, Japan, and the USSR are relatively low by worldwide standards. The highest rate for any of these countries in 1982 was in East Germany and Hungary (14), somewhat above the world average. The lowest rate in these regions was in Japan (6), and the other countries were bunched between these rates. Infant mortality rates for these countries were more disparate, being as low as 5 in Iceland and as high as 36 in the USSR. Almost all these countries had infant mortality rates of between 8 and 26, far below the world level of 85 in 1982.

Once relatively high levels were reached, expectation of life at birth approached stabilization. In the Soviet Union, it declined slightly in the late 1970s.[8] Not only the infant mortality rate, but most age-specific death rates in the Soviet Union, have been rising since the mid-1960s. This persistent reversal of mortality trends is unprece-

TABLE 3.1 **Trends in expectation of life at birth for selected developed nations since the turn of the century**

Country	Period	Expectation of Life at Birth (years)	Country	Period	Expectation of Life at Birth (years)
Austria	1901–1905	40.1	Spain	1900	34.8
	1930–1933	56.5		1930–1931	50.3
	1949–1951	64.4		1950	61.1
	1971	70.5		1960	69.7
	1975–1979	72		1975–1979	73
Belgium	1891–1900	47.1	Australia	1901–1910	57.0
	1928–1932	57.9		1920–1922	61.2
	1946–1947	64.7		1946–1948	68.4
	1959–1963	70.7		1956–1958	70.5
	1975–1979	73		1960–1962	71.2
				1975–1979	73
Hungary	1900–1901	37.5	USSR	1896–1897[a]	32
	1930–1931	49.8		1926–1927[a]	44
	1955	66.9		1957–1958	68
	1970	69.4		1968–1969	70
	1975–1979	70		1975–1979	69
Italy	1901–1911	44.5	United States	1900–1902	49.2
	1930–1932	54.9		1929–1931	59.7
	1954–1957	67.9		1949–1951	68.2
	1964–1967	70.7		1971	71.1
	1975–1979	73		1975–1979	74

Sources: United Nations, *Population Bulletin* no. 6, 1962 (New York: United Nations, 1963), pp. 22–23, 28, and 31; United Nations, *Demographic Yearbook,* (New York: United Nations, 1972), Table 27; and Population Reference Bureau, *1981 World Population Data Sheet.*
[a]*For European Russian.*

dented among industrialized nations. Even a statistically adjusted infant mortality rate of 26 per 1,000 in 1971 had risen to 36 by the late 1970s. Possible explanations are frequent epidemics of influenza, reduced health care, and growing environmental pollution.

Developing Regions of the World

It is characteristic of the bulk of countries in Latin America, Asia, and Africa that their mortality levels remained high for a longer period of time than those in modernized nations. When death control became more widespread, death rates in these countries fell more precipitously than they ever did in the developed countries. It is still the case, however, that important variations can be noted among the broad regions and individual countries (see the World Population Data Sheet in Appendix A).

Latin American mortality trends have been similar to those of developed nations, with some time lag. This would be especially true of countries such as Argentina and Uruguay, whose death rates at the turn of the century were already quite low, and to a lesser extent of Costa Rica, Puerto Rico, and Venezuela. With the exception of Haiti and Bolivia, other Latin American nations have experienced significant reductions in the death rate, and the prevailing rate in many of these lands is now below the crude death rates for the majority of modernized countries, partly because of mortality declines and partly because of favorable age distributions.

The downward course of mortality can also be documented for the major areas of Asia. Reductions have been observed since shortly after the turn of the century, with the steepest declines taking place in recent decades. In Japan, the death rate per 1,000 dropped from 21.8 in 1921 to 1925 to 7.8 in 1958 and has stayed at that low level. But decreases of the same order of magnitude are also shown by official data for most other Asian countries. Some of the sharpest reductions in mortality were recorded for Ceylon (now Sri Lanka), Malaysia, and Hong Kong. However, in 1982 death rates of at least 20 per 1,000 were estimated for Yemen, Nepal, Afghanistan, Bhutan, Laos, and East Timor.

The death rate for Africa as a continent stood at 17 per 1,000 in 1982, and virtually every country of Western and Middle Africa, as well as some in Eastern and Southern Africa, had death rates near that level or above. Where death rates were at least moderately low, they could be attributed partly to the presence of European settlers.

The overall picture in the developing countries is one of declining mortality, but with the decline at different stages of development. Latin American countries, by and large, have effected the mortality transition. Death control has been rapidly achieved in most parts of Asia. Only in Africa is such control lagging. Crude death rates there remain generally high, and infant mortality rates tend likewise to be sustained at levels far above those in most other parts of the world.

SHORT-TERM MORTALITY PATTERNS

We have been discussing the long sweep of mortality trends without paying attention to variations in death rates that take place within the calendar year and across just a few years. Closer examination of the trends, when death rates are plotted on a month-to-month basis, reveals fluctuations that are of significance to social life. Rosenberg has broken

FIGURE 3.2 United States death rates by month, raw data, and seasonal, cyclical, and irregular components, 1957–1960

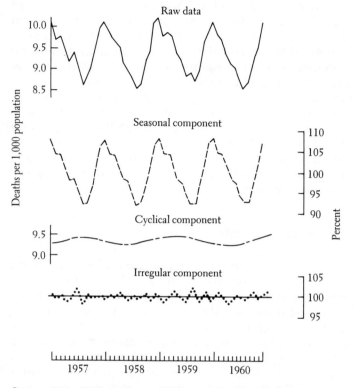

Source: Harry M. Rosenberg, "Seasonal Adjustment of Vital Statistics by Electronic Computer," *Public Health Reports,* 80, no. 3 (March 1965), 206.

down mortality patterns for the United States in the 1957-to-1960 period into three components.[9]

As depicted in Figure 3.2, the seasonal component, which consists of intrayear variations that are repeated more or less regularly each year, accounts for more than half of the month-to-month mortality variations. Year after year, one can observe peaks in the winter months and troughs during the summer months. The seasonal pattern in countries other than the United States may vary, depending on their locations and the climatic condition in the area. (Severe weather and the risks of respiratory ailments may occur in other calendar months.) The cyclical component, which incorporates continual longer alternating periods of increase and decrease spaced at least a few years apart, is relatively smooth. The irregular component, residual fluctuations that exhibit no recurrent pattern, accounts for about one-fourth of the total variation in the death rate. On balance, then, the level of the death rate at any point in time is composed of a significant and quite predictable seasonal pattern, a minor and somewhat predictable cyclical pattern, and a minor but most unpredictable irregular pattern, all superimposed on the long-term mortality trend. The nature and strength of these mortality components has remained fairly constant over time.

The seasonal pattern in mortality varies when different causes of death are examined separately.[10] For example, while the overall seasonal pattern is also observed for deaths due to heart diseases, vascular lesions, diabetes, influenza and pneumonia, and bronchitis, the pattern differs for malignancies (no significant seasonality), diseases of early infancy (peaks in summer), motor-vehicle accidents (rise throughout year), and suicide (peaks in spring).

THE AGE CURVE OF MORTALITY

The element of predictability found in both long-term and short-term mortality histories can also be discovered in age patterns of mortality. From birth to death, the human organism is subject to decreased functional capacity resulting from both the normal aging process and environmental factors.[11] The aging process, based on changes in tissues and cells of the human body, is fairly common among contemporary populations, even though different genetic characteristics of groups and individuals may alter the organism's ability to survive. Environmental factors, such as disease and accidents, are generally more variable in their impact on the human's chances of survival, but their effects are ordinarily of a smaller magnitude than those of the intrinsic processes of bodily change.

The net effect of these processes generates a human mortality curve that is characterized by four distinct phases: (1) rapid decrease in death rate during infancy and childhood; (2) a period roughly between 10 and 30 years of age during which there is a low or slowly increasing mortality rate; (3) a period of more rapid increase in mortality chances from about age 35 to 90; and (4) a slower increase in mortality after age 90.[12]

Most interestingly, as shown in Figure 3.3, the general age curve of mortality just described is standard for all times and populations for which data are recorded or estimated.[13] Six curves are presented in the figure, showing for each sex the death rate according to age (*age-specific death rates*) for three hypothetical populations. These populations

FIGURE 3.3   Models of age-specific death rates, for each sex, corresponding to three different values of expectation of life at birth (logarithmic scale)

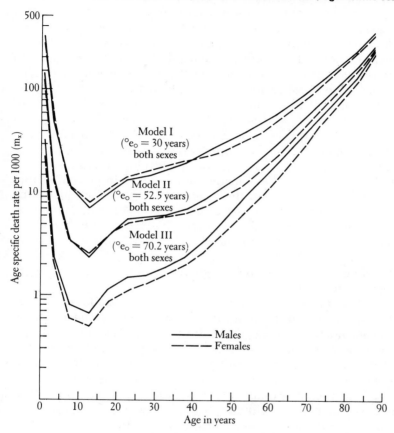

Source: United Nations, *Population Bulletin of the United Nations,* no. 6, 1962 (New York: United Nations, 1963), p. 52.

have mortality levels indicative of high, intermediate, and low life expectancies at birth in the modern world. In the case of Model I, a life expectancy of 30 years would be typical. Model II is characteristic of countries with a life expectancy of 52.5 years, while the average longevity of persons in Model III is 70.2 years.

The most impressive feature of the figure is the similarity in general shape of all the curves. Regardless of the level of mortality in the populations, death rates decline from infancy to teen ages and increase thereafter. (The fourth phase—after age 90—is not presented, but will be discussed later.) What does differ among the model populations is the level of death rates reached at various ages. Those countries with more favorable life expectancies have considerably lower death rates at the younger ages and somewhat lower rates at middle and older ages.

A country undergoing the mortality transition from a life expectancy at birth of fifty-two years to one of seventy years would experience reductions in the death rate of roughly 40 to 50 percent at ages up to forty, and even 20 to 25 percent after the age of seventy-five. This was the case for the United States between about 1915 and 1960, and is represented by a shift from the mortality curve of Model II to that of Model III. These are approximately the magnitudes of reductions in mortality at each age that will be necessary to bring the overall mortality picture in many of the developing countries of the world in line with what is now observed for many of the developed nations.

Not all countries that have made the transition in mortality from Model II to Model III have had the same pattern of reductions in the death rate at each age. In Europe, North America, Australia, and New Zealand, the decline of mortality initially affected mainly the death rates of infants and children, and that of young adults to a lesser extent. In the developing countries of Africa, Asia, and Latin America, adults up to age forty or fifty appear to have shared with children the benefit of mortality reduction.[14]

Even within these groups of countries the magnitudes of decline varied somewhat, and during short periods of time some mortality increases were noted. Considerable differences among countries still exist in the provision of health and medical resources and knowledge. Thus, reductions in mortality from more superficial means (such as spraying of insecticides on fields) tend often to be temporary.

The universality over time of the age curve of mortality is perplexing to some because one might suppose that lower death rates at the younger ages would lead to higher death rates at the older ages. The failure of that phenomenon to appear in Figure 3.3 may be due to the beneficial (or spillover) effect of environmental improvements directed at one age level on other age levels.[15] However, comparison of a large number of mortality curves reveals that the slopes (rates of incline) at the older ages (say, after age seventy) differ more than at the younger ages, thereby producing what is called a *crossover* effect in the curves.[16] This may be a function of the different rate at which populations approach phase four of the curve (described earlier). Subsequent discussion in this chapter will indicate disparities in the relative magnitude of certain causes of death at older ages in different populations that help to explain this phenomenon. More generally, one can refer to variations in individual frailty or vitality whose distribution changes with selectivity in mortality.[17] Thus, in some populations, those reaching older ages are susceptible to losing functional capacity more rapidly than in others.

Nevertheless, it is clear from available historical data that general improvements in survival have had no impact on life-span as yet, and have had only minor effects on the remaining life expectancy of those reaching older ages. In the first half of the twentieth century in Sweden, decreases in death rates amounted to between 64 and 81 percent at ages under forty-five, 27 percent at ages forty-five to sixty-four, and only 7 percent at ages sixty-five and over.[18] In the United States, expectation of life at birth increased from forty-nine to seventy-three between 1900 and 1978, an addition of twenty-four years of life. Only twelve years were added to life expectancy at age twenty (forty-three versus fifty-five years), and a mere four years were added at age sixty-five (twelve versus sixteen years).[19]

FACTORS AFFECTING MORTALITY

Now that we have surveyed the course of mortality as it has developed in all parts of the world, to what can we attribute the changes that have taken place? Which factors seem to have been most important, and how differently have the several factors operated to bring about alterations in death rates in various countries? In trying to provide the answers to these questions, we will return to the framework that distinguishes between macro, medial, and micro factors, and examine them in turn.

Macro Variables

Although a great number of global factors could be cited as affecting mortality, four broad categories are of particular relevance in understanding trends in the death rate. These are economic development and technological change, advances in public health and medical science, changing causes of death, and environmental factors.

Economic Development and Technological Change

A considerable amount of evidence points to these factors as contributing substantially to the reduction of mortality in Western countries. Various authors have recognized the importance of industrialization, commercial development, and the increasing efficiency of agriculture in providing the economic basis for a more abundant and more healthful life and for advances in public health and medicine that made the present low mortality rates possible.[20] The theoretical statement of the demographic transition hypothesized the important role of economic change in reducing deaths, and this relationship can be used to describe the history of mortality trends in industrialized nations. According to Coale and Hoover:

> *Economic development, according to the theory of the demographic transition, has the effect of bringing about a reduction in death rates. Economic development involves evolution from a predominantly agrarian economy to an economy with a greater division of labor, using more elaborate tools and equipment, more urbanized, more oriented to the market sale of its products, and characterized by rapid and pervasive changes in technique. It also involves improvements in transportation, communications, and productivity, and these improvements have had the effect (notably in Europe, the United States, Canada, Australia, and New Zealand, and later in Japan) of bringing a striking reduction in death rates. The reduction in death rates may be ascribed partly to greater regularity in food supplies, to the establishment of greater law and order, and to other fairly direct consequences of economic change. Other factors contributing to the decline— improvements in sanitation, the development of vaccines and other means of preventive medicine, and great and rapid strides in the treatment of disease—can themselves be considered as somewhat indirect consequences of economic change.[21]*

Economic change can be said to have contributed both directly and indirectly to long-term mortality reductions in what are now the industrialized portions of the world. But it is clear that economic factors have had less direct effect on declines in the death rates of developing countries. Many low-income countries, such as Sri Lanka, Malaysia, some of the Caribbean islands, and parts of Latin America, have attained low death rates without any major transformation in their resources. Most of these countries have borrowed death-saving technology and materials already developed in modernized nations and have benefited, to some extent, from economic aid from those countries.

It was long believed that economic progress in a country contributed to mortality reductions by a filter-down process, whereby the benefits of increased industrial and agricultural productivity first went primarily to the elite of the society, who had greater access to them, and then proceeded to be passed along to the lower social classes.[22] More recent evidence indicates that the relation of mortality declines and national economic gains, as reflected in national per-capita income or per-capita gross national product, can be misleading in that much of the economic benefit may be concentrated in the elite sector and not be distributed rapidly to other groups. In fact, in some countries where overall economic advancement is indicated, mortality levels have been slow to decline. We can now see that the economic gains must reach the whole population for real progress in death reductions to be achieved. This means not only raising average economic levels, but also distributing economic gains to all segments of the population.[23]

Advances in Public Health and Medical Science

It is increasingly being recognized that better health and medical improvements were major factors in the decline of mortality in both developed and developing countries. High levels of mortality had been maintained, in large part, as a result of epidemic disease and poor community-health conditions. The plague, smallpox, cholera, and typhus placed a heavy toll on the population, primarily in the earlier periods, and smallpox, tetanus, dysentery, typhoid, scarlet fever, tuberculosis, and pneumonia posed grave threats in later periods. Inadequate provisions for sanitary facilities, water, and sewerage systems contributed substantially to the existence of these diseases and the difficulty of controlling their spread throughout the population. Accordingly, control of these diseases was achieved by the introduction of vaccines and techniques of mass immunization; the development of bacteriology and the consequent prevention and cure of infections through *asepsis* (protection against bacteria) and *antisepsis* (inhibition or destruction of bacteria); *vector control* (the elimination of disease-carrying pests at points where they breed); improved standards of public sanitation; creation of more extensive water and sewerage systems; and expansion of health services, including the proliferation of hospitals, training of more physicians and auxiliary medical personnel, and growth of health-education programs.

The relative importance of health and medical advances, as compared with economic development, in accounting for the long-term decline in mortality is a matter of dispute among students of the topic. History has shown that many diseases, such as scarlet fever, diptheria, and measles, substantially diminished without active human control because of natural immunity developed in a society.[24] It may be, therefore, that medical science was greatly aided by tendencies inherent in the population to overcome certain diseases. McKeown has argued that a strong case can be made for early improvement in standards of living that were generated by economic change. He argues that gains in health in England and Wales were owed to a rising standard of living beginning in about 1770, to sanitary measures from 1878, and to treatment, both preventive and curative, dating from the second quarter of the twentieth century.[25] Preston claims that sanitary measures and medical treatment began earlier and may have been more powerful forces than living standards even during the nineteenth century.[26]

These explanations serve well for understanding, in macro terms, the modern mortality declines in industrialized countries. Developing countries, on the other hand, have reduced their previously high mortality rates primarily by "borrowing" the techniques of vector control and mass immunization already used in the Western world, and only secondarily through progress in classical medical services, sanitation, education, and level of living. The fact that many developing countries have not sustained mortality declines suggests that the latter processes are quite incomplete.

Changing Causes of Death

Long-term improvements in survival resulting from the diminution of many fatal diseases led to sharp changes in the distribution of causes of death of the population. Historical mortality declines were achieved mainly by controlling communicable diseases. As a result, such causes of death as cardiovascular-renal diseases and malignancies (cancers) became more prominent. This was partly because knowledge about heart and cancer ailments was limited, and partly because avoidance of the communicable diseases (heavily concentrated among infants and children) permitted many people to live to older ages, when the risks of cardiovascular-renal diseases and malignancies were greater.

Figure 3.4 illustrates what typically happens to cause-of-death patterns in a population as life expectancy increases from forty to seventy-five years. Causes of death are grouped into five categories, each of which includes causes that have reacted similarly to health improvements. As life expectancy at birth rises from forty to sixty years, a sharp decline is observed in Group I diseases (infectious and parasitic diseases, influenza, and pneumonia); a slight increase is noted for causes in Group IV (violence) and Group V (other causes such as diseases of the digestive system, children's diseases, and senility); while somewhat greater relative increases are recorded for Group II diseases (cancer) and Group III diseases (cardiovascular diseases and bronchitis after the age of five). An increase in life expectancy from sixty to seventy-five years accentuates the decline of communicable diseases and increases the importance of cardiovascular-renal diseases and cancers. Extension of the average life expectancy at birth beyond seventy is associated with continued reductions in the first set of causes, further prominence of the second and third sets, a higher rate of death by violence, and a rapid contraction of other causes.[27]

FIGURE 3.4 **Distribution, in a standard population, of deaths (all ages and both sexes) by cause-of-death groups for different levels of expectation of life at birth ranging from 40 to 76 years**

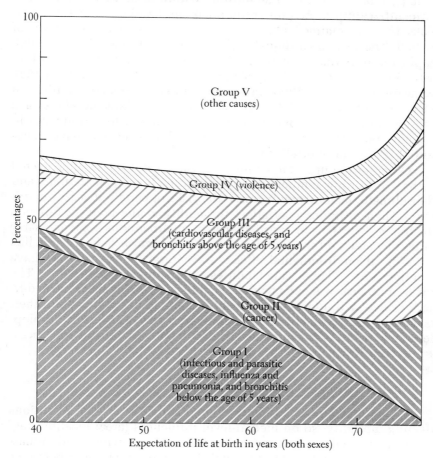

Source: United Nations, *Population Bulletin of the United Nations,* no. 6 (New York: United Nations, 1962), p. 110.

Environmental Factors

Throughout history, nations have been ravaged by the effects of environmental disasters or catastrophes, and the natural environment has also contributed to excess mortality in a more gradual way. Epidemics, famines, earthquakes, and floods have been known to exact a heavy toll from populations in many parts of the world. Before the great advances in mortality control, communicable diseases hit suddenly and affected large numbers of people in short periods of time. The infamous Black Death (bubonic plague) in Europe is reported to have killed one-fourth of the population, of 100 or so million, within three years, in the mid-fourteenth century. A similar outbreak in London over seventeen weeks in 1665 claimed about 80,000 lives, out of a population of 470,000. The Lisbon earthquake of 1755 is said to have killed 40,000 people, out of perhaps 250,000.[28] Famines resulted in about 9 million deaths in China from 1877 to 1879, close to a million in India in 1837 and again in 1863 and 1900, and roughly three-quarters of a million in Ireland around 1845.[29] Within the present decade, large numbers have been lost to famines in Bangladesh and Biafra and to earthquakes in Peru and Italy. These sudden environmental disasters can have a substantial impact on mortality levels.

Other environmental conditions can also lead to unexpected deaths. High or low temperatures or humidity, inadequate rainfall, and other climatic factors may increase the risks of certain diseases or ailments. High altitudes may affect the ability of the body to function effectively. The terrain (particularly in mountainous regions), large bodies of water, and soil deficiencies present hazards to health and life.

Not all environmental effects are natural, however. Wars have been the cause of large-scale fatalities at numerous points in time. The power of nuclear weapons, which demolished two Japanese cities during World War II, looms as a threat to mankind as nations build their arsenals of devastating weaponry. Some products of scientific development have resulted in contamination of the air, water, and soil necessary to sustain us.

Medial Variables

Just as macro-level variables act to establish or change conditions affecting mortality, so do medial-level influences (areal locations, aggregate memberships, and reference groups) with which individuals are associated, help to determine their life chances. These associations are important to mortality expectations both because opportunities for maintaining life are characteristic of each area or group and because individuals derive norms of behavior, including those affecting mortality, from the groups. Our discussion will focus on residential areas, the family and the sexes, socioeconomic status, race and nationality, religion, and government.

Residential Areas

Geographic variations in mortality are found to exist in every country. Differences in death rates can be discovered by region, among urban and rural areas, and even by areas within a city or town. In the 1975-

to-1977 period the infant mortality rate for white persons was as high as 16.2 per 1,000 in West Virginia and as low as 11.3 in Maine. For black persons, it varied from 29.8 in Illinois to 5.2 in Maine.[30] Some studies have reported higher mortality in urban than in rural areas and in the inner city than in the outlying areas.[31] Available evidence indicates that these variations in mortality according to where people live can be explained both by the characteristics of those who occupy the area (especially socioeconomic status) and the environmental attributes of the area (centers of cities are frequently the locus of pollutants because of factories and plants, which are situated there).

The Family and the Sexes

Examination of the family as a factor affecting mortality is crucial, because the formative years of life are a critical stage in the age curve of mortality, and the family is the principal institution determining behavior in these early years. From the time we are born, members of our family influence, sometimes explicitly and often subtly, the attitudes and behavior that partly determine our life expectancy. In nearly all families the infant and child is socialized to standards of health and avoidance of death. Parents and other family members instruct children in how to act, and exhibit behavior that the child may copy or use as a model. Some areas in which family behavior provides a guide for the child's own current and later behavior affecting mortality include toilet training, cleanliness, diet, dress, and knowledge about hazards, such as those in water, on roads, from poisons, and from smoking.

There has also been a study of how distinctive family patterns in food consumption emerge and shape the behavior of the child. Research on Southern rural families in the United States examined the role of mothers in imparting eating habits to their children:

> The mother's direct control of the eating habits of her children—her technique of control—is of great importance. Whether or not she displays her own food dislikes to her children, for them to imitate, or forces herself to eat foods she doesn't like in order to set a good example; whether or not she commands or entices or fools her family into eating what she thinks is good for them, or caters to their prejudices and cajoles their appetites; whether or not she insists on discipline at table; whether or not she uses food as reward or punishment—all of these are significant in the development of food habits. The process of socialization—the initiation into "the standard of expected performance"—both in regard to eating behavior and general behavior, which the child undergoes when growing up in a society, thus affect the child's experience with certain foods.[32]

The family socialization pattern undoubtedly varies among socio-economic strata as well as among other groupings of the population.

Family factors are also important in determining the extent of health care received by individuals. Although four-fifths of all Americans are covered by hospital and surgical insurance, there are variations according to age, race, and other personal characteristics.[33] Moreover, most families find it necessary to supplement health insurance with out-of-pocket health expenses, and such expenditures vary even more by family type and characteristics.[34]

Contributing to family patterns of mortality is the difference between the sexes in survival. In general, females have a greater life expectancy than do males. This differential can be observed in most countries of the world for a long period of time. However, it has been established that sex mortality differences have varied with level of economic development or modernization. In developed areas, "female life expectancy has been universally higher than male longevity for a period now approaching a full half a century."[35] In less-developed regions, the differences are small or favor males. This picture emerges when one examines either a country over time or different countries at the same point in time. Moreover, in developed countries women have extended their advantage in longevity until recently.

Preston has studied these trends by causes of death and concludes that the male disadvantage is attributable primarily to higher male mortality due to cardiovascular diseases, neoplasms, and influenza/pneumonia/bronchitis.[36] These are causes of death that are typical at older ages; hence, as both men and women increased their life expectancy, longevity rose more rapidly for females because of their greater resistance to those causes.

Since mortality is a result of both biological and socio-environmental forces, a debate has developed among students of sex-mortality patterns as to which set of explanations is better.

Support for the biological explanation comes from several sources. First, there is the information that sex-mortality differentials are also found among species other than humans. These species range from the mealworm to the rat. Second, sex differences in the death rate have been recorded not only at all ages of life but even during the prenatal period, when a much weaker case for the effect of socio-environmental effects can be made.[37] Third, a case for the biological position was made as a result of a study of the mortality patterns of religious teaching orders of brothers and sisters.[38] By selecting groups of men and women with similar styles of life, the research design controlled for a considerable part of the sociocultural differences between men and women in the general population. The men did not serve in the armed forces, nor were they apt to engage in illicit behavior. The women were not subject to the rigors of childbearing, nor were their occupations less stressful than those of the men. Diet, housing, and medical care were the same for the two groups, as was time allotted for sleep, work, study, and recreation. Of course, not all sociocultural differences between the sexes were eliminated, but they were at least diminished, and one would expect more similar mortality experience if sociocultural conditions were an important explanatory factor. A sample was drawn from twenty brothers' communities and forty-one sister's communities, and life records since 1900 were accumulated.

The study found that both sexes in the religious order enjoyed a greater life expectancy than their counterparts in the general population, but that the gap in life expectancy between the sexes was as apparent in the religious orders as in the general population. The similarity of life-styles of these men and women, which was greater than that of men and women in the general population, did not result in comparably similar mortality patterns.

The social arguments have been more widespread and just as compelling. Some have given more weight to environmental causes of death and to the generation by society of an increasing incidence of other causes (for example, automobile accidents).[39] Research on the Hutterites, a small religious sect in the United States that has a very low death rate and a very high birth rate, supports the socio-environmental argument. Contrary to the traditional sex differences in mortality observed in the wider population, death rates among Hutterite females are higher than those among males in the fifteen-to-sixty age bracket. The explanation for this unusual pattern can be found in the high birthrate among Hutterite women, which generally lowers their resistance to illnesses during the childbearing period and for a decade or so afterward.[40] In countries where males have had a more favorable life expectancy, a similar explanation involving high fertility performance among women, with its consequent weakening of the body (and often higher maternal mortality), can be given.

Additional support for the socio-environmental explanation of diverging sex-mortality trends comes from several large-scale surveys of the effects of social and psychological stress on the occurrence of several different diseases. Surveys of mental illness, heart disease, tuberculosis, arthritis, ulcers, alcoholism, diabetes, and many other diseases have all indicated that such diseases as these occur more often under stressful conditions mostly associated with men.[41]

Differences in the use of tobacco have been identified as a critical factor in the sex-mortality differential. Almost half of the sex difference in deaths at adult ages in the United States in 1962 could be accounted for by differences in smoking, and three-fourths of the widening gap between 1910 and 1962 was attributable to smoking patterns. The use of tobacco is apparently associated with the greater incidence among men of cardiovascular diseases and cancer.[42]

More generally, the differing sex roles in societies have been identified as leading to sex-mortality differences. The lower life expectancy of females in Bangladesh has been attributed to sex-biased health- and nutrition-related behavior favoring male children, which operates to affect sex-mortality differences through variations in malnutrition, disease, and nonrecovery from illness. This bias is related to the inferior status, role, and work opportunities of women in the country.[43]

It has been pointed out that the widening of sex differences in longevity has slowed down considerably in the 1970s in the United States. In fact, there has been narrowing of the differences in some age groups and some causes of death.[44] Indications are that many of the factors that led to the widening are no longer effective, and some may be reversing direction.

It is probable that both biological and social forces affect one's chances of dying, and that mortality differences between the sexes are the result of a combination of the two. Since there is little reason to suppose that the physiological makeup of males and females has been undergoing any significant change in recent time, the explanation for the widening gap, and any subsequent narrowing, must be found primarily in the changing levels and distributions of causes of death and environmental forces that affect the life expectancy of men and women. How much impact are such factors as greater similarity of smoking habits and work patterns having on these differentials?

Socioeconomic Status

Socioeconomic differences in mortality have been recognized for some time. Villerme reported on their existence as far back as 1828.[45] Data on the subject from the Registrar-General's Office of England and Wales go back at least to 1851. In the United States, the first census records showing mortality differences by occupation appeared in 1890.

Of all the studies linking mortality with socioeconomic status, the most prominent are those relating occupational categories to death rates (or other measures of mortality). Nearly all the early studies were of this type, mainly because occupational data were more readily available than were other socioeconomic data. In general, this research has found an inverse relationship between occupational status and mortality—the lower the status, the higher the death rate at a given age, or the lower the life expectancy.

Such a finding was made for the French population in 1907 to 1908. Mortality for managers and officials in industry was lower than for wage earners, either clerks or craftsmen. The mortality of craftsmen varied from one occupation to another, apparently because of different occupational risks. In the professions of law and teaching, mortality was much lower than for the total population. Statistics published by the French government for 1923 to 1928 confirmed these observations.[46]

Similar studies have been made at ten-year intervals since 1851 in conjunction with the British Census. The death rates calculated by comparing deaths and population in several hundred occupations have traditionally been adjusted to take account of differences in the age structure of different occupations. Since 1911, the various occupations have been grouped together into relatively homogeneous social classes. Analysis of these data over time suggests that the classic inverse relationship between socioeconomic status and mortality has been modified. For example, in 1921 to 1923 and 1930 to 1932 there was an uninterrupted upward gradient of mortality from social class I (professional) to social class V (unskilled), but at the later date the differences between classes were much less. By 1950, the inverse pattern was disturbed, the lowest mortality being in intermediate classes II and IV. However, the highest mortality was still in the lowest class.[47]

Studies in the United States through 1960 provide evidence of a continuing but narrowing occupational differential in mortality.[48] In Finland between 1971 and 1975, mortality differentials by both occupation and education were found to be rather large. Those with higher occupational status or education had a smaller risk of dying of almost any disease or nonnatural cause of death.[49]

Social-class variations in mortality do differ by age and cause of death in many countries. Figure 3.5 shows a typical age relationship for Norway in 1970 to 1973, covering ages twenty-five to sixty-nine. While higher social classes enjoy significant advantages at the younger ages, mortality differences become considerably contracted and confused at the older ages. Other analyses show a high lung-cancer rate for workers in the chemical industry, a high suicide rate for higher-educated women, and excess mortality from digestive and circulatory diseases among salesmen and clerks.[50] It can be hypothesized that these exceptions to the general relationship are a function of the life-style of particular social strata. For example, respiratory ailments take a greater toll among the lower social strata because persons in them have less adequate health and medical care and are more likely to live in environments that subject them to the risks of such ailments. Higher rates of

FIGURE 3.5   Age-specific death rates among Norwegian males for social groups as percent of the death rates for all occupied persons

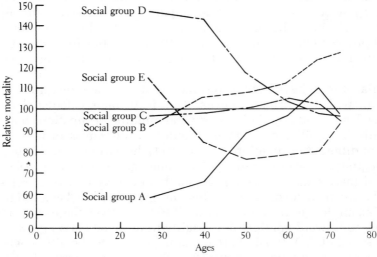

Note: Group A has high status; Group E has low status.

Source: Elsebeth Lynge, "Occupational Mortality in Norway, Denmark, and Finland, 1971–1975," in *Socio-Economic Differential Mortality in Industrialized Societies* (Paris: Committee for International Cooperation in National Research in Demography, 1981), p. 19.

coronary heart disease among upper-status men might be explained by their more excessive dietary habits and the physical and mental stress related to their life-styles.

For these reasons, one question that often arises in interpreting data on occupational differences in the death rate concerns whether the variations are primarily because of the differing risks of death associated with occupations or mainly a function of the socioeconomic levels of the occupations. This question has been answered using statistics for England and Wales that compare the mortality of men by occupation with the mortality of married women by their husband's occupation (Table 3.2). The mortality rates by social class and occupation are largely ranked in the same order for men and their wives, suggesting that mortality for the male population is affected to a greater extent by the level of living associated with an occupation than by the occupational risk itself.[51] However, for a number of occupations, the inherent risks are clearly important factors. Included would be such occupations as miner, steel-foundry furnaceman, "sandhog," and police officer.

TABLE 3.2 Standardized mortality ratios of men and married women by husband's occupation at ages 15–64 (England and Wales, 1961)

Occupation	Men Aged 15–64	Married Women Aged 15–64
All classes (occupied and unoccupied)	100	100
All occupations (active and retired)	99	100
Social Classes		
Professional etc., occupations (I)	76	77
Intermediate occupations (II)	81	83
Skilled occupations (III)	100	103
Partly skilled occupations (IV)	103	105
Unskilled occupations (V)	143	141
Unoccupied	63	45
Occupation Orders		
Farmers, foresters, fishermen	82	101
Miners and quarrymen	115	129
Gas, coke and chemical makers	92	107
Glass and ceramics makers	97	101
Furnace, forge, foundry, rolling mill workers	106	108
Electrical and electronic workers	102	101
Engineering and allied trades workers*	100	104
Woodworkers	91	100
Leather workers	109	109
Textile workers	116	116
Clothing workers	107	112
Food, drink and tobacco workers	103	108
Paper and printing workers	83	92
Makers of other products	82	87
Construction workers	93	102
Painters and decorators	103	107
Drivers of stationary engines, cranes, etc.	99	113
Laborers, n.e.c.	145	142
Transport and communications workers	107	108
Warehousemen, storekeepers, packers, bottlers	102	97
Clerical workers	98	86
Sales workers	90	88
Service, sport and recreation workers	118	105
Administrators and managers	70	72
Professional, technical workers, artists	75	76
Armed forces (British and foreign)	151	98
Inadequately described occupations	30	51

Source: The Registrar General's Decennial Supplement, England and Wales, 1961, *Occupational Mortality Tables* (London: Her Majesty's Stationery Office, 1971), p. 91.

*Those not classified elsewhere.

This interpretation of occupational mortality differences as being largely explained by styles of life at home as well as on the job raises a more fundamental question about mechanisms that produce socioeconomic differences and changes. Caldwell studied the process in Nigeria and found that, among all of the socioeconomic indicators related to child mortality, education of the mother exerts a strong and independent influence exceeding that of any other socioeconomic variable. He surmises that mother's education is at the root of socioeconomic variations, because it is the factor that most directly influences basic social and cultural processes that relate to health and survival. An educated mother may change feeding and child-care practices, she is more aware of health facilities and how to use them, and she can change the traditional balance of familial relationships, which frees her to be a more critical decision-maker in regard to her children.[52] As education and other developmental changes take place in societies, one can expect some narrowing of mortality differentials. Nevertheless, persistence of some differences will accompany continuing social stratification.[53]

Race and Nationality

Among the several differentials in mortality observed in various societies, race and nationality appear to be important variables. In the United States in 1970, mortality of several groups differed from that of whites both in level and age distribution (Table 3.3). Chinese-Americans and Japanese-Americans had age-adjusted mortality ratios below that of whites, whereas American Indians had a somewhat higher ratio, and blacks a considerably higher ratio, than whites. The favorable mortality ratios among the two Oriental groups were maintained through all age categories. For blacks and American Indians, however, the less favorable mortality ratios became more favorable at the older ages.

This crossover phenomenon, referred to earlier, reflects a selective process whereby higher death rates for some groups at the younger ages reduces the variability in the distribution of human conditions and improves the survival prospects of those who avoid death at an early age.[54] Higher death rates at earlier ages presumably relate to less desirable socioeconomic circumstances. With advancing age, the fact that the "heartiest" are most likely to survive probably becomes more important, and socioeconomic factors relatively less so. By older ages, the physiological selection has become so much more pronounced for the disadvantaged groups—the advantaged including many "weaker" persons who have survived to those ages because of socioeconomic benefits—that death rates begin to favor the traditionally disadvantaged. Despite these differences, the universal age curve of mortality is

TABLE 3.3 Mortality ratios according to race and age: United States, 1970

Age	RACE Black	American Indian	Chinese- American	Japanese- American
All ages, crude	1.06	0.76	0.50	0.45
All ages, age adjusted	1.54	1.18	0.73	0.49
Under 5 years	2.00	1.67	0.45	0.61
5–14 years	1.42	1.60	0.78	0.65
15–24 years	1.83	2.69	0.45	0.59
25–34 years	2.94	3.48	0.43	0.40
35–44 years	2.72	2.79	0.53	0.46
45–54 years	2.08	1.67	0.59	0.46
55–64 years	1.63	1.00	0.76	0.43
65–74 years	1.35	0.81	0.93	0.43
75–84 years	0.98	0.70	0.80	0.56
85 years and over	0.67	0.56	0.52	0.64

Source: National Center for Health Statistics, *Health, United States, 1979,* DHEW Publication no. (PHS) 80-1232 (Washington, D.C.: U.S. Government Printing Office, 1980), p. 10.
Ratios exclude deaths of nonresidents of the United States and are computed by dividing age-specific death rate of a specified racial or ethnic group by the death rate of the white population of that age group (not shown).

reported for each of the groups with slight departures from the expected curve, owing to the selective process.

Higher death rates of one group over another can generally be found for most causes of death; however, some causes are more distinctive for certain groups. Whites have higher rates of suicide and of malignant neoplasms of the respiratory system than do blacks. American Indians have an exceptionally high incidence of alcohol-related mortality. Genetic factors have an influence on distinctive cause-of-death patterns as well. Blacks suffer almost uniquely from sickle-cell anemia. American-born descendents of East European Ashkenazim Jews are particularly susceptible to Tay-Sachs disease. Other groups are reported to be subject to extreme probabilities or nonprobabilities of contracting other deadly diseases resulting from genetic origins.[55]

Religion

Religion also serves as an important mediating factor with regard to life and death. Although it is often difficult to separate the religious influence from broader ethnic and socioeconomic influences, distinctive religious teachings and practices relating to health and survival frequently have an effect on the death rate. Fatalism in traditional societies has been a source of resignation to death when modern techniques of control might have averted mortality at the time. The once-traditional practice of suttee in ancient India, in which a widow was expected, because of religious tenets, to sacrifice herself on the funeral pyre of her husband, still has some adherents.[56] In the past, it often took the form of mass suicide as the harems of deceased sultans followed the practice.

Some modern-day religions are very explicit about matters affecting health and longevity. The writings of Christian Science suggest that through mental health the life expectancy of followers of the religion will be increased. Christian Scientists shun most forms of medical aid, but they are required to avoid smoking and drinking of alcohol and beverages containing caffeine. Analysis of causes of death among Christian Scientists, as compared with the general population, indicates that they have a higher incidence of many forms of heart disease and malignancies but maintain a life expectancy similar to that of the general population.[57] How much of the mortality difference between Christian Scientists and other religious groups depends on the social-class, age, and marital-status composition of the groups and how much on their distinctive religious practices cannot be determined from available data; yet it seems clear that some practices modify the probability of death, perhaps increasing it in the case of shunning medical service and decreasing it in the case of avoidance of smoking and drinking.

Many contemporary religious denominations and sects support extensive medical and health work. They establish hospitals, clinics, and sanitariums; schools of medicine, nursing, dentistry, and medical technology; and health and medical publications. These activities are usually justified in terms of health as one aspect of the Gospel message and of Christian living. Seventh-Day Adventists, for example, believe that Christians should have a concern for health, for the practical reason that only in a sound body can they render the most effective service to God and to others. They cite Biblical verses on which they base their belief that each person is accountable to God for the preservation of health, and that the person who knowingly violates simple health principles, thereby bringing on ill health, disease, or disability, is living in violation of the laws of God.[58]

Ethnic and religious differentials in health and mortality seem to be declining with time as every group becomes exposed to the same advances in health care and medical technology. Only the differential economic ability to pay for services distinguishes the groups. Although the life expectancy at birth of blacks still lags behind that of whites in the United States (by about five years for males and four years for females in 1978), enormous gains have been made for both color groups, and differences are now smaller. In 1900 to 1902, black males could expect only thirty-two years of life, against forty-eight years for whites; by 1978, the figures were sixty-five and seventy years, respectively.[59]

Government

Mortality control has been achieved substantially through national and community effort; it is understandable, therefore, that governments have played a vital role. Although some form of organization for public health was known in ancient times, it was not until the modern era that what we now know as public health developed. At the turn of the nineteenth century in England, community sanitation programs were introduced, first through voluntary popular participation and later through compulsory appointment and activity of local boards of health.[60] A number of European countries began to build state hospital systems in the early 1800s. The American public-health organization followed that of the English, giving emphasis to administration by local authorities with the assistance, supervision, and support of state and national agencies.

Public health flourished after World War I as several countries modeled their systems after the existing ones, and it became almost universal after World War II.[61] The extent of the health needs of countries adopting systems during the latter period was much greater than of countries that adopted them earlier, and the means to meet the burden of sickness and suffering were as limited as needs were great. In the postwar period, the World Health Organization and other United Nations agencies emerged as supporters and facilitators of public health.

The origins of international collaboration in public health, like those of national public health, are found in the fear of epidemic spread.[62] Many nations adopted quarantine regulations in order to keep certain health hazards away from their shores. Although quarantine is still practiced selectively today, the emphasis in international public health has shifted to disease prevention and control. Technical commissions under the League of Nations studied the major causes of death and made recommendations for programs to contain them. It was not, however, until the World Health Organization was formed, following the establishment of the Charter of the United Nations, that international cooperation took place on a worldwide scale. That agency was designed to assist governments in strengthening health services, promoting improved health and medical standards and environmental hygiene, promoting and coordinating health research, and advancing knowledge concerning various aspects of health and medicine.

Although national and international efforts to improve health and longevity through general public-health programs have succeeded in reducing the death rate, their effects would have been limited without the inclusion of mass immunization campaigns. Moreover, it is inconceivable that such campaigns could have succeeded without the involvement of governmental organizations. Vaccination for smallpox was required of everyone in the United States until quite recently, and immunizations for yellow fever and cholera are required for travelers to countries where these diseases are prevalent. Immunization may be recommended for typhoid, tetanus, diphtheria, influenza, plague, and poliomyelitis, depending on location and circumstances. Through such health practices, and through health programs such as Medicare and Medicaid, the government units from the national to the local level are medial influences in translating macro developments in health and medical care into benefits for families and individuals.

Wherever mortality declines have been appreciable and extend to various segments of the population, the role of government as intermediary is manifest. It has been argued that the existence of sufficient political will and administrative capabilities among governments was more important than the quality or quantity of nutrition, per capita income, education, housing, or other level-of-living indicators.[63] The more rapid than expected mortality declines in Sri Lanka, Kerala, and Cuba were associated with common governmental programs that aimed explicitly at upgrading social and health conditions among the poorest sectors, achieving exceptionally high levels of literacy, and also achieving a relatively egalitarian distribution of health services and food.[64]

Of course, not all government actions serve to depress mortality. A glance at Figure 3.6 shows that the American white male population experienced a considerable increase in deaths during the periods of war. Groups born in 1896 to 1899 and 1916 to 1920 reached military age in World War I and World War II, respectively, and show excess mortality at early ages. However, the lucky cohort of men born between 1906 and 1910 generally missed both wars and do not show high death rates at early ages. A government's military involvement increases the death rate both of its own military population and of the general population against which it wages war. For instance, the Russian and German populations during World War II lost heavily among their fighting men but also lost substantial numbers of women and children who were victims of bombings.

Governments have also affected mortality rates through sanitation programs, police and other protective services, labor laws, social security and social-welfare legislation, food and drug laws, regulations

FIGURE 3.6   Mortality rates for cohorts born 1896–1900, 1906–1910, and 1916–1920 for white males in death-registration states, 1900–1968

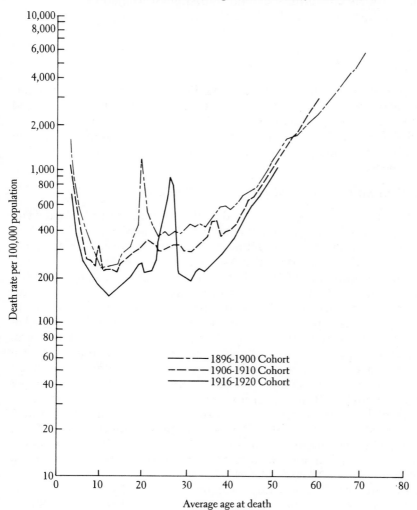

Source: U.S. Public Health Service, *Cohort Mortality and Survivorship: United States Death-Registration States,* 1900–1968, Vital and Health Statistics, Series 3, no. 16, p. 6.

regarding sewage disposal, provision and purification of water supplies, and laws concerning capital punishment. Depending on the direction of the action, the effect may be either an increase or a reduction
in mortality.

Micro Variables

In addition to the macro and medial factors, which help determine the chances of life and death, both biological and physical as well
as behavioral factors peculiar to the individual have an impact. The
individual can be seen as a focal point in a decision-making process on
which both psychological and social forces are brought to bear to affect
life chances.

Biological and Physical Makeup of Individuals

The individual at birth is endowed with a genetic and physical composition that influences life expectancy. Much fetal loss (deaths prior
to birth) occurs because the fetus is not properly formed or is genet-
ically unequipped for life. Likewise, many early infant deaths (those
taking place soon after birth, called neonatal deaths) are caused by the
same conditions. One of the most important factors in neonatal mortality is the maturity of the infant at birth. Those infants with low birth
weight, a critical measure of immaturity, have a much lower probability of survival than those weighing more. In the United States in
1960, among infants weighing 2,500 grams (about 5.5 pounds) or less at
birth, 172 per 1,000 died within four weeks after birth; among those
weighing more than 2,500 grams, the comparable death rate was 5 per
1,000. Although children with low birth weights accounted for only 8
percent of live births, deaths of these children accounted for three-
fourths of all neonatal deaths.[65] Interestingly, the mortal risks of low
birth weight are roughly equal for black and white infants, whereas
black infants have a significantly higher risk of mortality when birth
weights are above 2,500 grams.[66]

Closely related to low birth weight is prematurity (birth before the
end of the typical nine-month term of pregnancy of the mother). Statistics on mortality of infants on the basis of prematurity are similar to
those based on birth weight.

Some infant deaths are also traceable to physical difficulties experienced by the mother shortly before birth or during delivery. Causes of
death in this category are hypoxia (insufficient oxygen intake), intra-
cranial hemorrhage, and congenital (nonhereditary) malformations.
Blood conditions, particularly those resulting from matings of women

with Rh negative factor and men with Rh positive factor, can lead to disease of the newborn.

Physiological limitations are the primary cause of a significant number of deaths beyond infancy. At ages one to fourteen, congenital malformations and malignancies combined were exceeded only by accidents as a cause of death. At still older ages, such factors as being overweight, being crippled, high or low blood pressure, weak heart, urinary impairments, blindness, and deafness increase the risk of mortality.[67]

Individual Decisions and Actions

While macro and medial factors may exert influence on each individual's life expectancy, and biological and physical makeup may provide additional constraints, individuals affect their chances of living or dying through their own behavior—the extent to which they take account of these other factors in their daily living and their own idiosyncratic actions.

Individuals may avail themselves of health and medical care or not, they may take mortal risks or not, and they may enjoy nutritious diets and optimum physical activity or not. In a 1979 survey of the United States population at ages twenty to sixty-four, about seventeen percent admitted to doing no more than a fair or poor job of taking care of their health, two-fifths considered themselves overweight, more than half agreed that they exercised less than needed, 15 percent (but twice as many men than women) had no regular source of medical care, more than half had no general physical examination during the previous twelve months, one-third were current smokers of cigarettes and one-third of those smoked twenty-five cigarettes or more a day, one-fourth rarely or never eat breakfast, two-thirds seldom or never use seat belts when riding in a car, and one-fourth feel a great deal of emotional stress on the job.[68] Life expectancy will be determined partly by these choices people make, which are somewhat independent of societal and group forces.

Psychological variables have been more generally implicated in determining human longevity. One class of variables is concerned with psychological stress and its effects on creating or facilitating some types of diseases and ailments (including coronary attacks and neurological disorders). Some researchers have identified behavioral types (A and B) that differentiate the prospects for heart ailments. The Type A person organizes his or her life rigorously, according to time schedules and achievement goals, and works vigorously to meet them. The Type B person has a contrasting behavioral set.[69] Another emphasis relates psychological influences to the timing of death (such as apparent delays in death until after crucial birthdays, holidays, or other events, and suicidal waves associated with family dissolution or deaths of persons in public life). What is involved is a question of the "will to live." Various studies have provided empirical support for these phenomena,[70] but the methodologies of some of the studies have been questioned.[71]

FUTURE MORTALITY TRENDS

Further gains in life expectancy are bound to occur in nearly all parts of the world. Life expectancies at birth in the fifty-to-fifty-five-year range should be attained by nearly every low-income area within a decade or two. Those already in that range can expect to increase it by five or ten years, given reasonable assumptions about communicable-disease control and the absence of cataclysmic events. Smaller increases in longevity can be projected for developed countries, which have already attained low mortality levels. Only marked medical breakthroughs in the treatment of old-age and degenerative diseases could change the picture.[72]

Mortality in the United States has been projected to the year 2000, based on assumptions of continuation of recent cause-of-death trends that can be assumed as reasonable. These include further improvements in regard to cardiovascular diseases and infant deaths and further deterioration in some age groups of levels of deaths due to violence and cancer. The resulting life expectancy at birth in 2000 is eighty years, an increase of seven years over that in 1977. A substantial part of the gain would be at the older ages; hence, even the life expectancy at age sixty-five of twenty-two years would go up by five and a half years. A more modest assumption about continued reductions in cardiovascular deaths would still lead to a life expectancy at birth of nearly seventy-eight years, and at age sixty-five of nineteen years, by the turn of the century.[73]

These probable gains in life expectancy should not create an illusion that we are moving toward immortality. Life-span still seems fixed, and we are just staying healthy enough to survive a bit longer. Then those of us who live to an old age will see the functional capacities of our bodily organs rapidly deteriorate and, like the proverbial "One-Hoss Shay," we will suffer a total breakdown and celebrate the end of a long life.[74]

NOTES

1. Robert J. Myers, "Validity of Centenarian Data in the 1960 Census," *Demography* 3 (1966), 470–476; Jacob S. Siegel and Jeffrey S. Passel, "New Estimates of the Number of Centenarians in the United States," *Journal of the American Statistical Association* 71, no. 355 (September 1976), 559–566.

2. Edward S. Deevey, Jr., "The Probability of Death," *Scientific American*, 182 (April 1950), 58–60; Louis I. Dublin, Alfred J. Lotka, and Mortimer Spiegelman, *Length of Life* (New York: Ronald Press, 1949), pp. 28–29; G. Acsadi and J. Nemeskeri, *History of Human Life Span and Mortality* (Budapest: Akademiai Kiado, 1970).

3. Deevey, *Death*; Dublin et al., *Life*.

4. United Nations, Department of Economic and Social Affairs, *Population Bulletin of the United Nations, No. 6, 1962* (New York: United Nations, 1963), p. 20.

5. Ibid., p. 25.

6. Ibid., p. 30

7. Ibid., pp. 21, 27, 30.

8. Christopher Davis and Murray Feshbach, *Rising Infant Mortality in the U.S.S.R. in the 1970's*, Bureau of the Census, International Population Reports, Series P-95, no. 74 (Washington, D.C.: U.S. Department of Commerce, September 1980).

9. Harry M. Rosenberg, "Seasonal Adjustment of Vital Statistics by Electronic Computer," *Public Health Reports*, 80 (March 1965), 201–210.

10. Ira Rosenwaike, "Seasonal Variation of Deaths in the United States, 1951–1960," *Journal of the American Statistical Association*, 6, no. 315 (September 1966), 706–719.

11. Bernard L. Strehler, *Time, Cells, and Aging*, 2nd ed. (New York: Academic Press, 1977), p. 17.

12. Ibid., pp. 105–106.

13. United Nations, *Population Bulletin*, p. 51.

14. Ibid., p. 53

15. Ibid., p. 51

16. Charles B. Nam, Norman L. Weatherby, and Kathleen A. Ockay, "Causes of Death Which Contribute to the Mortality Crossover Effect," *Social Biology*, 25 (Winter 1978), 306–314; K. G. Manton, S. S. Poss, and W. Wing, "The Black/White Mortality Crossover: Investigations from the Perspective of the Components of Aging," *The Gerontologist*, 19, no. 3 (1979), 291–300.

17. James F. Fries and Lawrence M. Crapo, *Vitality and Aging* (San Francisco: W. H. Freeman & Company Publishers, 1981).

18. United Nations, *Population Bulletin*, p. 54.

19. National Center for Health Statistics, *Vital Statistics of the United States, 1978, Volume II, Section 5, Life Tables*, DHHS Publication No. (PHS) 81-1104 (Washington, D.C.: U.S. Government Printing Office, 1980).

20.   United Nations, Population Division, *The Determinants and Consequences of Population Trends* (New York: United Nations, 1953), p. 56.

21.   Ansley J. Coale and Edgar M. Hoover, *Population Growth and Economic Development in Low-Income Countries* (Princeton: Princeton University Press, 1958), pp. 9–10.

22.   Michael P. Todaro, *Economic Development in the Third World*, New York: Longman, 1977.

23.   G. B. Rodgers, "Income and Inequality as Determinants of Mortality: An International Cross-Section Analysis," *Population Studies*, 33, no. 2 (1979), 343–351.

24.   Hans Zinsser, *Rats, Lice, and History* (Boston: Little, Brown, 1935). p. 67.

25.   Thomas McKeown, *Modern Rise of Population* (New York: Academic Press, 1976).

26.   Samuel H. Preston, *Mortality Patterns in National Populations*, (New York: Academic Press, 1976), pp. 81–82.

27.   United Nations, Department of Economic and Social Affairs, *Population Bulletin of the United Nations, No. 6-1962*, (New York: United Nations, 1963), p. 111.

28.   Thomas H. Hollingsworth, "A Preliminary Suggestion for the Measurement of Mortality Crises," in *The Great Mortalities: Methodological Studies of Demographic Crises in the Past*, ed. Hubert Charbonneau and André Larose (Liege: Ordina Editions, 1979), p. 25.

29.   "Famine," *The World Book Encyclopedia*, Vol. 7 (Chicago: Field Enterprises Educational Corporation, 1972), 29.

30.   National Center for Health Statistics, *Health, United States, 1979*, DHEW Publication No. (PHS) 80-1232 (Washington, D.C.: U.S. Government Printing Office, 1980), pp. 92–93.

31.   Evelyn M. Kitagawa and Philip M. Hauser, *Differential Mortality in the United States: A Study in Socioeconomic Epidemiology* (Cambridge, Mass.: Harvard University Press, 1973), pp. 159–163. A recent study shows, however, that central city-suburb differences in cancer mortality rates have narrowed considerably in the past few decades. See Michael R. Greenberg, "A Note on the Changing Geography of Cancer Mortality Within Metropolitan Regions of the United States," *Demography*, 18, no. 3 (August 1981), 411–420.

32.   Margaret Cussler and Mary L. DeGive, *Twixt the Cup and the Lip* (New York: Twayne Publishers, 1952), pp. 56–57.

33.   National Center for Health Statistics, *Hospital and Surgical Insurance Coverage*, DHEW Publication No. (HRA) 77-1545 (Washington, D.C.: U.S. Government Printing Office, 1977).

34.   National Center for Health Statistics, *Family Out-of-Pocket Health Expenses*, DHEW Publication No. (PHS) 79-1555, (Washington, D.C.: U.S. Government Printing Office, 1979).

35.   George J. Stolnitz, "International Mortality Trends: Some Main Facts and Implications," in *The Population Debate: Dimensions and Perspectives*, vol. 1, Department of Economic and Social Affairs (New York: United Nations, 1975), p.231.

36.   Samuel H. Preston, *Mortality Patterns in National Populations*, (New York: Academic Press, 1976), p. 159.

37.   Dublin, Lotka, and Spiegelman, *Life*, pp. 129–130.

38.   Francis C. Madigan, "Are Sex Mortality Differences Biologically Caused?" *Milbank Memorial Fund Quarterly*, 35 (April 1957), 202–223.

39.   Philip E. Enterline, "Causes of Death Responsible for Recent Increases in Sex Mortality Differentials in the United States," *Milbank Memorial Fund Quarterly*, 39 (April 1961), 312–325.

40.   Joseph W. Eaton and Albert J. Mayer, "Man's Capacity to Reproduce: The Demography of a Unique Population," *Human Biology*, 25, no. 3 (1954), 34–35.

41.   Edward A. Suchman, "Public Health and Medicine," in *Survey Research in the Social Sciences*, ed. Charles Y. Glock (New York: Russell Sage Foundation, 1967), p. 458.

42.   Robert D. Retherford, *The Changing Sex Differential in Mortality* (Westport, Conn.: Greenwood Press, 1975), pp. 104–105.

43.   Lincoln C. Chen, Emdadul Huq, and Stan D'Souza, "Sex Bias in the Family Allocation of Food and Health Care in Rural Bangladesh," *Population and Development Review*, 7, no. 1 (March 1981), 55–70.

44.   Lois M. Verbrugge, "Recent Trends in Sex Mortality Differentials in the United States" *Women and Health*, 5:3 (1980), 17–18.

45.   Jean Daric, "Mortality, Occupation, and Socio-Economic Status," *Vital Statistics—Special Reports*, 33 (September 21, 1951), 177.

46.   Ibid., p. 179.

47.   W. P. D. Logan, "Social Class Variations in Mortality," *Public Health Reports*, 69 (December 1954), 1219.

48.   Edward G. Stockwell, "Socioeconomic Status and Mortality in the United States," *Public Health Reports*, 76 (December 1961), 1081–1082; Kitagawa and Hauser, *Differential Mortality*, p. 40.

49.   Tapani Valkonen and Hannele Sauli, "Socio-Economic Differential Mortality in Finland," in *Socio-Economic Differential Mortality in Industrialized Societies*, (Paris: Committee for International Cooperation in National Research in Demography, 1981), pp. 41–43.

50.   Elsebeth Lynge, "Occupational Mortality in Norway, Denmark, and Finland, 1971–1975," in CICRED, *Differential Mortality*, pp. 2–39.

51.   Daric, "Mortality," p. 181.

52.   J. C. Caldwell, "Education as a Factor in Mortality Decline: An Examination of Nigerian Data," *Population Studies*, 33, no. 3 (November 1979), 395–413.

53.   Calvin Goldscheider, *Population, Modernization, and Social Structure* (Boston: Little, Brown 1971), 268–269.

54.   Nam, Weatherby, and Ockay, "Mortality Crossover."

55.   Victor A. McKusick, "The Ethnic Distribution of Disease in the United States," *Journal of Chronic Diseases*, 20 (March 1967), 115–118.

56.   H. G. Rawlinson, *India: A Short Cultural History*, (New York: Praeger, 1952), pp. 58, 214, 407.

57. Gale E. Wilson, "Christian Science and Longevity," *Journal of Forensic Sciences*, 1 (1956), 43–60.

58. Don F. Neufeld, ed., *Seventh-Day Adventist Encyclopedia*, (Washington, D.C.: Review and Herald Publishing Association, 1966), p. 512.

59. National Center for Health Statistics, *Vital Statistics of the United States, 1978, Volume II, Section 5, Life Tables*, DHHS Publications No. (PHS) 81-1104 (Washington, D.C.: U.S. Government Printing Office, 1980), p. 4.

60. Fraser Brockington, *World Health* (Boston: Little, Brown, 1968), pp. 133–134.

61. Ibid., pp. 149–160.

62. Ibid., p. 169.

63. Stolnitz, "International Mortality," p. 234.

64. Samuel H. Preston, "Mortality, Morbidity, and Development," *Population Bulletin of the United Nations Economic Commission for Western Asia*, no. 15 (December 1978), 70.

65. National Center for Health Statistics, *A Study of Infant Mortality from Linked Records*, DHEW Publication No. (HSM) 72-1056 (Washington, D.C.: U.S. Government Printing Office, 1972).

66. Helen C. Chase, "Registration Completeness and International Comparisons of Infant Mortality," *Demography* 6, no. 4 (November 1969), 425–433.

67. Dublin, Lotka, and Spiegelman, *Life*, pp. 193–202.

68. National Center for Health Statistics, *Highlights From Wave I of the National Survey of Personal Health Practices and Consequences: United States, 1979*, Data from the National Health Survey, Series 15, No. 1, DHHS Publication No. (PHS) 81-1162 (Washington, D.C.: U.S. Government Printing Office, 1981), pp. 10–19.

69. Meyer Friedman and Ray H. Rosenman, *Type A Behavior and Your Heart* (New York: Fawcett Books Group—CBS Publications, 1974).

70. David P. Phillips and Kenneth A. Feldman, "A Dip in Deaths Before Ceremonial Occasions: Some New Relationships Between Social Integration and Mortality," *American Sociological Review*, 38 (1973), 678–696.

71. Richard Schulz and Max Bazerman, "Ceremonial Occasions and Mortality: A Second Look," *American Psychologist*, 35, no. 3 (March 1980), 253–261.

72. Stolnitz, "International Mortality," pp. 234–235.

73. Eileen Crimmins, "The Changing Pattern of American Mortality Decline, 1940–77, and Its Implications for the Future," *Population and Development Review*, 7, no. 2 (June 1981), 248–251.

74. Fries and Crapo, *Aging*, chap. 11.

SUGGESTED ADDITIONAL READINGS

ANTONOVSKY, AARON, *Health, Stress, and Coping*. San Francisco: Jossey-Bass, 1979. Valuable for its insights into the roles of tension and stress as they affect health and survival.

DUBLIN, LEWIS I., ALFRED J. LOTKA, AND MORTIMER SPIEGELMAN, *Length of Life.* New York: Ronald Press, 1949. A classic study of historical progress in health and longevity and contributing factors.

KITAGAWA, EVELYN M., AND PHILIP M. HAUSER, *Differential Mortality in the United States; A Study in Socioeconomic Epidemiology.* Cambridge, Mass.: Harvard University Press, 1973. The most comprehensive analysis of social and economic factors in mortality differences based on matched vital and census records.

MCKEOWN, THOMAS, *The Modern Rise of Population.* New York: Academic Press, 1976. Focuses on historical mortality decline in Europe and evaluates the contributions of various societal conditions.

PRESTON, SAMUEL H., *Mortality Patterns in National Populations.* New York: Academic Press, 1976. Examines determinants and consequences of mortality trends and differentials, with emphasis on cause-of-death patterns.

RETHERFORD, ROBERT D., *The Changing Sex Differential in Mortality.* Westport, Conn.: Greenwood Press, 1975. Explores causes of widening sex mortality differences in industrialized nations, with special attention to the role of smoking behavior.

UNITED NATIONS DEPARTMENT OF ECONOMIC AND SOCIAL AFFAIRS. *Population Bulletin of the United Nations No. 6-1962.* New York: United Nations, 1963. A somewhat outdated but fundamental analysis of world mortality trends.

TECHNICAL SUPPLEMENT NO. 3

Constructing a Life Table

Demographers calculate a variety of mortality measures, sometimes because different measures are more or less refined and not all countries have data that permit the refined measures to be computed, and sometimes because the questions to be answered necessitate different kinds of measures. If you want to know the number of war casualties among people in a given country in a given year, the number of deaths due to that cause, and its relation to the population, you would want to know the cause-specific death rate. If your interest is in the proportion of teenagers who died this year, you might calculate an age-specific death rate, say for the age group fifteen to nineteen. However, if your concern is with how long your newborn baby can expect to live, or with how many years of life you probably still have when you reach age fifty, then you need to get measures of life expectancy, and these come from a *life table.*

A life table is intended to represent the death and survival experience of a cohort of newly born babies as they age over time until the last one is deceased. We might follow the experience of an actual baby cohort in this way, wait about 100 years, and record our findings. But to gather such data for babies now born would leave few of us around to analyze the results. Unfortunately, there are very few instances where such survival histories have been collected in the past, so that *true cohort* life tables are rarities. Moreover, such tables would depict only the survival experience of that particular cohort over that range of time. (The mortality history of babies born in 1800 would not be a good expectation of the future course of mortality for babies born today.)

This methodological dilemma leads mortality specialists to rely on *current or cross-sectional* life tables. Such tables use as their basic data the mortality risks at each age in a current population. Arranging the age-specific death rates in a life-cycle fashion, an assumption is made that newborns will be subject to these mortal risks at each age as they proceed through life. Where mortality conditions are not likely to change very much, as in developed countries, that assumption seems fairly sound. Where mortality is still declining, future death rates are overestimated to some degree, and life expectancy is somewhat understated. In fact, current life tables turn out to be fairly accurate for most of our uses.

Yet how does one derive a life expectancy figure from a sequence of age-specific death rates? Several steps are involved, and at first the process seems complicated. But when it is completed, the results appear to be straightforward and simple to interpret.

Let us look first at the partial or discontinuous life table on pp. 102–103. (We have skipped some levels for convenience in presentation.) The first column tells us the age interval or time between birthdays. The second column gives the probability of dying between birthdays or a mortality rate specific to that age interval. These are based on reported death statistics and census population adjusted to those age categories. Column 3 starts with an arbitrary 100,000 babies born and shows the number surviving to each next birthday, assuming the age-specific death rates given. Column 4 is the number of deaths in each age interval, obtained simply by applying the death rate in a given age by the number who survive to the beginning of that age. Column 5 reports the number of person-years lived in that age interval. Those who live to the end of the age interval count for one each. Those who die during the interval are counted for only part of the year. The sum of the whole and part years lived by those who began the age interval (person-years lived) is sometimes referred to as the stationary population in that age category. Column 6 merely cumulates person-years lived from Column 5, from the oldest age interval to the youngest one. Hence, the number 7,074,927 on the first line means that the 100,000 babies born and subject to the age-specific mortality rates cited will have lived a grand total of that many cumulated whole and part years of life from birth until all have died. Similarly, the 5,125,689 for the 20-to-21 age interval are the cumulated person-years remaining for those who reach age 20. These are aggregate figures, which reflect the fact that some of these persons will die the following year, while others may live a very long life. Column 7 presents the life-expectancy figures. They are obtained by dividing the total person-years to be lived by an age category (Column 6), by the number of persons who began that age (Column 3). If 100,000 babies have 7,074,927 person-years of life to live, each has an average expectation of 70.75 years. If the 96,716 who reach age 20 have 5,125,689 person-years of life to live, each of them has an average expectation of 53 more years to live, or a total of 73 years (20 + 53).

As you can see, the life expectancies that come out at the end are a function of the age-specific mortality rates that are put in. Assuming a given number of babies born, all other statistics in a life table are products of that initial input.

TABLE 3.4 Life table for the total population: United States, 1969–71

AGE INTERVAL	PROPORTION DYING	OF 100,000 BORN ALIVE		STATIONARY POPULATION		AVERAGE REMAINING LIFETIME
Period of Life Between Two Ages	Proportion of Persons Alive at Beginning of Age Interval Dying During Interval	Number Living at Beginning of Age Interval	Number Dying During Age Interval	In the Age Interval	In This and All Subsequent Age Intervals	Average Number of Years of Life Remaining at Beginning of Age Interval
x to $x + t$	tq_x	l_x	td_x	tL_x	T_x	e_x
Years						
0–1	.02002	100,000	2,002	98,283	7,074,927	70.75
1–2	.00125	97,998	122	97,937	6,976,644	71.19
2–3	.00086	97,876	84	97,834	6,878,707	70.28
3–4	.00069	97,792	68	97,758	6,780,873	69.34
4–5	.00057	97,724	56	97,696	6,683,115	68.39
5–6	.00051	97,668	49	97,643	6,585,419	67.43
6–7	.00046	97,619	46	97,596	6,487,776	66.46
7–8	.00043	97,573	42	97,553	6,390,180	65.49
8–9	.00039	97,531	37	97,512	6,292,627	64.52
9–10	.00034	97,494	34	97,477	6,195,115	63.54
10–11	.00031	97,460	30	97,445	6,097,638	62.57
11–12	.00030	97,430	29	97,415	6,000,193	61.58
12–13	.00035	97,401	34	97,384	5,902,778	60.60
13–14	.00046	97,367	45	97,344	5,805,394	59.62
14–15	.00063	97,322	61	97,292	5,708,050	58.65
15–16	.00082	97,261	80	97,221	5,610,758	57.69
16–17	.00101	97,181	98	97,132	5,513,537	56.73
17–18	.00117	97,083	113	97,027	5,416,405	55.79
18–19	.00128	96,970	124	96,908	5,319,378	54.86
19–20	.00134	96,846	130	96,781	5,222,470	53.93
20–21	.00140	96,716	136	96,648	5,125,689	53.00
21–22	.00147	96,580	142	96,510	5,029,041	52.07

Age interval						
22–23	.00152	96,438	146	96,365	4,932,531	51.15
23–24	.00153	96,292	147	96,218	4,836,166	50.22
24–25	.00151	96,145	145	96,072	4,739,948	49.30
50–51	.00738	88,972	657	88,644	2,306,987	25.93
51–52	.00804	88,315	710	87,960	2,218,343	25.12
52–53	.00876	87,605	767	87,221	2,130,383	24.32
53–54	.00957	86,838	831	86,422	2,043,162	23.53
54–55	.01043	86,007	897	85,558	1,956,740	22.75
55–56	.01136	85,110	968	84,626	1,871,182	21.99
56–57	.01236	84,142	1,039	83,623	1,786,556	21.23
57–58	.01341	83,103	1,115	82,545	1,702,933	20.49
58–59	.01452	81,988	1,190	81,393	1,620,388	19.76
59–60	.01570	80,798	1,269	80,163	1,538,995	19.05
60–61	.01695	79,529	1,348	78,856	1,458,832	18.34
61–62	.01829	78,181	1,430	77,466	1,379,976	17.65
62–63	.01974	76,751	1,515	75,994	1,302,510	16.97
63–64	.02133	75,236	1,605	74,433	1,226,516	16.30
64–65	.02306	73,631	1,698	72,782	1,152,083	15.65
95–96	.25745	2,786	718	2,427	8,522	3.06
96–97	.26959	2,068	557	1,789	6,095	2.95
97–98	.28024	1,511	424	1,300	4,306	2.85
98–99	.28977	1,087	315	929	3,006	2.76
99–100	.29869	772	230	657	2,077	2.69
100–101	.30696	542	167	459	1,420	2.62
101–102	.31461	375	118	316	961	2.56
102–103	.32167	257	82	216	645	2.51
103–104	.32817	175	58	146	429	2.46
104–105	.33414	117	39	98	283	2.41
105–106	.33960	78	26	65	185	2.37
106–107	.34460	52	18	42	120	2.34
107–108	.34917	34	12	28	78	2.30
108–109	.35333	22	8	18	50	2.27
109–110	.35712	14	5	12	32	2.24

Source: National Center for Health Statistics, *United State Life Tables; 1969–71*, DHEW Publication no. (HRA) 75-1150 (Washington, D.C.: U.S. Government Printing Office, 1975). pp. 6–7.

ISSUES SUPPLEMENT NO. 3

Public versus Private Responsibility for Health Maintenance

Staying alive and avoiding death are universal desires; with few exceptions, they are held everywhere in the world. However, feelings about who should be responsible for achieving these goals are much less agreed upon. Some feel that it is solely the concern of each individual (or family). Others believe that it has to be at least a community matter, but that it should be up to private groups or organizations to provide the necessary means. Still others say that potential disease and illness must be a public matter, because their effects reach out to touch everyone, and at times it requires a compulsory effort to bring about controls.

Defend one of the above positions with regard to each of the following conditions:

a. an outbreak of poliomyelitis
b. location of a plant that produces a product emitting noxious fumes
c. smoking in public meeting rooms
d. providing health insurance

CHAPTER FOUR
FERTILITY: TRENDS AND DETERMINANTS

Madam, I should have thought one of those would have been more than enough.

During the last several decades, a substantial amount of demographic research and writing has been focused on fertility. In the developed countries, attention to fertility has been encouraged by the need to sharpen population projections and by the feeling that fertility is the most unpredictable of the population components. With death rates fairly low and stable and international migration regulated, fertility has been the most variable of the components. In addition, motivation to avoid death is rather constant, while fertility desires can fluctuate. In the developing countries, attention has been focused on fertility in an attempt to understand the reasons for its high level and how it might be reduced. Even in those developing countries where mortality is low or decreasing, fertility remains high. Great concern over the resulting high rate of growth of population has fostered attempts to understand what affects fertility.

Since the proliferation of literature on fertility has been so great, it would be impossible to be comprehensive in our review of it here. Rather, we shall attempt to illustrate the factors that affect fertility. As was the case with mortality, we shall first discuss trends in fertility in the world as a whole, and then in the developed and developing countries.

LONG-TERM TRENDS IN FERTILITY

It is really quite pretentious to claim to be able to trace fertility rates in the world over a "long term." In light of the data available to accomplish that task, any conclusions drawn must be tentative. As late as 1965, for example, 35 percent of the areas in Africa had incomplete birth-registration data.[1] In South America, 50 percent of areas lacked birth data. This is compared with 19 percent of areas in North America and 3 percent of areas in Europe lacking birth-registration systems in 1965. If this was the situation in the mid-sixties, data were even more incomplete at earlier dates. In Africa, 78 percent of areas had no data on births before 1935. The comparable figure in South America is 38 percent, and in Asia, 61 percent. By contrast, only 17 percent of North American areas and 15 percent of European areas lacked data on births before 1935. While demographers have techniques for estimating statistics on births without registration data, the uneven amount of direct information available on world fertility should be noted.

Early Fertility Trends

Given the inadequacy of birth data, the reader must already perceive the insecurity with which demographers discuss fertility rates in preindustrial or primitive times. In order to talk about the birthrate of primitive people, we must rely on archaeological evidence, any drawings or writings located from those times, and a good bit of surmising. It is fairly certain that the death rate was high, so that human beings must have had a high birthrate or they would have become extinct. One scholar has estimated, for example, that if the average expectation of life for females was twenty years, then almost a third of the female population would have survived to the childbearing years. Those who lived to the age of *menopause* (when menstrual periods cease) would have had an average of 6.5 children. This would mean a crude birthrate of 50 per 1,000, which is very high indeed.[2]

Such reasoning, while logical, is less satisfying than a census or vital-registration system. We might also look at relatively primitive peoples of today and draw some parallels with living conditions and their effect on fertility in earlier times. In such studies, fertility has been shown to be quite high, in the neighborhood of 55 or more births per 1,000 population.[3]

One interesting aspect of these findings is that fertility, even among primitive peoples, is often far below the biologically possible maximum. Techniques of contraception, abortion, and infanticide were known to such societies. The techniques used, while seeming crude or offensive today, were nevertheless effective. In many primitive societies, *lactation* (or breast-feeding) continued for several years after a child was born, reducing pregnancy risk. These factors combined with various cultural practices, such as sexual abstinence on certain special days, marriage and mating restrictions, and other taboos, to reduce the birthrate.

When looking at the fertility of societies prior to industrialization, we can also rely on church and government records. Church records of baptisms, burials, and marriages have been particularly useful in demographic research.[4] But the limitations of these records are numerous, since not all persons in a community are likely to be registered with a church, and we have very little information about how thorough the record keepers of those times were.

In spite of these data limitations, it appears that most countries had high fertility (50 per 1,000 or higher) prior to about 1650. Around 1650, and there is some dispute about the date, a tremendous growth in population began occurring in countries that were undergoing industrialization. This growth was apparently owed to a large decrease in mortality, although more recently there has been some evidence that birthrates rose slightly during the early stages of industrialization.

Following this period of rapid population growth, birthrates began to decline—in the seventeenth century in some nations, and not until the eighteenth or nineteenth century in others. Several reasons are postulated for this decline. It would appear that with industrialization replacing agricultural economies, children were not the asset they had been when they were needed to work the land. The decline in mortality meant that it was no longer necessary to have several extra children to ensure that a sufficient number survived to adulthood. Still other hypotheses include the greater use of coitus interruptus, the condom, and possibly abortion as methods of birth control. In any case, it seems that smaller families came to be more popular—at least in the countries that are now called developed. We turn now to an examination of twentieth-century trends in fertility rates in these countries and in the developing countries.

Developed Nations

It has often been said that no other single characteristic distinguishes developed areas from developing ones as clearly as does the birthrate. In the more-developed regions of the world, including Europe, North America, Australia, New Zealand, Japan, and the USSR, the average crude birthrate is 15 per 1,000. In the developing nations, however, the average crude birthrate is 33.[5] Still, there are no strict continental boundaries for developed and developing countries, and examples of countries with low birthrates can be found in nearly every region of the world.

In developed countries where birthrates have declined throughout this century, much variation in the pattern of decline is evident. Figure 4.1 shows crude birthrates for selected nations of the world from 1920 to 1981. Four countries on the graph are usually considered developed: Sweden, the United States, Japan, and the USSR. Nigeria, Guatemala, and India are developing countries, while Taiwan is a transition country, with urbanization and economic growth underway but relatively recent.

Close examination of the patterns in Figure 4.1 will illustrate the variations in birthrate decline evident in these nations. In the United States, the birthrate was 22.8 per 1,000 in 1920 to 1924, and then dropped to 17.2 during the Depression years of the early 1930s. Then, following World War II, it rose to 24.6. This was the period of the *baby boom*. Another decline began in the late 1950s and continued until 1968. While this is not shown in Figure 4.1, the birthrate rose slightly in 1969 and 1970 but began declining rather sharply again in 1971. This persisted (the *baby bust*) until very recently, when the birthrate began to rise again.

While the general shape of the birthrate curve is the same for Sweden, some interesting differences from the United States pattern can be noted. Sweden, too, had declining birthrates in the 1930s, with a

FIGURE 4.1 Crude birthrates for selected countries, 1920–1981

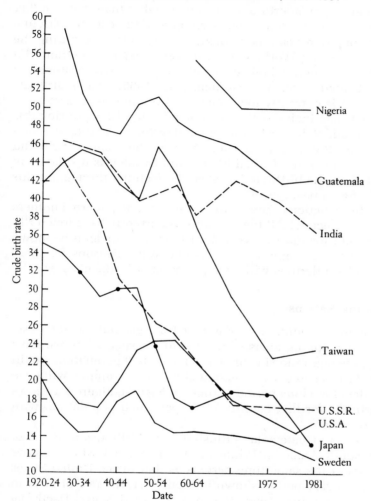

Source: Figures for these graphs are from *United Nations Demographic Yearbook, 1965,* New York, 1966, Table 12, pp. 276–299, and from Population Reference Bureau, *World Population Data Sheet,* 1969, 1970, 1975, and 1981.

return to slightly higher rates following the war. However, this rise after World War II was less prolonged in Sweden than in the United States. In addition, for every year from 1920 to 1981, Sweden's birthrates have been below those in the United States. This has been the common European pattern in these years.

Still a third pattern of birthrate decline in a developed country is shown by Japan. Japan's birthrate was much higher than that of either the United States or Sweden in the early part of the century. Decline during the Depression years is evident, as is a slight rise during the early 1940s. Following World War II, however, Japan experienced a marked decline, a pattern widely different from the postwar baby boom noted in the United States and Sweden. After 1960, Japan's birthrate rose slightly, but is currently lower than that of the United States.

Figure 4.1 also includes the birthrates for the USSR during this same time period. Relative to the other developed countries represented here, the USSR is quite deviant. None of the dramatic rises and falls evident in Japan, the United States, and Sweden is displayed in the USSR. Rather, the birthrate has steadily declined throughout this century and now appears level.

Each of these nations shows a different birthrate pattern, but there are also common factors. All these countries currently have low birthrates, and, except for the USSR, each of them has apparently shown responsiveness to economic conditions and wars. Reasons for these differences and similarities will be explored later in the chapter.

Developing Nations

The remaining countries in Figure 4.1 are generally called less-developed or developing areas of the world. In such areas we have noted that the average crude birthrate is 33 per 1,000 population, but in Africa it is a startling 46 per 1,000 population.[6] For example, while we cannot offer data for a long period of time for Nigeria, Figure 4.1 shows a current birthrate for that country of 50 per 1,000 population, with little recent decline.

The pattern in Guatemala is illustrative of birthrates in much of Central and South America. While the Guatemalan birthrate shows increases at about the same time periods as that in the United States and Sweden, in every period shown in Figure 4.1, the rate of birth in Guatemala was more than twice that in the United States. Declining from 62.6 per 1,000 in 1920 to 1924, the crude birthrate was 47.2 in the period 1940 to 1944. During the postwar period, it rose to 51.3 in 1950 to 1954 and has been declining steadily since that time.

In India the birthrate has also been high throughout the fifty years covered in Figure 4.1. While fluctuations are evident, it does not fall below 35 or rise above 47 per 1,000 during this entire period. Further, the rises and declines do not occur at the same time as those in Guatemala, the United States, or Sweden, indicating that different factors are influential. Nevertheless, the Indian, Guatemalan, and Nigerian birthrates, while somewhat different from one another, illustrate the common high level of fertility in developing nations.

Taiwan might be considered a transition country, both demographically and economically. From 42 per 1,000 in 1920 to 1924, the Taiwanese birthrate showed rises and declines until 1950 to 1954, when a period of steady and rather steep decline began. That decline has clearly placed it in a middle-ground position between the rather extreme highs of India and Guatemala and the lows of the United States, Sweden, Japan, and the USSR. We should note, however, that the Taiwanese decline apparently halted in about 1975. In the most recent years, the birthrate has risen slightly, calling into question whether the dramatic declines of the past will continue.

The trend of the birthrate in Taiwan and a good many other countries has led some authors to speculate that the previous sharp division between high- and low-fertility countries is disappearing as new countries enter the demographic transition.[7] In 1978, for example, Berelson suggested that at least thirteen countries with traditionally high fertility are likely to lower their birthrates to 20 per 1,000 population by the year 2000.[8] These countries include Taiwan, as well as South Korea, Chile, China, Brazil, Mexico, the Philippines, Thailand, Turkey, Colombia, Sri Lanka, Venezuela, and Malaysia.

While we have not included it in Figure 4.1, a special word needs to be said about the birthrate in the People's Republic of China. Since estimates of population in 1982 were about one billion people,[9] the impact of Chinese fertility on the world's population is substantial. However, until very recently only sparse and anecdotal data were available from China. The Population Reference Bureau estimates the current Chinese birthrate at 22 per 1,000, below the current rate in Taiwan. In addition, various reports indicate that the crude birthrate in China has declined drastically in the last ten years. There is much speculation about the future course of China's birthrate, but it is now certain that unprecedented efforts are being made toward further reductions.[10] We will discuss these efforts in more detail later in this chapter.

SEASONAL VARIATION IN FERTILITY

One of the most interesting short-term variations in fertility is by season. It has long been a source of curiosity that births, like deaths, show a seasonal fluctuation.[11] To illustrate this trend for the United States, Figure 4.2 shows seasonal indexes of live births, by color, for 1933, 1943, and 1963, as well as months of birth for 1980.[12] Two peak periods of birth are apparent: one centers around February, and the other,

FIGURE 4.2 **Seasonal indexes of live births, by color in the United States, 1933, 1943, and 1963, and birthrate by month, 1980**

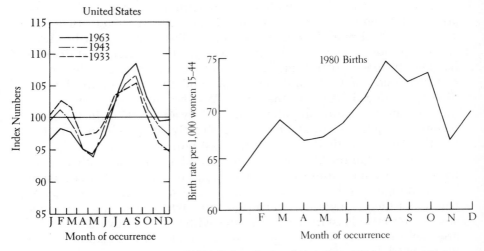

Source: National Center for Health Statistics, *Seasonal Variation of Births: United States, 1933–1963.* Series 21, no. 9, (Washington, D.C.: U.S. Government Printing Office, 1966). Births for 1980 are from National Center for Health Statistics, "Births, Marriages, Divorces, and Deaths for 1980," *Monthly Vital Statistics Report,* 24, no. 12 (March 1981).

around August and September. Since 1933, the September peak has become even more pronounced, while the February peak has declined.

For nonwhites, the peaks are even sharper, but the lessening of the February peak and the increase in the September peak are also evident. Regional data on seasonality of birth have shown that the South exhibits the most pronounced seasonality, while the Northeast exhibits the least. This is not owing to the concentration of nonwhites in the South, since whites in the South have a season-of-birth curve much like that of nonwhites in the area. Further, recent studies of seasonality of birth in the Southern United States indicate that this variation tends to be most pronounced among those with lower social status.[13] This finding perhaps helps to account for the tendency of children born in August and September to do less well in school, a deficit usually blamed on their younger age.

Other countries of the world have seasonal patterns of birth, but those patterns may differ greatly from those in the United States.[14] For example, in European countries there are more births in the late winter months, while in Mexico, the south Pacific and Gulf areas show birth peaks in December.[15]

No definitive answer to why births occur with greater frequency in some months than in others has been found. Writers have looked at seasonality of sexual relations, social customs such as religious holidays, climate, season of marriage, socioeconomic status, and even data-registration error, in an attempt to explain this phenomenon.[16] No one of these factors seems to be a total explanation. It may be that the causes of seasonality of birth are different for each society and that, within societies, influences on the birth curve vary in importance over time.[17] In any case, the importance of the patterns seems to be in creating a net reduction in the total birthrate because of reduced ability to conceive in some months.[18]

THE AGE CURVE OF FERTILITY

For several measures of fertility the assumption is made that ages fifteen to forty-four are the childbearing ages for women. For men, the ability to produce children lasts longer. While there are, of course, exceptions to this general assumption (that is, women who have children after age forty-four or before fifteen), they are relatively rare.

Between those ages, childbearing is not likely to be evenly distributed. In fact, fertility is usually concentrated quite heavily between ages twenty and twenty-nine. Figure 4.3 illustrates the differences between a hypothetical age curve of fertility, were women to distribute their childbearing throughout the fecund years, and an actual age curve of fertility, produced by using data from seventy-two countries. This figure demonstrates the uneven distribution of births within the years of potential fecundity.

The United Nations has identified three different age patterns of fertility that describe nearly every country for which there are data.[19] These patterns are early peaking, in which maximum fertility occurs between twenty and twenty-four years of age; late peaking, in which it occurs between twenty-five and twenty-nine; and broad peaking, in which fertility between age twenty and twenty-four differs only slightly from that between twenty-five and twenty-nine, with little fertility occurring at younger or older ages.

In low-fertility countries, births are concentrated in a much narrower range of ages than is the case in high-fertility countries. The contribution to the total fertility of the country from women below age twenty and above thirty-five is much higher in countries of high fertility than in those where fertility is low. The age curves of fertility for the United States and Mexico, shown in Figure 4.4, illustrate this difference between countries with an early peak, or low fertility, and a broad peak, or higher fertility. The fertility of women in the United

FIGURE 4.3 Hypothetical fecundity model and average age-specific birthrates in 72 countries

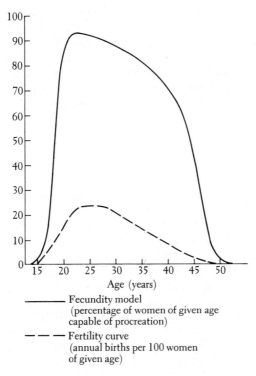

Age (years)

———— Fecundity model
(percentage of women of given age capable of procreation)

— — — Fertility curve
(annual births per 100 women of given age)

Source: Population Bulletin of the United Nations, no. 7, 1963, Figure 7.1, p. 101.

States is highly concentrated between the ages of twenty and twenty-nine, while Mexican women are more likely to bear children later. This is not to say that fertility rates are higher among women in the United States than Mexico at these ages, but only that a greater proportion of United States childbearing occurs between the ages of twenty and twenty-nine.

Earlier marriages in the high-fertility countries and less control over fertility in general account for these differences. It would seem that women in low-fertility countries can or do regulate their fertility more effectively, in order to concentrate it into a relatively small part of the total number of fecund years available. In the United States, for example, 64.6 percent of the total fertility in 1975 occurred among women twenty to twenty-nine years old.

FIGURE 4.4 Mean percent of total fertility contributed by women in each age group, United States, 1975, and Mexico, 1974

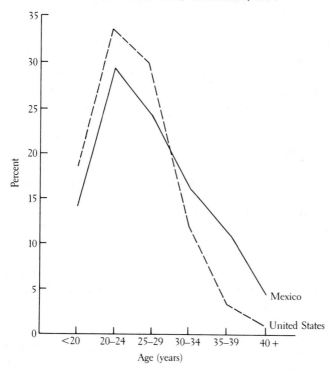

Source: Data for these graphs obtained from *Demographic Yearbook, 1979* (New York: United Nations, 1979), pp. 306–307.

In recent years in the United States and in other developed and developing nations, concern has arisen over the level of the birthrate at one end of the age curve; that is, births by teenagers. While in the United States these have been declining over the last decade, birthrates among older age groups have lowered more rapidly. Thus, births to teenagers have come to constitute a greater and greater proportion of all births. By the late 1970s, for example, births by teen mothers constituted nearly one-fifth of all births in the United States.

Another interesting characteristic of teenage births that has perhaps caused most of the concern is the number that occur out of wedlock. While there were 15.3 out-of-wedlock births per 1,000 unmarried teenage women in 1960, that figure had risen to 26.9 by 1979, a 76 percent increase.[20] Expressed as a ratio per 1,000 live births, about 46 percent of babies born to those between fifteen and nineteen in 1979 were to unmarried women.[21]

These trends in teenage births have been of concern to policy makers, because of the many demonstrated negative consequences of early childbearing for both young mothers and their children, as well as the resultant societal costs. Since they are less likely to obtain adequate prenatal care, teenage mothers run higher risks of pregnancy and delivery complications than women in their twenties.[22] In addition, the subsequent pace of childbearing among these early starters is more rapid, and their overall completed family size is higher than among women who postpone the onset of childbearing.[23]

Recent research has documented that teenagers are beginning sexual activity earlier than in previous generations and are thus in need of contraceptive services to prevent unwanted pregnancy.[24] The policy response to these trends in the 1970s emphasized greater access to such services, as well as provision of educational programs to acquaint teenagers with information about the risk of pregnancy and its consequences.

However, Federal policies in the early 1980s became more restrictive concerning access to contraceptive services for teenagers and the use of abortion, emphasizing instead the need to counsel young people to refrain from sexual activity. In addition, recently proposed rules from the Department of Health and Human Services require parental notification if teens are given prescription contraceptives. While some have been adamant that parents must be consulted and involved in the sex-related behavior of their children, others have noted that parental notification would only keep teenagers out of clinics and increase the number who become pregnant.

FACTORS AFFECTING FERTILITY

Theoretical Considerations

There have been many attempts to develop comprehensive theoretical frameworks to explain fertility. These frameworks have emphasized different factors as being most important, and, like the overall theoretical approaches to the study of population discussed in Chapter 2, they include consideration of macro, medial, and micro factors. Figure 4.5 illustrates one such framework.[25] Included in the framework are general environmental variables, such as health, food, or water supply. These are macro factors, which are important because they can

FIGURE 4.5 **An illustrative theoretical framework for the analysis of fertility**

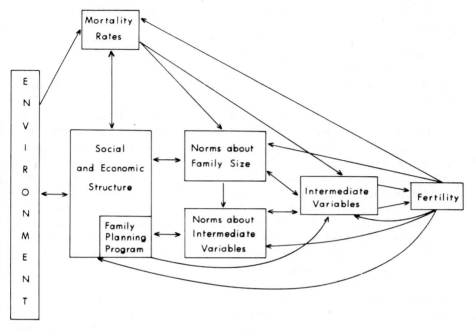

Source: Ronald Freedman, *The Sociology of Human Fertility* (New York: Irvington Publishers, Inc., 1975), p. 15. Reprinted by permission of Irvington Publishers, Inc.

so greatly limit the ability to conceive a child or carry it to term. Environmental factors, in turn, affect the mortality rate, and may cause couples to increase their overall childbearing so as to have the desired number of children survive to adulthood.[26] The social and economic-structure variables in the framework include other macro factors such as whether or not the society has a family-planning program, or its overall occupational or industrial structure.

Central to the framework, however, is the inclusion of medial factors such as norms. Societies enforce norms through positive and negative sanctions. In the case of fertility, many have argued that reproduction is so important that it would be "a sociological anomaly if normative cultural solutions were not developed to meet this problem.[27] In other words, societies have standards about family size, according to this theory, and enforce them through punishments of various kinds for those who have too few or too many children. These punishments may be quite mild, such as labeling couples "selfish" who remain voluntarily childless, or they may be quite strong, as in societies in which fines are levied against couples for having too many children.

Some economists have stressed the view that babies or children might be seen as consumer durables, like cars, refrigerators, or other goods.[28] Thus, these theorists reasoned, rises in income should lead to greater consumption of children, or in broader terms, to higher birthrates.

However, since, in fact, fertility rates seem to be higher among both low-income countries and low-income couples, the economic theory in this simple form attracted much discussion and debate.[29] Later revisions of this approach have stressed the importance of adding micro factors such as tastes or preferences to the medial variables in the model, and have made a distinction between the quantity of children a couple "consumes" and the quality of these children. With these additions it becomes easier to understand why a rise in income might produce a greater number of children, or it might produce only a greater investment in each child via greater expenditures on education, clothing, or other goods and services.[30]

Even later variations on these approaches have stressed that the determinants of fertility operate primarily through one or more of the following factors: (1) the demand for children; (2) the potential output of children (that is, their number) if no effort were made to control fertility; and (3) the costs of regulating fertility.[31] This latter variable is an important addition since the use of contraception involves not only monetary costs, such as those involved in the purchase of birth-control pills or other supplies, but other types as well, such as inconvenience, or health risks.

Figure 4.5 also includes a set of variables called "intermediate," as well as norms about those variables. The intermediate variables include three factors immediately preceding fertility: (1) factors affecting exposure to intercourse; (2) factors affecting exposure to conception; and (3) factors affecting gestation and successful parturition or birth.[32] For example, factors affecting exposure to intercourse include the usual age of entry into sexual unions, the number of persons who remain permanently celibate in a society, or abstinence from intercourse within marriage, due to separation. Included under factors affecting conception are voluntary and involuntary sterility or use of contraception. Finally, factors such as the rate of fetal mortality from both voluntary and involuntary causes affect both the gestational period and birth. Societies also have norms about each of these variables that are important in predicting fertility levels.

Explaining the fertility level of a society or group is a different task from seeking explanations for the childbearing of individuals or married couples. In an attempt to explain fertility variation among persons or pairs, micro variables have been added to other frameworks. It is important to emphasize again that these are not mutually exclusive approaches to the study of fertility, but only different emphases.

Figure 4.6 offers an example of a framework that adds attitudinal variables and family interaction to a theory of fertility.[33] Both the macro and medial variables discussed earlier are included in this framework. However, this approach argues that attention must also be given to processes within the family. These include the attitudes of family members toward fertility, as well as the social exchange between family members. For example, if a husband and wife differ on the appropriate number of children to have, their patterns of conflict or bargaining are important to understand in order to explain the final fertility outcome.

Perhaps these examples of approaches to the theoretical modeling of fertility will suffice to illustrate how complex such modeling may become. None of these frameworks is totally comprehensive, nor is a framework likely to emerge in the near future that would meet that standard. In fact, some authors have argued that all of these approaches suffer from being static and failing to recognize that each of these variables may assume different importance as each child is added.[34] If this is true, it may mean that a different model of fertility may be needed to explain a decision to add the second child, for example, than is needed to explain the decision to add the third. In any case, such frameworks are useful in pinpointing and organizing variables thought to explain fertility.

Macro Variables

In order to discuss some of the myriad factors affecting the patterns and trends of fertility just described, we shall return to the framework given in Chapter 1 of macro, medial, and micro influences. Certainly we will not mention all the variables that can affect fertility. Rather, we will attempt to mention the kinds that may affect fertility, and to give specific examples of how they operate.

We begin with a discussion of the larger influences in a society that affect nearly everyone living there, or the macro-level variables. Two such variables related to fertility are the natural environment and the level of development of the country.

Natural Environmental Factors

A considerable number of writers have been willing to maintain that the natural environment is the primary, if not the sole, cause of human behavior. The location of cities, religion, economic development, and

FIGURE 4.6 An illustrative theoretical framework including social psychological variables for the analysis of fertility

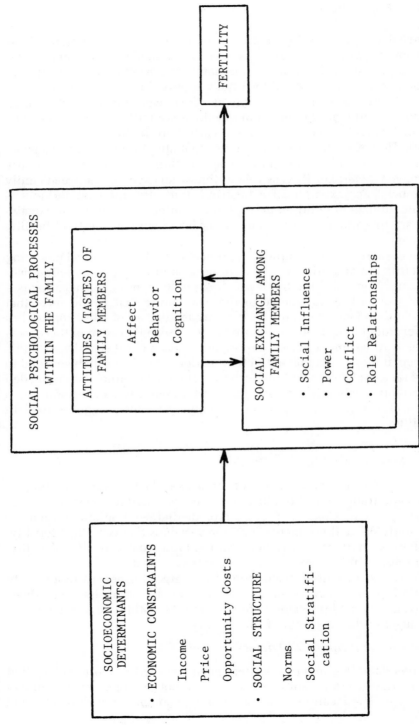

Source: R. P. Bagozzi and M. Frances Van Loo, "Toward a General Theory of Fertility: A Causal Modeling Approach," *Demography*, 15, no. 3 (August 1978), p. 303.

even reproductive behavior have been ascribed wholly or in part to the climate, resources, and topography.

In the realm of fertility, there has even been a popular fiction that peoples from warm climates are more sexually active, and hence more fertile, than those from colder climates. While the picture of a naked savage surviving on tropical fruits and warmed by the sun may conjure up ideas of virility to some, no reliable data are available to make this picture more than fantasy. In fact, there has been almost no research on the relationship of climate and fertility per se.[35]

The relationship of altitude to fertility has been explored in some depth by several authors, and an interesting debate has emerged. Some authors have found differences in the fertility of populations living at high and low altitudes in Peru.[36] These differences were first interpreted as resulting from cultural variations in mating practices or conscious attempts to control births.[37] Later analysis of these same populations suggested that the different altitudes at which they lived was the most important variable accounting for their fertility differences.[38] Some writers then proposed collaborative research by biologists and social scientists to explore the role of high altitude in fertility rates as well as in other demographic phenomena.[39]

Other aspects of the natural environment have been examined as possible sources of influence on fertility. Adequate food and water to support life are obviously essential. In addition, popular notions about what kinds of foods produce fecundity or increase sexual activity and, in turn, fertility have been abroad for some time. The food supply and its impact on fertility have been receiving more serious attention in developing countries in recent years, as part of the general examination of what factors influence high fertility rates in these countries. There has even been a fear on the part of some that increased food aid to developing countries might increase fertility.

In nations with little food, the infant death rate is likely to be high. Maternal health is weakened by nutritional deficiencies, affecting the child even before birth. Then, lacking resistance to disease because of vitamin or protein deficiencies, the child is vulnerable to death from even minor illnesses. Families in these countries are particularly interested in having children survive to adulthood, since that is the main form of social security for elderly parents. High infant mortality then encourages high birthrates to ensure old-age security. In India, for example, it has been estimated that a family must have 6.3 children to be 95 percent certain that one son, an especially valuable commodity, will survive until the father's sixty-fifth birthday.[40] If more food and more nourishing diets were available in these countries, lower mortality rates would produce higher population growth, at least in the short run. However, it is often argued that improved diets in the developing countries would be an important factor in lowering births over a long period of time.

It has also been suggested that the number of vitamins and amount of protein in the diet have a direct impact on fertility. De Castro has maintained that the birthrate is inversely related to the daily consumption of protein in societies.[41] He presents historical data to show that, statistically speaking, fertility and protein intake are related in this way. De Castro explains this relationship by hypothesizing that in countries where hunger is chronic but starvation not imminent, this hunger stimulates sexual appetites and speeds up the production of female hormones.

Critics of De Castro have noted that the birthrate is also negatively correlated with the number of motor vehicles, level of literacy, and telephones per 1,000 population in society. Karl Sax writes, "it would be just as logical to assume that people who spend much of their time riding, talking, or reading have low birth rates because they have so little time for reproduction."[42] Others have cited experimental studies of hunger and its apparent depressant effect on sexual activity, in order to refute De Castro.[43]

More recent analyses of the food-fertility linkage have examined carefully the difference in the impacts of severe malnutrition and chronic hunger.[44] It seems apparent that severe malnutrition can seriously impair fecundity. On the other hand, chronic, moderate malnutrition has only a minor impact on fecundity, thus decreasing fertility only slightly.

In examining the impact of food intake on fertility, it is also important to specify the variables through which the two might be connected and then to study whether or not the proposed intermediate relationships actually exist. For example, it has been argued that age at *menarche* (when menstruation begins) and duration of *lactational amenorrhea* (absence of menses due to lactation) seem to be directly affected by malnutrition, but that even among women with large differences in daily caloric intake, the fertility differences owing to these variables would be small.[45] Further, while current evidence is incomplete, it appears that other fertility-related variables are affected only minimally or not at all by chronic malnutrition. These include age at menopause, prevalence of sterility, ovulation, production of sperm, and miscarriage.

Taken together, the literature on natural environmental factors and their relationship to fertility does not seem to provide a substantial explanation of observed fertility trends. Indirect effects of climate, food, water, and other resources on fertility may be felt as these factors change the health of the population concerned. But the general level of health in the population seems to be most greatly affected by the economic development of the society, and so it will be discussed under that heading.

Economic Development

It is hard to live amid the current avalanche of materials on population and not know that fertility is related to the economic development of a society. Most people are aware that the poorer countries of the world have higher fertility rates than the more wealthy ones.

Even the terminology of the United Nations, which would like to avoid such implications, implies that "developed" nations are rich nations, while "underdeveloped" or, more gently, "developing" nations are poor ones. Indeed, the evidence that economically poorer nations have higher fertility rates is overwhelming.

Figure 4.7 graphically portrays this inverse relationship between economic well-being and the birthrate. Gross national product per capita has been used as the measure of economic development in this figure. The crude birthrate used does not take account of age differences in these nations, a factor that may make fertility appear somewhat distorted. Nevertheless, these two measures were chosen because they are virtually the only economic and fertility indicators available for this number of countries.

The inverse relationship between economic development and fertility is clear. Figure 4.7 also indicates that some countries might be considered middle range on both economic development and fertility, a reminder of the notion that some countries are now in transition in terms of demographic and economic development.

That this inverse relationship between economic development and fertility generally holds is well documented, but that this relationship always holds or has held in the past can be questioned. First, within the low-fertility countries, it is not those with the highest *gross national product* (GNP) per capita that have the lowest fertility. For example, Switzerland, with a very high GNP per capita, does not have the lowest crude birthrate. Even more startling exceptions can be seen in the cases of Kuwait, Qatar, or the United Arab Emirates. These countries have very high GNPs per capita, owing to oil wealth, while maintaining crude birthrates of 41, 44, and 37 per 1,000, respectively. While the general inverse relation between economic development and fertility may hold, then, other factors within a nation may cause deviation from this pattern. In fact, much of the analysis of the relationship between economic development and fertility has focused on how this relationship operates. Put another way, many have tried to discover what it is about economic development, exactly, that lowers fertility.

FIGURE 4.7 Crude birthrates and per capita gross national product for 80 countries of the world, 1981

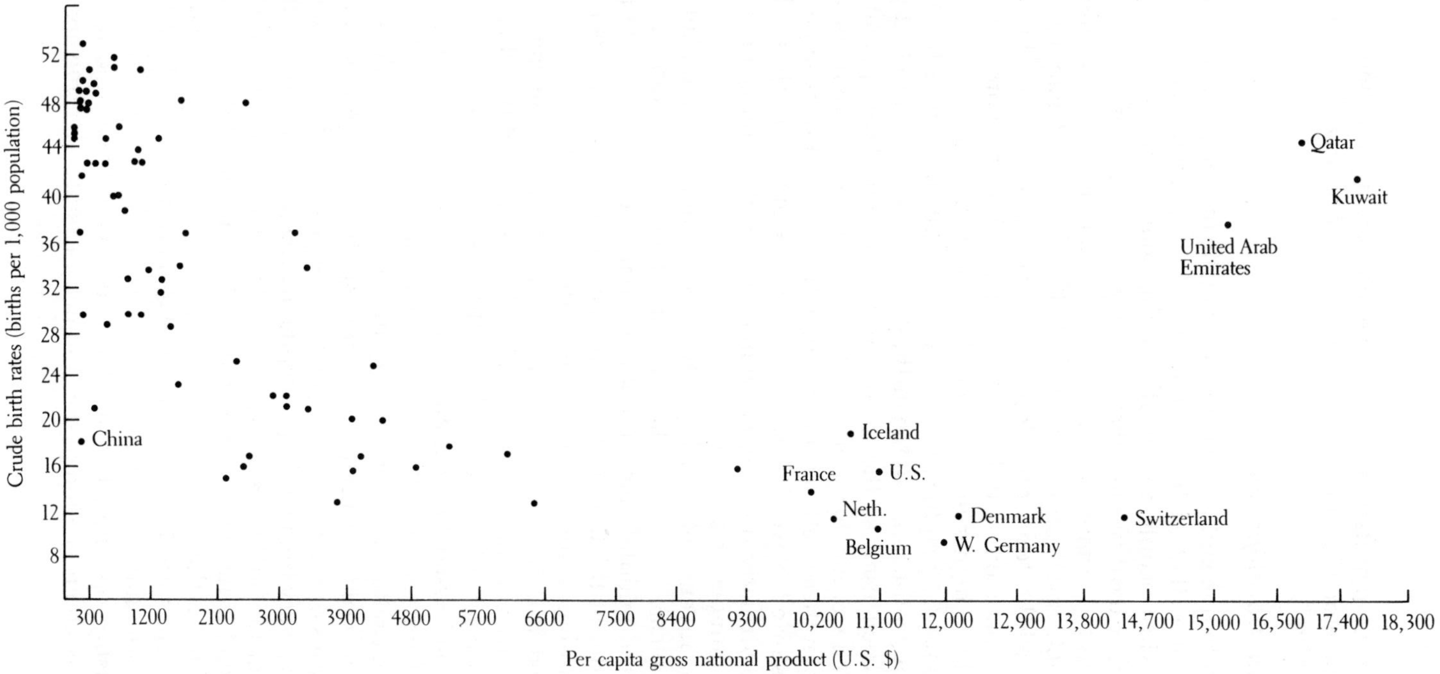

Source: 1981 World Population Data Sheet (Washington, D.C.: Population Reference Bureau, 1981).

In an early analysis in Latin American countries, for example, Heer and Turner found fertility inversely related to the proportion of the population engaged in agriculture, positively related to the proportion literate, and positively related to the proportion living in urban areas.[46] In trying to sort out the causation involved in these variables, Heer and Turner hypothesized:

> *An increase in the level of economic development leads to an increase in fertility as married couples become more optimistic concerning their future economic status. On the other hand, the increase in the level of economic development then sets in motion other forces, such as increased knowledge and use of birth control and increases in net economic cost of children, which tend to reduce fertility. In the long run, the forces depressing fertility tend to be stronger than the forces increasing fertility unless the increase in income per head continues at a high rate. Thus, many, if not most, nations exhibit the classic pattern of fertility decline with advancing industrialization.[47]*

Along this same line, others have examined the impact of land availability and agricultural employment on fertility. In rural Brazil, for example, it has been found that greater land availability is associated with higher fertility but that this relationship is not as strong as it may have been in nineteenth-century United States, because access to the land is greatly limited.[48]

Another investigation of socioeconomic factors led to the finding that the health and education levels of the population are determinative of fertility levels, holding economic development of the nation constant.[49] Thus it is suggested that economic development per se will not necessarily reduce fertility; it must be accompanied by other social changes in order to do so. Highest priority among these social changes would seem to go to the development of extensive educational programs, public-health services, and improvement in the status of women, all of which facilitate the spread of birth-control information and improve life-styles and life chances. In fact, it has been suggested that changing these factors directly may act as a "functional equivalent" to socioeconomic development.[50] We will discuss each of these factors in the following pages.

Education With regard to education, a recent analysis of the effect of schooling on the timing of fertility decline in developing countries argues that the mere reduction of illiteracy is not sufficient to insure fewer children.[51] Rather, mass education in the form of actual schooling seems to be necessary, and works in five important ways. First, schooling reduces a child's potential for work, because of the actual time spent in school and because schooling may make children less inclined to do ordinary work once they have found other pursuits. Secondly, schooling increases the costs of children, or what economists call the quality of children, not only because of the clothes or books they need, but also because school itself seems to alter tastes. Thirdly, the child must be viewed as a future producer while in school, rather than as a source of current family support. Each child therefore becomes, at least temporarily, less valuable. Schooling also speeds cultural change and creates new values, which may be compatible with lower fertility. Finally, this analysis argues, mass education via schooling, for better or for worse, perpetuates Western middle-class values and thus deemphasizes childbearing for the pursuit of other goals. Whether all of these factors operate in any given society or not, clearly many of them do, and perhaps they help to explain some of the mechanisms by which economic development lowers fertility.

Health It is apparent that the general health level of the population is also related to its fertility rate. We have already noted that parents in very poor societies, where the infant mortality rate is high, may wish to have large numbers of children in order to ensure that at least a few survive to adulthood. Conversely, raising the general health-education level of the society can further reduce the fertility rate, both by affecting infant mortality and by making family-planning programs part of the public-health services that are already trusted and used by the people.[52]

Poor health levels in a population can have a negative as well as a positive impact on fertility, as we noted in our discussion of malnutrition. Taking a somewhat different approach than examining food intake, some have discussed the role of three diseases known to produce *subfecundity*—pellagra, gonorrhea, and syphilis—in explaining historical rises and falls in birthrates among blacks in the United States.[53] Increases in the prevalence of these diseases apparently accounted for a decline in fertility among blacks from the end of the nineteenth century until about 1930. After that period, many blacks moved to urban areas and experienced improvements in their economic well-being. While these factors would seem to predict continued low fertility for blacks, their fertility rates rose, beginning in about 1940 and continuing for approximately twenty years. It is the contention of some that this fertility increase resulted primarily from improved health conditions. While other authors have disagreed with this judgment about the amount of subfecundity caused by venereal disease,[54] there is no argument that general health conditions among this population have influenced birthrates.

Status of Women   Another correlate of economic development in a society is improved status and opportunities for women. In recent searches for mechanisms to lower fertility in developing countries, the potential impact of programs targeted particularly at women has been examined,[55] because it is known that the traditional role of women in many societies has been the bearing and raising of children. If these activities are the primary ones through which women gain favor or status from their spouses and families, they are unlikely to lower their fertility without viable alternatives.

Table 4.1 illustrates some important differentials between males and females in the developed and developing nations, as well as showing the *total fertility rate* in these countries. We have already learned that fertility is more than twice as high in the developing countries as it is in the developed ones. The table also shows that in both developed and developing nations, women enjoy longer life expectancy than men but are less likely to be literate or economically active. However, the important point here is that the deficit of women relative to men is greater in the developing countries than in the developed ones, and even in the case of life expectancy, women enjoy only a three-year advantage over men in the developing countries, as opposed to one of seven years in the developed ones. In other words, fertility appears higher in those nations where the status of women relative to men is lower.

TABLE 4.1   Fertility and indicators of the status of women in more and less developed countries

	More Developed	Less Developed
Total Fertility Rate	2.0	4.3
Life Expectancy at Birth		
Females	75	60
Males	68	57
Ratio	1.10	1.05
Percent Adults Literate		
Females	97	36
Males	99	57
Ratio	.98	.63
Percent Aged 15–64 Economically Active		
Females	55	42
Males	84	86
Ratio	.65	.49

Source: "Fertility and the Status of Women" (Washington, D.C.: Population Reference Bureau, May 1981).

Another way of examining this relationship is to examine women's labor-force activity and their fertility. Some investigators have compared various nations in such an analysis, while others have studied female employment and fertility in cities. All of these studies show that the percentage of women employed and the number of economic opportunities for women are inversely related to birthrates or number of children ever born.[56] Indicators of this relationship turn up in other research as well. For example, a study of Filipino migrants to the United States indicated that as they began to think of employment or work as a major avenue for achievement, their attitudes toward children grew less favorable.[57] Further, these families often reported that lack of available child care in order to pursue their labor-force goals inhibited their fertility.

Economic approaches to the explanation of fertility have also included consideration of *opportunity costs* of the wife (other activities she must give up in order to bear children) in making fertility projections. Here the reasoning is that the more attractive opportunities a wife must give up in order to have children, the less likely she is to have additional births.[58] Finally, current predictions of future fertility in the developed nations argue that fertility will continue to decline as long as there is expansion of the economy, and particularly of women's wages.[59]

In other words, the ubiquity of the relationship between women's status, opportunities, and fertility seems clear. This has prompted some to suggest that fertility-reduction programs should not seek general economic development but rather the creation of economic opportunities for women, since without these, women are the ones who may seek status by becoming pregnant.[60] Even in the absence of economic opportunities, men cannot bear children to gain prestige.

On a more cautious note, it has not been entirely clear whether it is fertility that influences such factors as labor-force participation or the reverse. It is possible to reason that having more children leads women to drop out of the work force and assume greater responsibilities at home. On the other hand, it may be that the experience of employment leads to fewer children being born, because women are interested in careers, economic rewards, or other benefits of working. Some research has suggested that, in fact, this works both ways, but that the influence of fertility on employment is strongest.

In any case, there have been a growing number of programs targeted at women. Advocates of these programs have pleaded for more research and understanding about the way women themselves see their situations and the role of children in their lives. While it may seem obvious to others that much is to be gained in terms of health and economic well-being from reduced fertility among women in developing countries, there is a great deal of evidence that women themselves may not see their pregnancies as life-threatening events or their alternatives as particularly attractive.[61]

The factors we have been discussing have been primarily associated with long-term trends in economic development. However, improvements in education, health, and the status of women are important influences on fertility in and of themselves.

Economic Cycles The relationship of short-term trends in the economy to fertility has also been investigated at the macro level. Historical analyses of the postwar baby boom, for example, have interpreted it as a response on the part of native white couples to the exceptionally favorable job-market conditions during that time.[62] Others have examined fertility and marriage rates in relation to business cycles over longer periods. While the impact of business cycles on fertility varies at different times and for different nations, most of this literature argues that birth and marriage rates show a direct response to rising and falling conditions in the economy. This response has been shown among most population subgroups in the United States, including foreign-born, Catholic, nonwhite, and farm residents.[63] The relation of birth and marriage rates to business-cycle fluctuations has also been shown for the United Kingdom and Japan.[64]

Whatever the strength of the business-cycle impact, birth and marriage rates do show ups and downs that parallel business trends. During recent periods of birthrate decline in the United States, this has been one of the hypotheses advanced to explain the failure of the birthrate to rise just when the age distribution of the population would predict the opposite. Even if the baby-boom babies are now into the childbearing ages, current economic conditions may encourage them to postpone or forego having children.

Each of the variables we have considered—natural environment and long- and short-term states of the economy—is a factor that is generally society-wide in its impact. We turn now to a consideration of factors that have their primary effect through special group membership.

Medial Variables

The factors discussed here operate selectively, affecting individuals differently depending on the special groups of which they are members or the special combinations of group memberships that they possess. They are most easily grouped into institutional areas.

Marriage and the Family

In spite of new ideas about the institution of marriage and occasionally approved reproductive unions that are nonmarital, the primary unit in which births occur is the *family*. Indeed, the very definition of the family centers around the act of birth and the allocation of responsibility for children. In most societies, marriage is considered the usual, if not the legal, prerequisite for parenthood. Family units take many different forms. The pattern in the United States of a mother, father, and children living together is called a *nuclear family* and is actually a rather recent historical development. More common in history, and in many parts of the world today, is the *joint family*, in which one or more generations live together. Other forms of the family unit include clans, stem families, and other variations in the household unit, which might include uncles, in-laws, or multiple husbands and wives.

Some attempt has been made to determine the effect of each of these arrangements on fertility. This attempt has been somewhat thwarted, however, by lack of data from historical times and by the difficulty of separating out the effect of family composition. Certain forms of the family are more common with certain economic arrangements in societies, making it nearly impossible to separate the effect of, say, urbanization from that of nuclear-family living.

Nevertheless, in general it seems that joint families have higher fertility rates than nuclear ones.[65] This is apparently so because the nuclear-family system requires that the husband be able to support his family with land or housing of his own prior to marriage. Such economic independence is not necessary with a joint-family arrangement, since the young couple can live with the parents. This makes youthful marriages possible. Since marriages tend to occur later in societies with a nuclear-family system, it again becomes difficult to distinguish the effect of age at marriage from the effect of nuclear-family interaction. Besides promoting marriage at an earlier age, some authors have speculated, child care is easier within joint or other large families, and this may encourage parents to produce more children.

This discussion highlights two variables besides form of the family that are important: the percentage of women marrying and the age of first marriage. Data from the United States population may be used to examine these trends in relationship to fertility. Overall, Americans are a marrying people (see Table 4.2). In 1980, only 4.8 percent of women aged forty to forty-four were still single. This percentage has declined steadily since 1920. However, the proportion of single women in the younger ages has been increasing in this time period. This means that over this sixty-year period, more women are delaying marriage until

TABLE 4.2 Percent of women single, 15 to 44 years old, by age (United States)

| Age of Woman | YEAR | | | |
	1980	1960	1940	1920
15 to 19 years	—[a]	83.9	88.1	87.0
20 to 24 years	50.2	28.4	47.2	45.6
25 to 29 years	20.8	10.5	22.8	23.0
30 to 34 years	9.5	6.9	14.7	14.9
35 to 39 years	6.2	6.1	11.2	11.4
40 to 44 years	4.8	6.1	9.5	

Sources: Figures for 1920 to 1960 adapted from U.S. Bureau of the Census, "Fertility Indicators: 1970," *Current Population Reports,* Series P-23, no. 36, April 1971, Table 11. Figures for 1980 from U.S. Bureau of the Census, "Population Profile of the United States: 1980," *Current Population Reports,* Series P-20, no. 363, June 1981, Table 11.

[a]*Data for 1980 not reported in this age category. Among 19-year-olds, the percent single is 77.5.*

older ages, but eventually a greater percentage of women marry now than was the case in earlier years. In fact, median age at first marriage has exhibited variability. Between 1940 to 1944 and 1950 to 1954, years inclusive of the baby boom, median age at first marriage declined for Americans; then it began increasing slightly as the birthrate began decreasing.

Figure 4.8 shows data on this relationship for 70 countries of the world. Here it can be seen that in general, the more women who are married by ages 15 to 19, the higher is the total fertility rate in that society, or the average number of children born to a woman during her lifetime (see Technical Supplement No. 4). Women who marry early are exposed to the possibility of conception over a greater number of years. Of course, Figure 4.8 does not take into account the many other variables that affect fertility, but this relationship has prompted some to suggest that one of the most important ways to influence fertility in many countries would be to require a later age at marriage.

Another way to look at the marriage patterns is by using the cohort perspective. With this approach, the age at marriage or the proportions of individuals with similar birth dates ever marrying can be examined. This kind of analysis led to the conclusion in the 1970s that "a fundamental modification of life styles and values relating to marriage has been taking place" in the United States.[66] This conclusion is supported by findings that lifelong singleness was becoming more prevalent and that the proportion of women who end their first marriage in divorce had been rising for each successive birth group. For example, between

FIGURE 4.8 **Total fertility rate and percentage of women in union at ages 15–19 (70 countries of the world)**

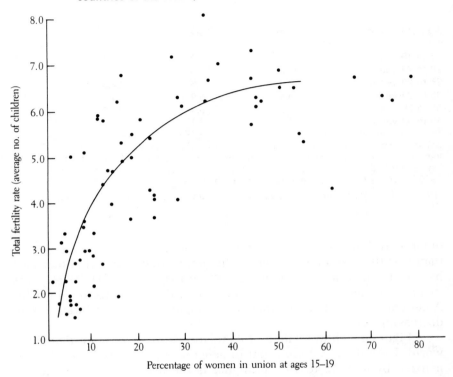

Percentage of women in union at ages 15–19

Source: "Fertility and the Status of Women" (Washington, D.C.: Population Reference Bureau, May 1981).

1970 and 1980, the number of divorced persons per 1,000 married persons aged thirty to forty-four increased from 47 to 125, a 266 percent increase.[67] Further, the number of children living with two parents dropped during this same decade from 85 to 77 percent.[68]

These trends have led to much investigation into the potential impact of divorce and remarriage on fertility. While it is possible that more divorce would lead to lower fertility because of less overall time spent in a marital union, remarriage might also lead to even higher fertility because couples in second marriages might start their child-bearing over again.

Recent data from the United States on these hypotheses indicate, first of all, that women who eventually separate have lower fertility in the two years prior to their separation than women who stay married.[69]

However, remarriage is followed by increased childbearing, so that for whites, total fertility is higher for the divorced and remarried than for those in stable marriages. Among blacks, however, the deficit in fertility created by divorce is never made up.

The impact of divorce and remarriage on fertility has also been studied in cities of Latin America where there is apparently a socioeconomic differential, rather than a racial one.[70] For women of higher socioeconomic status, reproductive time lost because of divorce seems to have a depressant effect on fertility. On the other hand, for women of low socioeconomic level, the effect of remarriage in raising fertility is more important, and fertility is higher among those married more than once than among those married once only.

Socioeconomic Status

Sociologists interested in the prediction of human behavior of many kinds have found that one of the most useful factors in such prediction is a person's socioeconomic status. *Socioeconomic status* (SES) refers to factors that contribute to the social and economic position of a person in a community, and may include education, occupation, income, style of life, place of residence, and many other variables. While SES has been measured in a variety of ways, it is repeatedly a good indicator of values, norms, attitudes, and behavior of individuals.

It is no surprise, then, that socioeconomic status is also related to fertility. Table 4.3 shows, by race or ethnicity, the average number of children born as of 1979 to women in the United States aged thirty-five to forty-four. The table employs three traditional measures of SES—educational attainment, family income, and occupation of husband. First, it can be seen that blacks and those of Spanish origin have more children than whites.

Second, the figures showing fertility by education and income indicate an inverse relationship between SES and fertility. In general, those with low education or income had more children than those with higher education and income. The same general inverse relationship holds when occupation is used as a measure of SES, but it is more difficult to rank occupations than income and education in order of status. Generally speaking, however, it can be seen that professionals, managers, and clerical workers have fewer children than farmers, laborers, service workers, or operatives.

There have been a variety of explanations for this inverse relationship between fertility and socioeconomic status in developed countries. These explanations are not unlike those used to account for the relationship between a society's level of socioeconomic development and fertility. One explanation has been that women in lower-income

TABLE 4.3   Average number of children ever born to wives aged 35 to 44 in married-couple families by socioeconomic status and race/ethnicity

Characteristic	Average Number of Children
Race/Ethnicity	
Whites	2.8
Blacks	3.5
Spanish Origin	3.3
Socioeconomic Status Measure	
Years of School Completed	
Elementary: 0–7 years	4.0
8 years	3.5
High School: 1–3 years	3.3
4 years	2.8
College: 1–3 years	2.6
4 years	2.3
5 years or more	2.0
Family Income	
Under $5,000	3.6
$ 5,000–$ 7,499	3.7
$ 7,500–$ 9,999	3.4
$10,000–$14,999	3.0
$15,000 & over	2.7
Occupation of Husband	
Professional, technical and kindred workers	2.5
Managers and administrators, except farm	2.6
Sales workers	2.6
Clerical and kindred workers	2.7
Craft and kindred workers	3.0
Operatives, including transport	3.1
Service workers, including private household	3.0
Laborers, except farm	3.3
Farm workers	3.4

Source: U.S. Bureau of the Census, "Fertility of American Women: 1979," *Current Population Reports,* Series P-20, no. 358, Tables 8 and 12.

groups, lacking education, simply do not know how to control their fertility should they desire to do so. This hypothesis may have some validity, since women with less education are more likely to report that they have unwanted births.[71] However, there have also been substantial increases in the percentages in all classes using contraception, and this increase has been particularly dramatic for black women.[72]

Another hypothesis to explain socioeconomic differences in fertility is that some women, rather than not knowing how to control their births, lack the motivation to do so. This hypothesis suggests that lower-class women greet new children with the same fatalistic attitude with which they view most of life. What chance would they have for better status, even if they controlled fertility? Sexual relationships, a pleasurable activity in what otherwise might be a difficult existence, are thus not likely to be interrupted or postponed in order to prevent future children. This hypothesis too would be consistent with lowered fertility in the future as it becomes increasingly possible to separate sexual activity from childbearing.

There are exceptions to this inverse relationship between SES and fertility. A direct relationship between SES and fertility has been noted in rural Bangladesh. Here the women with the least education, and those with the least land, are the ones with the lowest fertility rates.[73] Explanations for this finding have included the suggestion that couples with higher socioeconomic status have better health, lower fetal mortality, are less likely to breast-feed their children, and are more likely to have egalitarian role relations, leading to a greater frequency of sexual intercourse. In other words, higher SES in these villages seems to have its impact through the "intermediate variables" we discussed earlier. In any case, this finding of a direct relationship between SES and fertility in developing nations is important because it suggests that some improvement in socioeconomic status in such settings could mean at least a temporary rise in fertility.

Religion

Important as socioeconomic status is, the institutional area in society that defines morality, imparts values, and helps people cope with the unknown—namely, religion—is also important. Many studies in the United States have documented religious differentials in fertility. Historical data showed that Roman Catholics generally had higher fertility than either Protestants or Jews by the time they had completed their childbearing, and that Jews were conspicuously low in their fertility.[74]

In the past these differences were the result of many factors. It is widely known that the Roman Catholic church has looked with disfavor on the use of birth-control techniques. Studies have also shown, however, that the Catholic church encourages families to have large numbers of children in more positive ways than prohibiting the use of birth control. Large families have been seen as blessings from God, as the right and proper function of marriage, and as a means of increasing the membership of the church.

In spite of widespread changes in fertility among Catholics, this position is still espoused by church leaders. As Pope John Paul II asserted at the Mass on the Mall, in Washington, D.C., in October of 1980:

> *. . . all human life—from the moment of conception and through all subsequent stages is sacred. . . parents will remind themselves that it is certainly less serious to deny their children certain comforts or material advantages than to deprive them of the presence of brothers and sisters, who could help them to grow in humanity.*[75]

This encouragement of large families has by no means been confined to the Catholic faith. Certain Protestant denominations, while not prohibiting the use of birth-control techniques, are quite literal in their interpretation of the Biblical dictum, "Be fruitful and multiply." Fundamentalist sects, small in number and predominantly rural in location, may also be of this persuasion. The Church of Jesus Christ of Latter-Day Saints, or Mormon Church, is another example of a religious institution that encourages large families through the glorification of children.

However vehement and continuous these church teachings may be, there is substantial evidence, among Catholics at least, that church members may have other pressures on them to reduce fertility. Figure 4.9 documents what Westoff and Jones have called "the end of Catholic fertility."[76] It depicts the gradual convergence of Catholic and non-Catholic fertility in the United States between 1951 and 1975. This convergence has been expected, owing to increasing proportions of Catholic women deviating from church teachings on the use of birth control and abortion. The proportion of Catholic women between the ages of eighteen and thirty-nine who in 1955 were using methods of birth control other than rhythm was 30 percent. This figure had risen to 68 percent by 1970, and had increased by 17 percentage points between 1965 and 1970 alone. Among women aged twenty to twenty-four, those not conforming to church teaching had risen from 30 percent in 1955 to 78 percent by 1970.[77]

By 1979, Westoff and Jones suggested that in spite of what appeared to be consistent statements on the subject, some ambiguity surrounding the oral contraceptive in the 1960s had, in fact, facilitated the decline of Catholic fertility:

> *For several years, there was an atmosphere of belief that the Vatican would change its traditional stance . . . By the time that the Papal Encyclical of 1968 reaffirmed the traditional teaching . . . about a third of its members were using the pill. . . . the door had been opened for many Catholics and there was no turning back.*[78]

FIGURE 4.9 **Total marital fertility rates for Catholics and non-Catholics from survey data, 1951–75**

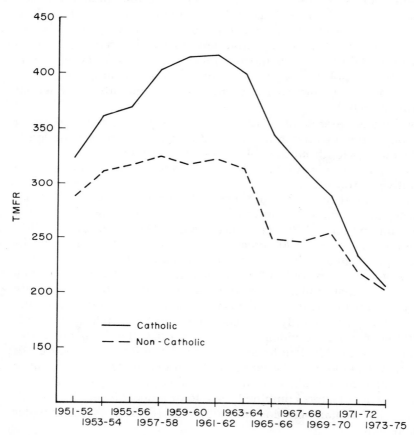

Source: Charles F. Westoff and Elise F. Jones, "The End of 'Catholic' Fertility," *Demography* 16 (1979), Fig. 2, p. 214.

In contrast with Catholics, the fertility of Jews has traditionally been lower than that of other groups. While it has been consistently lower than the fertility of other whites for many years, it has nevertheless been responsive to the same forces creating rises and falls in fertility during this period.[79] To explain low Jewish fertility, many authors have pointed to the high value placed on education by Jews, which tends to raise their age at marriage and lower fertility. More speculative suggestions that might explain low Jewish fertility include the hypothesis that as a minority group in America and one with a history of persecution, Jews might wish to limit their fertility in order to better the economic status of themselves and their children, thus protecting themselves against oppression. This is an interesting suggestion, since a minority group that perceived its position as precarious might also try to outnumber the majority by producing many children. Another attempt to explain the lower fertility rates of Jews suggests that these lower rates do not represent a religious differential at all, but are a reflection of the higher socioeconomic status and urban residential patterns of Jews.

Religious differentials between these groups in the United States are certainly not the only indication that religion has an effect on fertility. Several in-depth studies of religious subgroups and population processes have been conducted. We will cite only two of them here for illustrative purposes.

Moslem fertility has been noted to be generally high, very stable over time, and in many settings higher than the fertility of other groups in the same nations.[80] In fact, a recent study has noted that a nation whose population was 100 percent Islamic would have a crude birthrate four points higher than a comparable nation that was not Islamic.[81] In an exhaustive study of Moslem natality, Dudley Kirk has noted some of the factors that explain these findings. Not all of these factors are strictly religious in nature. Moslem countries are very often developing nations, with joint-family systems, high mortality rates, and agricultural economies in which sons are of great value. Religious influences include the Moslem belief that sexual relations are a God-given pleasure to be enjoyed, a belief in male dominance, encouragement of early remarriage for the widowed and divorced, and an early age at first marriage. These factors combined seem to produce the very high fertility rates observed among Moslem groups regardless of their particular national setting.

On the other hand, Moslems do not always have higher fertility than other religious groups, owing particularly to some religion-based customs. For example, among the Yoruba in Western Nigeria, Moslems have lower fertility than Christians.[82] This was true even though the Christians tended to have more education and higher socioeconomic status than the Moslems. One of the most important explanations for lower Moslem fertility seemed to be longer periods of postnatal abstinence from intercourse. Among Moslem women aged fifteen to twenty-seven, postnatal abstinence extended for an average period of twenty-three months.

A religious group that may have achieved something close to the biological limit of fertility is the Hutterites.[83] The average Hutterite woman has twelve children, which, when combined with low mortality and virtually no migration, creates a population increase of 4.1 percent per year. Such high fertility apparently comes about not because of any single factor, but because of the unique combination of many factors that are conducive to high fertility. Living in predominantly rural settings, the Hutterites avail themselves of good medical care. They believe that children have a very positive value and that use of birth control is sinful. Their communal economy and high level of productivity allow each new addition to the population to be assured of support, and marriage is nearly universal. There is little separation of husband and wife, making for maximum exposure to conception. There are a few negative factors operating in Hutterite society to depress fertility. These include prohibition of premarital sex, a later age at marriage than in some cultures, and occasional surgical interference with reproduction to protect a woman's health.

Another interesting religious group whose fertility has recently been studied is the Old Order Amish, located primarily in Pennsylvania.[84] Unlike the Hutterites, the Amish forbid the use of most modern technology, including telephones, automobiles, and electricity. They also forbid higher education. The average number of children born to Amish women is 6.8. This is lower than the Hutterite average, but is still considerably above the comparable average for other women.

Interestingly, analysis of the Amish birthrate over the twentieth century shows no decline, but does show some evidence of birth regulation among the older women. It is speculated that this regulation takes place through the use of sterilization and abstinence. Another factor lessening the number of births in this group is attrition. Amish families are apparently encountering increasing difficulty in obtaining farmland, and thus many are leaving the order.

The length of these lists of cultural practices influencing fertility makes it unclear whether the Hutterite or Amish fertility patterns should be interpreted more broadly as resulting from cultural, rather than only religious, practices. The cultural patterns shown here are certainly important, quite apart from their religious context.

Government

It has long been apparent to governments, as to religious groups, that the number of people in a nation heavily influences the options available. Depending on national goals, governments may find it advantageous to raise the birthrate or lower it, hoping for corresponding increases or reductions in the population.

Two authors have recently summarized the policies available to governments should they wish to intervene in fertility behavior, in either an antinatalist or pronatalist direction.[85] They may:

1. Manipulate access to methods of fertility control, making them either more plentiful or virtually inaccessible.
2. Try to change the socioeconomic determinants of fertility, such as education, industrialization, or the status of women.
3. Use propaganda in the desired direction and suppress opposing views.
4. Use incentives and disincentives such as maternity leaves, tax benefits, or fines.
5. Exert pressure or impose direct sanctions such as laws on age at marriage or allowable family size.

These strategies may also be used in combination, of course, to produce an even stronger effort.

Attempts to Raise the Birthrate. Pronatalist efforts may be motivated by several concerns. First, there may be imperialistic ambitions involved. If the nation is interested in conquering the world, or even a substantial portion of it, it becomes necessary to maintain a large occupation force, which can be spread out over acquired territory without crippling the forces left at home. When war was waged through hand-to-hand combat, it was especially important to be able to overwhelm the other side with superior numbers.

Besides imperialist ambitions, nations sometimes believe they need larger populations to facilitate economic development. Colonizing a new nation and trying to control and develop a large segment of land can be an impetus to greater births. Finally, national pride may equate the size of a nation with success and lead governments to encourage more births.

One of the most famous attempts to raise the birthrate was the campaign undertaken by Hitler in Germany in the early 1930s.[86] The main elements of Hitler's program included bonuses for having babies, suppression of contraception and abortion, and an intensive propaganda campaign emphasizing the building of a master race. Women were encouraged to leave the labor force, and couples who married were given loans for furniture, housing, and other commodities; part of these loans could be repaid by having many children. In addition, those with many children were given preferences in housing, travel accommodations, and the like.

Scholars are not in agreement on the success of these measures, although most cite German policies as more influential than many others.[87] The number of marriages and births in Germany did increase dramatically immediately after the policies went into effect. However, most of the increase in births came from first births. Although there was no appreciable long-term effect on the size of completed families, the collapse of the Nazi government abbreviated the time during which these policies were in effect.

France provides another historic example of a government that deliberately tried to raise the birthrate. The concern in France was prompted not by military ambitions, but by a real fear that the country would actually become depopulated.[88] The birthrate in France had fallen below replacement levels in the early part of this century, and government officials increased family allowances and payments to families based on the number of children they had. An attempt was made to keep the standard of living of couples with several children comparable to that enjoyed by those with none. While the family-allowance system may have achieved this goal, we have little evidence that it had a major impact on the birthrate in France.

More far-reaching population policies in France were enacted in 1939; the legislation was ahead of that of most other nations at the time.[89] The national family code included not only family allowances, loans for the establishment of households, and birth premiums, but also maternal and child-protection provisions, demographic and medical education, and the establishment of maternity homes. Even the promotion of induced abortion was prohibited, whether or not an abortion actually followed. Only in 1967 were laws repealed that prohibited the dissemination of birth-control information by mail or the sale of contraceptives. In addition, abortion is now available in France.

Some authors have contended that the birthrate in France fell at a slower rate than it might have in the absence of these measures. Nevertheless, the birthrate has continued to fall throughout the century. The only interruption in this decline was a brief post-World War II resurgence of births, common in many Western countries.

Sweden also provides a historic example of a pronatalist program.[90] In an attempt to bring the birthrate up to replacement levels during the late 1930s and early 1940s, the Swedish government enlisted the aid of a special Commission on Population, composed of experts in many fields. The commission took the view that every child in Sweden should be wanted and that the burden of replacement should be spread equally over all social classes in the country. Consequently, along with family subsidies, health centers for mothers and children, housing allowances, and free school books and lunches, the government also undertook an extensive birth-control-education program. Nevertheless, the Swedish birthrate has remained low, although high enough to ensure replacement.

A more recent attempt to raise the birthrate, in Romania, has had dramatic consequences.[91] Concerned about falling birthrates and possible labor-force shortages, the government of Romania issued a decree in 1966 banning almost all abortions and stopping importation of birth-control pills and intrauterine devices (IUDs). Romanian women had depended almost exclusively on abortion as a means of birth control, and many found themselves forced to carry to term pregnancies they had intended to have aborted. The result was that within eight months the birthrate doubled, and within eleven months it had tripled. The dramatic impact of this policy over the next 10 years can be seen in Figure 4.10. The birthrate in Romania has remained substantially above that in comparable Eastern European nations throughout the decade.

The impact of this pronatalist policy on the total population number in Romania has also been dramatic. In 1966 the population was 19.141 million, but by 1976 it had grown to 21.446 million—an increase of 12 percent.[92] It has been estimated that the excess births created by the repeal of abortion accounts for about half of this total increase. Overall, in terms of its own program goals, then, the Romanian policy is a major success. In fact, the pronatalist population policies in several countries of Eastern Europe have been generally successful, at least in the short run. While these policies may not increase

FIGURE 4.10   Trends in crude birthrate, 1957–76: Romania and average of five other Eastern European countries

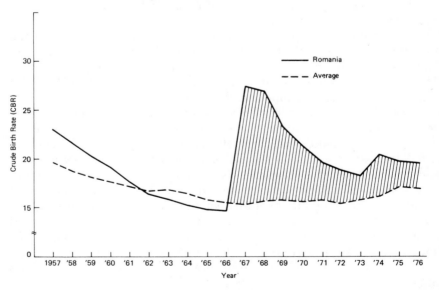

Source: B. Berelson, "Romania's 1966 Anti-Abortion Decree: The Demographic Experience of the First Decade," *Population Studies,* 33 (1979), Figure 1, p. 212.

the number of third births, they may be responsible for advancing the timing of the first and second ones.

The strategy of each of the pronatalist programs described has been different. Incentives, support services, penalties, and outright denial of services are used. Clearly the outstanding effect was achieved by the Romanian effort, a success made possible by both the far-reaching power of government and the excessive dependence of couples on one method of birth prevention. Likewise, the scope of these programs has varied from general family support and betterment to short-term raising of births in order to support the labor force, war, or other efforts. Some of the programs have sought replacement fertility, others very high fertility. In every case the strategy chosen has reflected the form of government, the birth-control and family histories, and the goals of the nations involved in these efforts.

Attempts to Lower the Birthrate. The reader is no doubt familiar with some of the more popular reasons why nations might undertake antinatalist campaigns. In many nations of the world today there is concern over lack of resources. Food, water, and fuel are in short supply in some countries and depleted in others. Governments have felt that reducing the birthrate might be the most direct way to slow down the consumption of such resources.

Some areas of the world are concerned about living space. Overcrowding has become a problem. There are large metropolitan areas in the United States suffering from high density. Some writers have gone so far as to propose that these density levels contribute to crime, juvenile delinquency, slums, and other problems. While it is not clear how much density itself contributes to these problems, governments have felt that some reductions would be desirable and have embarked on campaigns to reduce the birthrate. In the developing nations of the world, these problems have been particularly acute. As noted before, economic growth may be stifled by the press of population. A reduced birthrate should enable developing countries to use their resources for development as well as survival.

In still other countries, planners have been concerned over birthrate differentials among subgroups in the population. In the United States, for example, some have seen reduction of the birthrate as one way to reduce welfare rolls. In other nations, groups in power have feared being overrun from inside their own country by minority or immigrant groups that have higher birthrates than the indigenous population. Critics of programs to reduce birthrates in certain groups have charged that *genocide,* or the attempt to eliminate whole races of people, is the motivation behind such programs.

Each of these reasons for wanting to reduce the birthrate involves the belief that a growing population is not a benefit to society, either because of lack of space or resources or because a large population is felt to be aesthetically undesirable. Various programs for reducing the birthrate have been suggested.

The most popular movement, underway in many countries of the world now, is family planning. While developed countries often have family-planning programs or at least family-planning services available through private or public-health settings, the emphasis in recent years has, of course, been on programs for developing countries, where birthrates are high and most problematic. Table 4.4 indicates how many developing countries currently have official governmental policies favoring reduction in growth rates or support family-planning programs for other reasons, such as health of the population. About half of these nations currently have such policies, but this includes 91 percent of the population of the developing world.

In any of these countries, family-planning programs usually involve several features. An educational program may be launched to provide information as to what kinds of family-planning techniques are available and how they might be used. Propaganda campaigns may be instituted to encourage small families and create an atmosphere favorable to the adoption of family planning. Then some dissemination system is worked out so that the people may have access to the techniques they wish to use. In any case, family-planning programs, while orga-

TABLE 4.4   Government positions on population growth and family planning in developing countries, 1979

	All Developing Countries	North Africa	Balance of Africa	West Asia	East Asia and Oceania	South Asia	Latin America
Total	132	6	46	16	25	6	33
Policy to reduce population growth	35	3	5	2	11	5	9
Support for family planning for other reasons	31	2	15	2	1	0	11
Government position unknown	1	0	0	0	1	0	0
No policy	65	1	26	12	12	1	13

Source: Dorothy L. Nortman and Ellen Hofstatter. *Population and Family Planning Programs: A Compendium of Data through 1978* (New York: The Population Council, 1980).

nized and usually far-reaching, are generally seen as voluntary. Families wishing to reject the notion of family planning are free to do so.

In spite of some common denominators, family-planning programs vary a great deal from country to country. In developing nations, where such programs are most common, a recent summary has noted that they may differ on at least the following dimensions:

1. They may include all or only some of the major means of fertility control. Some programs, for example, may only attempt to distribute birth-control pills, while others offer a full range of contraceptive techniques.

2. They may give more or less attention to creating demand for these services. In many countries such efforts have seemed unnecessary, owing to great unmet need for services. In others, however, the population has expressed little interest in, and even resistance to, family planning.

3. Programs may use one method of service delivery or may incorporate many different efforts, such as marketing schemes or private and commercial channels.

4. Programs may or may not provide incentives or disincentives for potential users of contraception, such as money, free goods of various kinds, or fines for pregnancy or nonuse of contraception.

5. These programs may be integrated with other health, economic, or social programs, or may be uni-purpose in nature.

6. They may utilize a variety of different frameworks for actual service delivery, including clinics, mobile vans, household distribution, special camps, fairs, and drives.

7. Programs may be intended to cover the whole of a country or some smaller section, as funds or research interest dictate.[93]

In criticizing family-planning programs because of their voluntary approach, some have argued that couples are not able to plan a nation's population growth, but only the size of their individual families.[94] Insofar as people wish to have more children than replacement levels would dictate, population will continue to grow in spite of the fact that couples are having only the number of children they want.

It thus becomes important to ask how successful family-planning programs have been in developing countries. A careful answer to this question requires the separation of the impact of family-planning programs per se from other changes, such as improvements in health, education, economic status, or urbanization. In an examination of rates of fertility decline between 1965 and 1975 in ninety-four developing countries of the world, a recent report suggests that combining improvements in socioeconomic development with a strong family-planning program is most effective in producing fertility decline.[95] However, family-planning programs seem to make an independent contribution to fertility decline, even in the absence of socioeconomic development. For example, in countries with both a favorable social setting and a strong program effort, there was a decline in the crude birthrate during these ten years of 30 percent. In countries with only a strong program effort, the decline was about 20 percent, whereas in those countries with only a favorable social setting but no program, the decline was only 5 percent. Some authors have disputed whether the impact of family planning programs is this substantial,[96] but there appears to be no argument that these programs make some impact.

Program Examples: Developing Countries   A few examples of the kinds of programs that are currently operating in developing countries will perhaps make clear both the complexity and extent of variation in approaches to family planning. In Indonesia, for example, where the current crude birthrate is about 35 per 1,000 population, the program goal is to lower fertility by 50 percent by 1990.[97] In order to achieve this goal, emphasis has been placed on village-based programs in the rural areas. Village contraceptive supply posts have been created and are largely managed by contraceptive users and women's clubs.

The most popular method of contraception among Indonesian women is the pill. In some areas of the country, where the Islamic religion is strong, special efforts have been made to promote the pill to regulate the menstrual cycle. This strategy is employed in the fasting month of Ramadan, during which women are supposed to remain "pure" while fasting. The success of the pill in preventing menstruation during this month has apparently encouraged acceptance at other times. Certainly this strategy illustrates how essential it is to carefully tailor programs to local area customs and needs.

The Indonesian program, like many others, is paid for both by governmental funds and by international donor agencies. The United States Agency for International Development (AID), the World Bank, and the United Nations Fund for Population Activities contributed over a third of the funding for the Indonesian program in 1979 to 1980.

In evaluating the success of the program, two figures seem particularly important. The first is the percentage of married women using contraception. That figure was 19 percent in 1976 to 1977 but had risen to above 32 percent by 1982. The other important result has been a drop in the total fertility rate, from about 5.5 in the 1960s to below 4.0 by the late 1970s.

A less optimistic report on the success of family planning has come from Egypt.[98] After about ten years of program experience, acceptance rates were still low and discontinuation rates high, even for those women who gave contraception a try. The characteristics of the program blamed for this difficulty include the fact that it is a clinic-only, pill-only, physician-dominated program, with few personnel and little follow-up or outreach activity. In developing countries where physicians are in short supply, reliance of such programs on medical doctors rather than on midwives or other personnel can create serious difficulties and restrictions.

A different approach to family planning and control of fertility has now emerged in China, and apparently it has had dramatic results.[99] From a level of about 36 per 1,000 in the 1950s, the current level of the birthrate in China is estimated at about 14 in urban areas and 19 in rural areas.[100] While demographers have been extremely interested in watching fertility-control programs in China, the data have not been easily obtained. Although there are now several major works available on demographic processes in China, the data used are largely constructed from popular publications, statements by officials of the Chinese government, personal visits, and United States government estimates.[101] Nevertheless, what we know about fertility policies in China is quite interesting.

Since the Chinese Communist assumption of power in 1949, China has had a stop-and-go policy on fertility. At first, it was thought inconsistent with Marxist ideology to proclaim population a problem. Rather, if shortages of goods and services occurred, these were interpreted as reflecting an unequal distribution, not an inadequate absolute supply. Under the Marxist government, redistribution of wealth, goods, food, and other commodities would eliminate the problems that were thought to be connected to population growth.

Not until 1954 was there some evidence of concern about population growth on the part of the Chinese government. By 1956 there had been an increase in the number of popular articles in China that discussed the pros and cons of birth control, and the Ministry of Public Health was assigned the responsibility for implementing a campaign for its use.

Surprisingly, in 1958 the government abruptly reversed its stand on the use of birth control and returned to its original statement that family limitation was an unacceptable notion. Scholars are in disagreement as to whether birth-control programs disappeared entirely during this period or were simply downplayed.[102] In any case, this was the period of the Great Leap Forward, and the need for additional labor to undertake vast projects, plus general optimism, may have contributed to the ebbing of population-growth fears.

By 1962 a full-scale effort to reduce births was once again begun.

Financial difficulties and food shortages of huge proportions contributed to the reversal. Since 1962, the programs of the Chinese government have been rather consistently antinatalist. The most important emphasis of the current campaign in China seems to be the attempt to undermine traditional values.[103] The Chinese seem to be discrediting early marriage, preference for sons, and large families, and seeking to convince the population that the number of children born is a matter for state concern rather than just being a private decision.

In order to facilitate fewer births, the Chinese program has made a wide range of contraceptives available and has promoted and encouraged abortion, especially among couples who already have two children. There are also reports of a great deal of group pressure from neighbors to limit fertility, as well as the use of monetary incentives and disincentives, in the form of wages, housing, or privileges given to children depending on their birth order. It is not entirely clear what measure of coercion is included in all of this.

Nevertheless, there is agreement among the China-watchers that probably no greater effort at family planning and birth reduction has been undertaken by any government. While there remains a need for caution in proclaiming the success of this effort, preliminary estimates indicate that China may just have accomplished the fastest reduction in the birthrate yet recorded.

A discussion of attempts to reduce the birthrate in developing countries would be incomplete without some mention of India's recent experience with "emergency" control. The first nation to adopt a family-planning program, India recognized in the 1950s that its crude birthrate of about 40 per 1,000 per year and a death rate of 16 per 1,000 was giving rise to extremely rapid growth in a nation already poor and ill-equipped to provide basic amenities for its people. Thus, attempts were made to distribute contraceptives, and a variety of approaches to incentives for, and the delivery of, sterilization were tried in the 1960s and 1970s. These efforts met with little, or only moderate, success, in part because of lack of government commitment, but also because of the myriad problems associated with delivery of family planning in a rural nation with many different languages and very little socioeconomic development.

In 1976 and 1977, however, India set off in a different direction. Under extreme economic and political difficulties, Prime Minister Indira Gandhi declared a national state of emergency. In addition, the Central Ministry of Health and Family Planning announced a variety of new development and family-planning measures. These included making financial assistance to states partly dependent on family-planning performance, according higher priority to female literacy, increasing the minimum age at marriage, increasing the monetary reward for sterilization, and permitting individual states to enact compulsory sterilization laws. Perhaps this last recommendation was the most disruptive.

This national-level proclamation was followed by a variety of initiatives in states meant to implement all these directives. These included the following in individual states:

Government employees undergoing sterilization would get a raise.

Maternity leave would be withdrawn after two births.

No one with more than three children would get a government job without undergoing sterilization.

Teachers must be sterilized or lose a month's salary.

Government workers were given quotas of those they must persuade to be sterilized.

Food rations would be denied to those with more than three children.

Government loans were granted only to those who had small families or who were sterilized.[104]

There were other rules as well, some vigorously enforced and others apparently on the books but virtually ignored. In any case, the overall effort created something akin to panic for many. Mrs. Gandhi was soundly defeated for reelection in 1977, and the family-planning program returned to more voluntary measures. In the meantime, however, it had had a dramatic impact. In September 1976 alone, 1.7 million sterilizations were performed in India, a number that usually represents a year's total.

Was it worth it? That question is, of course, an ethical one, on which opinion is likely to be divided. It requires weighing the relative loss incurred when individual civil liberties are denied versus the loss of quality of life when rapid population growth is one of the villains in creating intense poverty and deprivation.

In between coercive measures and strictly voluntary programs are those efforts that offer some incentives to couples for family planning. For example, during the decade of the 1970s, women living on tea-growing plantations in South India were offered monetary payments deposited into a savings account for every month that they remained nonpregnant.[105] The account could only be drawn upon at the time of retirement, and payment into the account would be stopped for twelve months in the event of pregnancy. If a woman became pregnant with a third or higher-order child, she forfeited an amount in her account equivalent to the cost of that child to the State. The scheme seemed to be related to at least moderate declines in fertility, particularly in the one community where all women were invited to enroll.

In short, the variety of forms a family-planning program may take seems limited only by the imagination of the program planning personnel. The future is likely to see an increasing number of creative approaches to the lowering of fertility in developing nations.

Program Examples: Developed Countries We have already learned that developed countries have low and apparently stable birthrates, some of them at or below replacement level. It is difficult to talk about how effective programs were in bringing this about, since organized ones of the kind described in developing countries have never existed in developed countries. Rather, family-planning services most often have been offered in doctors' offices, hospitals, or clinics, as part of the overall private or public health-care delivery system. Further, the correspondence between the availability of birth-control technology and reduced fertility in these nations is not exact. By the time the modern methods of contraception became available in these countries in the 1930s, some European nations already had total fertility rates averaging two children per woman.[106]

Still, it is worth noting that in the countries of Western Europe and North America, recent analysis suggests that these low fertility rates have been brought about and are maintained by some changes that developing countries are now seeking. First, the ideal number of children in these nations seems to have dropped considerably. Occasionally the number of children women say they want to have falls below replacement level. Secondly, it appears that having children no longer constitutes the major reason for marriage. In many of the developed nations, procreation and marriage are not inseparable. Finally, childbearing has also been separated from sexual activity, owing to the effectiveness of contraceptive methods now available in these nations.[107]

The history of family-planning efforts in the United States is somewhat different from that in other countries, for these programs have been located primarily in the private sector, with public funding a relatively recent development. As recently as twenty-five years ago, the United States had no organized family-planning program, and in fact had no overall population policy of any kind. International migration was the only component of population change that was regulated directly. In 1959 President Eisenhower emphasized the hands-off policy of his administration by saying:

> *I cannot imagine anything more emphatically a subject that is not a proper political or governmental activity or function or responsibility. This government has not, and will not as long as I am here, have a positive political doctrine in its program that has to do with this problem on birth control. That's not our business.*[108]

Within ten years, that position had changed. A Commission on Population Growth and the American Future was established, and Eisenhower had become honorary chairman of Planned Parenthood. In addition, a new agency had been created as part of the Department of Health, Education and Welfare, specifically to deal with family planning. Federal expenditures for family planning increased from $8.7 million in 1965 to $56.3 million in 1969.[109] By 1979, federal and state governments spent $285 million on family-planning services.[110]

In its final report, which was issued in 1972, the Commission on Population Growth and the American Future stated:

> *Our immediate goal is to modernize demographic behavior in this country: to encourage the American people to make population choices, both in the individual family and society at large on the basis of greater rationality rather than tradition or custom, ignorance or chance. . . . The time has come to challenge the tradition that population growth is desirable: What was unintended may turn out to be unwanted, in the society as in the family.*[111]

This statement was radical in one way and neutral in another. It was radical in that it represented a departure from governmental silence on fertility and population-growth issues. It was neutral in that the recommendation of the Commission stressed freedom of choice for individuals and the desirability of changes that are good in and of themselves, apart from their population relevance. The response to the Commission report of then-President Richard Nixon was to reiterate his opposition to abortion and the availability of contraceptives to teenagers. Catholic church leaders strongly denounced the report. Reports by the press were largely favorable.[112]

Since these suggestions, the major governmental actions on abortion are the two 1973 Supreme Court opinions.[113] These opinions held that because abortion was no longer a high-risk procedure during the first trimester of pregnancy, the state did not have the right to interfere in a patient-and-doctor decision to terminate a pregnancy. During the second trimester, the state had the right to regulate who performs the abortion and under what conditions. In the third trimester, the Court held, every effort should be made to save the life of the fetus, since it is potentially viable in the seventh month. States may therefore prohibit abortion except to preserve the life of the mother during this trimester. These divisions were made by considering the interests of the state in the life of both the mother and the fetus. The almost unrestricted availability of abortion in at least the first three months of pregnancy is thus a relatively new development in the United States, although abortion has played a major role in the efforts of many other countries to control fertility.

Still, the Supreme Court action has not been without controversy. Since that ruling, some form of human-life amendment has been debated in Congress on several occasions. Basically such an amendment proposes personhood status for unborn fetuses, entitling them to equal protection under the law, including due process.

These proposed amendments have stirred up much controversy.[114] Some have argued that women who are pregnant might be considered criminally negligent in the case of certain miscarriages where the mother's activities may have exposed the fetus to danger. Babies conceived in the United States but born elsewhere might be considered citizens of the United States. Debates on the impact of the Supreme Court decision and this amendment have kept the abortion issue prominent.

Recent attempts to evaluate the effectiveness of the family-planning effort in the United States have centered on cost-effectiveness issues. One analysis, for example, suggests that in 1979 family planning programs prevented about 695,000 pregnancies, 370,000 of which would likely have terminated in abortion. This analysis also argued that savings from childbirth, postnatal and pediatric care, abortions, and welfare payments thus totaled about $570 million, or two dollars for every dollar spent in providing family planning services in organized programs.[115]

Whether or not such an estimate is correct, it emphasizes a shift in the criteria used to evaluate family-planning programs, away from contraceptive acceptance and reduced fertility. This is to be expected when fertility rates have already reached low levels.

Micro Variables

We have discussed macro- and medial-level influences on fertility. In the end, however, the birthrate in a society depends on actions of individuals. It is the individual who mediates and synthesizes these influences and ultimately controls fertility. It is difficult for any individual in a society to escape the societal-level variables discussed earlier. The effects of the natural environment and the economic development of the society are presumably about the same on everyone. Each individual has different group memberships, however. The normative influences that result from these memberships thus vary. In addition, each person has a peculiar combination of group memberships, interacting with the societal-level variables.

These two kinds of influences acting on individuals do not exhaust the kinds of factors that could affect fertility. First, there are biological considerations; for example, fecundity may be impaired. It is difficult to say how much influence biology has on the other factors we have already mentioned. There are also psychological variables to consider. The quality of the relationship with their parents or how well adjusted or stable individuals are could affect how many children they want to have.

Psychologists have recently shown increased interest in researching these problems and have employed the concepts attitude, value, motivation, and perception to describe factors relevant to fertility behavior. In measuring fertility preferences and attitudes, researchers have found it necessary to separate fertility desires from fertility expectations or intentions, since these may not be identical. In addition, it has been found that even among a group of women who all state the same initial fertility preference, there may be important underlying differences in their commitment to this preference or how they view it against other choices. For example, while two women may both state an initial preference for three children, when asked for their next choice, one may state that she would choose to have two, while the other would prefer four as a second choice. These underlying differences have been shown to be important for fertility prediction.[116]

There are other attitudes or individual preferences that may be important to fertility as well. For example, preference for sex of child has been much studied. The reasoning here is that if couples have strong preferences for, say, boys, they may continue to bear children until they reach their requisite number of boys, even if their total fertility exceeds their original goal. Such preferences are stronger in developing societies than in developed ones, but even in industrialized nations there is evidence of the impact of such attitudes on completed fertility.[117]

There are also sex-role attitudes that have an impact on fertility and bridge medial and micro influences. Traditionally women have been responsible for homemaking tasks and child raising. One of their primary duties has been the bearing of children. Some have argued that the extent to which a woman sees herself as feminine and suited for this role will influence her fertility.[118] An empirical test of this thesis with regard to American women lends support to this hypothesis.[119] This study found that women with more "masculine" self-concepts tended to have smaller completed families. Particularly important here was the extent to which women perceived themselves as competent, with those seeing themselves as more competent having smaller families.

Culturally defined sex roles of men may also have an impact on fertility levels in a society. In various contexts it has been noted that "manhood" may be defined by the number of children a man produces, or, more particularly, by the number of male children. Defining manhood in this way may encourage men to shun any method of birth control or to have more children should they have several girls.

All of these are ways in which the individual is important in the process of fertility. It is important to remember that each child who comes into the world is the result of a decision—or the lack of one—about fertility. Such decisions are made by individuals but have an impact on all society.

FUTURE FERTILITY

It should by now be obvious to the reader that the prediction of fertility is no easy task. Even if one were to gather information on all the factors we have mentioned for a given society, how should they be weighted? And what about changes in these factors over time? What elements have we left out?

Even if we know the present level of economic development in a society, there may be many different religious groups represented, changing government policy, changing business cycles, and so on. Which of these is most important? Could we expect the relative influence of these factors to be the same for each country?

All of these are questions that are dealt with in research and in theory by demographers and others who have been asked to supply such predictions. The demand for reliable fertility forecasting is growing. Fortunately the available research on which to base such predictions is also growing. The accuracy of past projections has not been particularly encouraging, however. While many countries were anticipating and taking measures to correct depopulation problems, the post-World War II baby boom occurred, surprising almost everyone. Birthrates rose drastically, and demographers began studying the phenomenon in retrospect.

Certainly our projections of fertility have improved in the last twenty years. The very demand for such projections has increased the interest in and effort devoted to their production. Most commonly, fertility projections are made on the basis of several assumptions. We might assume that fertility will continue at its present rate. We might assume that it will lessen or increase by a specified amount. We might use current survey data on fertility expectations. The accuracy of our projections then hangs on the accuracy of those assumptions or the reasonableness of expectations data. Changes that are not anticipated could invalidate the effort.

One of the most interesting variables used for future projections is *expected family size.* In the United States, interest has recently been sparked by reports of expected fertility that are lower than those of previous years, especially for younger cohorts. Figure 4.11 shows some of these data. For both white and black women aged twenty-five to twenty-nine, the average number of expected births has dropped since 1967. For whites, this drop was from 3.0 children to fewer than 2.2. For blacks the drop has been from 3.4 to something over 2.5, with a slight increase in lifetime expectations among those who were twenty-five to twenty-nine years of age in 1978. Still, these findings mean that the baby bust has been accompanied by a decrease in expectations as well, and may not merely be postponement of births that will be made up later.[120]

If women perform according to these expectations, fertility in the United States may fall even lower than current levels. However, at least

FIGURE 4.11   Average lifetime births expected by white and black currently married women aged 25 to 29 years, 1967 to 1979

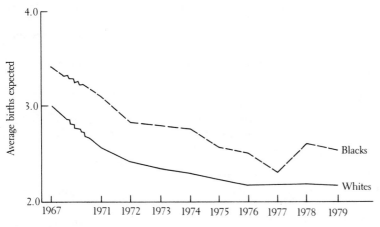

Source: U.S. Bureau of the Census, "Fertility of American Women: June 1979," *Current Population Reports,* Series P-20, no. 358, Table 1.

one author has suggested caution in that interpretation. Judith Blake has argued that since there is no indication of a greater acceptance of one-child or childless families, changes from expectations are likely to be in the upward direction, leading to higher fertility than these expectations would suggest.[121]

The reader should be aware that even accurate prediction of future fertility, were we capable of that, would not ensure its control. Deciding what will change fertility involves another set of assumptions and investigations into what kinds of policies will work. Much work is currently being done, on both an actual and a computer-simulated basis, to try out measures designed to control fertility. Governments and family planners have to surmise what would be the relative effects on the birthrate of raising the age at marriage or legalizing abortion. Their conclusions are based on all the factors that we have mentioned and many more.

NOTES

1.   These estimates are contained in the *United Nations Demographic Yearbook: 1965* (New York: United Nations, 1966), Table 12, p. 276.

2.   Ansley J. Coale, "The History of the Human Population," *Scientific American*, 231, no. 3 (September 1974), 40–51.

3.   See, for example, T. E. Smith, "Cocos-Keeling Islands: A Demographic Laboratory," *Population Studies*, 14 (1960), 94–130.

4.   A compilation of studies using such records is Maris A. Vinovskis, ed., *Studies in American Historical Demography* (New York: Academic Press, 1979).

5.   "1982 World Population Data Sheet" (Washington, D.C.: Population Reference Bureau, 1982).

6.   "1982 World Population Data Sheet" (Washington, D.C.: Population Reference Bureau, 1982).

7.   See, for example, Dudley Kirk, "A New Demographic Transition?" in *Rapid Population Growth: Consequences and Policy Implications* (Baltimore: Johns Hopkins University Press, 1971). Prepared by a study committee of the Office of the Foreign Secretary, National Academy of Sciences, with the support of the Agency for International Development.

8.   Bernard Berelson, "Prospects and Programs for Fertility Reduction," *Population and Development Review*, 4 (1978), 579–616.

9.   "1982 World Population Data Sheet" (Washington, D.C.: Population Reference Bureau, 1982).

10.   John S. Aird, "Fertility Decline and Birth Control in the People's Republic of China," *Population and Development Review*, 4 (1978), 225–253.

11. For an early discussion of this phenomenon, see Ellsworth Huntington, *Season of Birth* (New York: John Wiley, 1938). Huntington examines cross-cultural data to document seasonality of birth and discusses cultural and climatic factors as explanations of it. Attention is also given to subgroup differences in seasonality of birth and to the quality of those born in certain months.

12. For a discussion of the United States pattern, see Harry Rosenberg, *Seasonal Variation of Births: United States, 1933–1963*, Series 21, No. 9, National Center for Health Statistics (Washington, D.C.: Government Printing Office, 1966).

13. Charles W. Warren and Carl W. Tyler, "Social Status and Season of Birth: A Study of a Metropolitan Area in the Southeastern United States," *Social Biology*, 26 (1979), 275–288.

14. See, for example U. Cowgill, "Recent Variations in the Season of Birth in Puerto Rico," *Proceedings of the National Academy of Sciences, USA,* 52 (1964); or D. Kosambi and S. Raghavachair, "Seasonal Variation in the Indian Birth Rate," *Annual Eugenics*, 16 (1951–1952).

15. Ursula M. Cowgill, "The Season of Birth in Man," in *Man*, 1 (June 1966), 232–240.

16. See, for example, H. Rosenberg, *Seasonal Variation;* J. Richard Udry, and Naomi M. Morris, "Seasonality of Coitus and Seasonality of Birth," *Demography,* 4 (1967), 673–679; H. Hotelling and F. Hotelling, "Causes of Birth Fluctuation," *Journal of the American Statistical Association,* 26 (1931), 135–149; Huntington, *Season of Birth;* K. Chang et al., "Climate and Conception Rates in Hong Kong," *Human Biology,* 35 (1963), p. 366; or Melvin Zelnik, "Socioeconomic and Seasonal Variations in Births," *Milbank Memorial Fund Quarterly,* 47 (April 1969), 159–165.

17. For a discussion of this variable-cause hypothesis, see Cowgill, *The Season of Birth.*

18. Jane Menken, "Seasonal Migration and Seasonal Variation in Fecundability: Effects on Birth Rates and Birth Intervals," *Demography*, 16 (1979) 103–119.

19. United Nations, *Population Bulletin of the United Nations,* No. 7, 1963 (New York: United Nations, 1965), pp. 101–121.

20. Wendy H. Baldwin, "Adolescent Pregnancy and Childbearing: Growing Concerns for Americans," *Population Bulletin,* 31 (1976), 1–35.

21. National Center for Health Statistics, *Monthly Vital Statistics Report,* 30, no. 6, Supplement (2), September 29, 1981, Table 13, p. 19.

22. William Burr Hunt, "Adolescent Fertility: Risks and Consequences," *Population Reports,* Series J, no. 10 (1976), 157–175.

23. Larry Bumpass, Ronald Rindfuss, and Richard Janosik, "Age and Marital Status at First Birth and the Pace of Subsequent Fertility," *Demography,* 15 (1978), 75–86.

24. *Teenage Pregnancy: The Problem That Hasn't Gone Away.* (New York: Alan Guttmacher Institute, 1981).

25. Ronald Freedman, *The Sociology of Human Fertility* (New York: Irvington Publishers, Inc., 1975).

26.   Randall L. Olsen, "Estimating the Effect of Child Mortality on the Number of Births," *Demography*, 17 (1980), 429–443.

27.   Freedman, *Fertility*, p. 15.

28.   See, for example, Gary S. Becker, "An Economic Analysis of Fertility," in *Demographic and Economic Change in Developed Countries*, National Bureau of Economic Research (Princeton: Princeton University Press, 1960), pp. 209–240.

29.   See, for example, Judith Blake, "Are Babies Consumer Durables?" *Population Studies*, 22 (1968), 5–25.

30.   Arland Thornton, "Fertility and Income, Consumption Aspirations and Child Quality Standards," *Demography*, 16 (1979), 157–175.

31.   Richard A. Easterlin, "An Economic Framework for Fertility Analysis," *Studies in Family Planning*, 6 (1975) 54–63.

32.   Kingsley Davis and Judith Blake, "Social Structure and Fertility," *Economic Development and Cultural Change*, 4 (1956), 211–235. For a more recent revision of this framework, see John Bongaarts, "A Framework for Analyzing the Proximate Determinants of Fertility," *Population and Development Review*, 4 (1978), 105–132.

33.   R. P. Bagozzi and M. Frances Van Loo, "Toward a General Theory of Fertility: A Causal Modeling Approach," *Demography*, 15 (1978), 301–319.

34.   Michael Hout, "The Determinants of Marital Fertility in the U.S., 1968–70: Inferences from a Dynamic Model," *Demography*, 15 (1978), 139–159; Rudolfo Bulatao, "Values and Disvalues of Children in Successive Childbearing Decisions," *Demography*, 18 (1981), 1–25.

35.   One text does investigate this matter in detail. See Huntington, *Birth*.

36.   J. M. Stycos, "Culture and Differential Fertility in Peru," *Population Studies*, 16 (1963), 257–270; or David M. Heer, "Fertility Differences in Andean Countries: A Reply to W. H. James," *Population Studies*, 21 (1967), 71–73.

37.   David M. Heer, "Fertility Differences Between Indian and Spanish-speaking Parts of Andean Countries," *Population Studies*, 18 (1964), 71–84.

38.   W. H. James, "The Effect of Altitude on Fertility in Andean Countries," *Population Studies*, 20 (1966), 97–101.

39.   Gordon F. DeJong, "Demography and Research with High Altitude Populations," *Social Biology*, 17, no. 2 (1970), 114–119.

40.   Alan Berg, "Nutrition, Development, and Population Growth," *Population Bulletin*, 29, no. 1, Population Reference Bureau, Washington, 33.

41.   Josue De Castro, *The Geography of Hunger* (Boston: Little, Brown, 1952).

42.   Karl Sax, *Standing Room Only: The World's Exploding Population*, as quoted in Louise Young, *Population in Perspective* (New York: Oxford University Press, 1968), p. 74.

43.   See, for example, Marston Bates, *The Prevalence of People*, (New York: Scribner's, 1955).

44.   See, for example, W. H. Mosley, ed., *Nutrition and Human Reproduction*, (New York: Plenum, 1978); Beverly Winikoff, "A Discussion of Nutrition and Population," *Studies in Family Planning*, 10, (1979), 37–39.

45. John Bongaarts, "Malnutrition and Fecundity," *Studies in Family Planning*, 11 (1980), 401–406.

46. David M. Heer and Eba S. Turner, "Areal Differences in Latin American Fertility," *Population Studies*, 18 (1964), 279–292.

47. Ibid., p. 290.

48. Thomas W. Merrick, "Fertility and Land Availability in Rural Brazil," *Demography*, 15 (1978), 321–336.

49. David M. Heer, "Economic Development and Fertility," *Demography*, 3 (1966), 423–444.

50. William R. Kelly and Phillips Cutright, "Modernization and the Demographic Transition: Cross-Sectional and Longitudinal Analyses of a Revised Model," *Sociological Focus*, 13, no. 4 (October 1980), 315–329.

51. John C. Caldwell, "Mass Education as a Determinant of the Timing of Fertility Decline," *Population and Development Review*, 6 (1980), 225–255.

52. For a discussion of the interrelationship of these factors, see Carl E. Taylor and Marie-Francoise Hall, "Health, Population, and Economic Development," *Science*, 157 (August 1967), 651–657; Carl E. Taylor, "Health and Population," *Foreign Affairs*, 43 (April 1965), 475–486; and Deborah Maine, *Family Planning: Its Impact on the Health of Women and Children* (New York: Columbia University Press, 1981).

53. Reynolds Farley, *Growth of the Black Population* (Chicago: Markham, 1970); Phillips Cutright and Edward Shorter, "The Effects of Health on the Completed Fertility of Nonwhite and White U.S. Women Born Between 1867 and 1935," *Journal of Social History*. 13, no. 2 (1979), 191–217.

54. McFall, Joseph A., Jr., "Impact of VD on the Fertility of the Black Population, 1880–1930," *Social Biology*, 20, no. 1 (1973), 2–19.

55. Sondra Zeidenstein, ed., "Learning About Rural Women," *Studies in Family Planning*, 10 (1979), 309–422.

56. For example, see J. D. Kasarda, "Economic Structures and Fertility: A Comparative Analysis," *Demography*, 8 (1971), 307–317; Heer and Turner, "Latin American Fertility"; S. H. Preston, "Marital Fertility and Female Employment Opportunity" (Paper presented at the Annual Meeting of the Population Association of America, 1971); J. A. Sweet, "Family Composition and the Labor Force Activity of American Wives," *Demography*, 7 (1970), 195–209. For a summary of this earlier literature, see Geraldine B. Terry, "The Interrelationship Between Female Employment and Fertility: A Secondary Analysis of the Growth of American Families Study, 1960" (unpublished doctoral dissertation, Florida State University, 1973).

57. Josefina Jayme Card, "The Malleability of Fertility-Related Attitudes and Behavior in a Filipino Migrant Sample," *Demography*, 15 (1978), 459–476.

58. Bagozzi and Van Loo, "Theory of Fertility."

59. William P. Butz and Michael P. Ward, "Will U.S. Fertility Remain Low? A New Economic Interpretation," *Population and Development Review*, 5 (1979), 663–688.

60. Adrienne Germain, "Status and Roles of Women as Factors in Fertility Behavior: A Policy Analysis," *Studies in Family Planning*, 6 (1975) 192–200.

61.   George Zeidenstein, "The User Perspective: An Evolutionary Step in Contraceptive Service Programs," *Studies in Family Planning*, 11 (1980), 24–29.

62.   R. A. Easterlin, "The American Baby Boom in Historical Perspective," *American Economic Review*, 51 (December 1961), 869–911.

63.   Morris Silver, "Births, Marriages, and Business Cycles in the United States," *Journal of Political Economy*, 73, no. 3 (1965), 237–255.

64.   Morris Silver, "Births, Marriages, and Income Fluctuations in the United Kingdom and Japan," *Economic Development and Cultural Change*, 14 (April 1966), 302–315.

65.   For an example of a study that found this not to be true, see Moni Nag, "Family Type and Fertility," in *Proceedings of the World Population Conference*, vol. II (New York: United Nations, 1965), pp. 160–163.

66.   Paul C. Glick and Arthur J. Norton, "Perspectives on the Recent Upturn in Divorce and Remarriage," *Demography*, 10, no. 3 (1973), 301.

67.   U.S. Bureau of the Census, "Population Profile of the United States: 1980," *Current Population Reports*, no. 363, (Washington, D.C.: Government Printing Office, June 1981), p. 20, Table 12.

68.   U.S. Bureau of the Census, "Population Profile of the United States: 1980," Table 13.

69.   Arland Thornton, "Marital Dissolution, Remarriage, and Childbearing," *Demography*, 15 (1978), 361–380.

70.   Douglas Downing and David Yaukey, "The Effects of Marital Dissolution and Re-Marriage on Fertility in Urban Latin America," *Population Studies*, 33 (1979), 537–547.

71.   U.S. Public Health Service, "Wanted and Unwanted Births Reported by Mothers 15–44 Years of Age: United States, 1976," *Advance Data from the National Center for Health Statistics*, no. 56, January 1980; see also Susan Hill Cochrane, *Fertility and Education: What Do We Really Know?* (Baltimore: Johns Hopkins University Press, 1979).

72.   Norman B. Ryder, "Recent Trends and Group Differences in Fertility," in *Toward the End of Growth*, ed. Charles F. Westoff et al. (Englewood Cliffs, N.J.: Prentice-Hall, 1973), pp. 62–66. See also, National Center for Health Statistics, "Contraceptive Utilization, United States, 1976," *Vital & Health Statistics*, Series 23, no. 7, March 1981.

73.   John Stoeckel and A. K. M. Allauddin Chowdhury, "Fertility and Socio-Economic Status in Rural Bangladesh: Differentials and Linkages," *Population Studies*, 34 (1980), 519–524.

74.   U.S. Bureau of the Census, *Current Population Reports*, Series P-20, no. 79, February 2, 1958.

75.   As quoted in "Pope John Paul on Human Rights and Population," *Population and Development Review*, 5 (1979), 747–754.

76.   Charles F. Westoff and Elise F. Jones, "The End of 'Catholic' Fertility," *Demography*, 16 (1979), 209–217.

77.   Charles F. Westoff and Larry Bumpass, "The Revolution in Birth Control Practices of U.S. Roman Catholics," *Science*, 179 (1973), 41–44.

78.   Westoff and Jones, " 'Catholic' Fertility," p. 216.

79. Sergio DellaPergola, "Patterns of American Jewish Fertility," *Demography*, 17 (1980), 261–273.

80. Dudley Kirk, "Factors Affecting Moslem Natality," in *Family Planning and Population Programs*, ed. Bernard Berelson et al. (Chicago: University of Chicago Press, 1966).

81. Kelly and Cutright, "Modernization."

82. I. Sembajwe, "Religious Fertility Differentials Among the Yoruba of Western Nigeria," *Journal of Biosocial Science*, 12 (1980), 153–164.

83. Joseph W. Eaton and Albert J. Mayer, "The Social Biology of Very High Fertility Among the Hutterites: The Demography of a Unique Population," *Human Biology*, 25 (September 1953), 256–262.

84. Julia Erickson, Eugene Erickson, John Hostetler, and Gertrude Huntington, "Fertility Patterns and Trends Among the Old Order Amish," *Population Studies*, 33 (1979), 255–276.

85. Bernard Berelson and Jonathan Lieberson, "Government Efforts to Influence Fertility: The Ethical Issues," *Population and Development Review*, 5 (1979), 581–613.

86. Discussions of the German program may be found in Frederick Osborn, *Preface to Eugenics* (New York: Harper & Row, Pub., 1940), and in A. M. Carr-Sanders, *World Population* (Oxford: Clarendon Press, 1936).

87. See, for example, D. V. Glass, *Population Policies and Movements in Europe* (Oxford: Clarendon Press, 1940).

88. For a discussion of this possibility, see Joseph J. Spengler, *France Faces Depopulation* (Durham, N.C.: Duke University Press, 1938).

89. Jean Bourgeois-Pichat, "France," *Country Profiles*, The Population Council, New York, 1972.

90. For discussions of the Swedish program, see Halvor Gille, "Recent Developments in Swedish Population Policy," *Population Studies*, 2 (June 1948), 3–70; Gunnar Myrdal, *Population: A Problem for Democracy* (Cambridge, Mass.: Harvard University Press, 1940); and Gertrude Svala, "Sweden," *Country Profiles*, (New York: The Population Council, 1972).

91. Henry P. David and Nicholas H. Wright, "Abortion Legislation: The Romanian Experience," *Studies in Family Planning*, 2, no. 10 (1971), 205–210.

92. B. Berelson, "Romania's 1966 Anti-Abortion Decree: The Demographic Experience of the First Decade," *Population Studies*, 33 (1979), 209–222.

93. Walter B. Watson, "Family Planning Programs in Developing Countries," in *International Encyclopedia of Population*, ed. John A. Ross (New York: Free Press, 1982), pp. 205–215.

94. Kingsley Davis, "Population Policy: Will Current Programmes Succeed?" *Science*, 158 (November 1967), 730–739.

95. W. Parker Mauldin and Bernard Berelson with Zenas Sykes, "Conditions of Fertility Decline in Developing Countries, 1965–1975," *Studies in Family Planning*, 9 (May 1978), 89–148.

96. Donald J. Hernandez, "A Note on Measuring the Independent Impact of Family Planning Programs on Fertility Declines," *Demography*, 18, no. 4 (November 1981), 627–634.

97.   Suwardjono Surjaningrat, R. Henry Pardoko, Peter Patta Sumbung, and M. Soedarmadk, "Indonesia," in J. Jarrett Clinton and Jean Baker, eds. *Studies in Family Planning*, 11 (November 1980), 320–324.

98.   Mary Taylor Hassouna, "Assessment of Family Planning Service Delivery in Egypt," *Studies in Family Planning*, 11 (May 1980), 159–166.

99.   Pichao Chen and Adrienne Kols, "Population and Birth Planning in The People's Republic of China," *Population Reports*, Series J, no. 25 (January–February 1982), 577–618.

100.   Ansley J. Coale, "Population Trends, Population Policy, and Population Studies in China," *Population and Development Review*, 7 (March 1981), 85–97.

101.   Leo Orleans, "China: Population in the People's Republic," *Population Bulletin*, Population Reference Bureau, Washington, D.C., 27, no. 6 (1971), pp. 1–37. H. Yuan Tien, *China's Population Struggle* (Columbus: Ohio State University Press, 1973); also see a review of Tien's work by John S. Aird in *Demography*, 11 (1974), 695–701.

102.   Orleans, "China," and Aird, in his review of Tien, emphasize this reversal, whereas Tien, "China's Population Struggle," does not.

103.   John S. Aird, "Fertility Decline."

104.   Davidson R. Gwatkin, "Political Will and Family Planning: The Implications of India's Emergency Experience," *Population and Development Review*, 5 (March, 1979), 29–59.

105.   Ronald G. Ridker, "The No-Birth Bonus Scheme: The Use of Savings Accounts for Family Planning in South India," *Population and Development Review*, 6 (March 1980), 31–46.

106.   Henri Leridon, "Fertility and Contraception in 12 Developed Countries," *Family Planning Perspectives* 13 (March–April, 1981), 98–102.

107.   Ibid.

108.   Dwight D. Eisenhower, "The Presidential News Conference of December 2, 1959" (Washington, D.C.: U.S. Government Printing Office, 1960), pp. 787–788.

109.   "Fact Sheet on Birth Control," *Congressional Quarterly Weekly Report*, 26 (October 11, 1968), 2757, 2761.

110.   Mary Chamie and Stanley K. Henshaw, "The Costs and Benefits of Government Expenditures for Family Planning Programs," *Family Planning Perspectives*, 13 (May–June, 1981), 117–124.

111.   *The Report of the Commission on Population Growth and the American Future*, (New York: Signet, 1972), p. 7.

112.   Charles F. Westoff, "Recent Developments in Population Growth Policy in the United States," in *Toward the End of Growth*, ed. Charles F. Westoff et al. (Englewood Cliffs, N.J.: Prentice-Hall, 1973).

113.   *Roe v. Wade*, 410 U.S. 113 (U.S. Supreme Court, 1973); *Doe v. Bolton*, 410 U.S. 179 (U.S. Supreme Court, 1973).

114.   See, for example, Harriet F. Pilpel, "The Fetus as Person: Possible Legal Consequences of the Hogan-Helms Amendment," *Family Planning Perspec-*

tives, 6 (Winter 1974), 6–7; and Frederick S. Jaffe, Barbara L. Lindheim, and Philip R. Lee, *Abortion Politics: Private Morality and Public Policy* (New York: McGraw-Hill, 1981).

115.   Chamie and Henshaw, "Costs and Benefits."

116.   Lolagene C. Coombs, "Reproductive Goals and Achieved Fertility: A Fifteen-Year Perspective," *Demography,* 16 (November 1979), 523–534.

117.   Kathy Widmer, Gary McClelland, and Carol Nickerson, "Determining the Impact of Sex Preferences on Fertility: A Demonstration Study," *Demography* 18 (February 1981), 27–37.

118.   Davis, "Population Policy"; Judith Blake, "Demographic Science and the Redirection of Population Policy," in *Public Health and Population Change,* eds. Mindel C. Sheps and Jeanne C. Ridley (Pittsburgh: University of Pittsburgh Press, 1965).

119.   Frank E. Clarkson et al., "Family Size and Sex-Role Stereotypes," *Science,* 167 (January 1970), 390–392.

120.   Butz and Ward, "U.S. Fertility."

121.   Judith Blake, "Can We Believe Recent Data on Birth Expectations in the United States?" *Demography,* 11 (1974), 25–44.

SUGGESTED ADDITIONAL READINGS

Useful summaries of trends in fertility are contained in:

MAULDIN, W. PARKER,   "Patterns of Fertility Decline in Developing Countries," *Studies in Family Planning,* 9, no. 4 (April 1978), 75–84.

NATIONAL CENTER FOR HEALTH STATISTICS,   "Births, Marriages, Divorces and Deaths for 1980," *Monthly Vital Statistics Report,* 29, no. 12 (March 18, 1981). Monthly updates on the birthrate are also issued by the National Center for Health Statistics as part of this series.

U.S. BUREAU OF THE CENSUS,   "Perspectives on American Fertility," *Current Population Reports,* Series P-23, no. 70, July 1978.

An autobiographical account of the beginnings of the birth-control movement in the United States is:

SANGER, MARGARET,   *An Autobiography.* 1938. Reprint. New York: Dover, 1971.

Useful summaries on population policy, family planning, and abortion are found in:

CUCA, ROBERTO, AND CATHERINE S. PIERCE,   "Experimentation in Family Planning Delivery Systems: An Overview," *Studies in Family Planning* 8, no. 12 (December 1977), 302–310.

INTERNATIONAL CONFERENCE ON FAMILY PLANNING IN THE 1980's, "Family Planning in the 1980's: Challenges and Opportunities," *Studies in Family Planning,* 12 no. 6–7 (June–July 1981), 251–256.

NORTMAN, DOROTHY, AND ELLEN HOFSTATTER, *Population and Family Planning Programs* (9th ed.). New York: The Population Council, 1978.

TIETZE, CHRISTOPHER, *Induced Abortion: 1979* (3rd ed.). New York: The Population Council, 1979.

TECHNICAL SUPPLEMENT NO. 4

Period and Cohort Fertility

In studying fertility patterns in any nation, two major perspectives are employed: *period fertility* and *cohort fertility.* In the period approach to fertility, birthrates at any one period in time are calculated. The *crude birthrate* is an example of a measure computed in this way, since it is the number of births occurring per 1,000 population in one year.

For example, to calculate the crude birthrate for the year 1980, the following formula would be used:

$$\frac{\text{Births in 1980}}{\text{Population in 1980}} \times 1,000 = \text{Crude birthrate}$$

This measure is indeed crude, since it uses the entire population as the denominator, when clearly not all persons in the population contribute to the birthrate. Crude birthrates may thus vary widely between societies with differing age structures, even if women at each age have similar rates of childbearing. This is particularly a problem in special populations, where such a calculation might be misleading. For example, if a population were comprised almost exclusively of males, the crude birthrate would not really be comparable to other groups.

Another measure of period fertility, which is a refinement of the crude birthrate, is the *fertility ratio* or the *child-woman ratio.* This ratio is usually calculated as follows:

$$\frac{\text{Number of children under 5 in the population}}{\text{Number of women aged 15–44}} \times 100 = \text{Fertility ratio}$$

Unlike the crude birthrate, this measure can be calculated by the use of census data, whether or not vital-registration information from birth records is available.

While both of these measures provide an indication of relative fertility at any given point in time, the cohort approach to fertility measurement is somewhat different. It examines the total fertility of a group with a similar birthdate throughout its childbearing years. In this way, measures of completed fertility or final family sizes can be computed. The *total fertility rate* is a measure calculated in this way.

It represents the average number of children who would be born per woman in a cohort of women if they all survived to the end of their reproductive periods and bore children at the prevailing age-specific rates. This rate is usually expressed in terms of a cohort of 1,000 hypothetical women. The calculation would be as follows:

$$\Sigma \text{ (age-specific fertility rates)} \times 1,000 = \text{Total fertility rate}$$

Understanding the relationship of cohort and period fertility is crucial to an informed approach to fertility. For example, during any given time, period fertility may be falling even though cohort fertility does not change. This can occur, for example, when couples are postponing births because of wars or economic adversity. Even though the current birthrate or period fertility may be low, these births may be made up later, and the number of children these couples will eventually have may be no different from that of their parents' generation, making cohort fertility constant. Likewise, although period-fertility measures may indicate higher birthrates in one year than another, this fluctuation may only reflect changing age patterns of childbearing, and not signal altered cohort fertility levels.

ISSUES SUPPLEMENT NO. 4

How Soon and by What Efforts
Can World Fertility Be Decreased?

In the late 1960s and early 1970s, there was much discussion worldwide about the population explosion, and, in particular, the slow pace of fertility decline in developing countries. Sustained high fertility in these nations, coupled with low mortality in the classic pattern of the demographic transition, created very high growth rates in poor nations that could least afford them.

How soon would fertility rates come down? How could they be made to do so? These topics are still being debated, as demographers and others examine the mechanics of fertility control. Two recent entrants in this debate differ about not only when they foresee substantial fertility decline becoming a reality, but what the role of family planning programs will be in bringing about such a decline:

> By the end of the century, rapid population growth should be under control in most countries with the remainder following suit in the first quarter of the 21st century. The materialization of these projected trends will, to a large extent, depend on a strengthened role for the family planning movement. . . . the impact of family planning programs on the population problem can be realized in a shorter time than that of economic development and industrialization programs. (Amy Ong Tsui and Donald J. Bogue, "Declining World Fertility: Trends, Causes, Implications," *Population Bulletin,* 33, no. 4, Population Reference Bureau, October 1978, 39.)

> . . . the expectation of a generalized and precipitous fertility decline in the developing world during the rest of the century remains unsubstantiated, as is the claim that family planning programs provide a ready tool for triggering and sustaining such a decline. Considering further that even the highly optimistic extrapolations of present fertility trends underlying that forecast would leave the developing world in a state of rapid demographic expansion around the turn of the century, it is difficult not to conclude also that talk about the end of the population explosion is rather premature. (Paul Demeny, "On the End of the Population Explosion," *Population and Development Review,* 5, no. 1, March 1979, 157.)

CHAPTER FIVE
GEOGRAPHIC MOBILITY: TRENDS AND DETERMINANTS

By permission of Johnny Hart and Field Enterprises, Inc.

No model of demographic change is complete without consideration of geographic mobility. Moves of individuals and groups from one location to another not only affect the size of populations in different areas but have an impact on the composition, distribution, and characteristics of people in those areas as well.

MOBILITY CONCEPTS

A comparison of the three basic components of demographic change indicates that mobility is quite different in nature from mortality and fertility. First, birth and death are biological events, whereas mobility is not. The former involve physiological changes: people die just once, and a woman may have only as many births as is possible within her age range of fecundity. Mobility is possible for either sex at any age, and there is no biological limit on the number of moves one can make in a lifetime. Second, from a demographic point of view, fertility can only add to a population, and mortality can only subtract from it, but mobility involves a subtraction from one area's population and an addition to another's. Third, fertility and mortality are societal universals, in that births are necessary for the survival of a population, and deaths are inevitable, whereas a population can have no mobility for a long period of time and still survive.[1]

Our discussion in this chapter will include examination of various types of geographic mobility and their trends, the relationship of age to mobility, and the macro, medial, and micro factors that influence mobility.

The concepts and terms used in official statistics on mobility, and by demographers generally, are numerous and sometimes not in keeping with the popular vocabulary on this topic. First of all, a distinction needs to be made between *geographic mobility* (the physical movement of people across space) and *social mobility* (the changes of status in a social hierarchy either within one's lifetime or from one generation to the next). These two conditions are sometimes related, and demographers often are interested in both, but geographic mobility is fundamental to population analysis, since it constitutes one of the three basic components of population change.

People who move across space do so for various reasons and lengths of time. Some geographic mobility is quite temporary and does not involve a permanent change of residence. Such mobility may be for vacation or business trips, or commuting between home and work, school, service centers, and entertainment centers.

Since most concerns about population size relate to the relatively permanent population of an area, it is the people who move with the intent of changing their residence who are the prime subjects of geographic-mobility studies. People who change their residence are referred to as residential movers (or simply movers), and the process is regarded as *residential mobility*. People who change their permanent residence from one community to another, or from some other large geographical unit to another, are typically termed *migrants;* the process is referred to as *migration;* the intent of these terms is to define migrants as those who have severed connections with one area of residence and established them in another. Given the limited number of geographical distinctions that can be made in official data, one type of geographical unit (the county, in the case of the United States) is chosen as the base for defining movements that involve severance of community ties. People who change their residence but do not cross a critical boundary that would identify them as migrants are called *local movers*. Thus, someone who moves next door is a local mover, as is a person who moves several miles but does not cross a migration-defining geographical boundary (such as a county line in the United States). On the other hand, someone who moves only one block but thereby crosses a county line is regarded as a migrant, as is the person who shifts residence from one corner of a country to another. Actual distance moved is thus correlated with, but not an integral element of, the definitions. (In the popular language, migrant and mover are used synonymously.)

Although migrants can be classified in any number of ways (for instance, by distance moved, direction of movement, number of geographical units crossed), one distinction looms large in the demographic literature; namely, the difference between intersocietal and intrasocietal movement. Movement between countries (intersocietal) affects the population size and characteristics of the country; movement within a country (intrasocietal) leaves the country's population size unaffected but has an impact on the population size of areas within the country. The first type of movement is termed *international migration,* and the participants are called *immigrants* when they enter a country and *emigrants* when they leave one. The second type of movement is termed *internal migration,* and the people involved are called *inmigrants* when they enter an area and *out-migrants* when they leave one. At times, these terms seem to be arbitrary, but they have become conventional in demographic analysis and serve to highlight some important aspects of population change. A summary of them is presented on p. 172.

PROCESS	PERSONS INVOLVED
Geographic mobility	Geographic movers
Temporary mobility	Temporary movers
Vacation trips	Vacationers or tourists
Business trips	Business travelers
Commuting between home, work, and school	Commuters
Service and other trips	Service travelers
Residential (or permanent) mobility	Residential movers
Local mobility (within a community)	Local movers
Migration	Migrants
Internal migration (within a country)	Internal migrants
In-migration (into a county)	In-migrants
Out-migration (out of a county)	Out-migrants
International migration (between countries)	International migrants
Immigration (into a country)	Immigrants
Emigration (out of a country)	Emigrants

INTERNATIONAL MIGRATION

Migrations between nations have been taking place since very early times, but it is only in the modern era that we have been able to assess the magnitude of these movements.

Historical Patterns

Five major currents of international migration have been identified in modern times: (1) the emigration from Europe to North America beginning early in the seventeenth century and ending in the twentieth century (and numbering nearly 45 million persons); (2) emigration to Latin America since the beginning of the sixteenth century (involving about 20 million persons); (3) emigration of about 17 million Europeans to South Africa, Australia, and other areas of the South Pacific beginning in the nineteenth century; (4) importation of perhaps 15 million slaves from Africa to the New World starting in the sixteenth century; and (5) shifts of about 13 million in the Far East beginning in the seventeenth century, mainly from China and India to neighboring countries.[2]

These classic movements have largely completed their course in recent decades and have been replaced by migrations that are smaller in volume and different in direction but still significant in their impact. Typical of such movement was the readjustment of European peoples during and following the dislocations occasioned by World War II. Two general movements involving the resettlement of displaced persons were the return of approximately 12 million German nationals living outside postwar German territory who had to return to Germany in accordance with the Potsdam agreement, and the migration back to their native countries of about 4.5 million citizens of Poland, Czechoslovakia, and other European nations who had been uprooted from their homes during the war.

The end of the war also opened up some of the channels of transoceanic migration. The United Kingdom and Italy were prime contributors to this overseas movement of roughly 12 million persons directed largely toward North America and Oceania. In more recent decades, however, European nations have been receivers as well as senders of migrants.

The United States, Canada, Australia, New Zealand, South Africa, and Israel were the main receiving countries for emigrants from Northern and Central Europe and, later, Southern Europe. Latin America was also a destination for Southern Europeans. At the same time, there were shifts between European countries, those most affected being the United Kingdom, Sweden, Belgium, France, and Switzerland.

Current Patterns

Other significant international migrations have taken place in recent years in the Americas, Asia and the Middle East, and Africa. Dominant movements on the American continent have been the migrations from Mexico, Cuba, other Latin American nations, and Canada to the United States and a countermovement from the United States to Canada. Also observed in recent decades have been some sizable exchanges among South and Central American countries.

The most significant of the recent international migrations in Asia and the Middle East have been the shifts of nearly 15 million people between India and West and East Pakistan (now Bangladesh), involving largely the movement of Hindus to India and Moslems to Pakistan; the population exchanges between Israel, Jordan, Lebanon, Syria, and the Gaza Strip resulting from the partition of Palestine and subsequent conflicts of boundary adjustments; the migrations of East Asian people to Japan; and the flow of Chinese people to Hong Kong and Taiwan.

Finally, there have been the exchanges affecting Africa; namely, the emigration of Europeans from African countries gaining independence, and the mobility between African nations.[3]

The crossing of international boundaries takes place under a variety of circumstances. Most countries have laws that regulate immigration and emigration. At the same time, there can be special situations that allow for the temporary movement of persons across national borders, some may be admitted into a country under exceptional laws, and some may cross clandestinely.

An example of large-scale temporary movements is the flow of migrant workers into many Western European countries from areas of Southern Europe, Turkey, and the former French territories of North Africa.[4] France and Germany especially have been the recipients of manpower from these countries; such migration is encouraged because of labor shortages in the Western European nations and the labor available elsewhere. Many of these migrants are on twelve-month renewable permits, and others come for seasonal work. Those staying longer typically send part of their pay back home in the form of remittances. While some of the migrants may eventually establish new homelands in the countries in which they work, cultural differences lead most of them to return to their native lands at some point in time.

On a number of occasions, various countries have made exceptions to their existing laws in order to accommodate peoples who were victims of political or religious persecution or refugees from their native lands because of the effects of war or collapsed economies. The United States and other nations provided a haven, by special statute, for the Hungarians who were involved in political uprisings in the 1960s, for Vietnamese and other "boat people" who left their home countries in search of freedom in the 1970s, and for the Cubans, Haitians, and other Latin Americans who were classified as either political or economic refugees, also in the 1970s and in the early 1980s.

A case of clandestine movement involves some of the Mexican migration to the United States. While there are those who come under the provisions of the immigration acts, the number who wish to migrate to the United States for either temporary work or permanent residence far exceeds what is legally permissible. Because it is difficult for United States government border patrols to control movement across the border between the two countries (given the length of the border and the limited number of patrollers), undocumented movement takes place on a fairly large scale.

Low economic levels on the Mexican side and the magnet of job opportunities on the United States side provide the major catalyst. Some who enter the country in this way are caught and returned, but the vast majority are not apprehended and take jobs. For some it is seasonal work; others establish a new home in a foreign land. The growing Hispanic character of the Sun Belt (the southeastern and southwestern parts of the United States) makes the environment increasingly hospitable for these clandestine movers.

Estimates of the illegal alien population in the United States have ranged from 1 to 12 million, but a careful study of the situation indicates that there are fewer than 6 million and most likely between 3.5 and 5 million, or roughly 2 percent of the total population.[5] One reason for occasional larger estimates is the confusion between the total arrivals and the net arrivals (arrivals minus departures). For example, more than 1 million foreign-born persons who were legally in the country were estimated to have left the United States in the 1960-to-1970 decade,[6] and the number of illegal aliens who returned to their own country at some point is likely to have been exceedingly large.

International Migration and Population Change

All countries have experienced some immigration and emigration, yet international migration has had a significant impact on population change in only a minority of countries. For one thing, in many nations the inflow and outflow of people have substantially offset each other (for instance, in Ghana and Italy in recent decades). Second, the rate of natural increase has frequently been so great that the net effect of immigration is dwarfed (as in most developing countries). Third, international migration seems to be distributed unevenly over time; as a result, some countries are affected greatly by migration for only short periods of their history (the United States is one instance). Even so, there are some notable examples of countries whose populations were sharply increased (Israel) or decreased (Ireland) by migration.

Ireland was remarkable in this respect, for not only did it contribute sizably to the emigration from Europe to the New World in the nineteenth century, but its population was halved in the process. In the 1850s almost 1.25 million persons left Ireland, most of them headed for the United States, with some emigrating to Canada, Australia, and New Zealand. The movement was somewhat less voluminous in succeeding decades, but from 1846 to 1901 the Irish population was reduced from over 8 million to just under 4.5 million.[7] This decline took place despite a continuing excess of births over deaths. As Isaac has put it: "Irish emigration thereby achieved the unenviable distinction of being the only migration movement in modern history to have embraced a considerable proportion of a country's population and to have led directly to a definitive population decline."[8] Irish emigration tapered off

FIGURE 5.1   Legal immigration to the United States, 1820–1978

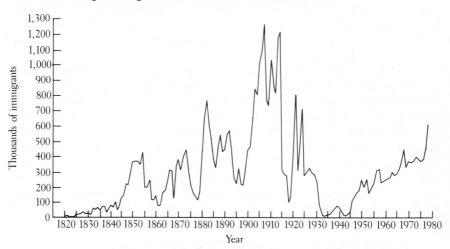

Source: U.S. Department of Justice, *1974 Annual Report, Immigration and Naturalization Service* (Washington, D.C.: U.S. Government Printing Office, 1975), p. 25.

during the twentieth century, and by 1970 natural increase had exceeded net emigration and produced population increase in Ireland, a phenomenon for a long time unknown in that country.

The United States, the principal receiver of Irish emigrants during the late nineteenth century, is a nation that flourished on immigrant settlements. In addition to the early Spanish and French settlements that accompanied the sparse Indian population, the growing European and African migrations and the natural increase of these immigrants and their descendents swelled the population of the country to nearly 4 million by 1790, the time of the first census.

Between 1820, when statistics on the topic first became available, and 1955, more than 40 million aliens entered the country (Figure 5.1). Except for periods of war and depression, the flow was substantial. The peak was reached just after the turn of the century; in each of six of the eleven years from 1905 through 1915 there were more than a million immigrants.[9] Restrictive immigration legislation (discussed later in the chapter) substantially curtailed movement into the country after 1920, yet significant numbers continued to enter.

In spite of these large numbers of newcomers, at most points in United States history, net immigration accounted for only a small proportion of the total population increase. Immigrants who had difficulty adjusting to the new environment or whose economic success would place them in an exceedingly favorable position in their native countries were good candidates for returning to their original locations. Consequently emigration was sometimes substantial. During the 1930s there was actually net emigration from this country.

At some points in time, however, the contribution of immigration to population growth was notable (Table 5.1). As much as two-fifths of population change during the 1880s could be attributed to the net effect of immigration. In recent years, as the rate of natural increase has dwindled, the continuing net movement of legal immigrants to the United States accounted for more than one-fifth of the population increase. Moreover, the volume of illegal or clandestine immigration is estimated to be as great or greater than that of legal immigration,[10] which is about 300,000 a year.

Israel is a nation that has experienced what is perhaps one of the most rapid population buildups through immigration of any nation in history. Before statehood, the nation (then Palestine) was relatively unpopulated and had modest numbers of Jewish residents. The first wave of Jewish immigrants came following a series of massacres in Czarist Russia in 1880 and 1881. Though numbering no more than

TABLE 5.1 Components of population change in the United States, 1810 to 1979

Period	Percent Due to Natural Increase	Percent Due to Net Legal Immigration
1810–1820	97	3
1820–1830	96	4
1830–1840	88	12
1840–1850	77	23
1850–1860	68	32
1860–1870	75	25
1870–1880	75	25
1880–1890	60	40
1890–1900	72	28
1900–1910	61	39
1910–1920	82	18
1920–1930	88	12
1930–1940	101	−1
1940–1950	90	10
1950–1960	90	10
1960–1969	84	16
1970–1979	76	24

Sources: Irene B. Taeuber and Conrad Taeuber, *People of the United States in 20th Century* (Washington, D.C.: U.S. Government Printing Office, 1971), p. 582; U.S. Bureau of the Census, *Current Population Reports,* Series P-25, no. 499, p. 1, and No. 870, p. 2.

20,000 to 30,000, these immigrants set a precedent for Jewish movement to the Holy Land. The second wave of immigration, from 1904 to 1914, added another 35,000 to 40,000, and brought with it the foundations of a new state.

Events associated with World War I led to the emigration of many Jews, but a third wave of immigrants, from 1919 to 1923, added 35,000 to the population, and a fourth wave, in the period 1924 to 1931, introduced 82,000 to the new land. In the fifth wave, during Hitler's rise to power, more than 217,000 Jewish immigrants entered Palestine, and smaller numbers came up until 1948, when Israel emerged as a new state.[11] Thus between 1919 and 1948 the Jewish population of Israel rose from 56,000 to 650,000, and 72 percent of this increase was attributable to net immigration.[12]

In the four-year period following independence, 687,000 immigrants entered Israel, more than the entire preindependence Jewish population of the country.[13] The new immigration included many non-Western as well as Western Jews. By the time of the 1961 census, the Jewish population approached 2 million, and more than two-thirds of the total growth was accounted for by net immigration.

INTERNAL MIGRATION

The movement of people within nations will not have a direct effect on the size and composition of the national population, but it can serve to redistribute people within the country. As a consequence, the population size of geographic units inside the nation will be changed. Internal migration can take place between geographic areas of various types and levels—urban and rural, city and suburb, city and city, small town and large town, county and county, state and state, and region and region. To qualify officially as migration, such moves must involve the crossing of a critical political boundary, such as a county.

The volume of internal migration generally exceeds that of international migration. It has been estimated that in Europe in about 1930, at least 75 million inhabitants were living outside their native communities, while only about 10 million were outside their countries of birth.

At the same time, the volume of local moves often is comparable to that of internal migrations. In about 1970, the five-year mobility experience of several developed countries (Australia, Canada, Great Britain, Japan, and the United States) showed that movement within local areas was roughly half of all residential movements in those countries.[14] In the United States in 1979, over the previous four years, 58 percent remained in the same place of residence, 23 percent moved but were not migrants, 17 percent were internal migrants, and 2 percent were movers from abroad. Thus nonmobility was most typical, but local mobility was one-third again as large as internal migration, which in turn was more than eight times larger than immigration.[15]

Migratory flows seem to change in intensity and characteristics as countries undergo the demographic transition, but data limitations and variability in size of geographic units frequently make comparisons very difficult. In Zambia about one-half of 1 percent of the population changes province of residence each year. The largest numbers gravitate toward the province containing the source of employment.[16] In Malaysia in 1970, about 3.3 percent of the population crossed a civil-division boundary during the previous year. The existing migration was heavily toward two dominant urban centers. This suggests less migration in developing than in developed countries. However, the nature of migration in particular areas and times is a consequence of the existing social structure and the character of social, economic, political, and cultural change.[17] Hence, exceptions to any generalized pattern may occur. Moreover, considerable mobility in developing countries is in the form of repeated movements between a home area and a distant area, usually for work reasons, and this *circulatory migration* may not get recorded as permanent migration.

Owing to the geographic pattern of societies and other factors that determine migration, movements of people are not random with regard to space or time. Since so many people are involved in the same kind of move, in terms of areas of origin and destination, one can discern what are called *migration streams* (flows of people from one point to another in a given period of time). These streams are significant on the basis of their direction and volume and have a bearing on the redistribution of population in a country or region. With some notable exceptions (for instance, the heavy cityward migration in developing nations), most migration streams compensate for one another to a large degree. That is, counterstreams between areas frequently are nearly equal in size.

LOCAL MOBILITY AND TEMPORARY MOVEMENTS

We have already indicated that residential mobility is dominated by local moves. Generally speaking, the incidence of mobility varies with distance. Availability of homes, jobs, and schools, and satisfaction or dissatisfaction with these and other environmental factors, lead people to change where they live with varying frequency. Because one's home is typically removed from one's place of work, school, or shopping or entertainment center, commuting and other forms of local travel are quite common in all countries of the world. Residents may become local movers in order to lessen the distance between home, work, and other sites frequently attended. Even so, commuting and other local travel occupies a significant part of our daily schedules.

A study done in the United States in 1975 showed that 97 percent of workers commuted to their jobs. The vast majority (65 percent) drove alone, 19 percent were in car pools, 6 percent used public transportation, and the remainder walked, bicycled, or used other means. The average trip from home to work was nine miles and took twenty minutes. Therefore, the better part of an hour was spent going to and from work.[18]

Traveling to school may involve similar or greater distances and times, as does going to shops and other service and entertainment centers. These travels can consume a significant part of the individual's day. Of course, if the individual judges these distances and times as being too great, a residential move may be considered in order to minimize subsequent temporary movement.

Travel related to vacationing and tourism includes more distance and time on a less frequent basis then commuting or other local travel. Such temporary moves often become the foundation for permanent moves. In Florida, for example, a large proportion of tourists either chose the state as a travel site because they were interested in it as an eventual residence or were attracted enough by their visits to think about moving there permanently.[19]

THE AGE PATTERN OF MOBILITY

As was the case with mortality and fertility, mobility is characterized by a typical age pattern. In contrast to mortality and fertility, the age configuration of mobility is not significantly determined by biological factors, but depends more heavily on social and cultural factors. It is thus the case that the age curve of residential change may be more variable than that of deaths and births. Yet there are still general tendencies toward a predictable pattern.[20]

In this typical age pattern, mobility rates are relatively high in early infancy, decline somewhat but remain above average until the mid-teens, rise to a peak in the early twenties, remain high but decline progressively with the approach of middle age, and attain a low but stable level from middle age onward (Figure 5.2). This reflects variations in life-cycle activities that are related to family and socioeconomic status. Thus a high mobility rate for infants suggests the need for families to provide more adequate housing for expanded family size;

FIGURE 5.2 Single year-of-age probabilities of making various types of moves during one-year periods, 1966–1971

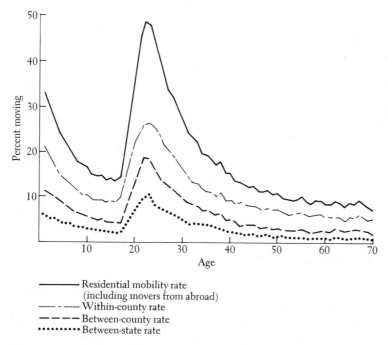

Source: Larry H. Long, "New Estimates of Migration Expectancy in the United States," *Journal of the American Statistical Association,* 68:341 (March 1973), 38.

the peak rate among those in their late teens and twenties is linked to finishing school, getting married, and taking a job; and the stabilization of the rate in later years is indicative of more settled familial and socioeconomic stages. These age patterns are just as common in Australia, Great Britain, and Japan as they are in the United States.[21]

The graphs in Figure 5.2 are shown for all residential moves and separately for moves between states, between counties, and within counties. It is clear that each of the graphs has the same form and that age patterns of mortality tend, therefore, to be the same regardless of the kind of move. The sharp peaks at infancy and, especially, in the early twenties are striking.

By converting such age-specific probabilities of mobility into a life-table form, we can calculate the lifetime or cumulative pattern of mobility, For example, the average United States resident makes about thirteen moves over a lifetime. While the age patterns in other countries are similar, the levels of mobility are lower. Consequently the average person in Great Britain makes only eight moves, in Japan only seven, in Taiwan six, and in Ireland three or four. The number of lifetime moves for someone from Canada or Australia is similar to that for the United States. Put in different terms, the average American makes as many moves after age twenty-two or twenty-three as the average person in Great Britain or Japan would make in a lifetime.[22]

That this age curve of mobility varies, even for national populations, can be seen in comparing the sexes and races. Women, largely because they marry slightly earlier than men, have somewhat higher mobility rates between ages fifteen and twenty-four, and because they are more likely to be widowed, also have higher rates at age sixty-five and over.[23] Blacks have higher rates of residential mobility than whites up to age nineteen and at age twenty-eight and over. This reflects the fact that blacks are less likely than whites to be migrants (between-county movement occurs frequently among people in their twenties), and what migration there is, takes place over a greater part of the young-adult age span.[24]

FACTORS AFFECTING MOBILITY

Attempts at developing explanatory frameworks for residential mobility go back to at least before the turn of the century. E. G. Ravenstein, after analyzing census data for several Western societies, listed certain generalizations that could be derived from those data, which he labeled "laws of migration." For example, he noted that

1. the bulk of these migrants proceed only a short distance
2. inhabitants of the countryside immediately surrounding a rapidly growing town flock into it; the gaps thus left in the rural population are filled up by migrants from more remote districts
3. each main current of migration produces a compensating countercurrent
4. natives of towns are less migratory than those of the rural parts of the country
5. females are more migratory than males.[25]

In succeeding years, others refined, modified, and added to these descriptive and relational patterns. These inventories of research findings did not provide a sufficient theoretical basis for studying mobility, however.

In the remainder of this chapter, we will concentrate on specifying the macro, medial, and micro variables and approaches that have emerged in twentieth-century studies.

Macro Variables

Analysis of migration patterns, both international and internal, have frequently focused on worldwide or societal changes that led to moving. Among the classes of variables that analysts have used are those related to spatial factors, environmental-organizational ones, and socioeconomic change.

Spatial Factors

It seems reasonable to assume that the longer the distance between two geographical points, the less likely people are to move between them. This basic assumption has been the foundation of several frameworks for predicting the size and direction of migration streams between areas. Thus, the number of migrants was determined by some to be a mathematical function of the size of the populations in areas of origin and destination and the distance between those areas.[26] An extension of this approach conceptualized the relationship in terms of the opportunities at a given place and the "intervening opportunities."[27] Much of this research eschewed the underlying factors that produced the movements and instead looked only for relational patterns.

Later attempts were made to build up the explanatory elements. Intervening opportunities were considered on the basis of the nature of opportunities and characteristics of potential movers as well as of the knowledge and communication networks involved.[28] Everett Lee elaborated this framework in a schematic way.[29] He first classified the factors that enter into the migration process under four headings: (1) factors associated with the area of origin; (2) factors associated with the area of destination; (3) intervening obstacles; and (4) personal factors. An individual was seen to be moving as a result of a decision based on perceptions of positive or negative evaluations of conditions in the two areas and of the intervening obstacles. The evaluations will be influenced by the individual's own characteristics and personal circumstances.

This neat formulation set the stage for subsequent development of theoretical work on geographic mobility, but, like its forerunners, the hypotheses generated from it were very general, and confirmation of them did not add depth to understanding about the mobility decision-making process or the social interactions that go into it.

Environmental-Organizational Factors

Classification of societal factors that affect migration served to isolate some important variables and to label types of migration that were unique because of the combination of sets of factors. Petersen categorized migrations into five types that were of historical significance:

(1) *primitive migration* (resulting from an ecological push to change the relationship between people and nature); (2) *forced migration* (deriving from a government policy affecting the relationship between people and the state that leaves the migrant no alternative); (3) *impelled migration* (also deriving from a governmental policy affecting tbe relationship between people and the state but granting the person some option about whether or not to leave); (4) *free migration* (based on the individual's will or aspiration, which may involve individuals, families, or relatively small groups); and (5) *mass migration* (in which the aspirations of large groups of people produce social momentum that generates their migration from an area).[30] These five classes of migration were further divided according to whether the movement was designed to retain a way of life (conservative) or to bring about a new one (innovating).

The so-called ecological approach to population analysis attempts to systematize the environmental and organizational factors in societies and communities, as well as technological change, in order to understand what creates migration flows.[31] Shifts and interactions of these categories over time are seen as providing the impetus for mobility of certain population groups. The ecological approach goes beyond the typological framework in generalizing to a variety of migration flows, and it helps us to advance from historical accounts (which typologies can indicate) to functional variables (which ecological orientations enable us to specify).

The natural environment, as opposed to the broader environment, which encompasses man-made factors, has often been identified as crucial to facilitating or impeding geographic mobility. For example, residents of a nation in the Himalayas, who have to deal with mountain crossings and severe weather, are less likely to be migratory than residents of plains countries, where it is likely that the climate is mild and travel relatively simple. Migration to the Sun Belt in recent years has been at least partly determined by preferable climatic conditions. Not only altitude and climate, but terrain, availability of water, natural resources, and condition of the soil are relevant to migration opportunities. Historically these factors influenced the wanderings of some early tribes and the sedentary life of other peoples. They enabled many in the past to reach desired destinations, and they constituted barriers to mobility for some who would have preferred to relocate.

Socioeconomic Change

If one looks at the developmental history of societies, it is clear that broad social changes, especially economic ones, precipitated a great deal of movement. The agricultural and industrial revolutions created differential opportunities, which drew people from areas of economic deficiency to those of economic sufficiency. The nineteenth-century mass movements to the New World represented a response to the shortages of accessible land and other sources of livelihood involving growing numbers of people.[32] The migration flow that evolved during the nineteenth and early twentieth centuries can be observed as the consequence of balancing the distribution of labor and capital on both sides of the Atlantic. Since labor and capital were plentiful in Europe, relative to land and natural resources, and scarce in America, freedom to move and the available means of transportation enabled many to migrate westward.[33] As the balance of these factors shifted over time, migratory flows were modified in volume and direction.

While the economy as a whole may be viewed as having an effect on migration, it can be seen more pointedly in terms of three separate economic effects—seasonal, business-cycle, and long-term.[34] The seasonality of international migration is related to the peak months of employment in receiving countries. The effect of the business cycle is reflected in the time lag between prosperity in America and increased immigration, as well as between depressions and decreased immigration. In addition to annual fluctuations, longer-term economic changes, such as those associated with home and factory construction cycles, were related to long-term swings in migration.

Internal migration can also be affected by broad economic changes. The Great Depression after 1929 reduced the attractiveness of the large cities, since jobs and resources were limited. Urban areas, which had registered a spectacular population growth during prosperity, showed little or no increase; on the other hand, rural areas in almost all states reversed their population trends and began to show marked growth. It was not until the Depression subsided and the economy was stimulated again that migration to urban areas was resumed in the United States. We are once more experiencing changes in the relative attractiveness of urban areas, which can be attributed in great part to imbalances in the availability of economic goods (see Chapter 6 for further discussion of that topic).

Socioeconomic change leading to migration involves more than just economic change. Political factors have weighed heavily at particular points in time in given countries. For instance, the revolution in Germany in 1848 led to the emigration of a number of refugees, the massacres in Russia in the nineteenth century were followed by a large-scale emigration of Jews, and the partition of India that created the country of Pakistan resulted in shifts from one area to another.[35] Especially in developing countries, a combination of economic and political determinants have been related to migration. Structural changes, in the form of investment patterns by nonnationals, land-tenure practices, foreign and domestic markets, and the location of military bases, have disturbed the status quo, providing more localization of capital and power in a limited number of large cities and an attraction to urban areas for persons from agricultural-poor rural areas.[36]

The extent and nature of migration can also be seen as a function of modernization processes more generally.[37] Relative stability was an integral part of the social fabric of traditional societies, which had little structural differentiation as well as strong kinship ties, which dominated activity within the society. The introduction of colonialism in many traditional societies brought about transformations in the social fabric and thus in the type and tempo of migration. Labor was directed to newly formed mines, plantations, and trading centers. Administrative control was centralized and eroded existing tribal-authority relationships in the rural villages. Social control by the older generation was diffused, and standards for rewards came to be based on more universal achievements. As these changes mounted, transportation, communication, and other services developed to facilitate mobility. With further socioeconomic development and industrialization, which typically accompany modernization, migration became more of a functional necessity and its volume increased.

Medial Variables

These global changes in societies affected people in a number of different ways. They became translated into action for individuals by establishing the normative bases and communal mechanisms for deciding if, when, and where to move. Illustrative of such group influences in the mobility process are factors associated with the family and kinship, socioeconomic status, ethnic affiliation, and governmental intervention. Each of these appears as a social-structural set of conditions an individual faces at different life stages and which guide decision-making.

The Family and Kinship

Mobility is often related to marriage, because two people who marry come from different residences and settle in one of them or in an entirely new location. During tight economic periods, newly married couples may "double up" with one set of parents until they can afford a home of their own. In the first stage, one of the partners has become a mover, and in the second stage, both have become movers. Migration at marriage may be culturally prescribed, as in traditional India. It is a widespread Hindu custom that a male take a bride from another village. Once married, the couple follows the practice of patrilocal residence; they reside in the same area as his relatives.[38] As a result, mobility is highly limited to women and serves to redistribute the female population extensively.

Even later in the family cycle, mobility is related to the structure and characteristics of family life among men eighteen to sixty-four years old in the United States (Table 5.2). Thus a high proportion of movers are those who move in family units, usually with wives and children following husbands to more favorable job opportunities. When people move because of different housing needs, it is typically the family as a unit that responds to those needs. Moreover, the decision to move takes account of the nature of interaction with the extended family after the move is completed.[39] The ties to one's relatives are a strong force in determining residential location, both in keeping some persons at their present locations and in providing incentives for others to locate where there are relatives.

As Table 5.2 shows, reasons for moving were linked to family situations, but the type of move was critical. Migration (or cross-country mobility) seems to occur primarily in response to circumstances relating to employment, whereas local mobility arises out of circumstances that might be termed the need for new living arrangements.[40]

Kinship (and friendship) affiliations can affect mobility propensities significantly. The presence of relatives and friends deters mobili-

TABLE 5.2 Reason for move by type of mobility for male movers 18 to 64 years old: United States, March 1963 (percent distribution)

Reason for Move	Intracounty Movers	Migrants
All reasons	100.0	100.0
Related to job	11.6	58.1
To take a job	2.7	23.6
To look for work	1.0	9.6
Job transfer	0.4	7.3
Commuting and Armed Forces	7.5	17.6
Easier commuting	6.7	6.7
Enter or leave Armed Forces	0.8	10.9
Not related to job	88.4	41.9
Housing	60.4	11.3
Better housing	55.3	10.7
Forced move	5.0	0.6
Family status	19.1	16.3
Change in marital status	11.0	4.0
Join or move with family	8.1	12.2
Other	9.0	14.3
Health	1.1	2.8
All other reasons	7.9	11.5

Source: U.S. Bureau of the Census, "Reasons for Moving: March 1962 to March 1966," *Current Population Reports,* Series P-20, no. 154 (Washington, D.C.: U.S. Government Printing Office, 1966), p. 4.

ty, and, conversely, the absence of relatives and friends encourages it. Kinship effects are related to migration, through the economic and emotional support systems and the informational base that families and relatives can provide at both present locations and potential future ones in terms of job-seeking and residential location.[41]

As the family advances in its life cycle and its size diminishes, children leave home or spouses die, and housing needs become more modest. Relocation might be an outcome. On the other hand, maintenance of the larger existing home may be the best way to provide a place for extended family members to visit and may enable those remaining in the household to continue their associations with kin and friends in a neighborhood.

Socioeconomic Status

Socioeconomic change may transform the migration prospects of a whole society, and the differing socioeconomic characteristics of individuals and families will further vary the probability of moving. Occupation, income, and education are three socioeconomic variables that have been studied in this respect.

Some research has shown that those seeking a better job will frequently have to relocate in order to maximize their opportunity, and must adjust their locale to their aspirations. Also, it is more economically feasible for those with higher status to move, particularly long distances, as a means of maintaining or enhancing that status. In addition, whereas the supply and demand for unskilled labor can be met within a local labor market, the more highly skilled the occupation, the more likely supply and demand for the skill will extend from local to regional to national levels.[42]

The highest mobility rates (especially of long-distance moves) are usually found among salaried professional workers and salaried managers and administrators; the lowest rates are found among self-employed professionals and proprietors of business.[43] Salaried employees frequently find themselves being relocated by their employers, a phenomenon not unusual in an economy in which businesses and industries standardize their employment activities but spread their commercial outlets and factories throughout the country. On the other hand, self-employed professionals will invest a great deal in capital equipment, clientele, customers, and actual or potential work and fringe benefits, which often tie them to a community and restrict their mobility.[44]

Economists tend to emphasize employment status and income as determinants of migration. Essentially a cost-benefit framework is assumed, in which these economic variables play a major role. The decision to migrate to an urban area of a developing country is hypothesized to reflect the perceived urban-rural income differential and the urban employment rate. It is not the absolute levels of these measures, but how they compare with one's present location, that is crucial. Thus the greater possibility of obtaining a job in another area and the net income benefit are evaluated as a basis for deciding on a move.[45]

Although wage rates may very well differ and provide incentives for moving, total income is not a meaningful differentiator of mobility patterns. Mobility levels vary to only a small degree among family-income categories, while varying considerably from one age group to another (see Table 5.3). The effects of income that are identified are strongly related to other socioeconomic factors; hence income alone affords little explanation of mobility patterns.

Education, on the other hand, appears to be a more potent factor in understanding population movement. Americans in the late 1970s had one chance in two of changing residence over a four-year period if they had gone to college, whereas the chances were only one out of four for those without some high-school education (Table 5.3). The tendency to migrate is greatest for the higher-educated; however, local mobility varies little among education groups and is actually highest for those with only a high-school background. Although specification of the aspects of education that make it important for mobility have not been thoroughly studied, it seems reasonable to assume that such factors as style of life, career aspirations, knowledge and awareness about alternative opportunities, and ability to meet travel needs and costs are involved.

Race and Nationality

Race and nationality are also related to mobility and to choice of specific destinations. We have already called attention to the fact that many historical movements of people, especially among smaller groups such as sects but also among such groups as Jews, were the result of religious persecution or ethnic discrimination. The ethnic linkage to mobility can come about as well because of factors that attract certain groups to particular places.

Ethnic groups of all types are affected to at least some degree by their cultural heritage and their ties to the traditions of the group; hence where they will move will be partly determined by the movement of the group as a whole and their interest in being within traveling distance of it. Such ethnic links have been nicely demonstrated by research that analyzed *chain migration* (a movement in which prospective migrants learn of opportunities, are provided with transportation, and have initial accommodation and employment arranged by means

TABLE 5.3   Mobility between 1975 and 1979 in the United States, by age of family head and family income and by education (percent distribution)

Age of Head, Family Income, and Education	Nonmovers	MOVERS All	Local Movers	Internal Migrants	Persons from Abroad
Age and family income					
Head under 25					
Less than $5,000	5.8	86.5	47.7	38.7	8.4
$5,000–$9,999	8.1	88.9	50.7	38.2	3.0
$10,000–$14,999	5.0	91.6	57.3	34.3	2.9
$15,000–$24,999	5.6	92.2	61.5	30.7	2.1
$25,000 or more	2.5	95.1	52.9	42.2	2.5
Head 25 to 34					
Less than $5,000	29.5	64.2	38.2	26.0	6.3
$5,000–$9,999	25.3	68.4	37.0	31.4	6.3
$10,000–$14,999	27.1	68.9	36.6	32.3	4.0
$15,000–$24,999	29.8	68.3	39.9	28.5	1.9
$25,000 or more	27.3	71.7	40.6	31.1	1.0
Head 35 to 44					
Less than $5,000	52.0	44.1	27.3	16.7	4.0
$5,000–$9,999	52.1	43.9	23.4	20.5	3.8
$10,000–$14,999	55.8	40.9	24.4	16.4	3.3
$15,000–$24,999	61.7	37.3	20.8	16.5	0.9
$25,000 or more	59.8	39.1	21.7	17.4	1.0
Head 45 to 54					
Less than $5,000	62.5	35.5	17.7	17.3	2.0
$5,000–$9,999	62.7	36.1	23.6	12.7	1.1
$10,000–$14,999	70.8	28.1	17.7	10.4	1.1
$15,000–$24,999	77.2	22.3	11.5	10.8	0.5
$25,000 or more	79.1	20.2	11.1	9.1	0.7
Education*					
None or elementary school	72.1	26.2	17.4	8.8	1.7
Some high school	61.6	37.6	24.3	13.4	0.8
High school grad.	58.7	40.0	24.0	16.0	1.3
Some college	52.2	46.1	23.9	22.2	1.7
College grad.	47.4	50.6	22.4	28.2	1.9
College postgrad.	49.2	48.3	21.0	27.2	2.6

Source: Based on U.S. Bureau of the Census, "Geographical Mobility: March 1975 to March 1979," *Current Population Reports,* Series P-20, no. 353 (Washington, D.C.: U.S. Government Printing Office, 1980), Tables 18 and 24, pp. 38–39, 47.

*Persons 18 and over.

of primary social relationships with previous migrants) as it related to Italian neighborhood formation in the United States.[46] There were three types of chain migration. First, some established immigrants who had achieved considerable status in the neighborhood helped male immigrants to get jobs in order to profit from them. They exploited the new immigrants directly or were paid a commission by American employers for providing labor. Second, new arrivals frequently went directly to the relatives and friends who had financed their passage and relied on them to find their first lodgings and employment. Such *serial migration* helped to ensure integration into the community. Third, there was *delayed family migration*. Typically, males preceded their wives and children, or prospective brides, so that they might first provide an economic base for the family. Chain migration thus made possible both the movement of people and their particular location in a homogeneous ethnic neighborhood.

These patterns of cultural cohesion have been repeated with black migrants from the South to the North and with Hispanic immigrant groups in the United States. In the case of the blacks, northern cities of the United States provided magnets for southern blacks who had lived under deprived conditions. Despite the fact that those who did move to the North were generally better educated than the average, their educational and economic levels were relatively low for the new location. Real-estate speculators encouraged the development of areas such as Harlem in New York City by black in-migrants, and a black community, with churches, social clubs, civic centers, and residences, emerged. Each succeeding wave of black migrants found the black community a logical place of entry to the North, since relatives and institutions were there to provide for them.[47] In recent years, much the same phenomena have developed to accommodate waves of Hispanic immigrants to south Florida, southern California, and the New York metropolitan area.

Cultural-mobility patterns are also common in other countries. In the case of Canada, the higher rate of British-origin than French-origin interprovincial migration spotlights the residential segregation of these groups and the cultural barriers that inhibit assimilation.[48] The economic causes of migration in Yugoslavia were considerably confounded by ethnic factors. Among the many ethnic groups in the nation, their movement was frequently conditioned by the presence of their ethnic community at the migration destination.[49] In Africa, Asia, and Latin America as well, the large streams of rural-urban migrants are attracted to areas where they find members of their own ethnic groups.[50]

The ethnic linkages are strong when mobility takes place, but the fact remains that minority groups are less likely to be mobile overall than is the majority group. A dominant reason is socioeconomic, since most minority groups have fewer resources and means for moving. Where such groups have relatively high mobility rates, such as within cities, it is often traceable to their more precarious housing status and their job insecurity.[51] The moves that take place are generally short-distance ones, which place them in affordable housing and greater proximity to work opportunities.

Government

We have already pointed out that governments have played a crucial medial role in bringing about sharp mortality declines in countries throughout the world, and they have played a lesser role, as much to impede as to facilitate, in fertility reductions. Government intervention regarding mobility is more diffuse and varies by type of movement. Governments have been most concerned about affecting crossings of their national borders, but some governments have also engaged in direct and indirect activities that influence mobility.

In considering appropriate policies on immigration, governments may specify the number of people who can be admitted, their areas of origin, and their characteristics. United States immigration practice has shifted over the years in this regard. In the earliest years, essentially unlimited migration prevailed, although restrictions were imposed on paupers, criminals, prostitutes, and other stigmatized persons. The familiar quota system was introduced in 1921 with the stipulation that immigration from European countries be limited to 3 percent of the number of foreign-born of each nationality resident in the United States in 1910. A revision of the law in 1924 reduced the quota to 2 percent and based the distribution of nationalities on the 1890 census. The aim of many in Congress was to further limit the numbers coming from the countries of southern and eastern Europe, whom they considered undesirable and who had migrated in large numbers after 1890. The change in the law succeeded in reducing the percent of immigrants from southern and eastern Europe from 45 to 12. The Immigration and Nationality Act of 1952 maintained the national-origins quota system but changed some of its features. For example, a preference system was introduced that gave first priority, within the quotas, to highly skilled immigrants and their families. Families of United States residents were next in order of priority. The Immigration Act of 1965, which was first implemented in 1968, abolished the national-origins quota system, continued a numerical ceiling on immigration (including that from the Western Hemisphere, which had been exempt earlier), changed the preference system to give greater priority to family relationships as a basis for selecting immigrants, and required employment clearances to ensure that a demand existed for a potential immigrant's skills. As a consequence of the latter act, a significant change in the origin of immigrants took place, so that southern European, Asian, and Caribbean immigrants made up a larger proportion of immigrants than previously.

Although internal migration in the United States has generally been a matter of individuals and families freely moving to where they prefer to live, governments have become more concerned with mobility patterns and have begun to exert controls on some types of movement. Thus, in an effort to restructure cities, urban-renewal programs have relocated large numbers of people from one part of a city to another. Public housing has provided mobility opportunities for some classes of the population, while excluding others. Changing levels of public-sector employment alter incentives for moving to new areas. Added to these factors affecting local mobility are government policies regulating interstate movements. Some states and counties are now passing legislation to monitor the flow of persons across their borders. Concern about the environment, energy use, and diminution of space and privacy have led many citizens to support such restrictions. A national survey conducted by the Commission on Population Growth and the American Future in 1971 shows that half of those questioned favored government action designed to slow the growth of large metropolitan areas.[52] Some states have set up growth-policies boards to shape legislation that will bring about a desirable population distribution. It is apparent that attention to matters of distribution and migration of people will increase as preoccupation with population size is moderated.

Governments may attempt to move people in order to achieve a better balance of population and resources. This may take the form of forced migration (such as the displacement of political prisoners to work camps)[53] or of impelled migration (such as the transmigration project in Indonesia, in which the government provides incentives for people to move from highly populated Java to the Outer Islands).[54] Moves are also made when military forces are redeployed by a country from one base to another or are sent into combat. Civilian employees of a government likewise can be reassigned from one location to another because of administrative or functional needs.

Micro Variables

As broad societal changes take place and various group structures and processes provide both guidance and pressures for action, the individual is engaged in a decision-making process that leads to mobility or nonmobility. Many of the decisions that are made are not entirely voluntary, in the sense that being imprisoned, evicted from a home, or ordered into military service prevents the people involved from acting in an independent fashion. Similarly, a rational decision on the part of an individual as to whether or not to move may be tempered by the desires of family members and friends who impose constraints on the final outcome or by the individual's physical condition at the time. However, the decision about whether, when, and where to move are typically made by an individual in the context of these other forces.

This decision process has been examined in a variety of different frameworks. We have grouped the major approaches into three categories—microeconomic, family-locational, and social psychological.

Microeconomic Approach

This basic approach uses the familiar economic cost-benefit framework, in which mobility takes place only when the individual expects to be better off by doing so. Disadvantages of moving include "out-of-pocket" expenses such as transportation and shipping of goods; "opportunity" costs, such as loss of earnings during the moving process; the greater expense of new housing; and the psychic pain of leaving friends and neighborhoods. Benefits may include a better job and a more congenial environment. The decision-maker considers the expected net benefits and costs of moving to each potential destination and chooses to move, if at all, to the one where expected benefits most exceed expected costs.[55]

Since greater attention is given to economic than noneconomic variables in this approach, the empirical studies based on it have contributed most in the area of economic participation and rewards. For example, the nature and length of a wife's employment carries a good deal of weight when a couple is deciding whether and where to move. So does the difference between expected real income at points of origin and destination, the extent of location-specific capital (for example, home ownerships with a favorable mortgage rate), and information about a prospective area of destination. *Return migration* (moving back to one's earlier general location) is quite frequent, because expectations about the place are generally more realistic and knowledge greater than for other areas not visited or studied.[56]

Family-Locational Approaches

Microeconomic analysts focus on the actual behavior of individuals. A decision by married couples or families is based on a joint calculus, which uses the same essential cost-benefit framework applied to individuals. Although family factors are recognized as important, the noneconomic family aspects of decision making are not dealt with directly.

William Kenkel has conceptualized the moving-decision process for families in terms of several steps: (1) some circumstance or event raises the possibility of moving; (2) the family engages in a discussion in which the advantages and disadvantages of moving are elaborated; (3) a determination about moving is made, first by each family member and then by the family as a group; (4) if the decision is to move, the family selects the date, time, and location of movement.[57] Clearly, mobility decisions are not always made in such a logical fashion. Heads of families may decide about moving themselves and notify the family only after commitments have been made. Conflicts among family members may keep a group decision from being reached. Or the calculation of pros and cons of a move may be imperfect; that is, done without knowledge of some of the relevant information. Moreover, those who simply desire to move may create their own opportunities. Other family structures and functions affect moving decisions as well.[58]

Since jobs and housing are principal items for consideration in moving decisions, they are the concerns about which family discussions most often take place. The relative satisfaction or dissatisfaction with jobs or home locations leads to examination of alternatives. Some imperfect cost-benefit calculation may be involved, and economic considerations are merged with emotional ones. Alden Speare found residential satisfaction to be a critical factor in mobility decisions.[59] As long as people are satisfied with their living quarters, it is not very likely that a move will be seriously contemplated or take place.

Location has also been viewed in a broader perspective. *Place utility* refers to an individual's or family's overall level of satisfaction or dissatisfaction with respect to a given location.[60] When the place utility of one's present location falls below some threshold, another location with greater place utility may be substituted for it. Knowledge of alternatives is crucial in this framework. Thus the cognitive or "mental map" of an area is the perception or awareness of its net benefits. Candidates for new locations can then be selected for further investigation as desirable living places.

Social-Psychological Approach

Because the mobility decision involves thought processes, various social-psychological mechanisms have been cited as important elements. Mobility decisions are rarely snap judgments, although intense dissatisfaction with a place may at times lead to an impulsive decision. In fact, most moving decisions are weighed for a considerable period of time, during which comparisons and evaluations are being made that call into play several psychological concepts.

One set of factors relates to personality traits, such as willingness to take risks, feelings of being in control of situations, and adaptability

TABLE 5.4 Summary of major motives related to migration from the empirical and theoretical literature

| Major Motive for Migration | Direction of Relationship with Decision to Move | ESTIMATED STRENGTH OF MOTIVE | | | Potential Migrant Groups Most Affected |
| | | Developing Nations | Developed Nations | | |
			Long-distance Moves	Short-distance Moves	
Economic motive	positive	strong	strong	weak	working ages, males
Social mobility/social status motive	positive	moderate	moderate to weak	weak	young adults, lower and middle SES, some families with children
Residential satisfaction motive	positive (with level of dissatisfaction at area of origin)	weak	moderate	strong	young families, renters
Motive to maintain community-based social and economic ties	negative	strong	moderate	moderate	middle and older ages, clientele and capital-intensive occupational groups
Family and friends affiliation motive	positive	strong	moderate	moderate to weak	women; occupational groups not in national labor market; young adults
Motive of attaining life-style preferences	positive	weak	weak but increasing	moderate to weak	retired, higher SES

Source: Gordon F. DeJong and James T. Fawcett, "Motivations for Migration: An Assessment and a Value-Expectancy Research Model", in *Migration Decision Making,* ed. Gordon F. DeJong and Robert W. Gardner (Elmsford, N.Y.: Pergamon Press, 1981), p. 40.

to change. People who have such traits are seen as more likely to hold values and have expectations that favor geographic mobility. Basic values or goals that might be maximized as a result of a mobility decision are wealth, status, comfort, stimulation, autonomy, affiliation, and survival. These can be associated with major motives for moving, such as income maximization, social mobility and social-status aspirations, residential satisfactions, influences of family and friends on attainment of life-style preferences, and maintaining community-based social and economic ties.[61] This motivational structure, as conditioned by personality and value orientations, has been shown to correlate with the decision to move, particularly for certain groups and situations. These relationships are summarized in Table 5.4.

People's mental set and the psychological processes involved in mobility decision-making are micro-level factors that are shaped by the macro and medial forces in the world around them. Societal conditions, socialization forms, localized situational factors, and the uniqueness of the individual combine to produce mobility (or nonmobility) outcomes that determine where someone will be located at a future point in time.

FUTURE MOBILITY PROSPECTS

Those responsible for making population projections for states and local areas are faced with the difficulty of estimating future population mobility patterns as one component of population change. Traditionally mobility is assumed to follow some past trend. For some periods of time and for some areas, this assumption of continuing past patterns of movement is valid; however, often it is not, and causes many inaccurate population projections for small areas. Better data sources are essential if estimates and projections are to be improved as guides for planning and programs.

The volume of immigration has been generally predictable in most countries because of government controls. Emigration has been less predictable, but levels have been fairly stable. Within nations, the movements of people are much too varied to be estimated accurately from past trends. As more surveys are taken that delve into people's desires and expectations concerning mobility, and as data are collected regularly regarding changing employment opportunities, housing development, and government actions in regard to residential location and mobility, we will have a basis for better predictive models of migratory behavior.

In the absence of such systematic information, we can only speculate about future mobility patterns for specific areas. It is safe to say, nevertheless, that mobility will become an even more important component of population change in the future than it has been in the past, owing to an increasing balance of births and deaths and further development and facility of modes of travel and relocation.

However, large-scale movements, especially those involving clandestine border-crossings and refugee displacements, can be expected as political activities make living arrangements untenable for large groups of people throughout the world. Likewise, social and economic changes will result in altered incentives and disincentives for moving at local and regional levels, particularly in developing nations. Mobility is likely to affect more sizable percentages of the population than in the past, and thus become a more focused area of population study.

NOTES

1. Calvin Goldscheider, *Population, Modernization, and Social Structure* (Boston: Little, Brown, 1971), pp. 48–50.

2. W. S. Woytinsky and E. S. Woytinsky, *World Population and Production* (New York, Twentieth Century Fund, 1953), pp. 67–83. Also see Kingsley Davis, "The Migrations of Human Populations," *Scientific American*, 231, no. 3 (September 1974), 92–105.

3. "International Migration," in *The Determinants and Consequences of Population Trends*, vol. 1, (New York: United Nations, 1973), pp. 225–261.

4. Ian M. Hume, "Migrant Workers in Europe," *Finance and Development*, 10, no. 1 (March 1973), 2–6; Leon F. Bouvier, Henry S. Shryock, and Harry W. Henderson, "International Migration: Yesterday, Today, and Tomorrow," *Population Bulletin*, 32, no. 4 (September 1977), 11–13.

5. Charles B. Keely, "Illegal Migration," *Scientific American*, 246, no. 3 (March 1982), 41–47.

6. Robert Warren and Jennifer Marks Peck, "Foreign-Born Emigration from the United States: 1960 to 1970," *Demography*, 17, no. 1 (February 1980), 71–81.

7. Arnold Schrier, *Ireland and the American Emigration, 1850–1900* (Minneapolis: University of Minnesota Press, 1958), p. 3.

8. Julius Isaac, *Economics of Migration* (New York: Oxford University Press, 1947), p. 143.

9. Conrad Taeuber and Irene B. Taeuber, *The Changing Population of the United States* (New York: John Wiley, 1958), pp. 48–52.

10. The lack of adequate annual statistics on illegal immigration makes this statement quite speculative, but most estimates place the figure at or above the level of legal immigration.

11. Judah Matras, *Social Changes in Israel* (Chicago: Aldine, 1965), pp. 22–29.

12. Moshe Sicron, *Immigration to Israel, 1948–1953,* vol. 11 (Jerusalem: State of Israel Statistical Supplement, 1957), Tables A2–A3.

13. Matras, *Social Changes,* pp. 32–38.

14. Larry H. Long and Celia G. Boertlein, "The Geographical Mobility of Americans: An International Comparison," *Current Population Reports,* Series P-23, no. 64, (Washington, D.C.: U.S. Government Printing Office, 1976), p. 20.

15. U.S. Bureau of the Census, "Geographical Mobility: March 1975 to March 1979," *Current Population Reports,* Series P-20, no. 353 (Washington, D.C.: U.S. Government Printing Office, 1980), p. 10.

16. Patrick O. Ohadike and Habtemariam Tesfaghiorghis, *The Population of Zambia* (Paris: Committee for International Cooperation in National Research in Demography, 1974), p. 73.

17. Goldscheider, *Population,* pp. 215–217; Wilbur Zelinsky, "The Hypothesis of the Mobility Transition," *Geographical Review,* 61 (1971), 219–249.

18. U.S. Bureau of the Census, "The Journey to Work in the United States: 1975," *Current Population Reports,* Series P-23, no. 99, (Washington, D.C.: U.S. Government Printing Office, 1979), pp. 4–8.

19. David F. Sly, "Tourism's Role in Migration to Florida: Basic Tourist-Migration Relationship," Florida State University, *Governmental Research Bulletin,* 2, no. 4 (December 1974), 2.

20. In fact, the age curve for all three processes may vary depending on the geographic area and characteristics of those involved. One needs to distinguish, however, between the age distribution of a particular set of movers and the propensity to move at a given age. We are concerned here with the latter.

21. Long and Boertlein, "Geographical Mobility," p. 13.

22. Ibid., pp. 14–15.

23. U.S. Bureau of the Census, "Geographic Mobility: March 1975 to March 1979," *Current Population Reports,* Series P-20, no. 353 (Washington, D.C.: U.S. Government Printing Office, 1980), p. 14.

24. Larry H. Long, "New Estimates of Migration Expectancy in the United States," *Journal of the American Statistical Association,* 68 (March 1973), 37.

25. E. G. Ravenstein, "The Laws of Migration," *Journal of the Royal Statistical Society,* 48 (June 1885), 167–235, and 52 (June 1889), 241–305.

26. Leading exponents of this approach were John Q. Stewart, "A Measure of the Influence of Population at a Distance," *Sociometry,* 5 (February 1942), 63–71; and G. K. Zipf, "The P_1P_2/D Hypothesis: On the Intercity Movement of Persons," *American Sociological Review,* 11 (December 1946), 677–685.

27. Samuel A. Stouffer, "Intervening Opportunities: A Theory Relating Mobility and Distance," *American Sociological Review,* 5 (December 1940), 845–867.

28. Samuel A. Stouffer, "Intervening Opportunities and Competing Migrants," *Journal of Regional Science,* 2 (Spring 1960), 1–26.

29. Everett S. Lee, "A Theory of Migration," *Demography,* 3, no. 1 (1966), 47–57.

30. William Petersen, "A General Typology of Migration," *American Sociological Review,* 23 (June 1958), 256–266.

31.   Amos H. Hawley, *Human Ecology* (New York: The Ronald Press, 1950); David F. Sly, "Migration and the Ecological Complex," *American Sociological Review*, 37, no. 5 (October 1972), 615–628.

32.   Joseph J. Spengler and George C. Myers, "Migration and Socioeconomic Development: Today and Yesterday," in *Internal Migration: A Comparative Perspective*, ed. Alan A. Brown and Egon Neuberger (New York: Academic Press, 1977), pp. 14–15.

33.   Brinley Thomas, "International Migration," in *The Study of Population*, ed. Philip M. Hauser and Otis Dudley Duncan (Chicago: University of Chicago Press, 1959), p. 531.

34.   Ibid., pp. 526–527.

35.   United Nations, *The Determinants and Consequences of Population Trends* (New York: United Nations, 1953), p. 123.

36.   Alan Simmons, Sergio Diaz-Briquets, and Aprodicio A. Laquian, *Social Change and Internal Migration: A Review of Research Findings from Africa, Asia, and Latin America* (Ottawa: International Development Research Centre, 1977), p. 10.

37.   Goldscheider, *Population*, pp. 182–220; Wilbur Zelinsky, "The Hypothesis of the Mobility Transition," *Geographical Review*, 61 (1971), 219–249.

38.   Kingsley Davis, *The Population of India and Pakistan* (Princeton: Princeton University Press, 1951), pp. 111–112.

39.   Gerald R. Leslie and Arthur H. Richardson, "Life-Cycle, Career Pattern and the Decision to Move," *American Sociological Review*, 26 (December 1961), 894–902; Felix M. Berardo, "Kinship Interaction and Communications Among Space-Age Migrants," *Journal of Marriage and the Family*, 29 (August 1967), 541–554.

40.   A more recent study of interstate migration suggests that reasons for longer-distance movement have not changed with time. See Larry H. Long, "Reasons for Interstate Migration," *Current Population Reports*, Series P-23, no. 81 (Washington, D.C.: U.S. Government Printing Office, 1979), p. 6.

41.   P. Neal Ritchey, "Explanations of Migration," *Annual Review of Sociology*, 2 (1976), 389–393.

42.   R. Paul Shaw, *Migration Theory and Fact* (Philadelphia: Regional Science Research Institute, 1975), p. 24.

43.   Larry H. Long, "Migration Differentials by Education and Occupation: Trends and Variations," *Demography*, 10 (May 1973), 248.

44.   Jack Ladinsky, "Occupational Determinants of Geographic Mobility Among Professional Workers," *American Sociological Review*, 32 (April 1967), 253–264.

45.   Simmons et al., *Social Change*, pp. 21–24, 48–52, 78–79; Michael P. Todaro, *Internal Migration in Developing Countries* (Geneva: International Labor Office, 1976).

46.   John S. Macdonald and Beatrice D. Macdonald, "Chain Migration: Ethnic Neighborhood Formation and Social Networks," *Milbank Memorial Fund Quarterly*, 42 (January 1964), 82–97.

47.   Stanley Lieberson, "A Reconsideration of the Income Differences Found Between Migrants and Northern-born Blacks," *American Journal of Sociology*,

83, no. 4 (January 1978), 940–966; Louis H. Masotti, Jeffrey R. Hadden, Kenneth F. Seminatore, and Jerome R. Corsi, *A Time to Burn?* (Chicago: Rand McNally, 1969), p. 80.

48. Shaw, *Migration Theory*, p. 32.

49. Oli Hawrylyshyn, "Ethnicity as a Barrier to Migration in Yugoslavia: The Evidence from Interregional Flows and Immigration to Belgrade," in *Internal Migration: A Comparative Perspective*, ed. Alan A. Brown and Egon Neuberger (New York: Academic Press, 1977), pp. 379–399.

50. Simmons et al., *Social Change*, pp. 29, 57–58, 88.

51. Ronald J. McAllister, Edward J. Kaiser, and Edgar W. Butler, "Residential Mobility of Blacks and Whites: A National Longitudinal Survey," *American Journal of Sociology*, 77 (November 1971), 452–453.

52. Sara Mills Maizie and Steve Rawlings, "Public Attitude Towards Population Distribution Issues," in ed. Sara Mills Maizie, *Population Distribution and Policy*, vol. 5 of Research Reports of the U.S. Commission on Population Growth and the American Future. (Washington: U.S. Government Printing Office, 1972), p. 612.

53. Aleksandr Solzhenitsyn, *The Gulag Archipelago* (New York: Harper & Row, Pub., 1974).

54. Mayling Oey and Hananto Sigit, *Migration, Economic Development, and Population Growth: A Case Study of Transmigrants in Lampung, Indonesia* (Jakarta: University of Indonesia, 1977).

55. Julie DaVanzo, "Microeconomic Approaches to Studying Migration Decisions," in Gordon F. DeJong and Robert W. Gardner, *Migration Decision Making* (Elmsford, N.Y.: Pergamon Press, 1981), pp. 90–129; Jerome Rothenberg, "On the Microeconomics of Internal Migration," in *Internal Migration*, ed. Brown and Neuberger, pp. 183–205.

56. DaVanzo, "Microeconomic Approaches," pp. 114–119.

57. William F. Kenkel, "The Family Moving Decision Process," in *Family Mobility in Our Dynamic Society*, ed. Iowa State University Center for Agricultural and Economic Development (Ames, Iowa: Iowa State University Press, 1965), p. 180.

58. Sarah H. Harbison, "Family Structure and Family Strategy in Migration Decision-Making," in *Migration*, eds. DeJong and Gardner, pp. 225–251.

59. Alden Speare, Jr., "Residential Satisfaction as an Intervening Variable in Residential Mobility," *Demography*, 11 (May 1974), 173–188. Also see Peter H. Rossi, *Why Families Move*, (New York: Free Press, 1955); and Leslie and Richardson, "Decision to Move."

60. Lawrence A. Brown and E. G. Moore, "The Intra-Urban Migration Process: A Perspective," *Yearbook of the Society for General Systems Research*, 15 (1970), 109–122.

61. Gordon F. DeJong and James T. Fawcett, "Motivation for Migration: An Assessment and a Value-Expectancy Research Model," in *Migration*, eds. DeJong and Gardner, pp. 13–58.

SUGGESTED ADDITIONAL READINGS

Some recent overviews of the mobility process include:

GREENWOOD, MICHAEL J.,   "Research on Internal Migration in the United States: a Survey," *Journal of Economic Literature*, 13 (1975), 397–433.

RITCHEY, P. NEAL,   "Explanations of Migration," *Annual Review of Sociology*, 2 (1976), 363–404.

SHAW, R. PAUL,   *Migration Theory and Fact*. Philadelphia: Regional Science Research Institute, 1975.

Useful references on international migration are:

KEELY, CHARLES B.,   *U.S. Immigration: A Policy Analysis*. New York: The Population Council, 1979.

TAPINOS, GEORGES, ED.,   *International Migration*. Paris: Committee for International Coordination of National Research in Demography, 1974.

Comparative studies of internal migration can be found in:

BROWN, ALAN A., AND EGON NEUBERGER, EDS.,   *Internal Migration: A Comparative Perspective*. New York: Academic Press, 1977.

SIMMONS, ALAN, SERGIO DIAZ-BRIQUETS, AND APRODICIO A. LAQUIAN,   *Social Change and Internal Migration: A Review of Research Findings from Africa, Asia, and Latin America*. Ottawa: International Development Research Centre, 1977.

For a good summary of recent U.S. migration trends, see entire issue of:

BIGGAR, JEANNE C., "The Sunning of America: Migration to the Sunbelt," *Population Bulletin*, 34, no. 1 (March 1979).

The micro perspectives are well covered in:

DEJONG, GORDON F., AND ROBERT W. GARDNER, EDS.,   *Migration Decision Making; Multidisciplinary Approaches to Microlevel Studies in Developed and Developing Countries*. Elmsford, N.Y.: Pergamon Press, 1981.

TECHNICAL SUPPLEMENT NO. 5

Problems in Measuring Geographic Mobility

The conventional sources of demographic data do not lend themselves well to measuring geographic mobility. When we study mobility, we are usually interested in the frequency, direction, and distance of moves, and in the characteristics of movers, nonmovers, and the places they move to and from. Vital registration covers only births, deaths, marriages, and divorces. Censuses (and most surveys) necessarily limit the number of mobility-related questions, so that only limited types of information about population movement can result. A question may be asked about place of residence (city or county) at birth and/or at an intervening point in time, such as one year ago or five years ago. The analyst then can infer mobility from differences in residential locations at the different points in time. This provides, at best, a partial history of lifetime or recent migration, because the number and kinds of interim moves are excluded. In fact, a person with the same city of residence at two points in time may have moved several times within the city or even moved away from the city and back again before the time of the second inquiry.

Three demographic data sources offer possibilities for more extensive mobility information. The population register found in some countries (see Chapter 1) typically includes a record of each and every change of residence made in the country. A compilation of such data can lead to detailed descriptions of moves in terms of frequency, direction, and distance. Characteristics of movers are generally not well covered in population registers, and most countries lack such registers, so that other data sources must be sought. In some countries, certain administrative records include keeping track of residences and their changes (for instance, social security records). It is possible, therefore, to derive residential histories. But coverage is frequently limited in administrative records of this type, and up-to-date reporting of residential relocations is not regularly maintained. A social survey that focuses on geographic mobility but still measures population characteristics might encompass a lifetime or complete recent residential history, such that all of the desired information about mobility (frequency, direction, distance, and characteristics of people and places) can be obtained. These data are restricted only by problems of recall and by the survey sample size, which may not allow for analysis of mobility in specific areas.

Gathering such data on the flows of mobility permits us to derive measures of gross and net mobility (that is, the total movement and the excess movement in one stream as compared with a counterstream). Sometimes (as when our interest is in knowing the contribution of migration to an area's population growth or decline) a measure of net migration is sufficient. Demographers have devised a number of schemes for estimating such information. These include accounting for births and deaths in the population-balancing equation and deriving net migration as a residual, or monitoring, change in variables correlated with mobility (for instance, utilities connections or changes in school enrollments).

If mobility is indeed becoming a more and more crucial element of population change, it will be necessary to enlarge our sources of required data through further inquiries of these various kinds and by developing newer means of collecting relevant information.

ISSUES SUPPLEMENT NO. 5

Should Communities Control the Mobility of Their Citizens?

Historically, Americans have enjoyed the right to migrate anywhere in the country without any form of official sanction or intervention. Each citizen's right of access to the social, economic, and physical resources of the nation has been vested in the right to migrate and, for generations of migrants, geographical mobility has indeed meant upward social mobility. . . . But increasingly, the rights of migrants are being called into question by those who feel their rights are being impinged upon by migrants' traditionally unlimited access . . .

Cities and towns that have felt inundated by new settlers are now stubbornly challenging certain basic, heretofore inalienable, rights in actively seeking to regulate further increases in population. Recent years have seen a proliferation of local efforts to impose population ceilings. These have taken various forms: restricting the number of new dwelling units that can be built; making new residential construction contingent upon the provision of additional educational, sewage-disposal, and water-supply facilities; or simply legislating a maximum allowable population (without specifying the fate of the next arriving migrants). (Peter A. Morrison, *Migration and Rights of Access: New Public Concerns of the 1970's.* Santa Monica: The Rand Paper Series, The Rand Corporation, 1977, pp. 3–4, 11.)

How do you think this apparent conflict between the rights of migrants and the rights of community residents (or their governments) to control their demographic futures can be resolved?

CHAPTER SIX
POPULATION COMPOSITION AND DISTRIBUTION

Drawing by Phil Frank. Copyright © 1982 Creative Media Services, Berkeley, CA.

In the preceding five chapters we have reviewed the major trends and components of population change. We turn now to a discussion of the structural components of population that can serve as both causes and consequences of its change. These are the composition and distribution of the population.

POPULATION COMPOSITION

The composition of a population refers, as we have already stated, to the basic demographic characteristics by which the population may be divided or described. While there are many such characteristics we might consider, our discussion will be limited to those found to be most fundamental to population change—age, sex, and race or ethnic status.

In discussing fertility, mortality, and residential mobility, we noted that age, sex, and racial or ethnic status are important explanatory variables related to these major components of population change. Each of the components varies among older and younger populations, among men and women, and among whites and nonwhites. In this chapter we will discuss in more depth how the age composition of a population, for example, can affect its birth and death rates. Fertility, mortality, and residential mobility can, in turn, change the composition of populations within small areas or within a whole country. Selective residential mobility by age, sex, and race can change the population composition of a nation. These and other ways in which population composition can be a consequence of population change or an influence on it will be examined.

While we discuss population composition as both a cause and a consequence of population change, the way in which population composition and change are related is really more of a circular process. High birthrates, for example, may create a younger population, which in time may again contribute to high birthrates or low mortality rates. The intertwining of these factors makes population composition an important structural component to consider in studying the process of population change in any society.

Age-Sex Composition

The age and sex compositions of a population are two factors that seem to be important as both causes and consequences of population change. We will discuss them together, since various combinations of age and sex have special effects we might not notice, were we to study them separately.

Age-Sex Distribution as a Consequence of Population Change

Age-Sex Pyramids   One of the most useful devices for showing the past and present age-sex composition of the population is the age-sex pyramid. This device allows us to look at the percentage of the population in each age-sex category. Figure 6.1 shows these pyramids for the United States for 1900, 1940, 1960, and 1980. In the 1900 pyramid, for example, the bottom bar shows that males less than five years of age constituted 6.1 percent of the total population during that year, while females constituted 6.0 percent. If we compare the bars vertically, we are looking at the relative proportions of each age group in the population, while horizontal comparison allows us to see whether there were proportionally more males or females at each age.

Theoretically, age-sex pyramids are handy devices that allow us to compare the age-sex distribution of a population at a given time with the distribution at other times. In a population with constant birth and death rates and no migration, the figure should be a perfect pyramid, since usually there are fewer individuals surviving to each higher age level. The pyramid for the year 1900 illustrates this pattern very well. The bars on the graph for 1900 become progressively shorter at each higher level, although sometimes by uneven amounts. That is why, even though not all the drawings in Figure 6.1 actually look like pyramids, they have been so named.

By 1940, however, the age-sex pyramid for the United States had lost this theoretical shape and had a narrow base. This small base reflects the low birthrates prevailing during the 1930s. The 1940 age-sex distribution also shows the effect of a pronounced sex differential in mortality at the older ages. At age seventy-five and over, there are more females than males in the population. This effect of the sex differential in mortality did not appear in the 1900 pyramid.

The 1960 age-sex pyramid almost looks like two pyramids instead of one. The indentation that was noticeable at the bottom of the 1940 pyramid has advanced farther up the 1960 pyramid as the population aged. Those twenty to thirty years of age in the 1960 pyramid were the children born from 1930 to 1940, years of low birthrates. Also reflected in the 1960 pyramid are the years of the baby boom. The children under age fifteen in 1960 were born during this period. The effect of the sex differential in mortality is even more apparent in the 1960 pyramid. Females constitute a greater proportion of the population than males at every age after twenty-five.

This male-female difference would be even more pronounced if it were not for the number of surviving earlier immigrants to the United States, primarily over age sixty at the later date. Since immigration

FIGURE 6.1 Age-sex pyramids for the United States: 1900, 1940, 1960, and 1980

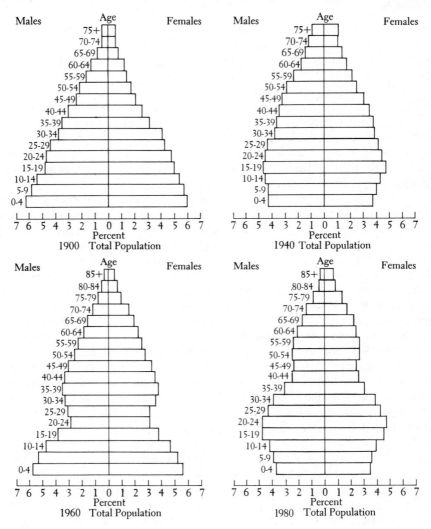

Source: Data are from U.S. Bureau of the Census, *U.S. Census of Population: 1960,* Final Report PC(1)-1B; *General Population Characteristics: U.S. Summary,* Washington, 1961, Table 47, p. 153. The 1980 pyramid is from U.S. Bureau of the Census, *1980 Census of Population,* Supplementary Reports Series P.C80-51-1.

during the first part of this century favored young males, there are currently more males at the older ages shown in the pyramids than there would have been without immigration.

Finally, the 1980 pyramid shows each of the things reflected in the 1960 pyramid advanced twenty years, but a change in the shape of the diagram has again taken place. Like the 1940 pyramid, the 1980 pyramid has an indented base because birthrates during the fifteen years before were lower than those during the twenty years that preceded that period. If birthrates continue to remain low, the 1990 age-sex pyramid will begin to look inverted.

Comparing the pyramids through this eighty-year period, another interesting phenomenon can be noted. The changing age composition results in a population that, as a whole, gets older during some periods and younger during others. A population is getting older when its average age rises and the proportion of older people increases. A population is getting younger when its average age declines and the proportion of younger people increases.

Examination of the sequence of age pyramids for the United States reveals continuing increases in the proportion of the population aged sixty-five and over. Also, as noted in Table 6.1, from 1900 to 1950 the median age of the population rose. By both of these criteria, the United States population was getting older during the first half of the twentieth century. Between 1950 and 1970, however, an apparent inconsistency in these criteria of aging can be noted. The percentage of the population at older ages continued to increase, while the median age declined. This anomaly was due to the fact that the decline in the birthrate in the

TABLE 6.1   Median age of the population by sex: United States, 1900–1980

Year	MEDIAN AGE IN YEARS		
	Total	Males	Females
1980	30.0	28.8	31.3
1970	28.1	26.8	29.3
1960	29.5	28.7	30.3
1950	30.2	29.9	30.5
1940	29.0	29.0	29.0
1930	26.4	26.7	26.2
1920	25.3	25.8	24.7
1910	24.1	24.6	23.5
1900	22.9	23.3	22.4

Source: U.S. Bureau of the Census, *Census of Population: 1970, General Population Characteristics,* Final Report PC(1)-B1, United States Summary, Table 53; and "Population Profile of the United States: 1980," *Current Population Reports,* Series P-20, no. 363, Table 4.

1960s and 1970s had reduced the relative numbers at the younger ages, yet the earlier birth cohorts were still below the middle age groups. Thus the population has been getting both younger and older during those decades. By 1980 the population median age had risen to thirty, a full seven years older than in 1900.

Similar trends in aging can be noted in many countries of the world (see Table 6.2). Projections of the populations of developed countries to the year 2000, for example, anticipate that the median age of the populations in these areas will rise to almost thirty-five. This can be contrasted with an anticipated median age of 23 in developing nations by the year 2000.

Another way to look at this phenomenon of aging in developed and developing countries is to examine the percentage of the total population that is under fifteen or over sixty-four years of age. In Table 6.2 it can be seen, for example, that while the percentage of the population over age sixty-four is less than 5 in each of the less-developed areas shown, that percentage is as high as 14 in Western Europe.

These differences in age composition between more- and less-developed countries can also be depicted for the present and the future by the use of age-sex pyramids, as seen in Figure 6.2. These pyramids display a startling contrast in the age structures of these populations

TABLE 6.2 Summary measures of age composition for selected developed and developing regions and countries

	MEDIAN AGE		PERCENT OF TOTAL POPULATION	
	1975	2000	Under 15 Years	65 Years and Over
More-developed areas	30.3	34.9	24	11
Japan	30.5	36.6	24	8
USSR	28.9	33.0	26	9
United States	28.8	36.0	22	11
Western Europe	33.1	34.4	22	14
Eastern Europe	30.9	34.4	23	12
Less-developed areas	19.1	23.2	39	4
Bangladesh	16.8	18.8	43	3
Nigeria	17.4	17.2	47	2
Mexico	16.2	19.4	42	4
Latin America	18.5	21.1	40	4
Africa	17.8	18.5	45	3

Source: Data on median age from U.S. Bureau of the Census, "Illustrative Projections of World Populations to the 21st Century," *Current Population Reports,* Series P-23, no. 79 (January 1979), Table E.; other figures from *1981 World Population Data Sheet* (Washington, D.C.: Population Reference Bureau, 1981).

FIGURE 6.2 **Age-sex composition of more-developed and less-developed regions, 1975 and 2000**

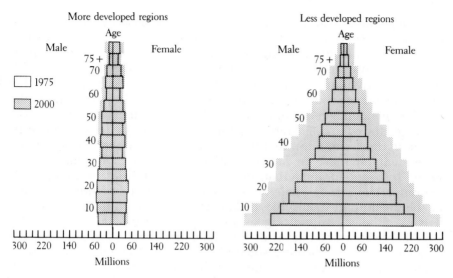

Source: U.S. Bureau of the Census, "Illustrative Projections of World Populations to the 21st Century," Current Population Reports, Series P-23, no. 79 (January 1979), Figure E.

both now and in the future, one that has implications for many societal processes and possibilities. In developing nations, the momentum for future population growth is substantial, since, between 1975 and 2000, the increase in children under five years of age will exceed the total number of living children at these ages in developed countries.

The greater proportion of older people and the higher average age in developed than in developing countries is principally due to the long-term decline in fertility. Lower birthrates mean relatively smaller numbers of people at the younger ages, with the reciprocal effect of relatively larger numbers at the older ages. One would also expect mortality reductions to contribute to the aging of a population. In fact, lengthening of life does add to the older segment of the population more people who would not otherwise have survived, but mortality reductions are usually even greater during infancy and childhood than at older ages. Consequently it is typical of societies proceeding through the demographic transition that mortality control will lead to even younger populations. In any event, in shaping the age structure, changes in fertility over time are more important than changes in mortality. Selective age patterns of migration can also affect age composition, but historically they have had a rather small impact except in a few countries for short periods of time when immigration or emigration was very heavy.

Dependency Ratios Another way of looking at the age composition of a population is in terms of the *dependency ratio.* Dependency ratios are calculated by taking the ratio of the number of persons under fifteen and over sixty-four years of age to the number of persons aged fifteen to sixty-four, multiplied by 100. *Aged dependency* refers to the ratio of just those sixty-five and over to those fifteen to sixty-four, while *youth dependency* refers to the ratio of just those under fifteen to those fifteen to sixty-four. The term dependency is perhaps unfortunate. It is based on the assumption that those under fifteen or over sixty-four are dependent on those in between for economic or other sustenance. While some might argue that this is a reasonable rule of thumb, there are numerous cases of people between fifteen and sixty-four who are unable to support themselves. Likewise, many individuals over sixty-five are quite self-supporting, as are some under fifteen.

These shortcomings aside, the dependency ratio is another shorthand method of indicating something important about the age composition of the population. Table 6.3 shows these ratios for the United States from 1900 until the present. The youth dependency ratio in the United States moved steadily downward from 1900 until the decade 1940 to 1950, when it increased. High birthrates during this period created a rise in the youth dependency ratio that continued until the years 1960 to 1970, when it began to decrease again.

TABLE 6.3 Dependency ratios in the United States, 1900–1980

Year	Total	Youth	Aged
1980	51.4	34.3	17.1
1970	62.2	46.2	16.0
1960	67.6	52.1	15.5
1950	53.9	41.4	12.5
1940	46.8	36.8	10.0
1930	53.4	45.1	8.3
1920	57.5	50.2	7.3
1910	57.3	50.5	6.8
1900	62.6	56.0	6.6

Source: U.S. Bureau of the Census, *Census of Population: 1970, General Population Characteristics,* Final Report PC(1)-B1, United States Summary, Table 53; and "Population Profile of the United States: 1980," *Current Population Reports,* Series P-20, no. 363, Table 5.

The youth dependency ratio is defined as the ratio of population under fifteen to that fifteen to sixty-four years old. The aged dependency ratio is defined as the ratio of population sixty-five and over to that fifteen to sixty-four years old. The total dependency ratio is the sum of the youth and aged dependency ratios.

The aged dependency ratio, conversely, has been steadily rising throughout this century. This reflects the aging population already discussed. The rise in the proportion of aged persons in the population was quite small, however, between 1960 and 1980. This small increment is partly a reflection of the leveling off of mortality rates during these decades.

Sex Ratios   Sex ratios are another summarizing device for looking at the sex composition of a population. A *sex ratio* is the number of males per 100 females in the population. A sex ratio greater than 100 thus indicates more males than females, while a sex ratio of less than 100 indicates fewer males than females.

In the United States, the sex ratio at birth is on the order of 105 males to 100 females. There are differences among subgroups of the population; for example, the sex ratio is about 106 for whites and 103 for blacks. Research on fetal deaths indicates that many more male than female fetuses die; therefore, the sex ratio prior to birth is even larger than that found at birth.

Table 6.4 shows the sex ratio of the United States population in

TABLE 6.4   Sex ratios for the United States population, 1900 to 1970, and by age for 1980

Date and Age	Sex Ratio
1980 total	94
0–4 years	105
5–14 years	104
15–24 years	102
25–34 years	98
35–44 years	96
45–54 years	93
55–64 years	88
65–74 years	76
75+ years	55
1970	95
1960	97
1950	99
1940	101
1930	103
1920	104
1910	106
1900	105

Source: U.S. Bureau of the Census, *Census of Population: 1970, General Population Characteristics,* Final Report PC(1)-B1, United States Summary, Table 53; and "Population Profile of the United States: 1980," *Current Population Reports,* Series P-20, no. 363, Table 4.

1980 by age and the overall ratio at ten-year intervals between 1900 and 1980. At the youngest ages, the number of males exceeds the number of females by 5 per 100. By ages fifteen to twenty-four, however, the sex ratio has dropped to 102 and continues downward to about 55 at ages seventy-five and over. The effect of the sex differential in mortality on the sex composition of the population can be clearly seen in these figures. Table 6.4 also indicates that the sex ratio in the total population has been dropping since about 1910. As we noted in our discussion of differential mortality, the overall sex differential in death rates did not appear until about that time, but it has been increasing ever since.

A population component other than mortality has also played a role in determining the sex ratio. Prior to 1920, and before the cessation of massive immigration to the United States, the sex composition of the population was being affected by the selectivity in this migration. These migrants tended to be young, and about 60 percent of them were male.[1] The sex ratio of immigrants to the United States has become more balanced in recent years. Since 1920, with a great reduction in the numbers of migrants received each year, this component has played less of a role in changing the age-sex composition of the population.

Age-Sex Distribution as a Cause of Population Change

We have been discussing some of the ways in which change in the population components of fertility, mortality, and residential mobility can change the age and sex composition of the population. We turn now to some of the ways in which the age-sex composition of the population can have a direct impact on these components of population change.

Fertility   In 1969 and 1970, the rising birthrate was a good example of how changing age-sex composition can affect fertility. As those born during the baby boom in the United States reached prime childbearing years, the birthrate rose slightly, resulting in a temporary departure from the recent trend.[2] Increased numbers of women of childbearing age in the population can cause such a rise in the birthrate, but that factor alone may be more than compensated for by other factors, as was true of the birthrate trends after 1970.

Failure to take into account the changing age structure of a population can cause very misleading interpretations of changing birthrates. In Hong Kong in the 1960s, for example, the crude birthrate fell from 35.5 to 28.8 in four years.[3] This startling decline was due almost entirely to changes in the age structure of the population, which left a smaller proportion of persons at reproductive ages, and not to real changes in fertility rates at each age level. Had this factor not been taken into account, demographers might have sought as explanations for the decreased fertility, changing ideals, business-cycle changes, or some of the myriad other factors discussed earlier that might cause fluctuations in fertility rates.

Future Growth   The irregular age structures of populations also have an impact on future growth potential. In the United States, for example, even if women restrict themselves to an average of two children each (approximately the level of replacement), it will take about seventy years for the nation's population size to level off. The reason for this phenomenon is that the number of females reaching reproductive age will vary over time. During some periods, the proportions of women of reproductive age will be unusually large (for example, when the baby-boom cohorts reach that age), and if each woman has two children, the total number of births will be relatively high. As a result, the population growth rate will fluctuate, being moderate at some times and higher at others. After a number of decades (about seven), the constant number of births per woman will lead to greater stabilization of the age structure.

Marriage Patterns   Another less direct, but still important, way in which age-sex composition can affect birthrates is through changes in the number of men and women available to marry during a given period. Since women in the United States traditionally marry men somewhat older than themselves, a fluctuating birthrate can produce what demographers call a *marriage squeeze.* Since there were many more females born in 1946, for example, than there were males born in 1944, when those children reached marriageable age, in the 1960s, there was a shortage of marriage partners for that cohort of women.[4] These women must then marry men their age or younger, or men considerably older, or remain unmarried. While these temporary imbalances in the sex ratios of potential marriage partners do not seem to produce long-term changes in marriage patterns, and hence in fertility rates, they are important on a short-term basis.

Like fluctuating birthrates, deaths of young males in wartime may also produce a marriage squeeze. An example of a country with an historic imbalance resulting from this effect is East Germany. In 1965 the sex ratio at ages twenty to forty-nine in this country was 85, as a result of very high losses of males during the two world wars.[5]

Mortality   The age-sex composition of a population can also have a direct influence on its mortality rate. Since death rates usually increase at each older age after the first thirteen or so years of life, older populations will tend to have higher death rates than younger ones.

TABLE 6.5   Percent of population over 65, 1979, and crude death rates for selected states, 1978

State	Percent Aged 65 and Over (1979)	Crude Death Rate (1978)
Alaska	4.1	2.6
Hawaii	5.1	7.7
Utah	6.0	7.7
Arizona	8.1	11.8
Arkansas	10.1	13.7
Florida	11.0	18.1

Source: *1981 United States Population Data Sheet,* (Washington, D.C.: Population Reference Bureau, 1981).

This effect of age composition on the death rate can be seen clearly in Table 6.5. In the six states shown, the death rate varied consistently with the percentage of the population over sixty-five. Looking at just the crude death rates, without knowing the age composition of these states, we might be led to hypothesize that Alaska has a healthier environment than does Florida, a hypothesis that does not have much intuitive appeal and is not consistent with comparisons of death rates at each age. We might also hypothesize, when looking at just the death rates, that Alaska has better medical-care facilities than Florida, and so on. While age is certainly not the only factor that explains the differences in death rates appearing in Table 6.5, it is one of the most important.

International differences in death rates can also be attributed partly to differing age compositions of populations. A few areas in 1981 had death rates as low as 4 per 1,000.[6] Fiji and Brunei (in Southeast Asia) are examples of such areas. These areas also had a very large percentage of their population under fifteen years of age.

Failure to take into account the age-sex composition of the population might also lead to errors in explaining cause-of-death patterns. Some causes of death are more characteristic of one age group than another. An older population might show higher rates of death due to heart disease, while younger populations might show higher rates of death due to accidents.

Migration   Since migration also shows selectivity by age and sex, the changing age-sex composition of a population might affect residential mobility rates. Interstate migration, for example, is more frequent among the young, with the peak rate occurring at age twenty-three.[7]

Populations that are younger will therefore have greater potential for mobility.

Future Changes in Age-Sex Composition

Determination of the future age-sex composition of the population is, of course, a complex matter. We have a reliable basis for estimating the older segments of the population (which are already born), but we have a less reliable basis for estimating the younger ones (especially those not yet born).

In making projections of the population by age and sex for the United States and other countries, the Bureau of the Census often combines different estimates of future births, deaths, and migration to arrive at population counts for given years. In a recent set of projections of this kind, the census estimated that if every 1,000 women in the United States had an average number of births of 4,866 in the years 1995 to 2000, the number of children below age five would be 24 million. On the other hand, if the average number of births per 1,000 women was only 2,816, the number under age five would only be 14 million.[8] A similar contrast between high and low total fertility rates of 4.7 and 3.0 in Mexico in the year 2000 would change the percentage of the population under age fifteen from 33 to 30.[9]

The changes in sex ratios of the populations of developed countries are not expected to be great. However, if birthrates become lower, the sex ratio is also likely to be lower, since decreasing birthrates mean an older population. We have already noted how much lower the sex ratio is among older than younger persons in the United States and other developed nations. The pattern of lower sex ratios at older ages may be modified further in the future, depending upon the extent to which mortality differences between the sexes change and the volume and selectivity by sex of immigrants is altered.

Racial-Ethnic Composition

The racial-ethnic composition of a population is another important variable in some countries as both a cause and a consequence of demographic change. Racial-ethnic composition encompasses several different variables. For example, the *color* or *race* of persons in the United States, as measured by the Census Bureau (on which we are dependent for most of our data), is not based on biological classifications. Rather, the racial categories used in the census are a combination of color and nationality. Thus, census data may include information on the following racial groups: white, Negro or black, American Indian, Japanese, Chinese, Filipino, and several groups in the "all other" category such as Malayans, Polynesians, and Koreans. Obviously some of these are nationality groups. The tabulations by race, therefore, reflect social convention as to what constitutes separate racial groups more than they do biological characteristics. Further, since recent census data are gathered principally by self-enumeration, they reflect the racial grouping that people recognize for themselves.

Ethnic origin of the population, on the other hand, has traditionally been determined by looking at data on place of birth, country of origin, language spoken, surname, and the like. More recently the Census Bureau has been reporting data on the ethnic origin of the population based on self-report. The ethnic-origin classifications are based, by and large, on nationality. Because it now includes one in every sixteen Americans, the category "Spanish origin" is often included in official government tabulations on ethnic origin.

Another census variable that is useful in analyzing racial-ethnic composition is *nativity*. Nativity indicates the place where the person was born and is generally differentiated by the categories "foreign-born" and "native." Included as native in the United States are all those born in the United States, Puerto Rico, and outlying areas of the United States, and persons not reporting their country of birth.

Racial-Ethnic Composition as a Consequence of Population Change

A recent ambitious analysis has attempted to describe changes in the racial composition of the world population during the last two decades.[10] The analysis is ambitious because of the scarcity and inaccuracy of data available to make such estimates and the continuing controversies over how to classify peoples. Nevertheless, the results are interesting, because they provide some global perspective on the racial/ethnic composition of the population and how it has changed.

Table 6.6 indicates that the percentage of the world's population in each racial group has increased, since population has grown steadily. However, it is also clear from these estimates that the racial groups are not increasing at even rates. For example, from 1961 to 1975 the percentage of the world's population estimated to be of the "Negroid great race" has changed from 5.3 to 6.4, an increase in absolute numbers of 54 percent. On the other hand, the increase in numbers of those in the "Caucasian great race" has only been 26 percent, and their proportion of the world's population has declined from 46.4 to 45.5 percent. Perhaps most striking in Table 6.6 is the large increase in the mixed and transitional forms, a phenomenon to be expected over time, because of increased intermarriage.

These changes in the racial and ethnic composition of the world's population have occurred, by and large, because of the uneven rates of natural growth of these peoples through differential fertility and mor-

TABLE 6.6 Changes in the size of human races

Human Races	1961 Size (millions)	1961 Percent of World Population	1975 Size (millions)	1975 Percent of World Population	1975 Population as Percentage of 1961 Total
World population	3,068	100.0	3,947	100.0	129
Negroid great race	163	5.3	251	6.4	154
Mixed and transitional forms between the Negroid and Caucasian great races	263	8.6	353	9.0	134
Ethiopian type	35	1.1	44	1.1	126
South-Indian type	164	5.4	217	5.5	132
Mulattoes	45	1.5	66	1.7	147
Other types	19	0.6	26	0.7	136
Caucasian great race	1,426	46.4	1,794	45.5	126
Northern branch	127	4.1	140	3.6	110
Transitional and mid-European forms	546	17.8	616	15.6	113
Southern branch	753	24.5	1,038	26.3	138
Mixed forms of the Caucasian great race and the American branch of the Mongoloid great race	80	2.6	120	3.0	150
Mixed and transitional forms between the Caucasian great race and the Asian branch of the Mongoloid great race	33	1.1	45	1.2	136
Mongoloid great race	580	18.9	705	17.8	122
American branch	22	0.7	33	0.8	150
Asian branch	558	18.2	672	17.0	120
Pacific (eastern) Mongoloids	551	18.0	664	16.8	121
Other types	7	0.2	8	0.2	114
Mixed and transitional forms between the Asian branch of the Mongoloid great race and the Australoid great race	508	16.6	657	16.6	129
Types of the South-Asian group	411	13.4	542	13.7	132
Japanese type	94	3.1	111	2.8	118
Other types	3	0.1	4	0.1	133
Australoid great race	7	0.2	9	0.2	129
Other racial and unidentified types	8	0.3	13	0.3	162

Source: S. Brook, "Ethnic, Racial and Religious Structure of the World Population," as reprinted in *Population and Development Review,* 5, no. 3 (September, 1979), 505–534. Originally in *The World Population Today* (Moscow: USSR Academy of Sciences, 1977), Chap. 8.

tality. In smaller regions of the world, particularly, these factors plus differential migration rates can cause drastic alteration in the racial/ethnic composition of the population.

The particular importance of migration is well illustrated in the United States, which has often been called a nation of immigrants. We have already mentioned the important role that the quota system played in shaping the patterns of immigration to the United States. In 1850 those who were born outside the United States came almost entirely from Europe, most particularly from northern and western Europe. By 1940 this picture had changed, in that, while the majority of the foreign-born were still from Europe, a greater proportion of them came from southern, central, and eastern Europe. The foreign-born coming from other American nations, such as Central and South America, had increased also. Asian, African, and other nations were still contributing relatively small numbers to the population. Currently the proportions from Europe have dwindled even further, and those from Asia and the Americas have increased appreciably. Thus the United States has increasingly become a "melting pot" of ethnic groups.

The racial composition of the United States population from 1790 through 1980 has also undergone significant change (see Table 6.7). The percentage of blacks in the population declined progressively from 19 percent to 10 percent between 1790 and 1920,was stable for several decades, and now has risen slightly. The decrease in the percentage of blacks largely reflected the heavy in-migration among whites until 1920. Since that time, growth rates have been somewhat higher for blacks than for whites, primarily because of differential fertility patterns for these two color groups. Since the period prior to World War II, the fertility of blacks has exceeded that of whites by a substantial amount. Very recently the fertility differences among the racial groups have narrowed.[11] While the death rate for blacks has traditionally been higher than for whites, this differential is narrowing and is not enough to compensate for the higher birthrate of blacks.

More dramatic than black-white differences in fertility are the current differences between birthrates among Hispanics and non-Hispanics in the United States and the changes in ethnic composition that they portend for the future. In 1970 persons of Spanish origin comprised 4.5 percent of the population, but by 1980 they were 6.4 percent.[12] Fertility rates for the Spanish-origin population were about 119 births per 1,000 women aged eighteen to forty-four in 1979, whereas the comparable rate for those not of Spanish origin was only 73 births per 1,000 women.[13] Another way to look at this difference is to note that during this same period of time, about 10 percent of all births were to Hispanic women, whereas Hispanics constituted only about 6 percent of all women in this age group.

TABLE 6.7 Population size and annual growth rates for whites and blacks, and the percentage of blacks in the total population: United States, 1790–1980

Year	POPULATION (000)		AVERAGE ANNUAL GROWTH RATES FOR INTERCENSAL PERIOD (PERCENT)		Percentage of Total Population Black
	White	Black	White	Black	
1790	3,172	757	—	—	19
1800	4,306	1,002	3.06	2.80	19
1810	5,862	1,378	3.08	3.19	19
1820	7,867	1,772	2.94	2.51	18
1830	10,537	2,329	2.92	2.73	18
1840	14,196	2,874	2.98	2.10	17
1850	19,553	3,639	3.20	2.36	16
1860	26,923	4,442	3.20	2.00	14
1870	33,589	4,880	2.22	0.94	13
1880	43,403	6,581	2.56	2.99	13
1890	55,101	7,389	2.39	1.25	12
1900	66,809	8,834	1.92	1.79	12
1910	81,732	9,828	2.01	1.07	11
1920	94,821	10,463	1.48	0.63	10
1930	110,287	11,891	1.51	1.28	10
1940	118,215	12,866	0.70	0.79	10
1950	134,942	15,042	1.33	1.56	10
1960	159,467	18,916	1.67	2.29	11
1970	177,749	22,580	1.15	1.94	11
1980	188,341	26,488	0.60	1.73	12

Source: For figures through 1960, Reynolds Farley, Growth of the Black Population (Chicago: Rand McNally, 1970), p. 22. For 1970 and 1980, U.S. Bureau of the Census, "Population Profile of the United States, 1980," Current Population Reports, Series P-20, no. 363, Table 3, p. 9.

In some states the number of births to Hispanic women makes a particularly large contribution to overall births, and hence will gradually change the ethnic composition of the area. In 1978, for example, 28.8 percent of all children born in Arizona had at least one Hispanic parent, and 34.1 percent of births in California were in this category.[14] The potential impact of this phenomenon on the ethnic composition of these areas is clear.

In selected areas of the United States, the different migration patterns of blacks and whites are beginning to create racial compositions very different from those that had previously existed. The greatest change in racial composition has been taking place in the South. While blacks made up 24 percent of Southern residents in 1940, they comprised only 19 percent of that population in 1980.[15]

Probably the most dramatic example of the effect that differential migration can have on the racial composition of an area is found in suburban–central-city movement. In recent years, for example, black populations in central cities increased, while the proportion of whites declined as a result of out-migration. Such a trend would eventually produce greater residential segregation than has ever existed before, with whites living almost exclusively in the suburbs and blacks almost exclusively in the central cities. However, most recently there has been a net migration of blacks to the suburbs. Between 1970 and 1977, for example, the number of whites living in the suburbs increased by 10 percent, but the number of blacks living in these areas rose by 34 percent.[16]

Racial-Ethnic Composition as a Cause of Population Change

We have already seen that as the population components of fertility, mortality, and residential mobility operate to change the racial-ethnic composition of nations and areas, so the racial-ethnic composition in those areas and nations can influence fertility, mortality, and residential mobility.

Areas of the United States with high percentages of blacks or Hispanics, for example, generally have higher birthrates. As minorities constitute a greater proportion of the population of central cities, and if their birthrates remain higher than those of other groups, then central cities, which have long been known for low birthrates, will become areas of high ones. On the other hand, it must be recognized that changes in social conditions can affect the fertility desires and behavior of groups with previously high fertility and lead to a decline in fertility.

Another example of the effect of ethnic composition on population processes can be found in the USSR. In the republics of Central Asia and the Transcaucasus the population growth rates are more like those displayed in developing countries than in the Soviet Union as a whole.[17] This is apparently because these regions are inhabited predominantly by persons of Islamic origin, a group with high birthrates. Births to persons of Islamic origin are coming to constitute a greater and greater proportion of all births in the Soviet Union, such that the government has considered various policy interventions to prevent the proportion of these peoples from increasing so greatly.

Future Changes in Racial-Ethnic Composition

For the past three decades in the United States the percentage of the population that is black has been steadily increasing. This increase, while primarily due to the relatively high birthrates of blacks, as was already pointed out, is also the result of this group's declining death rate. The main problem in projecting the future racial-ethnic composition of the population is in estimating whether this birthrate differential will persist or decline. Indeed there is some evidence to support a narrowing of the differential.

Still, an outstanding characteristic of the present black population of the United States is its young age. High birthrates produce younger populations, which in turn put more women of childbearing age into the population at successive dates. Thus even if the average number of births of blacks were to decline, in proportion to whites there would still be more black women bearing children for some time to come, and the overall birthrate levels would differ. It is most likely, therefore, that the percentage of the population that is black will continue to increase for a number of years.

Changes in ethnic composition of the population are likewise difficult to predict. As a result of the enactment in 1968 of a new immigration policy in the United States, it is likely that over many years the ethnic origin of the population will not be so heavily Northern and Western European. As in the past, wars, natural disasters, and other events that stimulate refugee movements may be expected to contribute temporary influxes from a variety of nations.

We have already noted that perhaps the most dramatic ethnic change will come from the increasing proportion of the population of Spanish origin. Not only will this proportion increase through immigration, but it seems likely that the substantially higher birthrates of this group will continue. Among women eighteen to thirty-four years old, for example, Hispanic women currently expect an average of 2.35 births, whereas this figure is only 2.05 for white and 2.24 for black women.[18]

Racial and ethnic composition will also be affected by the rate of intermarriage among groups. Although marriage among people in different racial categories has been rare in the United States, the rate has been increasing. Among whites, marriage across nationality and religious lines is much more frequent and also increasing. Because of these trends, racial and ethnic categories of the population will become even less "pure" in the future than at present.

POPULATION DISTRIBUTION

In the past, concerns about population have been related mostly to its size. Are populations getting too large or too small? Are they growing too rapidly or too slowly? Is population size in keeping with the resources available? In recent years, the focus of concern has shifted somewhat to population structure and its consequences, particularly the effects of changing age composition on the society.

Governmental and public attention has also been turning to questions about population distribution and redistribution. These phenomena can be examined quite independently of changes in population size. Even if a country were to attain a zero rate of population growth or stability in size, there would probably continue to be shifts in population distribution.

The distribution of a population refers to how that population is spread over a given land area. Our discussion of population distribution includes the relative numbers of people in different geographical units, the extent to which people tend to be heavily concentrated in some areas, and population redistribution (the patterns by which population distribution changes over time).

It will be clear from the following discussion that population distribution at a point in time is the result of initial settlement patterns in an area, subject to subsequent modifications by births, deaths, and residential mobility. The basic processes of population change thus serve to determine population distribution. In turn, the basic population processes are affected by the distribution of population, because, as indicated in earlier chapters, distinctive cultural and social-structural factors associated with particular areas have an influence on fertility, mortality, and residential mobility.

World Population Distribution

The distinction that can be made between *international* and *intranational population distribution*, like that between international and intranational (or internal) migration, is based partly on the extent of available data and partly on the different distributional patterns that can be observed in the world and within nations. The lack of adequate population information for some parts of the world makes world population distribution difficult to describe except in the broadest terms. In particular countries, especially those with advanced demographic reporting systems, the information on population distribution is generally more complete and more complex, thereby permitting more detailed analyses. Also, the increasing specificity of areas (that is, the ability to identify smaller units and their linkage to other units) enables us to describe distributional patterns and processes and understand their causes and consequences more readily. It is only through the intensive study of individual nations that this can be accomplished.

In our examination of world population distribution, we will follow the framework elaborated earlier, paying attention to relative numbers of people in different areas, the extent of population concentration, and the components of population redistribution.

The Spread of Population among Nations

The topic of world population distribution is not new; it was discussed in the overview of population trends in Chapter 1. A glance back at that section and at Appendix A will show the uneven distribution of people among nations and broader regions of the world. Table 1.1 acquainted us with the fact that populations of some areas of the earth have been growing in size at a more rapid rate than those of other areas, and that as a consequence there have been shifts in population distribution among nations and regions over time.

The percentage distribution of world population in Table 6.8 highlights those changes. Although Asia contained more than half of the world's population in 1950, the proportion of population in that continent had actually been declining over the previous two centuries.

TABLE 6.8 Percentage distribution of the world's population among major areas, 1750–1982

Area	1750	1800	1850	1900	1950	1981
World total	100.0	100.0	100.0	100.0	100.0	100.0
Asia (excluding USSR)	63.0	64.4	63.5	56.1	54.9	58.2
China (mainland)	25.2	33.0	34.1	26.4	22.3	21.8
India, Bangladesh, and Pakistan	24.0	19.9	18.5	17.3	17.3	19.6
Japan	3.8	3.1	2.5	2.7	3.3	2.6
Indonesia	1.5	1.3	1.8	2.5	3.1	3.3
Remainder of Asia (excluding USSR)	8.5	7.1	6.9	7.2	9.0	10.9
Africa	13.4	10.9	8.8	8.1	8.8	10.9
North Africa	1.3	1.1	1.2	1.6	2.1	2.5
Remainder of Africa	12.1	9.8	7.6	6.4	6.7	8.3
Europe (excluding USSR)	15.8	15.5	16.5	17.9	15.6	10.8
USSR	5.3	5.7	6.0	8.1	7.2	5.9
America	2.3	3.2	5.1	9.5	13.0	13.8
North America	0.3	0.7	2.1	5.0	6.6	5.6
United States	0.2	0.5	1.8	4.6	6.0	5.1
Remainder of North America	0.1	0.2	0.3	0.4	0.6	0.5
Middle and South America	2.0	2.5	3.0	4.4	6.4	8.2
Oceania	0.3	0.2	0.2	0.4	0.5	0.5

Source: John Durand, "The Modern Expansion of World Population," *Proceedings of the American Philosophical Society,* Philadelphia, June 1967, p. 137; *1982 World Population Data Sheet* (Washington, D.C.: Population Reference Bureau, 1982).

This decline was most noticeable in the most populated areas of the continent, the People's Republic of China and the combined areas of India and Pakistan. By 1981, however, rapid population increase in the smaller countries of Asia helped to raise Asia's share of total world population. A decrease in the relative share of world population can also be observed in Africa between 1750 and 1900. During the twentieth century, Africa increased its proportion, with the most rapid increases taking place in central and southern Africa. Europe's share of world population grew most perceptibly during the nineteenth century, but by 1950 it was about the same as it had been during the earlier periods, and by 1981 its proportion was considerably smaller. Sharp increases over time in the percentage of world population are noted for the USSR and the Americas, and a small rise in its proportion was recorded for Oceania. The USSR reduced its share during the twentieth century, and North America declined relatively after 1950. The greatest relative increases were in Middle and South America.

Thus, during two hundred years of the modern era, a modification of the world's population distribution took place that shifted relative numbers of people away from Asia and Africa toward the developing areas of the world, most notably the USSR and the Americas. After 1950 this process began to change as population growth started to stabilize in North America and the USSR, and rapid population growth took place in parts of Asia, Africa, and Middle and South America.

Concentration of Population: International Comparisons

When we speak of the relative numbers of people in different countries, it is obvious that we are not assuming that the population is spread out over the same distance in each country. The size and shape of land varies among nations, and the relationship of population to land area provides us with another dimension of world population distribution. Among a number of measures of population concentration, we shall examine two that are widely utilized in demographic analysis: population density and urbanization.

The first measure, *population density*, refers to population per square unit of land area. A glance at Table 6.9 shows that countries with large population sizes do not necessarily have the largest population densities. Conversely, some countries with small populations are densely settled. For example, India's over 688 million people had a density of only 194 per kilometer of total surface area, and the over 200 million in the United States represented a population density of merely 23 per kilometer of total surface area. On the other hand, Hong Kong had a comparable population density of 4,408, and for Malta it stood at 1,075.

When arable land, rather than total land, is used as the base for these calculations, densities become larger. For example, in a country such as Egypt, there are only 40 persons per square kilometer of surface area, while there are 1,533 persons per square kilometer of arable land. In Singapore the comparable density figures are 4,018 and an incredi-

TABLE 6.9   Population size, 1982, percent urban in 1970s, and population density, 1978, for selected countries of the world

Country	Population Estimate (millions)	Percent Urban	Persons per Sq. Km. of Surface Area	Persons per Sq. Km. of Arable Land
Argentina	28.6	82	10	16
Australia	15.0	86	2	3
Bahrain	0.4	78	555	6,383
Bangladesh	93.3	10	588	954
Brazil	127.7	63	14	58
Canada	24.4	76	2	35
China	1,000.0	13	97	309
Cuba	9.8	65	84	185
Egypt	44.8	45	40	1,533
France	54.2	78	97	169
Ghana	12.4	36	46	90
Hong Kong	5.0	90	4,408	62,675
Iceland	0.2	88	2	10
India	713.8	22	194	381
Indonesia	151.3	20	72	524
Ireland	3.5	58	46	60
Israel	4.1	89	178	321
Italy	57.4	69	188	326
Japan	118.6	76	309	2,145
Kenya	17.9	14	26	273
Malta	0.4	83	1,075	2,486
Mexico	71.3	67	34	71
Netherlands	14.3	88	341	694
Nigeria	82.3	20	78	178
Pakistan	93.0	28	95	356
Peru	18.6	67	13	59
Philippines	51.6	36	155	538
Saudi Arabia	11.1	67	4	12
Singapore	2.5	100	4,018	30,250
Thailand	49.8	14	88	273
United Kingdom	56.1	77	229	304
United States	232.0	74	23	53
Zaire	30.3	30	12	97

Sources: 1982 World Population Data Sheet (Washington, D.C.: Population Reference Bureau, 1982); United Nations, *Demographic Yearbook, 1978* (New York: United Nations, 1979), pp. 98–104.

ble 30,250 persons per square kilometer of surface and arable land, respectively. Furthermore, not all arable land is equally productive, since grassland supports fewer persons than croplands.

Comparisons of population densities cannot be properly interpreted without considering the social and cultural setting in which the ratios exist. That is, such densities must be viewed not only in terms of the degree of intensity of physical contact, but also with regard to social organization, values, and life-styles; the individual's status and class position within the society; and personal and social expectations regarding a desirable way to live. For these reasons, moderate population densities (such as those in the United States) may not indicate any greater carrying capacity than high population densities (such as those in the Netherlands).[19]

The second measure of population concentration, *urbanization*, refers to the proportion of a population resident in urban areas or in areas with at least a given concentration of people. In a more dynamic sense, urbanization can be viewed as a process involving the multiplication of points of concentration and increases in the size of individual concentrations.[20]

Although there were a few cities in the world as early as 4000 B.C., they were generally small and had to be supported by rural populations. Societies in which a high proportion of the population lived in cities developed only in the nineteenth and twentieth centuries. Urbanization as a world phenomenon began increasing rapidly in about 1800. At that time 1.7 percent of the people lived in cities of 100,000 or more. That percentage grew to 5.5 percent by 1900 and 13 percent by 1950. The population in all urban places having 5,000 or more persons rose from 3 percent in 1800 to 30 percent in 1950.[21]

Today it is estimated that 37 percent of the world's population lives in areas termed urban by the country. The figure rises to 69 percent for the more-developed nations of the world and is 26 percent for the less-developed countries (Appendix A). But "rapid urbanization has seized one country after another in the less developed regions and it is now gathering immense force in all the countries that have hitherto remained less developed."[22]

As Table 6.10 shows, the rate of urban growth in developing areas outpaces both the rate of rural growth in developing areas (thus leading to continuing urbanization) and the rate of urban growth in more-developed regions.

In the more-developed regions, the continued growth in urban population has been occurring in part at the expense of a net decrease in rural population; thus, during the period 1970 to 1975, urban places gained 65 million inhabitants, but since the total population of the

TABLE 6.10 Amounts and annual rates of growth in urban and rural population by world regions, 1970–1975

Region	1970–1975 POPULATION GAIN (MILLIONS)		1970–1975 ANNUAL GROWTH RATE (PERCENTAGE)	
	Urban	Rural	Urban	Rural
More-developed regions	65.5	−17.8	1.7	−1.0
Europe[a]	21.2	−7.2	1.4	−0.9
North America	13.4	−2.9	1.5	−1.0
Soviet Union	17.1	−4.8	2.3	−0.9
Japan	9.1	−2.4	2.3	−1.6
Temperate South America	3.2	−0.5	2.1	−1.3
Australia and New Zealand	1.5	0.0	2.2	−0.1
Less-developed regions	140.6	169.2	4.0	1.7
South Asia[b]	45.1	91.8	4.1	2.1
East Asia[c]	34.9	37.9	3.4	1.2
Latin America[d]	31.7	6.7	4.3	1.1
Northern Africa and Western South Asia	16.1	8.1	4.7	1.5
Africa[e]	12.5	24.5	4.8	2.1
Pacific Islands[f]	0.2	0.3	6.4	1.6

Source: United Nations Department of Economic and Social Affairs, *World Population Trends and Policies: 1977 Monitoring Report, Volume I, Population Trends* (New York: United Nations, 1979), p. 114.
[a]*Excluding the USSR.*
[b]*Excluding Western South Asia.*
[c]*Excluding Japan.*
[d]*Excluding Temperate South America.*
[e]*Excluding Northern Africa.*
[f]*Melanesia, Micronesia, and Polynesia.*

more-developed regions grew by only 48 million, this entailed an absolute decrease of approximately 18 million in the rural population.

In the less-developed regions, despite the much more rapid growth of the urban population, the amount of population gain in the rural areas was even larger. Thus between 1970 and 1975 the urban population increased by about 141 million and the rural by 169 million.[23] Thus, the basis for still further urbanization in developing areas, through adverse rural conditions and consequent rural-urban migration of large numbers, is profound.

We have long become accustomed to thinking of New York, Chicago, Los Angeles, London, Tokyo, and Paris as among the world's major urban areas. Many cities of the less-developed world have been growing at a much more rapid rate and are expected to maintain that growth rate into the future. The populations of big cities in developed countries are growing very slowly or even declining. Growth rates in excess of 3 percent per year are found in Peking, Calcutta, Cairo, Seoul, Rio de Janeiro, and Sao Paulo; in excess of 4 percent per year in Bombay, Jakarta, Manila, Bogota, and Mexico City; in excess of 5 percent per year in Karachi; and over 6 percent per year in Kinshasa and Lagos. Mexico City's population, estimated as under 3 million in 1950, is projected to be about 32 million in the year 2000.[24]

The rapid expansion of these cities in developing countries is partly related to the fact that many of them are the dominant cities (sometimes called primate cities) of their countries. Such places often become magnets for the rural population and those people who reside in smaller urban places. A measure of *primacy* (the largest city's population divided by the sum of the next three largest) is large and increasing for many Asian cities. The measure for Manila grew from 4.91 in 1960 to 5.31 in 1970. For Jakarta, it went from .87 in 1955 to 1.34 in 1971. Bangkok is 32 times bigger than the next largest city in Thailand.[25]

Components of World Population Redistribution

Each of the basic processes of population change (mortality, fertility, and residential mobility) can account for variations in population distribution among nations over time. Although migration between countries is the most obvious redistribution process, population distribution can also be modified by differences in rates of births and deaths. In areas like North America and Oceania, high net immigration levels, combined with substantial natural increase, raised their share of the world's population significantly until 1950. In areas like China, India, and Pakistan, moderately high death rates and emigration were more than compensated for by high birthrates and immigration, but the net effects were not as great as in other areas, thus reducing their share of the world's population. Indonesia's relatively high birth levels and sharply declining death levels accounted for its increased percentage of the world's population. It is therefore apparent that any combination of the basic population components might produce a population change rate that differs from the world average and thereby leads to population redistribution.

The urban-rural balance is likewise affected by the several basic components of population change. The effects of natural increase (excess of births over deaths) and net migration are complemented by reclassification of areas. That is, areas that were once rural become classified as urban because of their population buildup. In most cases the population growth leading to reclassification was due to earlier migration from other rural areas, which helped to create an urban place.

As a component of urban population growth, net transfers (due to either migration from rural to urban areas or reclassification of rural areas to urban) during the early 1970s accounted for over half of the urban growth in Europe, the USSR, East Asia, and the Pacific Islands, but less than 40 percent in temperate South America, the remainder of Latin America, and in Australia and New Zealand, where natural increase was a greater force.

The decline of rural population in more-developed regions occurred because a substantial natural increase was overcome by an even greater transfer of people from rural to urban areas. In the less-developed regions, rural population grew because natural increase was large enough to more than balance net transfers out of rural areas.[26]

Future Changes in World Population Distribution

There is every reason to expect that the trend of urbanization experienced in the recent past will continue during the next few decades. Some slackening of natural increase in rural areas combined with further transfers of population from rural to urban areas may accelerate the trend. Projections put more than half of the world's population in urban areas by the year 2000. In the more-developed regions, it is expected to be close to 80 percent. In less-developed regions, it will be fast approaching 45 percent.[27] Only in countries of Asia and Africa, which have large rural populations, will urbanization attain lower levels, and in most of these countries the growth of cities is in an early and emerging phase.

This growing world urbanization has caused concern to many who see the disadvantage of large numbers of people flocking to places that cannot accommodate them socially and economically, and perhaps not physically. Proposals have been made for relocating such urbanites (for instance, the transmigration of Indonesians in Jakarta to the outer islands under government programs), for halting or limiting movement to the cities by law, and by developing rural areas to make them more desirable as living places, so that people are less eager to escape them.[28]

With regard to population distribution among nations, the slowdown in international migration in recent years will shift attention to natural increase or decrease as the principal determinant of population shifts. The proportions of the world population in Asia, Africa, and Latin America should increase, while those in the USSR, Europe, and

North America should decrease. The United States's share of world population will probably continue to decline as a result of declines in natural increase and limitations on immigration.

Population Distribution Within Nations

The description of distribution patterns within societies requires considerably more detailed information than is necessary for the description of overall national distribution character. How extensive that information should be is a function of the kinds and numbers of geographical units that are meaningful for analysis.

Typically, official population statistics are provided for divisions of a country along political as well as nonpolitical lines. The classification system for the United States is representative of those for nations with a broad land area. Included among politically defined areas are states, counties, cities, towns, smaller urban places, and minor civil divisions. The importance of these units for the analysis of population distribution rests on the significance of legal residences and governmental functions. The population base of an economy, the population eligible to vote in an election of governmental representatives, people holding automobile licenses, the number of property owners, and the number of children attending schools are examples of demographic statistics that are keyed to political boundaries.

Political units may be combined in various ways for statistical purposes even though the combined area has no political identity. Metropolitan areas or other functional groupings of counties with urban character give us a basis for describing urbanization trends that go beyond city boundaries. Regions of the country are groupings of states corresponding to broad sections of the nation that have historical as well as contemporary importance (such as the South and the West).

Often these political units and their groupings are not adequate for indicating general distribution patterns or changes in population. Farm-nonfarm residential distinctions are an important part of distributional analysis. The simple urban-rural dichotomy in demographic data does not respect political boundaries. Some large urban conglomerations are more accurately defined by a land area that cuts across geographical lines. An urbanized area in United States Bureau of the Census parlance is that area encompassing a large city and its urban hinterland; it does not necessarily conform to county boundaries.

Finally, we are often interested in population distribution within the smallest political units, particularly where populations are very concentrated and we wish to describe or explain their distributional forms. How is population distributed over city blocks or *census tracts* (groups of blocks that correspond to neighborhoods or other subsegments of a city)? How geographically patterned are land uses and the characteristics of residents of an urban area?

The Spread of Population among Geographical Units

Illustrations of population distributed across these several types of units, and changes over time, can be given for the United States. The uneven distribution and dynamics of change may not be characteristic of all societies at all periods of time, but these illustrations serve to point out that the distribution of population by area has significant implications for the study of demographic and social changes in a nation.

Figure 6.3 shows vividly the shifting proportions of population in the four major regions of the United States over time. At the time of the first census, in 1790, with only the eastern coast of the present land area then settled, almost half of the population was in the Northeast and half in the South. Development of the north central region and its incorporation into the nation led to an increasing share of the country's people being in that area. With the settlement of the West, beginning in the mid-1800s, that region's share of the national population began to increase. By 1980 the four regions were approaching parity in their proportions of the United States population, although significant differences remained.

An examination of county populations in the United States will likewise show disparities in population size and changes in them over time. One would expect differences because of unequal amounts of land areas among counties and variations in economic bases, but these factors can account only in part for the distribution changes from one point in time to another.

The urban or rural character of counties is a major factor in determining variations in total population sizes. While four-fifths of the United States population was classified as living in urban areas in 1980, a number of counties contained no urban population whatever, and a vast majority had an urban percentage that was less than the United States average. There was a tendency for most of the American people to congregate in a limited number of metropolitan areas that cover a very small portion of the nation's land area. About 73 percent of the population lived in such areas, which cover roughly 15 percent of the land.

County population change has not been unidirectional over time, however. For the longest period, the urban counties kept increasing demographically, while the rural counties had a decrease in the number of people. Changes were observed between 1960 and 1970 that showed obvious losses in the rural heartland and other agricultural areas. This was a replication of the process that had been observed for a number of decades. As shown in Figure 6.4, the picture changed between 1970 and 1980. It had earlier been noted that many large cities had stabilized in size or declined in numbers, but the apparent reason

FIGURE 6.3   Percent distribution of population by region, 1790–1980

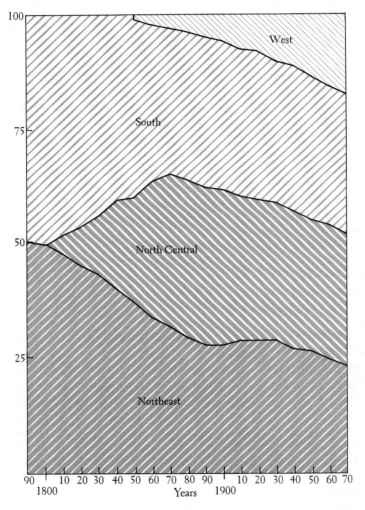

Source: U.S. Bureau of the Census, *U.S. Census of Population, 1970,* Final Report, PC(1)-A1 (Washington: U.S. Government Printing Office, 1971), p. 19; and U.S. Bureau of the Census, "Population Profile of the United States: 1980," *Current Population Reports,* Series P-20, no. 363, Table 6, p. 11.

FIGURE 6.4   Percent change in total population by counties: United States, 1970–1980

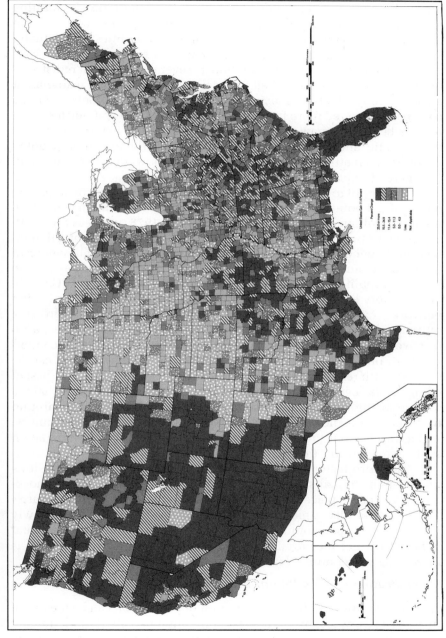

Source: Bureau of the Census, *Summary PC80-1-A1* (Washington, D.C.: U.S. Department of Commerce, 1982), Figure 12.

was the growth of *suburbs* (those built-up areas just outside cities). Since the suburbs were generally joined with the cities in forming metropolitan areas, populations of metropolitan counties continued to expand. Now many of the larger metropolitan counties had actually lost population, and nonmetropolitan counties were gaining it.

The *population turnaround* reflects several population redistributional tendencies in the United States. First is the regional realignment already referred to, but especially the growth of the Sun Belt. Migrants have been attracted there from the older northeastern and north central regions because of new economic development and job opportunities, the climatic and life-style advantages (especially for older people), changed racial attitudes in the area, an overall lower cost of living, and commercial expansion.[29]

The population turnaround also reflects the decision by large segments of the population to locate away from the large urban centers, in nonmetropolitan counties. Between 1970 and 1978, whereas one-sixth of all metropolitan areas lost population, three-fourths of all nonmetropolitan counties gained it. This pattern occurred in all regions of the country, and the nonmetropolitan gains were in counties remote from metropolitan areas as well as in those adjacent to them.[30] Contributing factors have been improved transportation and communication networks, extended services and consumer-goods outlets, a growing retirement population not dependent on access to work places, a rediscovery of the natural environment, and some new economic enterprises in outlying areas. Nonmetropolitan residential location can be coupled with relatively easy access to urban centers, so that "the best of both worlds" can be enjoyed. Some researchers are discovering that the demise of the central cities has made the metropolitan rings around those cities the new "hub of life" of the metropolitan community, which reaches out to both the older city and the emerging population settlements beyond the metropolitan area.[31]

The third factor involved in the population turnaround is a slowing of the historical suburbanization trend and a simultaneous movement to smaller places and rural areas outside metropolitan areas.[32] These smaller places may have existed for some time or may be newly established in open country. In any event, the result of this movement is net urban deconcentration in the nation. The average American is increasingly becoming identified with modest-size places.

Concentration of Population: Intranational Comparisons

As already indicated, the concentration of population can be measured in at least two ways: by comparing population density (population per square unit of area), and by comparing levels and rates of urbanization.

Population densities vary considerably from one part of the United States to another. Compared with an average density of about 53 per square kilometer of surface area in the United States, densities are as low as 1 per square kilometer or less in many rural areas and perhaps as high as about 50,000 per square kilometer in New York County (Manhattan Island), and still higher in some neighborhoods within it.

Measures of urban level and change indicate what population densities do not; namely, the attraction of people to a small number of areas and the differential multiplications of the size of areas. Figure 6.5, which shows the urban percentage in each county in 1980, reveals that the population turnaround discussed earlier has hardly altered the picture of the United States as a country where many people are located on a limited portion of the land and vast expanses of land are much more sparsely occupied. One can picture the East Coast, West Coast, Sun Belt, and Great Lakes urban build-up, as well as the parts of the West and Alaska where there appear to be wide open spaces. However, the newer reversals of large city and metropolitan growth since about 1970 represent a change in a trend that saw the most urban areas growing the most rapidly. Between 1900 and 1960 in the United States, while total population increased two and a half times, urban population increased almost fourfold, the population of metropolitan areas (which include central cities of 50,000 or more and the surrounding area that is socially and economically integrated with the city) increased more than fourfold, and large metropolitan areas (those with 1 million or more people) increased fivefold.[33]

As metropolitan areas expanded geographically as well as demographically, the merging of once-discrete metropolitan areas took place in certain parts of the country. The term *megalopolis* has been introduced to refer to the densely populated consolidated urban chains that extend from Boston to Washington, Chicago to Pittsburgh, and other sections of the nation.

We have suggested that growing urbanization can take place even while a population is becoming more dispersed. That is, concentrations may be developing in a number of places even though the greatest concentrations are in a few areas. This phenomenon applies very well to the black population of the United States. In 1910 nine-tenths of the blacks were located within the southern region; by 1980 the proportion had been reduced to just over half. However, while southern blacks were mainly in rural residences, the growing number of blacks have become a numerical majority or near-majority in many of the nation's largest cities. They have not, however, emerged in great numbers in the suburbs or more outlying areas, a phenomenon reflecting important social processes of the past decades.[34]

FIGURE 6.5   Percent urban by county: United States, 1980.

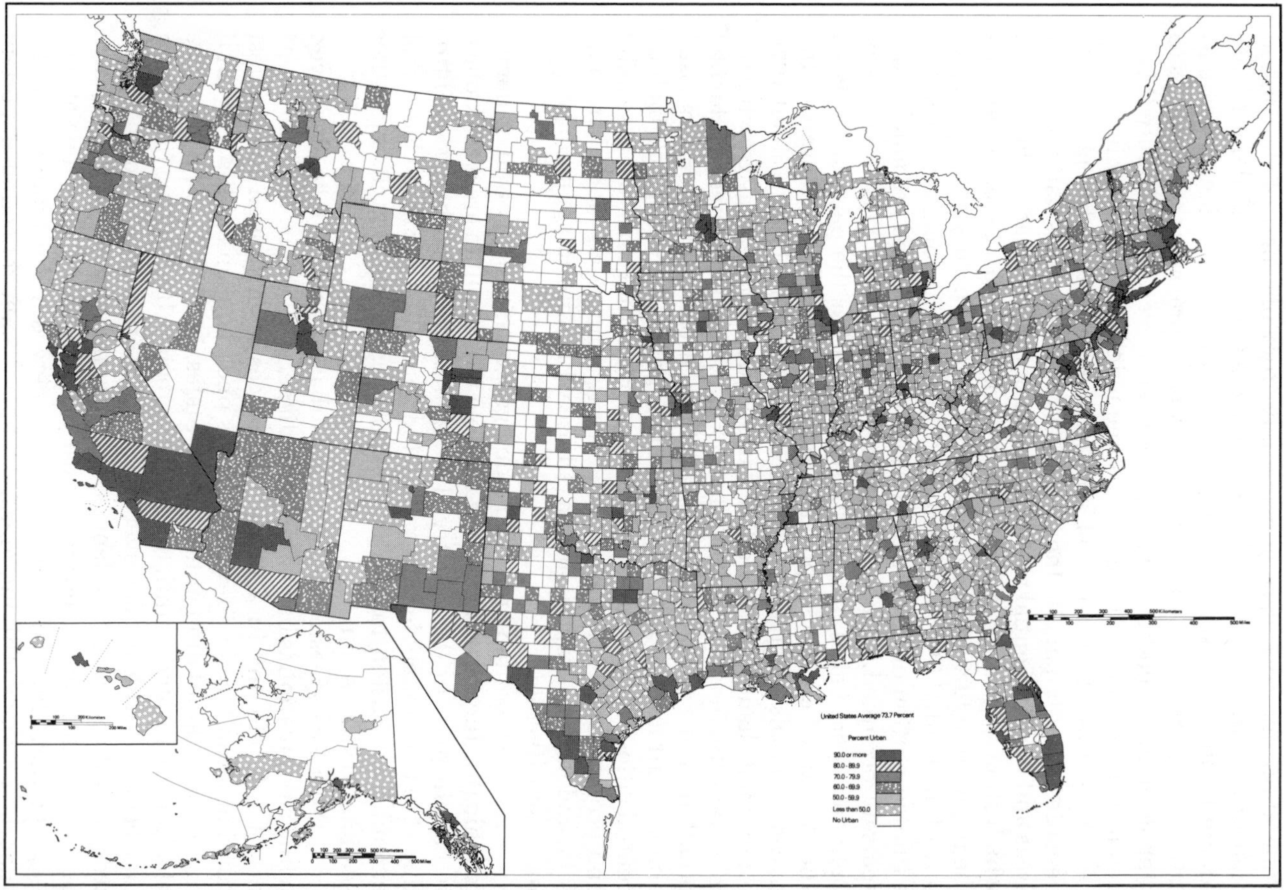

Source: Bureau of the Census, Summary PC80-1-A1 (Washington, D.C.: U.S. Department of Commerce, 1982), Figure 24.

These urbanization patterns have been duplicated, with some variation, around the world. In countries like Thailand, India, and the Philippines, the overall level of urbanization is relatively low, but urban increase is continually taking place. While only 17 percent of Thailand's population is urban, the urban population is growing at almost twice the rate of the rural. Of all the municipalities, the primate city of Bangkok continues to grow most rapidly. Likewise India's urban population is about 21 percent of the total, but the urban is growing half again as fast as the rural sector. The percentage urban in the Philippines is up to 36 percent, with the urban population increasing roughly twice as fast as the rural one.[35]

Population Distribution Within Urban Areas   The changing population balance in metropolitan areas between central cities and the surrounding territory is, of course, not the only significant aspect of intraurban population distributional change. Populations within cities assume varying geographical patterns, and these often shift over time.

There have been numerous attempts to describe the population structure of cities in general terms. Burgess surveyed some large North American cities and, on the basis of these, posited a concentric zonal hypothesis, saying that there will be a differentiation of functions as one moves away from the center of cities. Concentric layers emanating from the central point will form the central business district, industrial areas, lower-class working homes, areas of better residences, and commuter suburbs. Burgess provided a reasonably accurate portrait of many American cities that were growing during the first part of the twentieth century. Later studies in Latin America showed its cities traditionally had a different gradient pattern, with higher-status residences in the center of the city and lower-class residences toward the periphery. With population growth and changes in social and economic organization, these cities changed their population spatial form and began to assume the North American pattern.[36]

Alternative descriptions of population distribution have been offered. Some researchers have emphasized sector development resulting from arterial transportation patterns. Others have pointed to the effects of both natural features of the land (for example, water, parkland) and cultural effects (such as ethnic neighborhoods that cut across social lines) on land use. In any event, all cities may exhibit some common demographic features as well as some unique ones that result from the particular set of historical events that affected the city, its age, and the precise period of time during which it developed. In recent years much attention has been devoted to the intervention of governments in restructuring cities and thus altering population distribution. Urban renewal, subsidized housing, environmental control, and tax incentives and disincentives are examples of government policies that have had some impact on the distribution of people within urban areas.[37]

Most people occupy their residences for only part of each day. Knowing where population is located at different times is of interest, and sometimes of vital importance, to traffic engineers, city planners, civil-defense administrators, businessmen, and others. Table 6.11 shows the temporal patterns of population distribution at selected hours of the day and night for an aggregate group of American cities around 1950. It is unlikely that these distributions have changed much over time, although the increased labor-force participation of women and suburbanization of some urban activities may have altered the patterns to some extent. By early afternoon, only about two out of three residents were found in residential areas, and some of these may have been away from their own homes. One-sixth of the population was in industrial areas during most of the day, and another one-sixth in commercial areas or on the streets at those times. These data are meaningful because population distribution is dynamic, with regard to both residential patterns over the year and locational patterns during the day and week.

TABLE 6.11 Mean percent of resident population present in functional areas at selected hours in five United States cities*

Hour of Day	Commercial Areas	Industrial Areas	Residential Areas	Streets**
3:00 A.M.	4	7	89	1
6:00 A.M.	3	7	89	2
9:00 A.M.	9	16	73	3
12:00 noon	13	16	68	4
3:00 P.M.	13	16	66	6
6:00 P.M.	5	9	78	9
9:00 P.M.	5	9	76	9
12:00 midnight	3	8	85	5

Source: Donald L. Foley, "Urban Daytime Population: A Field for Demographic-Ecological Analysis," *Social Forces,* 32, no. 4 (May 1954), 327; based on "Population Distribution-Spatial and Temporal," (unpublished report of the Institute for Research in Social Science, University of North Carolina, September 1952), Table 5, p. 76. Copyright © The University of North Carolina Press.

*Cities included were Philadelphia-Camden, Minneapolis-St. Paul, Grand Rapids, Flint, and Erie.
**Peak street percentages occurred at 8:00 A.M. with 6 percent, and at 5:00 P.M. with 10 percent.

Future Changes in Population Distribution within Nations

Most developed nations are highly urbanized, and the majority of those that still contain substantial rural areas are seeing them become converted to urban ones. In the United States, for instance, non-metropolitan growth is creating urban places where rural area once existed. As cities remain unattractive for residence, as transportation channels continue to improve, as suburban areas take on many of the former functions of the cities, and as business and industry set up establishments outside the metropolis, the further growth of non-metropolitan areas probably will mean the spread of urbanization.

Extended urbanization will depend heavily on what happens to American cities, particularly the large ones. If they continue to suffer economically and retain other negative features, such as high crime rates and decayed housing, they should further lose population, and what national population growth takes place will be elsewhere. On the other hand, if cities become revitalized through urban redevelopment and renewed economic investment, some displacement of their present populations and possible relocation in cities of some who had previously migrated away will occur. These developments will hinge, to a great extent, on federal, state, and local policies affecting immigration, internal migration, housing, and economic opportunity.

In developing countries, the continued growth of primate, as well as secondary and tertiary, cities, seems inevitable so long as national population growth rates are high and employment and income prospects appear brighter in urban areas. However, maintenance of high growth rates suggests continued rates of population growth in rural areas as well. Many programs for stimulating rural development, if carried out successfully, could shift the relative advantages away from major cities and slow down traditional urban growth. One additional consequence of such an event would be the rise of smaller cities and towns.

NOTES

1. See U.S. Bureau of the Census, *Historical Statistics of the United States: Colonial Times to 1957* (Washington, D.C.: U.S. Government Printing Office, 1960), p. 62.

2. National Center for Health Statistics, *Monthly Vital Statistics Report; Annual Summary for the United States, 1971*, 20, no. 13 (August 30, 1972).

3. For a discussion of the Hong Kong situation, see Ronald Freedman, D. N. Namboothiri, and A. Adlakha, "Hong Kong's Fertility Decline: 1961–68," *Pop-

ulation Index, 36 (January–March 1970), 3–18; and Sui-Ying Wat and R. W. Hodge, "Social and Economic Factors in Hong Kong's Fertility Decline," *Population Studies*, 26 (November 1972), 455–464.

4. For calculations on the marriage squeeze over time, see Donald S. Akers, "On Measuring the Marriage Squeeze," *Demography*, 4, no. 2 (1967), 907–924.

5. U.S. Bureau of the Census, "Projections of the Population of the Communist Countries of Eastern Europe, by Age and Sex: 1965–1985," *International Population Reports*, Series P-91, no. 14 (1965), p. 44.

6. See "1981 World Population Data Sheet" (Washington, D.C.: Population Reference Bureau, 1981).

7. Larry H. Long and Kristin A. Hansen, "Reasons for Interstate Migration," *Current Population Reports*, Series P-23, no. 81 (March 1979).

8. U.S. Bureau of the Census, "Projections of the Population of the United States: 1977 to 2050," *Current Population Reports*, Series P-25, no. 704 (July 1977), p. 7.

9. U.S. Bureau of the Census, "Illustrative Projections of World Populations to the 21st Century," *Current Population Reports*, Series P-23, no. 79 (January 1979), p. 67.

10. S. Brook, "Ethnic, Racial, and Religious Structure of the World Population," *Population and Development Review*, 5, no. 3 (September 1979), 505–534. Reprinted from *The World Population Today* (Moscow: USSR Academy of Sciences, 1977), Ch. 8.

11. U.S. Bureau of the Census, "Fertility of American Women: June 1979," *Current Population Reports*, Series P-20, no. 358 (December 1980), Table D, p. 5.

12. U.S. Bureau of the Census, "Population Profile of the United States: 1980," *Current Population Reports*, Series P-20, no. 363 (June 1981), Table 3, p. 9.

13. U.S. Bureau of the Census, "Fertility of American Women," p. 5.

14. National Center for Health Statistics, "Births of Hispanic Parentage, 1978," *Monthly Vital Statistics Report*, 29, no. 12, Supplement (March 20, 1981), Table 1, p. 2.

15. U.S. Bureau of the Census, "Demographic Social and Economic Profile of States: Spring, 1976," *Current Population Reports*, Series P-20, no. 334 (January 1979), Table 1, pp. 10–21.

16. U.S. Bureau of the Census, "Social and Economic Characteristics of the Metropolitan and Nonmetropolitan Population: 1977 and 1970," *Current Population Reports*, Series P-23, no. 75 (November 1978), p. 11.

17. David M. Heer, "Three Issues in Soviet Population Policy," *Population and Development Review*, 3, no. 3 (September 1977), 229–252.

18. U.S. Bureau of the Census, "Fertility of American Women," p. 11.

19. Alice Taylor Day and Lincoln H. Day, "Cross-National Comparison of Population Density," *Science*, 181 (September 14, 1973), 1,016–1,023.

20. Hope Tisdale, "The Process of Urbanization," *Social Forces*, 20 (March 1942), 311.

21. Kingsley Davis, "The Origin and Growth of Urbanization in the World," *American Journal of Sociology*, 60, no. 5 (March 1955), 429–437; Philip M. Hauser, "Urbanization: An Overview," in *The Study of Urbanization*, ed. Philip M. Hauser and Leo F. Schnore (New York: John Wiley, 1965), p. 7.

22. United Nations Department of Economic and Social Affairs, *World Population Trends and Policies: 1977 Monitoring Report, Volume I: Population Trends* (New York: United Nations, 1979), p. 111.

23. Ibid., p. 112; Glenn Firebaugh, "Structural Determinants of Urbanization in Asia and Latin America, 1950–1970," *American Sociological Review*, 44 (April 1979), 199–215.

24. George J. Beier, "Can Third World Cities Cope?" *Population Bulletin*, 31, no. 4, Population Reference Bureau, Washington, 1976, 9.

25. Robert A. Hackenberg, "New Patterns of Urbanization in Southeast Asia: An Assessment," *Population and Development Review*, 6, no. 3 (September 1980), 394.

26. United Nations, *World Population*, p. 117.

27. United Nations, *Patterns of Urban and Rural Population Growth*, Population Studies No. 68 (New York: United Nations, 1980), p. 16.

28. Beier, "Third World Cities," pp. 25–32; Michael P. Todaro with Jerry Stilkind, *City Bias and Rural Neglect: The Dilemma of Urban Development* (New York: The Population Council, 1981), pp. 40–79.

29. John D. Kasarda, "The Implications of Contemporary Redistribution Trends for National Urban Policy," *Social Science Quarterly*, 61, nos. 3 and 4 (December 1980), 376.

30. Kasarda, "Redistribution Trends," p. 380.

31. David F. Sly and Jeffrey Tayman, "Changing Metropolitan Morphology and Municipal Service Expenditures in Cities and Rings," *Social Science Quarterly*, 61, nos. 3 and 4 (December 1980), 595–611.

32. Tim B. Heaton and Glenn V. Fuguitt, "Dimensions of Population Redistribution in the United States Since 1950," *Social Science Quarterly*, 61, nos. 3 and 4 (December 1980), 508–523.

33. Philip M. Hauser, "Urbanization—Problems of High Density Living," in *World Population—The View Ahead*, ed. Richard N. Farmer (Bloomington: Indiana University Graduate School of Business, 1968), p. 191.

34. Reynolds Farley, "The Urbanization of Negroes in the United States," *Journal of Social History*, 2 (Spring 1968), 241–258.

35. United Nations, *Patterns of Urban and Rural*, p. 269.

36. Leo F. Schnore, "On the Spatial Structure of Cities in the Two Americas," in *Urbanization*, ed. Hauser and Schnore, pp. 349–398; Ray M. Northam, *Urban Geography* (New York: John Wiley, 1979), pp. 238–246, 319–337; Brian J. L. Berry and John D. Kasarda, *Contemporary Urban Ecology* (New York: Macmillan, 1977), pp. 85–93.

37. Donald L. Foley, "Urban Daytime Population: A Field for Demographic-Ecological Analysis," *Social Forces*, 32, no. 3 (May 1954), 326–327.

SUGGESTED ADDITIONAL READINGS

BERRY, BRIAN J. L., AND JOHN D. KASARDA, EDS., *Contemporary Urban Ecology.* New York: Macmillan, 1977. An interdisciplinary approach to urban ecological issues that includes attention to demographic, social, and ecological aspects of regional, metropolitan, and city structures.

BERRY, BRIAN J. L., AND LESTER P. SILVERMAN, EDS., *Population Redistribution and Public Policy*. Washington, D.C.: National Academy of Sciences, 1980. An interdisciplinary review of the linkages of population redistribution to various sectors of American society.

GOLDSTEIN, SIDNEY, AND DAVID SLY, EDS., *Basic Data Needed for the Study of Urbanization* and *The Measurement of Urbanization and Projection of Urban Population*. Working Papers 1 and 2 of the International Union for the Scientific Study of Population (IUSSP), Committee on Urbanization and Population Redistribution. (Dolhain, Belgium: Ordina Editions, 1974 and 1975). Examination of data and measurement of urban concepts on an international basis.

————, *Patterns of Urbanization: Comparative Country Studies*. Dolhain, Belgium: Ordina Editions, 1975. 2 volumes. Review of urbanization measurement and patterns in a number of developed and developing countries throughout the world.

TECHNICAL SUPPLEMENT NO. 6

Measuring Urban Concepts

Among the several concepts that are used to describe population distribution, those relating to the terms *urban, rural,* and *urbanization* seem to be the most widely used. These are intended to convey a sense of population clustering, or the lack of it, in different geographical areas.

Urban typically refers to a place that has a fairly substantial population. Various countries measure urbanness in terms of one or more criteria—population size, population or housing density, administrative structure or function, or other urban-related characteristics. Population size is the most frequent criterion, and is recommended by the United Nations. Where this is the criterion, a minimum size is selected, and any place having at least that many people is regarded as urban; those who live there constitute an urban population. The minimum-size cutoff varies by country; hence it is very difficult to approximate the world's urban population by any standard definition.

In the United States Census, a cutoff of 8,000 people was used to define a place as urban from 1850 to 1880, at which time the qualifying size was reduced to 4,000. In 1906 it was further reduced to its present minimum size of 2,500 people. In fact, the urban definition used in the decennial census is more complex, including special rules that allow for the inclusion in an urban population of those who live outside of places with 2,500 or more but within the sphere of a large population cluster such as an urbanized area.

By definition, any area that is not urban is considered rural. This may include places with concentrations of fewer than 2,500 people as well as space that is sparsely inhabited. For this reason census definitions were elaborated some years ago to separate the rural component into "rural farm" and "rural nonfarm," with a definition of acreage or sale of produce determining farm status. Today there is more interest in scaling geographic places by their population size as a measure of degree of urbanness.

Urbanization, on the other hand, refers more to a population distributional *process* than a population distributional *status.* Several measures have been developed to capture the rate at which urban population is expanding absolutely and relatively. The percent of the total population that is in urban areas and how that is changing are common indicators of urbanization. So are the percentages living in agglomerations of at least a given population size beyond the urban minimum.

The tendency for people to be most concentrated in a relatively few number of places led to specification of other urban terms that describe some of these concentrations. A *metropolitan area* has a central city of 50,000 or more people and includes the remaining part of the central county and any other adjacent counties that are socially and economically integrated with the central city. Thus a metropolitan area may be viewed as a market area or commercial sphere even though its outlying part includes rural territory and population. An *urbanized area* has the same central city, but the remaining part of the area is only the densely settled adjacent area. Hence no rural area is included, and the boundary of an urbanized area can be quite irregular and may not conform to political boundaries.

The many aspects of measurement of urban concepts have produced a great number of variations in measures that attempt to relate the indicators to the changing realities of population distribution.

More elaborate discussions of this topic can be found in: Eduardo, Arriaga, "Selected Measures of Urbanization," in *The Measurement of Urbanization,* eds. Sidney Goldstein and David Sly (Dolhain, Belgium: Ordina Editions, 1975); Henry S. Shryock, Jacob S. Siegel, and Associates, *The Methods and Materials of Demography,* vol. 1 (Washington, D.C.: U.S. Government Printing Office, 1973); United Nations Secretariat, "Statistical Definitions of Urban Population and Their Uses in Applied Demography," in *Basic Data Needed for the Study of Urbanization,* eds. Sidney Goldstein and David Sly (Dolhain, Belgium: Ordina Editions, 1974).

ISSUES SUPPLEMENT NO. 6

Should We Make Cities Less Attractive?

"How you gonna' keep 'em down on the farm . . . ?" asks the old song. Indeed, the attraction of "city lights" has long been recognized by weary city planners trying to keep up with migrant in-flows and by discouraged parents losing their children to a way of life they find both strange and frightening.

There have been many incentives to move to the city in both developed and developing areas. Besides entertainment and other consumer amenities, cities have also offered the possibility of better jobs, higher wages, superior housing, and improved services of many kinds. Now, however, in many parts of the world, cities are becoming old and crowded. In developed countries, urban deterioration and the flight of many of the more wealthy to suburban locations have called into question the survival of these cities. In developing countries, urbanization is occurring so rapidly that the slums and poverty of the city have become their dominant characteristics.

In order to combat this trend, some have argued that population policies that have favored urbanization should now be changed to favor rural areas. Without a thriving countryside and a strong agricultural economy, some suggest, cities cannot prosper. Michael Todaro has recently expressed these sentiments:

> *Two policy approaches, undertaken simultaneously, are necessary. The first, rural development, is now widely accepted—in theory, if not always in practice. Its aim is to increase employment and incomes in the countryside so that fewer people feel compelled to migrate in search of a livelihood. But that step is not enough, for the cities have a running head start. The subsidized jobs, incomes, and amenities of modern urban life are firmly established in one form or another in many countries. Consequently, unless urban-biased policies are gradually dismantled, rural areas and smaller cities will never become an attractive alternative to the principal urban areas. . . . In order to eliminate the urban bias in development policies, three equally dramatic and perhaps unpopular steps need to be taken. The first is to end the special tax breaks, subsidized interest rates, excessive tariff protection, and other privileges enjoyed exclusively by urban large-scale industry. The second is to modify minimum wages by holding them to the level of average agri-*

cultural incomes while simultaneously slowing the growth of urban real wages at all levels in both the public and private sector. Third, governments must curtail the expansion of urban public services and instead provide for them in rural towns and small-city service centers. (Michael P. Todaro with Jerry Stilkind, *City Bias and Rural Neglect: The Dilemma of Urban Development.* New York: The Population Council, 1981, pp. xiii–xiv.)

Who would object to such programs? Who are the persons in power in a city? Do you think such programs are necessary and workable?

CHAPTER SEVEN
POPULATION IMPACTS:
EDUCATION,
THE ECONOMY,
AND THE ENVIRONMENT

"I ask you, what's wrong with the environment?"

Drawing by Alan Dunn: © 1972 *The New Yorker* Magazine, Inc.

In the preceding chapters we examined some of the factors that influence population size, growth rates, composition, and distribution. In addition, we looked at macro-, medial-, and micro-level influences on fertility, mortality, and mobility. But that is only half the picture. Demographic processes in turn influence these various factors. This chapter and Chapter 8 will explore some of the ways in which population size, growth rates, composition, and distribution influence other processes in society.

Specifically, we shall examine how demographic processes affect education, the economy, the environment, the polity, religion, and the family. While it should be obvious on reflection that population size, growth rates, composition, and distribution must have important effects on these societal institutions, the impacts of these demographic factors are often overlooked. For example, since crime is more prevalent among some age groups than others, larger numbers of young people in a population would ordinarily lead to rising crime rates, all other things being equal. Similarly, declining numbers of young people should lead to a lessening of criminal activity. Ignorance of this important relationship might lead local communities to conclude that declining numbers of police, a breakdown of moral standards, lack of parental discipline, or a multitude of other causes should be blamed for crime upswings. When crime decreases, many agencies would be eager to claim credit. Of course these other causes of social change are not to be ignored or downplayed. Still, it is important to appreciate how a simple change in some demographic factor can produce widespread social change.

Some population processes are more important than others for each institutional area. For example, the size of the population may be an important factor in determining the form of the educational or political system. However, the growth rate of the population may be more important than its size in determining the economic patterns in the society. Similarly, the level at which population influences each institutional area also varies. For example, population growth may affect the economic development of a nation, a macro-level impact, or affect the socioeconomic status of groups or individuals, impacts felt at the medial and macro levels.

POPULATION AND EDUCATION

There are those who argue that increased education in a society is the key to all other aspects of economic development. Indeed, education provides not only basic literacy but also high-level training to make possible utilization of and advances in technology. Through education the population broadens its work capabilities, its productivity, and its opportunities. Education may also change the degree to which people are exposed to new ideas and may, in turn, lead to the development of different tastes and values. All of these impacts of education are important to overall economic development.

When societies were small and undifferentiated and residential mobility was low, education usually consisted of apprenticeship. Fathers passed skills along to sons, mothers to daughters; or, in a more developed form, masters of given trades agreed to train a limited number of apprentices in their occupation. Education was thus highly individual and very different from the large classes common in universities at the present time.

As societies grew, it became more efficient to organize education at specific locations and to license or certify those who were educators. With growing populations, more skills and specialization became necessary. Societies needed to separate those who were most able to learn given skills from among all those who wanted training.

As population grew still larger, one-room schoolhouses containing all six elementary grades gave way to single grades in multiclassroom schools. Training thus changed from individual tutelage, to small classes for the elite, to large schools where students may number in the thousands.

As schools accommodated more and more students, they also became more formalized. There was a need not only to teach and evaluate great numbers of students, but to develop procedures to select teachers as well. Volunteer teachers or those selected by community consensus were replaced by teachers trained in the school system specifically to assume these positions. Whether these changes are seen as beneficial to education or not, their connection, at least in part, to growing population is clear.

Some societies have simply not been able to provide more places in schools and more educators for the greater number of children in each generation; in other nations, the amount of educational expenditure per child has decreased. In either case, three measures of educational status show the effects of population growth: *school enrollment* or the number or percentage of those in the population enrolled in school by age, sex, or other characteristics; *educational attainment* of the population, or years of school completed; and *literacy*, or the number or percentage of those in the population who are able to read and write in any language. These measures are not independent of one another but are different in some senses.

The overall literacy rate in a population is a crude measure, since ability to read and write is a rather minimal standard against which to measure educational achievement. School enrollment is a measure of how many persons in the population are currently receiving formal education, or if projected, how many persons may be expected to receive it. The educational-attainment measure, on the other hand, reflects the level of education achieved by people already old enough to be out of school. Both school-enrollment data and figures on educational attainment refer to participation in the formal educational system, and do not include other kinds of learning. We will use each of these measures to describe population and education relationships in developed and developing societies.

Developing Nations

The mere size of a population is perhaps not as important for the development and maintenance of its educational system as the rate at which the population grows and the stability of the growth pattern. Rapid or erratic growth creates problems for educational systems, as it does for other societal institutions.

Examples of *rapid* population growth influencing education are plentiful in the developing nations. In an analysis of the development and cost of education in the United States, Sweden, and Latin America, for example, one author makes a startling statement:

> The handicap that the Latin American demographic characteristics have represented for educational purposes will continue in the future. The goals for rapid educational development will be jeopardized by the high fertility of these populations. Even those Latin American countries that will rapidly reduce fertility up to the year 2000 . . . will have an education cost 47 percent higher than that in the Swedish case in 1965.[1]

These costs occur because, in rapidly growing populations, more and more resources have to be consumed to maintain a constant standard of living for each generation. Thus, increased expenditures for education to provide instruction to a greater *proportion* of children becomes more difficult when the *number* of children is also increasing. Thailand illustrates this problem well. About 4.3 million children were enrolled in school there in 1960.[2] This number had grown to 6.1 million in 1970, but because of rapid population growth, this large increase in the number of children enrolled in school represented only a very slight increase in the proportion of children enrolled.

As if these modest gains in enrollment were not discouraging enough, the monetary costs of providing education under conditions of

FIGURE 7.1   Total costs of education as a percent of GNP under three projections, assuming improving enrollment rates: Thailand, 1970–2000

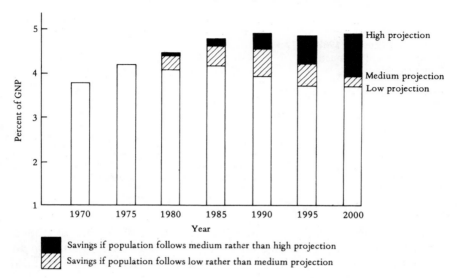

Savings if population follows medium rather than high projection
Savings if population follows low rather than medium projection

Source: Gavin W. Jones, "Educational Planning and Population Growth," in *Population and Development Planning,* Warren C. Robinson, ed. (New York: The Population Council, 1975), Figure 4.3, p. 79. Reprinted with permission of The Population Council.

unabated population growth are staggering. Figure 7.1 shows how these costs will be different in Thailand from 1970 to the year 2000 if population growth follows low, medium, or high growth. The cross-hatched and dark sections of each bar show the savings that result from lower growth. These savings become greater as time goes on. In Table 7.1 the education costs of higher rather than lower fertility are shown for sever-

TABLE 7.1   Additional costs of education with higher rather than lower fertility in selected developing countries

	PERCENTAGE INCREASED COST	
Country	After 15 Years	After 25 Years
Ghana	7	25
Pakistan	10	30
Thailand	16	33
Sri Lanka	17	54

Source: Gavin W. Jones, "Educational Planning and Population Growth," in *Population and Development Planning,* Warren C. Robinson, ed. (New York: The Population Council, 1975), Figure 4.3, p. 79. Reprinted with permission of The Population Council.

TABLE 7.2 **Population growth and school enrollment in more and less developed nations of the world**

	More Developed	Less Developed
Population growth (1982)		
Annual percent increase	0.6	2.1
Years to double	116	33
Percent enrolled in school (1975)		
Males 6–11	94	70
Females 6–11	94	53
Males 12–17	84	42
Females 12–17	85	28

Source: Growth figures from Population Reference Bureau, *1982 World Population Data Sheet.* School enrollment from Population Reference Bureau, *World's Children Data Sheet,* 1979.

al developing nations. Particularly after twenty-five years of higher fertility rates, and assuming gradually improving school-enrollment rates, the percentage difference in educational costs incurred by these nations is substantial.

Table 7.2 summarizes these differences in the educational opportunities afforded to children in the developed and developing nations, and also demonstrates that the educational deficits for women are particularly large. Particularly in Islamic countries, women are often denied educational opportunities available to them in developed nations. Clearly, one of the most important contributors to these educational problems is the persistent high fertility in many of the developing nations.

Developed Nations

Pressure on school systems to accommodate more and more young people has been felt in developed nations as well. Perhaps more important, however, erratic population growth produced by rising and falling fertility rates has also required adaptations of the educational system.[3] Fluctuations in the number of young people change the needs for teachers, classroom space, and monetary expenditures from year to year, making effective development of the educational system difficult. In the United States, for example, the post-World War II baby boom filled classrooms to capacity as these children reached school age. Portable classrooms, temporary teachers, and buildings designed for other purposes were all pressed into service to meet the demand. By the 1960s the educational system had nearly caught up with this demand, only to be faced with a period of declining fertility. Many of the extra classrooms and facilities built to cope with baby-boom children were relatively empty in the 1970s, following ten years of fertility decline.

Even among developed countries, relatively small differences in fertility rates can have lasting impacts on costs. One analysis has demonstrated, for example, that the education cost per worker in the United States was 10 to 18 percent higher than in Sweden, owing to slightly higher levels of fertility and mortality from the 1800s to the 1960s.[4] While in developing countries much attention is directed toward the acquisition of primary and secondary education, in developed nations population impacts are also felt at higher levels of the educational system. Figure 7.2 illustrates this phenomenon in the United States by showing projected college-enrollment figures from 1973 to the year 2000.

The four population projections in Figure 7.2 were made by assuming different levels of fertility between now and the year 2000. In addition, Figure 7.2 assumes that the proportion of young people going to college will continue to grow as it has in the past. The series E projection is the lowest, and assumes an average of 2.11 children per woman. The series B projection, on the other hand, assumes an average of 3.10 children per woman. Before 1985 these figures are shown as a single line, since the children to be enrolled in college in 1985 are already born and this projection can be made rather safely. Notice, however, that by the year 2000, the number of persons enrolled in college will be vastly different under the different fertility assumptions. Even the difference between 2.11 children and 2.45 children (series E and D) would make a difference of about 1.7 million students enrolled in college. If fertility assumptions differ by as much as one child per woman (series E and B), the college enrollment difference by the year 2000 would be about 5 million students.

It is possible that fertility will remain below even the 2.11 children per woman offered by the census as its lowest estimate for these projections. In fact, in the most recent years, college enrollment has leveled off, giving rise to speculation as to the cause of this phenomenon. Again, demographic factors seem important. It appears that this downturn in college enrollment corresponds with an increase in the proportion of households with two or more children of college age. These households are part of the famous baby-boom cohort.[5]

Perhaps, it is argued, families with more than one child of college age simply cannot afford to send them all to college. If this interpretation is correct, then it illustrates once again the pervasive and long-term impact of demographic processes for the educational system. Moreover, this particular impact was unpredicted (as can be seen by the projections in Figure 7.2). Even once uncovered, without consideration of the demographic patterns of the nation, explanations might have suggested decreasing interest in college, a return to "traditional" values wherein a high-school education is considered sufficient, or a myriad of other hypotheses.

FIGURE 7.2   Projections of college enrollment, 1973 to 2000 *

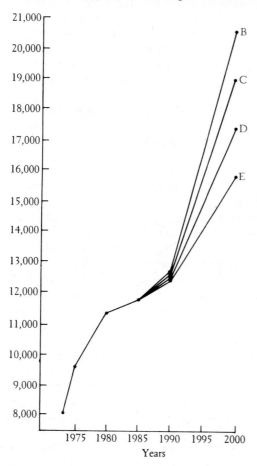

Sources: 1973 data are from U.S. Bureau of the Census, "School Enrollment in the United States: October, 1973," *Current Population Reports,* Series P-20, no. 261, March 1974, Table 4, p. 6. All other data are from U.S. Bureau of the Census, "Projections of School and College Enrollment: 1971 to 2000," *Current Population Reports,* Series P-25, no. 473, January 1972, Table A-2, p. 14.

**Projections based on the assumption that women will bear the following number of children, on the average, during their lifetime: B = 3.10; C = 2.78; D = 2.45; E = 2.11.*

An interpretative challenge of this sort is offered by yet another educational trend in which demographic processes may be implicated. There has been much documentation of the national decline in Scholastic Aptitude Test (SAT) scores among American youth. Deteriorating quality of education has been most often blamed for this drop.

However, a recent controversial analysis suggests that this drop corresponds to a rise in the average birth order of the population.[6] It is already known that higher birth order (that is, being, for instance, a fourth rather than a second child) is associated with lower intelligence. As Figure 7.3 shows, the higher the average birth order of various cohorts, the lower has been their national average on the SAT. Still, this analysis only shows a parallel trend and does not demonstrate causation. Decreasing scores may also reflect the changing composition of the population of test-takers, more of whom are now from deprived and lower socioeconomic status groups. Whatever the cause, this phenomenon appears to be another example of an important, and unanticipated, potential consequence of population processes for education.

FIGURE 7.3   **Average SAT score and average birth order for annual birth cohorts of 1940 through 1960**

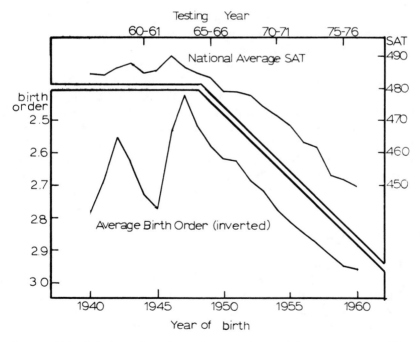

Source: Richard A. Easterlin, "What Will 1984 Be Like? Socioeconomic Implications of Recent Twists in Age Structure," *Demography,* 15 (November 1978), Figure 8, p. 412.

We have seen that both the number of people to be educated and the rates at which that number changes are important considerations. What kinds of persons are to be educated, where they come from, and where they are located are also important. For example, the racial-ethnic composition of the population may also influence the educational system. In cities where a heavy influx of immigrants is common, needs for curriculum changes may emerge, such as teaching English as a second language. In central-city schools, greater proportions of black students give rise to requests for more teachers who can satisfy the curriculum needs of those students.

The great movement of citizens from rural to urban areas has, of course, created burdens for the urban schools, but problems have arisen in rural systems as well. Where these systems have become depopulated, the demand for teachers is lessened. In addition, teachers in rural schools are more likely to need broad skills in a variety of areas than are teachers in urban schools, who may teach only one subject to a variety of classes each day. Recent population movements out of central cities may shift demands on schools in yet new directions.

In each of the ways we have discussed, and in many more, population size, growth rates, composition, and distribution have an impact on the educational system. In spite of the importance of the population variables, it is ironic that the educational system itself is at present doing very little to educate students about these processes. In a survey conducted for the U.S. Commission on Population Growth and the American Future, it was found that knowledge about population processes and facts among Americans was very low.[7] In addition, few secondary schools have courses or even units included in the curriculum to teach students about population processes.[8] While it is not entirely clear that knowledge about population processes would make a difference in, say, the fertility or mobility behavior of individuals,[9] it would seem that since it is one of the major recipients of population consequences, the educational system would profit from exploring ways of spreading knowledge about those processes and their results.

POPULATION AND THE ECONOMY

For residents of many developed countries, and for Americans in particular, "bigger" has long been synonymous with "better." Towns have pointed with pride to the new residents and industry they have been able to attract. More people has meant larger markets for goods and services, ensuring economic growth. Truly, the major part of the nation's history reflects a belief in the growth ethic.

Only recently has the inevitability of the connection between population growth and economic growth been questioned. This questioning has taken place not only in the developing countries, where growth has become a rather obvious burden, but also in developed countries, where "more" has sometimes meant "dirtier" and "poorer" as well.

The issues involved in the more recent discussions of population changes and economic development vary, depending on whether the nation in question is developed or developing. For developing countries, some have argued that priority should be given to developing the economy in order to lower birth and death rates, while others have maintained that lowering high birthrates first would greatly aid these nations in developing their economic structures. On the other hand, there is little disagreement that economic development of these nations suffers from rapid population increase.

In developed countries, the debate seems to center around whether economic stagnation would result from slowly growing or even decreasing populations. The impact of increasing numbers in these countries is seen as primarily related to demand for goods and services, the composition of the labor force, and potentials for creative technological development.

Because concern over the economic impact of population processes has taken different forms in societies at different stages of development, we will discuss these concerns separately for developed and developing countries. In addition, we will consider population processes that influence nations in somewhat the same way, regardless of their economic-development level.

Developing Nations

The economic growth rate of some of the less-developed countries during the past few years has been impressive. Gross national product (GNP) is the most common summary measure of economic well-being; it refers to the total volume of goods and services produced in a society during a given period of time. We have used unadjusted gross national product and gross national product per capita in Figure 7.4 to illustrate the role of population in the economic development of a nation. This figure shows the average annual growth in each of these measures for low- and middle-income developing countries. Note that, particularly in the middle-income developing areas, the growth in gross national product has been rather large. But the difference between the change in gross national product and the change in gross national product per capita is the portion of this growth taken away by increasing population. Figure 7.4 shows rather clearly that, had population remained

FIGURE 7.4   Growth rate of GNP and GNP per capita; selected low- and middle-income countries, 1970–1978

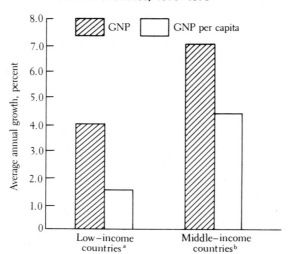

Source: Nancy Birdsall, "Population Growth and Poverty in the Developing World," *Population Bulletin,* vol. 35, no. 5 (Washington, D.C.: Population Reference Bureau, 1980), Table 1.

aIncludes Bangladesh, India, Sri Lanka, Zaire, Pakistan, Kenya, and Indonesia.

bIncludes Egypt, Thailand, Philippines, Nigeria, Morocco, Peru, Colombia, South Korea, Turkey, Mexico, Taiwan, Costa Rica, Brazil, and Venezuela.

constant and GNP been the same, the percentage gain in gross national product per capita in each set of countries would have been larger. This is a phenomenon we noted with regard to educational gains. As one author states the problem, "It is a matter of running up the down escalator; it is possible to reach the top, but the effort involved is much greater than it would be if the escalator halted."[10]

The connection between population growth and economic development in these developing nations has been described as cyclical. As some writers reason, having too many children makes it difficult for a family to accumulate savings and thus limits investments. Lack of investments prevents capital from growing, does not help unemployment, and further perpetuates the cycle of poverty. With lowered fertility, the cycle should be broken, since the family would then have greater savings and would be able to make more investments in such items as education for their children.

This reasoning has led to debates over whether a decline in fertility necessarily will have a favorable impact on the rate of social and economic development. For example, growing populations can contribute to economic growth by stimulating demand for goods and services, creating larger and larger markets, or by permitting economies of scale. A growing population may or may not also encourage technological innovation.[11]

Furthermore, a debate still exists about the degree to which reduced fertility and savings are linked.[12] Some arguing this point say that the relative contribution of household savings to total savings of a country is very small. Also, family investments are only a small part of total national investment. In making investments, there is no guarantee that families will use what additional savings they have for long-term investments, such as education, that would really help the national economy.

Moreover, it is clear that in some countries children contribute valuable labor, so that at least from the perspective of their parents, they are not purely economic liabilities. In Bangladesh, for example, male children become net producers by age twelve and compensate for their cumulative consumption by age fifteen.[13]

To make the issue even more confusing, there are historical examples of countries whose economic development seems to have been helped by increases in population. In Guyana, for example, the rice industry was apparently able to develop because of an expansion in the labor force and the demand for goods, both largely furnished by population increase.[14] Furthermore, some have suggested that specific aspects of economic development in developing countries are even now aided by population growth. Included here would be arguments that population growth has a substantial positive effect upon agricultural investment by farmers in poor countries and that transportation infrastructures, such as roads, are more likely to develop in countries with greater population density.[15]

The other point of contention with regard to the effects of reduced population growth on economic development is how long-term such effects would be. Some say that increased savings by families after fertility is reduced would only be temporary.[16] Others have suggested that in the long run decreased fertility may lower the time countries require to develop economically, but in the short run it will worsen unemployment because of lower demands for goods and services.[17]

A rather thorough debate on these issues occurred in China during the 1950s. As noted in Chapter 4, China's birth-control policies have been erratic, in part reflecting ideological debates on the propriety of introducing birth-control programs in socialist states. It will be recalled that Marxian philosophy indicates that the Malthusian view of population processes is not correct; that is, population problems arise from unequal distribution of resources, not from the numbers of people alone.

China has had economic-development goals that have been seen by some as incompatible with an indefinitely increasing population. Thus arguments ensued over the necessity and/or desirability of bringing down the birthrate to facilitate economic development or for some other purposes. In support of many births as a facilitator of economic development, one Chinese writer argued:

> In the past, many Malthusian scholars once displayed a "scientific" facade and concluded that the territory of China could supply consumption materials to maintain at most 200 million to 280 million persons. This fallacious thesis has been shattered by actual events. Because of the revolutionary victory and the expansion of production, we have within a short period of time abolished hunger for the first time in the history of our nation as well as solved, step by step, the unemployment problem and appreciably raised the level of living of the entire people, though our nation's population has passed 600 million. Moreover, since national liberation, under comparatively backward technological circumstances, we have rapidly made large strides in the national economy. This would have been inconceivable had there not been such a massive source of manpower.[18]

But that view was not to be the prevailing sentiment in China. It remained for others to justify birth planning and limitation for ideologically acceptable reasons. Current programs in China stress the one-child family to promote economic development:

> If population growth is not controlled, there will be a dizzy peak (in the next two decades), making it virtually impossible for the economy and all our social institutions to cope . . . the State Council deems it necessary to launch a crash program over the coming 20 or 30 years calling on each couple . . . to have a single child . . .[19]

This statement reflects concern with a standard of living for individuals, as well as with the general economic growth of the society. It argues, as does Figure 7.4, that while economic growth may be possible with a rapidly growing population, improvement in the level of living will be accelerated if population growth is curtailed. Still, the conditions are different for each country at different points in time.

A more middle-ground approach to the question of the relationship between fertility control and economic development of the developing nations was taken by Easterlin:

The existing state of knowledge does not warrant any clearcut generalizations as to the effect of population growth on economic development in today's less developed areas. Some theoretical analyses argue that high population growth creates pressures on limited natural resources, reduces private and public capital formation, and diverts additions to capital resources to maintaining rather than increasing the stock of capital per worker. Others point to positive effects such as economies of scale and specialization, the possible spur to favorable attitudes, capacities, and motivations of younger populations compared to older ones. The actual evidence . . . does not point to any uniform conclusion.[20]

While the majority of writers would argue that reductions in fertility would bring economic benefits of some kinds, even if only short-run, to the developing nations, others say that only if economic conditions are improved will fertility go down.

Developed Nations

In the economically developed countries, recent concern has centered on falling birthrates, the aging of the population, and the impact of these trends on several features of the economy: composition and size of the labor force, consumption patterns, and savings.

These are not entirely new concerns in these nations. We noted in our discussion of fertility that low birthrates in the earlier part of this century motivated several nations to institute pronatalist programs.

However, by the early 1970s the Commission on Population Growth and the American Future was prepared to conclude:

We have looked for, and have not found, any convincing economic argument for continued national population growth. The health of our economy does not depend on it. The welfare of the average person certainly does not depend on it. In fact, the average person will be markedly better off in terms of traditional economic values if population growth follows the two-child projection rather than the three-child one.[21]

Still, there are those who have maintained that rapidly achieved stable population growth would mean a disrupted, if not a stagnant, economy.[22] What are the mechanisms, then, by which population processes affect the economy? How can we sort out these arguments?

First, it seems clear that the volume of goods and services produced in these nations is larger with rapid population growth than with zero population growth. However, lower overall growth of the GNP affects industries differently. Families with two children clearly require fewer diapers, jars of baby food, pediatricians, and cribs than do three- or four-child families. Industries catering to the needs of young children, at least in some cases, suffer from reduced fertility.

The decreased business of these industries is buffered in at least two ways. First, many companies make not only baby food, but other products such as ketchup, mustard, and hot dogs. These are "leisure foods," commodities for which demand is increasing and should increase further as families decrease fertility and have more money and time for leisure activities. Secondly, parents tend to spend more money on the first child, requiring other children to reuse or share toys, furniture, or other items. Replacing the three-child family with the two-child family thus creates greater problems for those industries producing nonreusable or nontransferable goods for children.

Other sectors of the economy, on the other hand, would benefit. We have already mentioned leisure foods. Likewise, sporting-goods manufacturers and retailers, travel industries, and other recreational businesses will have more customers. Businesses specializing in goods and services for the aged should likewise experience upswings in demand as the population continues to age. Thus the effect on the GNP will not be totally negative.

More important than the total GNP, however, is the GNP per capita. How will material well-being for the average citizen change? One argument is that it will be improved because there are not more and more people in each generation to share incomes. Well-being should also improve, however, because of the changed age composition of populations with low or zero growth. Since they contain a greater proportion of middle-aged people relative to dependent aged or young people, these populations have more workers available to produce goods and services to share with nonproducers. With larger incomes per family, even the business of child-related industries may increase.

On the other hand, some have argued that there will not be much perceptible improvement in average material well-being because the cost of supporting aged dependents is much greater than that of supporting young dependents. Further, it has been suggested that the rate of technological progress will also decline with zero or slow population growth, thus depleting potential gains in well-being.[23]

The second area of concern is labor-force size and composition. The past few years have been difficult ones for the relatively large baby-boom cohort as its members entered the labor force. This "glut" of young workers has produced higher unemployment for this age group, at least in the short run.[24] Such an oversupply is destined to change, however, as the baby-boom cohort marches inexorably through the age pyramids of developed countries. New cohorts of young workers are smaller; thus, demand for their talents will be greater.[25]

The net impact of these changes will be an aging work force. While some analysts have stressed the possibility of lower productivity as a consequence, others have emphasized the greater experience and job commitment older workers would possess. The evidence for either scenario is not overwhelming.

One of the resources any nation has for its economic and general social development is those citizens who are especially gifted, bright, or creative. Such persons innovate, lead social change, and develop technological and social tools that help the society. This resource is important for both developing and developed economies. Some people have argued that decreased population growth lessens the number of such persons in a society. In addition, this argument contends that some population pressure, by producing a continual need to cope with problems, stimulates creativity. Young people often provide an impetus for social change. If the population becomes older, these people fear, society will become stagnant and conservative, not open to new ideas and ways.

Such speculations are, of course, hard to validate. It is possible to reason in the opposite direction—that decreasing the dependency burden and rate of social change will lead to creative and intelligent, rather than emergency, solutions for problems. Further, a study of Nobel Prize winners has found that the age of maximum creativity and production for them is thirty-five to forty-four.[26] Such a finding seems to suggest little need for concern over the aging of the labor force.

Another labor-force factor that requires consideration is the number of women who enter or leave, and the impact of childbearing on these trends. It has seemed clear that higher fertility is associated with decreases in labor-force participation by women. For example, one estimate indicates that the net average effect of a baby is the loss of over 400 hours of work per year from young mothers.[27]

Another way to look at this effect is to examine how many women are employed and at work during the months immediately preceding and following a first birth. Figure 7.5 shows data of this kind for a sample of black and white women in the United States. The birth of the first child is associated with a precipitous drop in working for both racial groups, with blacks returning to work somewhat sooner than whites. Even ten months after the first birth, not all of the white women have returned to work. In spite of these interruptions, there are now more women with small children at work than has been the case in earlier decades, so that the net loss of time and income due to child-

FIGURE 7.5   Percentage of prospective and new mothers employed and at work before and after first birth by race

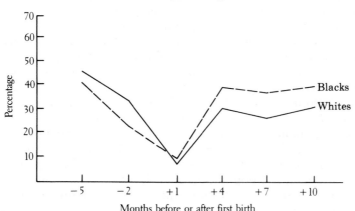

Months before or after first birth

Source: Adapted from David Shapiro and Frank L. Mott, "Labor Supply Behavior of Prospective and New Mothers," *Demography,* 16, no. 2 (May 1979), Figure 2, p. 203.

bearing in the developed countries is somewhat less. In addition, lower birthrates as a whole act to temper these losses.

Another area of speculation in developed countries concerns the potential impact of lower fertility on savings. Some economists have argued, along what seems a plausible line, that fewer children should mean greater savings on the part of families. Fewer expenditures on the necessities for children should provide some surplus income, which might become savings. Further, as we have just discussed, fewer children should mean greater labor-force participation by one or both parents, which should lead to an increase in savings.

On the other hand, this extra income may not become savings but instead may be allocated to the purchase of other consumer goods. Children may even promote savings, it has been reasoned, by working themselves, by encouraging parents to work harder or longer, or by providing an impetus for parents to accumulate an inheritance.

A recent study argues that these effects are different depending on duration of the marriage when the children are born.[28] Children born early in the marriage seem to decrease assets, while those born to marriages of nine or more years seem to increase assets slightly. This is partly because childbearing seems to decrease consumption of some items and increase it of others. For example, young families may feel the need to purchase a home when children are born, a major expense that is likely to decrease savings. For those who postpone having children, this substantial expenditure may already be out of the way. Thus, in evaluating the impact of demographic processes, particularly fertility and age composition, on the economies of developed nations, there is not a simple answer. It is not clear that reduced fertility or population aging will drastically affect consumption patterns, labor-force problems, or savings. In fact several countries that have already achieved population stability have, nevertheless, vibrant economies. In summarizing such a conclusion, one writer states that

> it is difficult to conclude from available evidence that there is any obvious and strong correlation between the rate of population growth and economic well-being for the group of developed countries. . . . A transition to zero population growth will require some readjustments, but with proper anticipation and planning, there need be no insurmountable problems.[29]

POPULATION AND ENVIRONMENT

In assessing the impact of population on the natural environment, the economic factors just discussed make conclusions difficult. It is clear that it is people who pollute, use resources, invent chemicals with adverse side effects, and create waste. Without people there would be no environmental catastrophes such as filthy rivers, dirty air, or poisoned animals and plants. The difficult question is not whether people create pollution, or even whether more of them create more pollution, but how many environmental problems are caused by the numbers or distribution of people and how many by the ways in which those people live. It has been asked whether changes in population processes or economic systems will produce the greatest impact, while many argue that alterations in both are ultimately necessary.

In the developing nations, the primary environmental problems seem to be resource shortages, particularly of food and living space. In developed nations, environmental problems include energy and mineral shortages, pollution, and difficulties arising from population concentrations in certain areas. We will discuss these problems separately.

Developing Nations

In the late 1960s a host of writers predicted that massive famine would occur in much of the developing world within ten years. The following illustrates such projections:

> The battle to feed humanity is over. Unlike battles of military forces, it is possible to know the results of the population-food conflict while the armies are still "in the field." Sometime be-

tween 1970 and 1985, the world will undergo vast famines—hundreds of millions of people are going to starve to death. That is, they will starve to death unless plague, thermonuclear war, or some other agent kills them first. Many will starve to death in spite of any crash programmes we might embark upon now. And we are not embarking upon any crash programme.[30]

Such predictions, while not very optimistic, were rather common. Then, for a brief period, it seemed these estimates were in error. Because of something called the *Green Revolution*, the threat of massive famine appeared to have abated. This revolution refers to the development of new, higher-yielding strains of wheat, rice, and other grains from the same amount of land that formerly produced less. The change in the amount of food produced by some nations was so dramatic that some net importers became self-sufficient or even exporters.

The Green Revolution was not a permanent answer to the pressure of population on food supplies. These new grains required massive amounts of fertilizer and water, and new techniques of agriculture had to be learned if the farmer was to use them effectively. In addition, in the most tradition-bound societies, where fertility is the highest, commitment to the old agricultural ways is also strong. The impact of the Green Revolution was further limited by the inefficiency with which governments distributed the grains and provided the instruction necessary for their cultivation. Even when seed and fertilizer were supplied by other nations, the bureaucratic morass in some countries prevented their utilization.

Norman Borlaug, who won the Nobel Prize for developing these grains, estimated that the Green Revolution, if used to its utmost, would stave off famine for thirty years.[31] Thirty years is a relatively short period of time, but even if massive famine for the entire developing world can be staved off for that long, famine may already have engulfed some countries and food shortages affected others. The problem is again one of trying to run up the down escalator. Figure 7.6 illustrates this problem for Africa, where drought and population growth have combined to produce severe starvation conditions. Food production per capita has steadily declined, despite an optimistic period of increase in absolute food production as a whole from the 1950s to 1970.

Another example of this continuing race between population growth and food supply is provided by the construction of the Aswan Dam in Egypt. The dam improved the arable land in that country by a third. However, during the decade required to build the dam, population grew from 26 to 33 million, and food output per capita has hardly increased at all.[32]

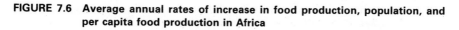

FIGURE 7.6 **Average annual rates of increase in food production, population, and per capita food production in Africa**

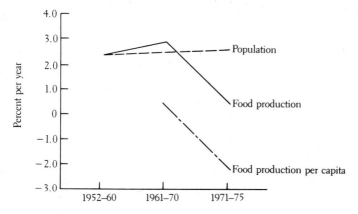

Source: Keith Abercrombie and Arthur McCormack, "Population Growth and Food Supplies in Different Time Perspectives," *Population and Development Review,* 2, nos. 3 and 4, p. 483.

In spite of the time bought by some advances in agriculture, recent estimates of the supply of key biological resources are not optimistic.[33] Table 7.3 looks at per-capita production of the world's forests, fisheries, grasslands, and croplands from 1960 to 1978. In each case, production has begun to decline or has been declining for many years. The production of firewood is especially important in developing nations, where it is a major source of fuel. In many areas forests have become depleted, and local residents use dried cow dung for fuel. This in turn deprives the soils of nutrients and lowers its quality for growing future crops.

Still another indicator of the relationship between population growth and food supply is provided by a comparison of per-capita calorie supply in developed and developing nations. In developed nations, that daily supply is 132 percent of requirements. In developing nations, however, it is only 96 percent of requirements.[34] More distressing yet are the nations where this figure falls below 80 percent, such as Mali, Upper Volta, and Chad in Africa, and Bolivia in Latin America.

All of these indicators have led writers to speculate about whether the developed nations can continue to feed both themselves and these developing nations indefinitely. The answer to that question is probably no. What is in doubt is how much more time technology or foreign aid can buy for those rapidly growing nations that face continual food shortages.

Another serious problem in developing nations is crowding and

TABLE 7.3 **World production per capita of key commodities of biological origin, 1960–1978, with peak year underlined**

	FORESTS	FISHERIES	GRASSLANDS			CROPLANDS
Year	Wood	Fish	Beef	Mutton	Wool	Cereals
	(cubic meters)			(kilograms)		
1960	—	13.4	9.43	1.91	0.86	287
1961	0.65	14.3	9.67	1.91	0.85	278
1962	0.66	14.5	9.90	1.90	0.85	292
1963	0.66	14.7	10.25	1.89	0.83	286
1964	0.67	16.1	10.12	1.84	0.81	297
1965	0.67	16.2	10.09	1.82	0.79	288
1966	0.67	17.1	10.39	1.80	0.80	308
1967	0.67	17.7	10.59	1.92	0.79	308
1968	0.66	18.4	10.86	1.92	0.80	318
1969	0.66	17.7	10.90	1.88	0.79	316
1970	0.66	19.5	10.80	1.90	0.76	314
1971	0.66	19.2	10.57	1.91	0.74	335
1972	0.65	17.6	10.75	1.92	0.73	319
1973	0.66	17.5	10.63	1.83	0.67	337
1974	0.65	18.1	11.16	1.80	0.65	322
1975	0.62	17.6	11.49	1.80	0.67	321
1976	0.62	18.2	11.81	1.79	0.65	342
1977	0.62	17.4	11.53	1.78	0.63	333
1978*	0.61	16.6	11.21	1.77	0.64	340

Source: Lester R. Brown, "Resource Trends and Population Policy: A Time for Reassessment," *Worldwatch Paper* 29 (May 1979), p. 9.

*Preliminary estimates.

the consequent environmental damage. In the cities of India, for example, millions live in the streets, with sanitation facilities sadly lacking and disease rampant.

These nations are not even free of the pollution problems that haunt developed countries. In India, for example, the sacred river Ganges, believed to wash away sins, has been declared unfit for bathing. A recent report estimates that only 8 out of 142 major cities in that country have effective sewerage systems, and 72 cities have no facilities at all.[35]

That problems of environmental strain and food shortage exist in these nations, no one denies. Differences in viewing these problems center on the degree of urgency perceived and the solutions envisioned. These differences are not unlike those we found when we examined economic issues. Some authors suggest that direct attacks on population growth rates are the key. Others argue that assaults on the environment will have greater impact. Still others believe that only with massive economic aid for development can either population or environmental issues be attacked. However, everyone agrees that the three areas are inextricably intertwined.

Developed Nations

As we noted above, growth in GNP has been the goal sought after by most developed nations. But this growth has exacted certain prices—among them, environmental deterioration. This problem received great attention in the 1960s and early 1970s, when many gloomy forecasts were made regarding the future of the environment. For example, to call attention to the problems of economic growth for the environment, one author wrote:

> More important than what the GNP is, however, is what it is not. It is not a measure of the degree of freedom of the people of a nation. It is not a measure of the health of a population. It is not a measure of the state of depletion of natural resources. It is not a measure of the stability of the environmental systems upon which life depends. It is not a measure of security from the threat of war. It is not, in sum, a comprehensive measure of the quality of life.[36]

Because of these links between prosperity and environmental damage, some even suggested that nations forego some amount of economic growth to insure the maintenance of other valued goods and conditions.

Population changes, too, were seen as contributing to environmental damage, although the Commission on Population Growth and the American Future estimated that in almost all environmental areas, the impact of economic growth was much greater than that of population growth. Relative to consumption of valuable resources, one estimate for the United States was that "a one percent reduction in population would reduce consumption of resources in the year 2000 by 0.2 to 0.7 percent, whereas the equivalent percentage reduction in per capita GNP would reduce consumption in that year 0.6 to 3.5 percent."[37]

Still, population processes play an important role in several environmental areas, even if not as vital a one as economic development. In the United States, for example, several minerals will shortly be, or are at present, in limited supply. Using a two-child rather than a three-child family model, it has been estimated that demand for these minerals will be reduced by between 1 and 8 percent by the year 2000. By the year 2020, the demand would be reduced by 14 percent.[38]

Another way to look at the supply of minerals, and of energy in general (resources of central concern to developed economies), is to examine the dates when their world prices are likely to rise because of shortages. In other words, these estimates do not attempt to predict an absolute end to their supply, but rather recognize that in advance of that end, world markets will reflect scarcity. Price adjustments can, in turn, cause rather drastic changes in the world economy, much as has occurred with regard to oil since the late 1970s.

Table 7.4 gives such dates for seventeen nonfuel minerals and four major energy sources. For all but a few of these, the time of projected price rise based on currently known reserves is relatively short.

TABLE 7.4 Dates when price must rise to avoid exhaustion of selected resources

	Based on Currently Known Reserves Only (Year)	Based on Reserves Plus Prospective Reserves (Year)
Nonfuel minerals		
Aluminum	2025	2038
Chromium	2048	2095
Cobalt	2004	2016
Copper	2010	2041
Iron	2053	2094
Lead	2000	2016
Manganese	2061	2112
Molybdenum	2014	2480
Nickel	2014	2032
Phosphate rock	2034	2120
Potash	2104	2368
Sulfur	2010	2036
Tin	2003	2030
Titanium	2043	2151
Tungsten	2009	2037
Vanadium	2060	2180
Zinc	1993	2065
Energy		
Coal	2050	3000
Petroleum	1995	2010
Natural gas	2005	2024
Uranium	2005	2030–2070

Source: Ronald G. Ridker and Elizabeth W. Cecelski, "Resources, Environment and Population: The Nature of Future Limits," *Population Bulletin,* 34 (August 1979), Table 6, p. 26.

These projections are based on the "standard world case" from the above source and assume that recycling rates remain unchanged and that the rate of growth in demand during the 2015–2025 period remains constant thereafter.

Even these estimates are likely to be optimistic, since they suggest that petroleum prices should rise in 1995, a date we now know is grossly in error! The world supply of petroleum is in itself a matter of such grave concern that it deserves special attention. Oil is not only important to the industrialized economies in developed nations, but it has assumed tremendous importance in the developing world as well.[39] Kerosene serves as a substitute for firewood where the latter has been in short supply. Gasoline is required to power tractors and irrigation pumps in agricultural economies, and farmers use fertilizer produced from petroleum in croplands that have been depleted. Petroleum-based products are used to produce synthetic rubber and to make plastics to substitute for wood, paper, and leather. As the population continues to grow and the world's supply of petroleum dwindles, the issue becomes much more serious than whether one should use a few gallons of gasoline to power a big American car during a summer vacation.

In looking at pollution control, it is again clear that lower economic growth rates would produce greater benefits than reduced population growth. In addition, an active attack on pollution in the form of an abatement or regulatory policy produces greater impacts on clean air, water, and the like, than would population control. One estimate, for example, suggested that by 1975 the cost of pollution damages in the United States would amount to 8.6 percent of the GNP. Those damages were only 3.2 percent, however, because of control policies costing about 1 percent.[40] Nevertheless, those areas with the greatest pollution problems have high population concentrations. As population concentrates more and more in urban areas, strategies such as staggered work hours, forced use of mass transit, or special taxes on car use may be required in order to keep hydrocarbon emissions at acceptable levels. These changes alter our style of life and are clearly made necessary by population changes as well as by economic activity.

Moreover, there is no guarantee that even the regulations currently enacted to reduce pollution will remain in effect. We have just seen a period of time in the United States when various restrictions on hydrocarbon emissions have been suspended in order to allow some relief from gasoline shortages.

In addition to these environmental considerations, there is a set of pollutants about which little is known except that they are extremely dangerous. These include radioactive wastes, pesticides, and various chemicals emitted by industry, all of which continue to have an impact over a long period of time. The environmental damage wrought by them may be far worse than the standard emissions from combustion processes, because of their long-lasting nature and their ability to affect large areas, and because their effects take a long time to appear. Nevertheless utility companies argue that they must employ nuclear technology to keep pace with consumer demands. Such solutions are adopted under pressure before we even know how to dispose of the nuclear wastes created by these processes. While it is difficult to project the exact impact, in this case, of reducing population growth, at least there would be more time in which to carefully test and evaluate advanced technology and its side effects.

Each of these environmental problems is influenced by population processes. Some of them are tightly bound to population growth; others are more loosely connected through economic processes. In every case, few environmental benefits seem to result from continued population growth. Even larger improvements in the environment would result from slower economic growth—a difficult voluntary solution for the developed nations.

The World Outlook

Developed and developing nations share the burden of unequal distribution of people and resources. Many of the countries with the largest populations have the fewest environmental resources. The inequality of population and resource distributions creates problems of support for the haves and problems of scarcity for the have-nots. Both problems contribute to tension in international relations.

Table 7.5 indicates, for example, that in 1972 the developed regions accounted for 84 percent of the world's energy consumption but had only 29 percent of the population. By the year 2025 energy consumption in the developed regions is predicted to drop to 53 percent of the world total, and population should be only 15 percent. The developed regions will still be overconsuming energy in relationship to their proportion of the world's people, but the disparity will not be as great.

In the developing regions, on the other hand, with 71 percent of the world's people, energy consumption was only 16 percent of the world total in 1972. Energy consumption in these nations is projected to rise to 47 percent by the year 2025, while the population percentage will rise to 85 percent. In short, the disparity between the developed and developing regions is likely to continue for many years.

In addition, both developed and developing nations have pressing environmental problems that could be alleviated by slower rates of population growth. In developing nations, the frantic search for newer technological developments to push back the ever-present specter of famine could be alleviated in part by slower population growth. The developing nations must implement new programs without taking the time to watch for side effects or to test other results. The wholesale introduction of fertilizer, for example, may create water quality problems or ground damage.

TABLE 7.5 Estimated and projected world energy consumption and population, developed and developing regions

	Energy Consumption (Percent)	Population (Percent)
Developed Regions		
1972	84	29
2000	67	20
2025	53	15
United States		
1972	32	5
2000	20	4
2025	14	3
Developing Regions		
1972	16	71
2000	33	80
2025	47	85

Source: Ronald G. Ridker and Elizabeth W. Cecelski, "Resources, Environment and Population: The Nature of Future Limits," *Population Bulletin,* 34, no. 3 (August 1979), Table 5, pp. 24–25.

In developed nations, too, time is often precious. Energy crises, made worse by large populations, demand instant solutions. Such solutions sometimes have devastating long-range effects. As we noted in discussing education and economic development, the effect of technological gains is lessened by increasing populations, so that overall progress is slow.

To say that the economy, education, and environment can develop indefinitely if population keeps growing rapidly is absurd. To say that the world's population will die from starvation or pollution tomorrow, or to argue that developed economies can never cope with stable populations, is equally silly. The middle ground seems to be the recognition that population processes play a part in educational, economic, and environmental well-being. This acknowledgment can be the first step toward making effective planning decisions to reach societal goals in these areas.

NOTES

1.   Eduardo Arriaga, "Impact of Population Changes on Education Cost," *Demography,* 9 (May 1972), 283.

2.   Manasvi Unhanand et al., "Thailand," *Country Profiles,* The Population Council (March 1972).

3. For analyses of these effects see Richard A. Easterlin, "What Will 1984 Be Like? Socioeconomic Implications of Recent Twists in Age Structure," *Demography*, 15 (November 1978), 397–432; and Thomas J. Espenshade, "Zero Population Growth and the Economies of Developed Nations," *Population and Development Review* (December 1978), 645–680.

4. Arriaga, "Population Changes," p. 279.

5. David Goldberg and A. Anderson, "Projections of Population and College Enrollment in Michigan 1970–2000" (paper presented to the Governor's Commission on Higher Education, Lansing, Michigan, 1974).

6. R. B. Zajonc, "Family Configuration and Intelligence," *Science*, 192 (1976), 227–236.

7. Carl C. Hetrick, A. E. Keir Nash, and Alan J. Wyner, "Population and Politics: Information, Concern, and Policy Support Among the American Public," in *Governance and Population: The Governmental Implications of Population Change*. Research Report of the U.S. Commission on Population Growth and the American Future (Washington, D.C.: U.S. Government Printing Office, 1972), pp. 301–332.

8. Stephen Viederman, "Population Education in Elementary and Secondary Schools in the U.S.," in *Aspects of Population Growth Policy*. Research Report of the U.S. Commission on Population Growth and the American Future (Washington, D.C.: U.S. Government Printing Office, 1972, pp. 433–458; Carl A. Huether and Susan O. Gustavus, "Population Education in the United States," *Population Reference Bureau Report*, 3, no. 2 (March 1977), 1–11.

9. A study for the U.S. Commission on Population Growth and the American Future, for example, found that knowledge about population was not related to concern about it. See Hetrick et al., "Population and Politics."

10. Gavin W. Jones, "Effect of Population Change on the Attainment of Education Goals in the Developing Countries," in *Rapid Population Growth: Consequences and Policy Implications*, ed. Roger Revelle (Baltimore, Johns Hopkins University Press, 1971), p. 317.

11. Nancy Birdsall, "Population Growth and Poverty in the Developing World," *Population Bulletin*, 35, no. 5 (December 1980), 1–48.

12. As noted in Eric R. Weiss-Altaner, "Reviews of Papers Presented to the Conference: Angel Fucaraccio, 'El control de la natalidad y el argumento del ahorro y la inversion,' and Paul Israel Singer, 'Cambios de poblacion y produccion,'" *Concerned Demography*, 2 (January 1971), 8–11.

13. Mead T. Cain, "The Economic Activities of Children in a Village in Bangladesh," *Population and Development Review*, 3, no. 3 (September 1977) 201–227.

14. Jay R. Mandle, "Population and Economic Change: The Emergence of the Rice Industry in Guyana 1895–1915," *Journal of Economic History*, 30 (December 1970), 785–801.

15. Julian L. Simon, *The Economics of Population Growth* (Princeton: Princeton University Press, 1977).

16. John Isbister, "Birth Control, Income Redistribution, and the Rate of Saving: The Case of Mexico," *Demography*, 10 (February 1973), 85–97.

17. Richard Blandy, "Population and Employment Growth: An Introductory

Empirical Exploration," *International Labor Review*, 106 (October 1972), 347–366.

18. Yang ssu-ying, "The Premise of Birth Control Advocacy is Not Malthusianism," quoted in H. Y. Tien, *China's Population Struggle* (Columbus: Ohio State University Press, 1973), p. 222.

19. G. Hua, Speech at the Third Session of the Fifth National People's Congress, September 7, 1980, quoted in Pichao Chen and Adrienne Kols, "Population and Birth Planning in the People's Republic of China," *Population Reports*, Series J, no. 25 (January–February 1982), p. 582.

20. Richard A. Easterlin, "Effects of Population Growth on the Economic Development of Developing Countries," *The Annals of the American Academy of Political and Social Science*, 369 (January 1967), p. 98.

21. Commission on Population Growth and the American Future, *Population and the American Future* (New York: Signet, 1972), p. 53.

22. Arguments of this sort are made by Harold H. Barnett, "Population Problems: Myths and Realities," *Economic Development and Cultural Change*, 19 (July 1971), 545–559. A suggestion that rapidly achieved stability would be disruptive is made by Ansley J. Coale, "Man and His Environment," *Science*, 170 (October 9, 1970), 132–136.

23. For a review of these arguments see Espenshade, "Zero Population Growth."

24. James P. Smith and Finis Welch, "No Time to Be Young: The Economic Prospects for Large Cohorts in the United States," *Population and Development Review*, 7, no. 1 (March 1981), 71–83.

25. Easterlin, "1984."

26. Alan R. Sweezy and Aaron Owens, "The Impact of Population Growth on Employment," *American Economic Review*, 64 (May 1974), 45–50.

27. James C. Cramer, "Employment Trends of Young Mothers and the Opportunity Cost of Babies in the United States," *Demography*, 16, no. 2 (May 1979), 177–197.

28. James P. Smith and Michael P. Ward, "Asset Accumulation and Family Size," *Demography*, 17, no. 3 (August 1980), 243–260.

29. Espenshade, "Zero Population Growth," p. 668.

30. Paul R. Ehrlich, "Paying the Piper," *New Scientist*, 36 (December 14, 1967), 652–655.

31. Population Reference Bureau, "The Techno-Population Race: Who Needs It," PPB Selection No. 40 (July 1972).

32. Ronald G. Ridker and Elizabeth W. Cecelski, "Resources, Environment and Population: The Nature of Future Limits," *Population Bulletin*, 34, no. 3 (August 1979), 1–43.

33. Lester R. Brown, "Resource Trends and Population Policy: A Time for Reassessment," *Worldwatch Paper* 29, May 1979.

34. "World's Children Data Sheet," (Washington, D.C.: Population Reference Bureau, 1979).

35. Sunanda Datta-Ray, "Pollution Spreads to India's Sacred River," *Earthwatch*, no. 3 (1980), 3–4.

36. Paul R. Ehrlich and Anne H. Ehrlich, *Population, Resources, Environment: Issues in Human Ecology* (San Francisco: W. H. Freeman & Company Publishers, 1979), pp. 279–280.

37. Ronald G. Ridker, "Resource and Environmental Consequences of Population Growth in the U.S.: A Summary," *Population, Resources and the Environment*, Vol. III. Research Report of the U.S. Commission on Population Growth and the American Future, (Washington, D.C.: U.S. Government Printing Office, 1972), p. 23.

38. Ibid.

39. Brown, "Resource Trends."

40. Ridker and Cecelski, "Resources."

SUGGESTED ADDITIONAL READINGS

An analysis of demographic effects on education can be found in:

JONES, GAVIN, *Population Growth and Educational Planning in Developing Nations.* New York: Irvington, 1975.

Studies of the relationships of population processes and the economy include:

EASTERLIN, RICHARD A., *Birth and Fortune: The Impact of Numbers on Personal Welfare.* New York: Basic Books, 1980.

HAUSER, PHILIP M., *World Population and Development: Challenges and Prospects.* Syracuse: Syracuse University Press, 1979.

SUMMERS, GENE F., AND ARNE SELVIK, EDS. *Nonmetropolitan Industrial Growth and Community Change.* Lexington, Mass.: Heath, 1979.

THOMAS, ROBERT N., AND JOHN M. HUNTER, EDS. *Internal Migration Systems in the Developing World: With Special Reference to Latin America.* Boston: G. K. Hall, 1980.

Interesting views of the current environmental situation are contained in:

CATTON, WILLIAM R., JR. *Overshoot: The Ecological Basis of Revolutionary Change.* Champaign: University of Illinois Press, 1980.

GILLAND, BERNARD, *The Next 70 Years: Population, Food, and Resources.* Tunbridge Wells, England: Abacus Press, 1979.

TECHNICAL SUPPLEMENT NO. 7

How Unemployment Is Measured

When economic analysts assess the state of the economy, they are likely to examine a host of indicators, three of which are given major attention—the inflation rate, the rate of interest on money to be borrowed, and the unemployment rate. While the first two indicators relate to fiscal matters at the governmental, business, and household levels, the last indicator is a measure of the extent to which the population fully participates in the world of work. A high unemployment rate suggests that the economy is not providing enough jobs, which renders some individuals and families (those with unemployment problems) incapable of earning adequate income.

In the United States and other countries, we are given monthly reports on unemployment. The unemployment rate is a familiar measure usually cited in the media when the government releases that statistic. We sense that it is bad for the economy when it is rising and good when it is falling. But do we know how it is calculated and what are some of its limitations?

The unemployment rate is, in fact, a demographic item of information. It relates to a population characteristic and is based on census or household survey data. In the U.S., the Current Population Survey (referred to in Chapter 1) is the data source for monthly unemployment figures.

The concept of unemployment is a relatively modern one, and its measurement has been modified with time. When the economic depression of the late 1920s and early 1930s struck, many people were obviously losing jobs, yet we had no well-defined basis for assessing the extent of unemployment. At that time, censuses and surveys reported the numbers of people with gainful (paying) occupations, which could be shown as a percentage of the total population, or those in certain age groups. The number who lost their gainful jobs during the Depression divided by the population was not really a measure of unemployment, because many in the population were too young, too old, or too infirm to work, or simply uninterested. A truer unemployment rate would be one that revealed what percentage of those who were ready, willing, and able to work did not have jobs.

A new conceptual scheme was developed, which divided the population into three categories: (1) those not in the labor force (people who were not ready, willing, and able to work); (2) the employed (those who had jobs); and (3) the unemployed (those who were ready, willing, and able to work but could not find employment). The last two categories together constitute the *labor force* (the potential total employment when jobs are plentiful). The unemployment rate is then measured as the unemployed divided by the labor force (and multiplied by a constant 100 to convert it to a percentage). If 100 people in an area are either working or actively seeking work, as indicated by various forms of job search, and 8 are unsuccessful in finding work at a given time, the unemployment rate for that area is 8 percent (8/100 × 100).

The concepts seem clear-cut enough, but a number of decisions have to be made in classifying people properly. People are regarded as employed if they did any work for pay or profit during the week when unemployment was counted, whether it was part-time or temporary or full time and year-round. Persons who, during the study week, are on vacation, ill, involved in an industrial dispute, prevented from working by bad weather, or on personal leave, are still counted as employed, because they have a job to which they can return. Also included as employed are those who do not work for pay or profit but participate in a family-operated business or farm.

People are regarded as unemployed if they have actively looked for work in the past four weeks, are currently available for work, and do not have any type of job. Actively seeking work means registering at a public or private employment office, being interviewed for a job, advertising for a job or writing letters to prospective employers, checking with relatives or friends, or being on a union or professional register. Also included in this category are those waiting to start a new job within thirty days and those workers waiting to be recalled from a layoff, even if they are not actively seeking work.

The unemployed thus are not only those who have lost jobs but those who may never have had jobs but want them, quit one job to look for another, or were employed some time ago and now wish to return to work.

There is a minimum age for defining labor-force status (at least sixteen years of age, although formerly it was fourteen) but no maximum age. Institutionalized populations are excluded from consideration. Labor-force status is determined regardless of other statuses the individual may hold. If you are a student sixteen or older, you can be employed, unemployed, or not in the labor force. Likewise, spouses who stay home, whose housework or child-care duties ordinarily would not qualify for an employed designation, may be elsewhere employed, unemployed, or not in the labor force. The same is true of someone over sixty-five who once retired from a job.

Fluctuations in the unemployment rate can reflect various conditions in the community or society. The general availability or supply of jobs is certainly crucial, but work may be plentiful in some segments of the economy and not in others, and the skills and demand may be great in the areas of job shortages, leading to a higher unemployment rate. The "fit" between jobs and qualified workers may be at the root of the rise in unemployment. Or people may stop looking for work after some months, because they do not expect to find any in their field during bad economic times. These "discouraged workers" are no longer counted as unemployed, which gives us a deceptively lower unemployment rate. Or an economic recession may cause many full-time workers to shift to only part-time work, and yet the unemployment rate is unaffected. Such conditions, as well as demographic changes in population composition, distribution, and other characteristics, means that it is hard to "fine tune" the unemployment rate as a major economic indicator.

Even though the communications media typically issue one overall figure, statistical publications on unemployment are usually designed to assist data users in interpreting the information. For example, they provide tabulations to show variations by personal and family characteristics of the population, to enable the user to see if an unemployment level is pervasive or situated disproportionately in some segments of the population. Also, monthly unemployment rates are usually "seasonally adjusted" to standardize for the seasonal variations in employment supply and demand that are not protracted aspects of the economy (for instance, added business employment during holiday seasons, a surge of employment demand when schools let out for summer vacation).

Because of difficulties in measuring unemployment, government commissions and study groups have periodically reviewed the way the concept is defined and operationalized, and occasionally they have suggested methodological improvements. The more searching question for economic analysts, government decision-makers, and the general public, however, relates to the usefulness of unemployment data more generally. Is there a population-related characteristic that is more germane to indicating the healthfulness of an economy?

ISSUES SUPPLEMENT NO. 7

What Shall We Do About Social Security?

The "graying" of America, some have called it, as a greater and greater percentage of the population reaches sixty-five and over. While that percent was 4.1 in 1900, it is now up to 11.2 and should rise to about 18 percent in the year 2030. The famous baby-boom cohort will soon turn into a retirement boom.

Such a dramatic change in age structure will apparently require some rethinking about traditional modes of financing for the retirement years. The present Social Security system was designed so that the contributions of current workers would provide funds to support those who are currently retired. But consider the implications of such a system. As the number of retired persons grows larger relative to the number of workers, the pool of Social Security payments becomes smaller and must be spread among a larger number of older persons. In 1980, for example, three workers made payments to support the needs of one retiree. By 2010 only two workers will be available to provide such support.

The Social Security system is also in trouble because of changes in other demographic processes. Retired persons are now spending more years in retirement and thus collecting benefits longer. Lower mortality rates, or greater expectation of life, has strained further Social Security assets. Even though workers have been asked to accept greater and greater payroll deductions, these increases have not kept pace with increased demand.

From the point of view of the elderly, Social Security is something they have counted on, and indeed earned, since they provided retirement funds for the generation ahead of them. Almost 50 percent of all income received by senior citizens comes from Social Security. Moreover, this income is already so minimal that it hardly provides for a luxurious life-style. Decreasing the amounts of these benefits can hardly be considered, since 30 percent of the elderly who depend almost entirely on Social Security have incomes below the poverty line.

What can be done to save the Social Security system in the face of these demographic changes? One solution is to raise the amount of money currently deducted from workers' paychecks. It has already risen from 1 percent in 1935 to its current level of 6 percent. Furthermore, even if these deductions are increased, those currently working will not get back an amount matching their own contributions, since the cohort just behind them will be smaller. These are problems created by changing birthrates.

Another possibility would be to change the system by which payments go into and out of the Social Security fund. Perhaps instead of having current workers support current retirees, current workers could make payments that would then be paid out to them when they retire. Were such a system to be adopted, future imbalances in birthrates would not jeopardize Social Security.

Another money-saving plan for Social Security would be to encourage senior citizens to stay in the labor force longer. This might be done by making work requirements and schedules more flexible for older persons or by offering retraining and continuing-education programs.

None of these solutions is simple, however, and will require some time for implementation. In the meantime, elderly persons continue to be concerned about their well-being and young workers increasingly resent having to support them when their own incomes may already be limited.

What would the nation be like without any governmental system for old-age support? How would working people prepare for retirement if there were no Social Security? Would they even be encouraged to have more children so that they could be assured of support in their old age?

CHAPTER EIGHT
POPULATION IMPACTS: THE POLITY, RELIGION, AND THE FAMILY

"You don't need anyone to play house with. Be a single parent household."

Reprinted by permission of the Tribune Company Syndicate, Inc.

In Chapter 7 we examined some of the ways in which population processes influence societal changes in education, the economy, and the
environment. Now we turn to three other important institutional areas:
the polity, religion, and the family. These are the institutions that regulate the use of authority and power, morals and conceptions of ultimate
meaning, and sexual behavior and reproduction, respectively. We will
begin with the polity, an institution that has its impact mostly at the
macro level, and later discuss religion and the family.

POPULATION AND THE POLITY

It is certainly true that population processes affect the form, effectiveness, and relative world positions of governments. Although the following is not an exhaustive consideration of the ways in which this
occurs, we will examine three primary influences of population on the
polity: (1) population effects on national power, a macro impact; (2)
population effects on governmental processes, also a macro-level effect,
and (3) population effects on internal political disputes within nations,
an impact at the macro and medial levels.

Population and Power

The sheer size of its population has long been thought an important determinant of a nation's strength. Ancient Romans, for example,
were strongly pronatalist, since conquering territory for the empire
required vast armies. Even in the present day, when power is not as
absolutely determined by the number of fighting men, population is an
important contributor. One historical analysis argued that large population size contributes to a nation's power in four major ways. First, it
provides a larger labor force to make economic contributions to a nation. Second, in a large population there are greater advantages of scale
from a system of mass production and distribution, making modern
economies more profitable. Third, a larger military force can be maintained for defense and security purposes. Finally, if new territory is
gained by military or other action, large occupational forces can be sent
to the new land to maintain its allegiance to the state.[1] These factors
have been cited by other authors as well. A study of developing countries found a strong relationship between a nation's military power and
the size of its population.[2]

A more refined examination of the relationship between national
power and population size was accomplished for the U.S. Commission
on Population Growth and the American Future.[3] This study suggested

that to measure the relationship of population to power in a nation, one must consider only those who contribute to the furthering of national goals, the "effective" population. People effectively utilized by a country contribute to its influence over others, whereas those who only consume and drain a country do not. When looked at in this more refined way, population seems to be related to power in a conditional way.

A cross-national study of the relationship of population size and growth rates to the power of a country has also concluded that this relationship is somewhat conditional.[4] By looking at forty countries of the world, it was found that economic capability was an important variable that intervenes between population and power; that is, nations with greater economic capability can be small in terms of population and still have great power.

How many people a country needs to effectively achieve political or other goals varies with its social organization and technological development. The personnel requirements of different technologies are not the same. A large population may be an asset in some settings and a liability in others, depending upon the circumstances.

Nevertheless what nations believe about population and power has enormous practical consequence for population growth and decline. Nations that believe their power to be directly connected to their level of population growth or the size of their population would, of course, pursue different fertility, mortality, and migration-control policies than those that feel extra people are an additional burden.

Population and Governmental Processes

Just as a nation's population makes a difference in international politics, so the number of people being governed in a nation affects the possible forms of internal government. For example, participatory democracy, in which every member of society votes on each issue, is not a feasible form of government when the population is large and/or widely dispersed. Recent technological innovations have raised questions about whether we might not all be able to vote on each issue pending in Congress by remote computer, but this suggestion remains in the realm of science fiction for the present.

In the United States, several authors have analyzed the growth of the nation and the result of that growth on its governmental processes.[5] For example, in 1870 the number of representatives in the Congress was 106. The present number in the House of Representatives is 435. That fact alone changes the nature and form of deliberations possible for the House.

The work load for each session is now greater, and the time it takes each legislator to do what was originally conceived of as a part-time job has grown longer. Politics has now become a career, with less turnover in office. More and more committees become necessary, as do more and more rules for writing bills and conducting debate. Legislators are not often available to their constituents, since even in the smallest states the number of people represented by a senator or a representative is quite large. Data such as these are not, of course, measures of the quality of representation or government. These changes may have resulted in the same quality of government or even raised the quality of representation. They are nevertheless changes made necessary by population dynamics.

These considerations have led some authors to speculate on how large governmental units should be if they are to communicate effectively with people and deliver needed services. One writer, for example, has estimated that for local governments to function effectively in communication and delivery, their optimal population should be 40,000 to 200,000, a size many communities exceed.[6] States, says Elazar, should have approximately 2.5 to 10 million persons to facilitate these two goals. Larger size results in greater concentration of power in the hands of a few. Whether these numerical estimates are correct or not, the important point is the recognition that population size does influence the nature of governmental processes.

The cost of government services has also escalated tremendously. This is true not only because of the growth of the population, but because of other population processes as well. One author puts the argument succinctly:

> There is no question that population change has a profound impact on the costs of state governmental services. If only people did not migrate, have so many babies, or wait so long to die, government costs could be reduced . . . the mere movement of population from state to state and even from country to country produces conditions eventuating in increased government costs.[7]

Since governments often provide maternal and child health subsidies, retirement benefits, and unemployment or other benefits to new migrants, it is easy to see how demographic processes can cause escalation of government spending.

Population redistribution also affects governmental processes. For example, in the 1980s for the first time, the southern and western regions of the United States will have a majority of seats in the House of

Representatives.[8] This is quite a change, and something of a shock, to the northeastern urban centers, which have long dominated the House. Since the days of Franklin D. Roosevelt, for example, New York State has lost ten seats in the House. While Florida had three seats at the turn of this century, it will probably have nineteen in the decade of the 1980s.[9]

There has also been speculation on how migration to the Sun Belt is likely to affect politics in those regions and in the United States as a whole. While most of the migrants to these areas are more liberal than the indigenous population, they will not be a majority for some years to come, if ever. Thus their votes are likely to be subsumed by the majority, making the country as a whole more conservative. Further, the number of votes being cast in presidential elections by residents of the Northeast and North Central states has remained relatively stable, while the number of votes cast in the South and West has risen.

The changing age composition of the United States and of other developed nations has also influenced political processes. In this country, for example, the number of young voters has risen dramatically over the last decade.[10] This is due to both extension of the vote to eighteen-year-olds and the baby-boom cohort's reaching voting age. However, whether this group will make a substantial impact on the American political future is in doubt. Traditionally, younger people have been less likely to vote than older ones. Perhaps this large cohort will only make a noticeable impact on the political scene as it ages. If its peak impact is at middle age, then more conservative politics are likely.

The importance of all these demographic trends has not been unnoticed by modern politicians. Since many office-seekers are now marketed via mailing, mass media, and carefully programmed strategies, demographic data on voters have become essential to these "targeting" efforts. Even the political analyses of the mass media have begun to include more and more data on population factors in order to forecast trends and winners. These uses of demographic data attest to the importance of population trends in political processes.

Population and Conflict

We have seen ways, then, in which population processes affect international and domestic politics. However, population also has an impact on political processes and conflict within and between nations. Some research has tried to assess whether nations with larger populations tend to experience greater internal and external conflict than smaller ones. This is a plausible notion, since research on small groups has shown that as they become larger, conflict and disagreements increase.

In a study of seventy-five nations, it was found that the larger their population size, the more likely they were to experience various symptoms of internal conflict.[11] These symptoms included riots, revolutions, people killed as a result of internal military action, antigovernment demonstrations, and purges of political opposition. Similarly, various indicators of conflict with other nations were also more prevalent in the nations with the greatest population size. The most populous countries had more military troop movements, more persons killed in conflict, more military actions, more recall or expulsion of diplomats, more use of negative sanctions, accusations, and threats in dealing with other countries, and more antiforeign demonstrations.

Some authors have gone so far as to suggest that trends in world population growth and distribution create civil unrest and constitute a substantial threat to national and world security, and they must be met with programs to abate that threat.[12] It is argued that as population continues to grow and resource imbalances between developed and developing nations continue to be aggravated by differential rates of growth between them, more regimentation will be required to maintain life-styles at an acceptable level. Furthermore, the great influx of illegal immigrants to nations like the United States is not only costly, but is likely to lead to military buildups. Soldiers may soon be used to ensure supplies of materials to some nations and to maintain domestic order. Perhaps, it is suggested, a NASA-type agency with military organization and "a wartime sense of urgency" should be created.

The impact of population processes on internal conflict can be illustrated in a variety of countries. For example, the very high growth rate of the Arab population in Israel is causing much concern among Israeli Jews. The annual rate of natural increase of the Israeli Arab population is 3.7 percent, so that their population doubles every eighteen years.[13] Among Israeli Jews, however, the annual rate of natural increase is only 1.7 percent, requiring forty-one years' doubling time. What this means in terms of family size is that Jews have an average of 3 children per couple, while Arabs average 6.5. Furthermore, among Arabs on the West Bank and in Gaza, improvements in medical care and nutrition introduced by the Israelis have now brought the total fertility rate up to about 9 children.

Such population growth imbalances mean, in effect, that Israel faces the ironic situation of becoming Arab as a result of internal processes. If we ignore migration to Israel, the population within the current boundaries of the nation claimed by Israel will be 53 percent Arab by the year 2000. It seems quite likely, however, that net immigration will enable the Jewish population to maintain its majority position, at least for a time.

The United States provides another example of how population processes and population policies affect ethnic fears and disputes. Some prominent black leaders in the nation have claimed that the family-planning movement is genocidal in its intent, as far as blacks are concerned.[14] Indeed, some research has reported that the percentage nonwhite in areas and the presence of subsidized family-planning services are positively related in the United States.[15] A quote from the Black Panther publication illustrates this view:

> Black people know that part of our revolutionary strength lies in the fact that we outnumber the pigs—and the pigs realize this too. That is why they are trying to eliminate as many people as possible before they reach their inevitable doom.[16]

Within the black community, and among researchers, this view has been challenged. The following illustrates some of the counterarguments to this genocidal interpretation:

> At this point a few members of my community will tell me that legalized abortion is simply another white man's trick to foster racial genocide. They will say that we need to reproduce as many black children as possible—which only adds numbers. There is no magic in a home where someone has reproduced five or more black babies and cannot manage economically, educationally, spiritually nor socially to see that these five black babies become five highly trained black minds.

> . . . under slavery, blacks were encouraged to reproduce to assure an adequate supply of muscle energy people. Wake up, brothers and sisters, America no longer needs muscle energy people.[17]

This argument seems to be more appealing to the majority of the black community. Black women have been receptive to family-planning programs in their communities. In addition, as early as 1960 national fertility surveys found that 90 percent of black women had either used or intended to use contraception.[18] Furthermore, there is apparently no separate impact of race on the availability of family-planning services, once age and socioeconomic status of the population are taken into account.[19]

The white community, on the other hand, has also voiced fears of the relative balance of ethnic power being changed by population processes. Feeling threatened by the larger natural increase of blacks in the nation, whites have on occasion argued for increased white reproduction. In addition, the redistribution of the black and white populations, creating a black majority in some central cities in the nation, has had political repercussions. These changes have fostered fears not only about who will be elected to various offices from such districts, but also "takeovers" as well.

At an earlier time in United States history, changing population distribution also contributed to changes in power. Farley has pointed out that "slavery was not compatible with an urban environment."[20] In the cities, blacks could more easily escape, get other jobs, and congregate with other blacks for protection.

The nation of South Africa provides yet another example of internal conflict between blacks and whites being aggravated by population processes. While the black population in South Africa currently outnumbers the white population by a ratio of 3 to 1, that imbalance is expected to increase to 5 to 1 by the year 1990.[21] This differential growth seems likely to have contributed to the current political struggles in South Africa. The African population is demanding a one-person-one-vote government, while there is substantial resistance to that idea among whites.

Further, some analysts have argued that the distributions of the black and white populations in South Africa are likely to further aggravate political turmoil. At present whites hold 87 percent of the land, while Africans occupy only 13 percent. This imbalance will probably lead to more and more crowding of the black population and further confrontations.

There has been some response to these trends on the part of the South African government. First, the nation has adopted a whites-only immigration policy. However, in only twenty-four days, the natural increase of the African population overcomes the entire annual average immigration of whites. Furthermore, the nation has adopted an intense family-planning program—which some claim is aimed only at the African population, while whites are offered money to have extra babies.[22]

What appears in each of these situations, then, is fear on the part of ethnic groups within a nation that differentials or changes in population processes will contribute to differentials in power between their own group and others. Open warfare, attempts at regulation, or resistance to population policies may be the results of such fear.

The USSR, on the other hand, illustrates how population processes such as migration and distribution patterns may contribute to greater communication between various ethnic groups in a nation. Brian Silver has examined how the process of "Russification," or the learning of Russian in addition to one's native tongue, has been impeded or speeded up by various patterns of migration and population distribution in the USSR.[23] His analysis showed that those who had migrated outside of their native area or who lived in urban places learned Russian more often than those who did not migrate or live in urban locations. In addition, Silver found that those who lived in urban areas outside of their native ones experienced the greatest impact of Russification. These migratory and population distribution patterns may then have an effect on nationalistic ties.

We would not suggest here that the panacea for nations' political ills is to reduce population growth or redistribute it. What seems to be clear, however, is that population processes have a definite and important impact on political processes—effectiveness, forms, and power—within and between nations.

POPULATION AND RELIGION

In earlier chapters, it was noted that religion has an important impact on population processes. The ways in which population can in turn affect religion may be less obvious. Three current influences will be discussed here: (1) that of population size on religion, (2) of population distribution on religion, and (3) of population on religious doctrine and commitment.

Population Size and Religion

As big towns are different from small ones, so large churches are different from small ones. Whether people become members as a result of birth or conversion, their impact can be substantial.

Sociologists have studied how the size of a religious group is related to how it can be organized and what it can offer its members. The large church may have several ministers, a paid education staff, paid directors of choirs or music programs, and various service personnel to tend church buildings and facilities. Large churches may be able to offer youth programs, Bible schools, day care, educational programs for members of all ages, and a variety of other events and services. In short, the large church may become something of a bureaucracy. Small religious groups, on the other hand, generally cannot afford such elaborate staff or programs.

Because of concern with decline, the Jewish community in the

United States has recently studied the possible impacts of current birthrates and changes in age composition on its religious activities and institutions.[24] As we noted in Chapter 4, the birthrate of the Jewish population has traditionally been lower than that of other religious groups, so that the median age of that population is now between forty-five and forty-eight, compared to a total population median age of thirty. It seems likely that a decreased proportion of the Jewish population that is young will have an impact in many ways. First, synagogue affiliation is strongly related to the presence of children in a family. It is estimated that 22 percent of young married couples with no children are synagogue members, but 56 percent of young couples with children under age fourteen are members.

Furthermore, there has been speculation that the increasing numbers of working women with no children will weaken the membership in various women's organizations such as Hadassah. Indeed, the supply of volunteers in many organizations has been crippled by the increasing numbers of women who are employed full time. Another potential impact of demographic trends in the Jewish community will be on education. Will communities be able to afford Jewish education or will the increasing proportion of the Jewish population that is aged force a reordering of priorities from the young to the elderly?

These problems, while not unique to the Jewish community, are easily illustrated by this group. In religious organizations, as in many other institutions, the size and composition of the population can have a great impact.

Population Distribution and Religion

Originally the population of the United States was almost entirely Protestant, with few Catholics, Jews, or members of other religious groups. However, because of changing immigration patterns and differences in natural increase of religious groups, the population is now more heavily Catholic. Particularly in urban areas, where large numbers of Jewish and Catholic immigrants settled, the Protestant majority has been scaled down.[25]

In addition to these consequences of international migration, internal residential mobility also influences religion. We have noted the rural-to-urban movement of people in many countries. Earlier analyses of the phenomenon from a religious point of view were quick to make the connection between urbanization and secularization—a worrisome trend from their point of view. In an urban environment, it was suggested, religion became a private matter, with no place in public life.

The city and its varied life-styles might convince people that their religious views could be wrong, and therefore they might be concerned with other, more important issues than a peculiar or particular faith.[26]

Of course, places to worship continue to exist in even the largest metropolis today, so that secularization has clearly not stamped out religion in urban areas. The urban-rural-suburban exchanges of population have created other problems, however.

For example, in the United States, the central cities have become increasingly populated by blacks, members of other minority groups, and low-income whites. In addition, high proportions of older people are left there. Such movement has an impact on the formerly large and wealthy churches located in central-city areas. Left with congregations that have low incomes, these churches may no longer be able to support the large buildings and varied programs that were offered before the exodus of higher-income and younger families.

In addition, however, people of different social classes are not distributed evenly among religious denominations. People of higher economic status, for example, are more often Episcopalian, Unitarian, Congregationalist, or Presbyterian, while people of low economic status more often join small sect groups or fundamentalist branches of the Baptist or Lutheran churches. As the concentration of people of low economic status in central cities has increased, there has been a large growth of storefront churches and sects of various kinds in these areas. Such groups tend to be temporary, and turnover of leaders and members is high. The practices and beliefs of such groups may be tailored to the needs and circumstances of the central-city resident. Their financial position is, of course, tenuous.

Still another impact on religion has been made by the migrants to these central cities. Lenski has noted that in Detroit, for example, southern rural migrants have often found the central-city churches uncomfortable. Here the migration experience must be responded to by the churches.

> . . . the transition from the semirural South to a modern metropolitan community is in many respects a change comparable to that experienced by a first-generation immigrant from abroad. The metropolis is a new world filled with unfamiliar institutions. The established white Protestant churches seem strange and unfamiliar by rural southern standards, and hence not especially attractive. A few congregations have been organized which seek to recapture the spirit and flavor of the rural, southern congregations, but such efforts are, at best, only partially successful.[27]

These are examples of the responses of the religious institutions to the changes in population composition and distribution brought about by migration. But what about migration itself? Does the process of pulling up roots and moving from one place to another affect religion in any way? In lamenting the impact of mobility on organized religion, one author wrote: "Let us admit at once that high mobility does play havoc with traditional religion. It separates people from the holy places. It mixes them with neighbors whose gods have different names and who worship them in different ways."[28]

In fact, data on the relationship between migration and church attendance seem to provide some support for that sentiment. In one study of Catholics and Protestants in the United States, for example, it was found that international migration, regional migration, residential mobility, and moving between rural, urban, and suburban areas all were associated with decreased church attendance.[29] This pattern was found among younger persons as well as older ones. Since mobility of these types is very prevalent in many countries, this finding has broad implications for religion.

Population and Religious Doctrine

Religions, like other institutions in society, do change their doctrines, practices, and membership in response to social change. Since religion has traditionally been the institution that sets moral guidelines for societies, these changes become very important at the medial and micro levels, or even at the macro level if societal members have a common religion.

Some have suggested that population processes have played a role in molding doctrines of the Roman Catholic Church and particularly influenced it to evaluate repeatedly its stand on the use of birth-control devices. We will present this argument here briefly as an example of the more subtle ways in which population processes can be at least one influence on doctrinal changes of this kind.

While the controversy in the Catholic Church over the use of birth control has been well publicized, one recent analysis has suggested that population pressures, at least in part, accounted for the emergence of a negative policy on use of birth control in the first place.[30] During the period 1879 to 1930, birthrates were falling in many countries and international movements between countries were of staggering proportions. During this period, pastoral letters from bishops, writings of theologians, preaching, and various other official statements all reacted to these trends. Some began to claim that those who were using contraceptives were selfish, materialistic, or desirous of luxury. Use of birth control could therefore not be condoned as having any legitimate or good purpose.

By the 1960s two quite different population-related factors were in evidence. First, in many countries that were predominantly Catholic, population growth rates and the pressure on resources generated by them became very great. Poverty in Latin American countries, for example, was acute. Second, the development of the birth-control pill made effective contraception possible and provided a way of eliminating unwanted children and hence relieving some of the pressure generated by large families.

In 1962 the meetings of Vatican Council II began. This series of meetings among bishops of the Catholic Church was intended to deal with a variety of social issues, among them birth control. One of the goals of these meetings for Pope John XXIII was to demonstrate that the Church was responsive to these issues and could be relevant in contemporary society. Indeed, the attitude of the Council seemed generally liberal on the issue of birth control, suggesting that, in considering how many children to have, a couple should take into account the "material and the spiritual conditions of the times as well as of their state of life."[31] Certainly such a statement does not sound like an injunction prohibiting the limitation of family size.

Further, Vatican Council II also affirmed the obligation of governments to deal with population issues and indicated that the people at large should be informed of scientific advances in birth control. However, its members asserted that the final decision about how many children to bear must not be usurped by any government but belonged instead to parents.

In the meantime, the Commission for the Study of Population and Family Life was preparing its report to Pope Paul, submitted in 1966. While officially the report was kept confidential, media sources indicated that the Commission had recommended by an overwhelming majority a change in the Church's doctrine on birth control. Taken together, these events seemed to portend imminent liberalization of the Church's traditional negative stand on birth control. By 1968, however, Pope Paul issued his famous encyclical reaffirming the church stand opposing the use of any method of birth control except rhythm.[32] According to some analysts, the encyclical relied on tradition and papal supremacy rather than on scriptures or other sources for its rationale.

Even among the leaders of the Church, the encyclical became very controversial and even sparked rebellion. Some priests continued to teach parishioners that contraceptive decisions must be left to their own consciences, and official statements arguing with the Pope were issued by theologians in the United States.

The reactions of Catholic women to the encyclical, at least in developed countries where they are documented, were overwhelmingly negative. Some women left the Church entirely rather than give up the use of effective contraception; others curtailed their involvement in the Church or simply disobeyed its view. Currently over 80 percent of Catholic women in the United States are using some form of contraception prohibited by their Church. We are also reminded of the convergence of Catholic fertility rates with those of other groups, as was shown in Figure 4.9. What ultimate effect these trends will have on the long-term cohesiveness of the Catholic Church remains to be seen.

With the election of Pope John Paul II in 1978, hope was renewed among those who sought a liberalization of church teaching on the use of birth control. In 1980 the meeting of the Synod of Bishops chose as its theme, "The Role of the Christian Family in the World of Today." That choice seemed to pave the way for reexamination of the issue.

Indeed, the Synod meeting was marked by much debate on the issue, with pleas on the part of some bishops for the Church to recognize the pressure of population growth on many of the world's poor. However, the Pope closed the meeting with a strong restatement of the traditional stand prohibiting the use of birth control. Confusion and controversy were sustained.

In spite of the unchanging stance of the Catholic hierarchy, some have suggested that the Church must finally reckon with the "population problem" or continue to suffer from its own internal conflict on the matter.

> *The refusal of the Church's officials to accept the horrifying fact that some ten million human beings enter the world each year without the slightest possibility of achieving the human dignity being proclaimed by the Pope in countless talks is an enigma beyond the understanding of most Vatican observers.*
>
> *Close analysis of previous crises in Church history suggests a solution. It is only after an indignant attempt on the part of Rome to prevent turnabouts in its teaching, such as that required by the drastic event of the "population explosion," that the sensus fidelium (mind of the faithful) will finally assert itself.[33]*

It is, of course, entirely possible to interpret this sequence of events as the result of technological developments in birth control, political processes within the Church, or other events quite distinct from population processes. It is also possible to suggest that population processes and pressures, on the family as well as the societal level, were at least partly responsible for a change in adherence to religious teaching, if not an alteration in religious doctrine.

While religion has exerted stronger effects on population processes than the reverse, the foregoing examples suggest that religion as an institution is not free from the effects of population growth, size, composition, and distribution.

POPULATION AND THE FAMILY

We began discussing the influences of population processes on other institutions by looking at societal impacts on education, the economy, and the environment. In this chapter we have moved from societal and group political effects of population to a consideration of population influences on religion for both the society and particular religious groups. We come finally to the family, the site of many decisions relating to fertility, mortality, and residential mobility. It is within this context that many of the educational, economic, environmental, political, and religious consequences we have discussed have their impact on individuals.

We will examine three examples of this process: population effects on (1) the societal structure and importance of families, (2) the formation and composition of families, and (3) children and parents within families.

Population and Family Structure

The family has long been an important unit in society. It has been the mechanism by which status and privilege are defined and the most basic unit of social organization. As other changes in social structure occur, so do changes in the importance and form of the family. Population processes can also contribute to these changes.

In countries or continents experiencing accelerating urbanization, historical analyses have demonstrated a tendency for the social structure to become based on contracts and formal associational arrangements rather than kinship. In Africa, for example, the family has become less important in defining social status and rights and privileges than was the case before high rates of mobility and urbanization occurred.[34] On the Ivory Coast these same population processes have eroded ethnic differences in family customs.[35] Women who move to urban areas tend to have about the same rates of marriage and to engage in roughly the same child-rearing practices, thereby blurring distinctions in these phenomena that existed between ethnic groups before the population was concentrated in urban areas.

There are other ways in which urbanization, modernization, fertility, and family structure become intertwined. For example, two common characteristics of traditional societies are a preference for a large number of children and for sons over daughters. In some countries a woman's status is tied to the number of sons she produces. Those wishing to reduce fertility have often recognized these impediments to their success and have tried to alter such attitudes. However, urbanization and migration from rural to urban areas also undermine these attitudes, at least to some extent.

Recent studies in Taiwan[36] and Bangladesh,[37] for example, indicate that, while there have been increases in the number of women using birth control, in many rural areas preferences for a large number of children and for males remain stable. If programs or urbanization succeed in altering these preferences, there will doubtless be long-term implications for the structure of families and for the ways in which women earn status within them.

One of the principal duties of the family has traditionally been child rearing. These practices too can be influenced by population processes. A study of Basque society reported that land could not be subdivided between children upon the death of the parents, because there would then not be enough land to support the growing population of the region.[38] To cope with this problem, Basque custom specifies that family farms will be inherited by the oldest son or daughter only. Thus subsequent children are taught to be self-reliant and aggressive in finding other ways to support themselves. The study goes on to speculate that this practice predisposes the migrating Basque children to success in entrepreneurial careers.

Ireland is another country where limited amounts of land and high birthrates have combined to lead to special family practices. Robert E. Kennedy has argued that one of the traditional reasons for lowering fertility in Western countries has been the desire to raise "quality" children.[39] This means, among other things, being able to provide educational and occupational opportunities for children as they grow up. In Ireland, where all children but the eldest can be expected to emigrate, because only the eldest can inherit land, Kennedy suggests that parents are not likely to plan far into the future with regard to the welfare of these younger children. Relieved of this burden, motivation to limit fertility is not strong.

In each of the foregoing cases, population pressure induced by a shortage of land has led to family inheritance or child-rearing practices that in turn influence demographic processes. In this way population influences the family, and the family influences population patterns.

The Formation and Composition of Families

Because the family is such an important unit in terms of demographic processes, those interested in studying population have seen the description of family processes to be important, quite apart from the impact of population on the family per se. The rate at which families form and dissolve and their resultant composition is both a cause and a consequence of demographic patterns. Because of the importance of these topics, we will describe family formation and composition in some detail, using the United States as an example. Then we will explore life-cycle approaches to the study of the family, and finally consider special demographic circumstances that can influence family formation and composition patterns.

Interesting trends with regard to the prevalence and form of the family in the United States are beginning to emerge. First, while the number of households and families in the United States has been increasing, Table 8.1 shows that families constitute a smaller and smaller proportion of households. A *household* consists of all persons who occupy a housing unit, while *family* refers to two or more persons living together who are related by blood, marriage, or adoption. In 1940 families constituted 92.0 percent of households; in 1980 only 73.8 percent.

Further, the number of unmarried couples living together in the U.S. has been steadily increasing over the last two decades. In 1960 there were 439,000 such couples, but by 1977 this number had increased to 957,000.[40] This latter figure is about 4 percent of all couple households.

TABLE 8.1 Household and family characteristics: United States, 1940–1980

Year	Percent of Households That are Families	Average Population per Family	Average Population per Household
1940	92.0	3.76	3.67
1950	90.2	3.54	3.37
1960	85.4	3.67	3.33
1970	81.4	3.58	3.14
1980	73.8	3.28	2.75

Source: For 1940–1970 figures, U.S. Bureau of the Census, "Households and Families by Type: March 1974," *Current Population Reports,* Series P-20, no. 266, Tables 1 and 5. For 1980 figures, U.S. Bureau of the Census, "Households and Families by Type: March 1980," *Current Population Reports,* Series P-20, no. 357, Tables 2 and 3.

The average population per family, also shown in Table 8.1, declined from 1940 to 1950, then rose until 1960, when it again declined. This reflects rising and falling birthrates during this period. The average population of households has declined from 1940 to 1980, owing both to decreased fertility and to an increase in the number of adults living alone.

These trends in the formation and composition of families and households are further amplified in Figure 8.1, which shows the first-marriage rate, the divorce rate, and the remarriage rate for the United States population from 1921 to 1980. The pattern of first marriages looks much like the pattern of fertility during this time period. After declining in the Depression years, the rate of first marriages rose after World War II and has declined since that time.

Divorces and remarriages, on the other hand, show a similar pattern until after World War II, when, instead of declining, these rates

FIGURE 8.1 Rates of first marriage, divorce, and remarriage for U.S. women, 1921–1980

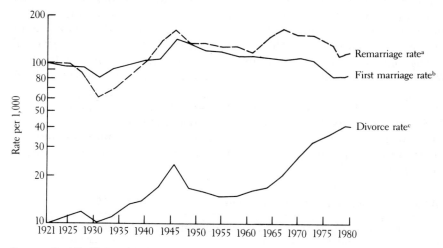

Source: Paul C. Glick and Arthur J. Norton, "Marrying, Divorcing and Living Together in the U.S. Today," *Population Bulletin,* 32 (October 1977), Figure 1, p. 5; courtesy of the Population Reference Bureau, Inc., Washington, D.C. Updated figures to 1980 supplied by Arthur J. Norton.

In 1980 the Census began to tabulate marital status for women aged 15–44 rather than 14–44. In order to keep the above rates comparable, the 1980 denominator for the first-marriage rate includes an estimated 2,075 single women age 14, an estimate reflecting the difference between the number of single females aged 14–17 in 1979 (7,822) and the number of single aged 15–17 in 1980 (5,747). Divorce and remarriage rates are not as affected by this change and refer to women aged 15–44 in 1980, without adjustment.

TABLE 8.2 Percentage of families with female heads by color: United States, 1955–1980

Year	Total	White	Blacks
1955	10.1	9.0	20.7
1960	10.0	8.7	22.4
1965	10.5	9.0	23.7
1970	10.9	9.1	28.3
1975	13.0	10.5	35.3
1980[a]	14.6	11.6	40.5

Source: Figures for 1955–1970 are from U.S. Bureau of the Census, "Female Family Heads," *Current Population Reports,* Series P-23, no. 50, July 1974, Table 1, p. 6. Figures for 1975 and 1979 are from U.S. Bureau of the Census, "Household and Family Characteristics: March 1975," *Current Population Reports,* Series P-20, no. 291, February 1976, Table 1, p. 7, and "Household and Family Characteristics: March 1979," Series P-20, no. 352, July 1980. 1980 figure is from U.S. Bureau of the Census, "Households and Families by Type: March 1980" (Advance Report), *Current Population Reports,* Series P-20, no. 357 (October 1980).
[a]*Figures for whites and blacks are for 1979.*

continued to rise. Taken together, these trends have meant more and more families headed by females. Table 8.2 indicates that between 1955 and 1980 the percentage of families headed by females increased from 10.1 to 14.6. Among whites, females head 11.6 percent of families, while among blacks, the figure is 40.5 percent. Looked at from the point of view of children's living arrangements, this means that about one-fifth of all children do not live with two parents.[41] If divorce and remarriage are considered, then about one-third of children in the United States are not living with both biological parents. Surely the magnitude of these numbers forces a careful reconceptualization of the meaning of family.

Family Life Cycles

Figure 8.2 presents the family life events experienced by typical mothers over the last eighty years. This figure permits at least two kinds of comparisons: the trend in age at each of these events can be seen over time, and the relative space in years between each of these events can be examined for each birth cohort.

We examined some of these trends in Chapters 3 and 4. For example, the average age at first marriage was late during the Depression years but earlier during the 1950s. Similarly, over this time period, mothers had their first children some 1.3 to 2.1 years after marriage.

On the other hand, the age for mothers at the birth of the last child has moved rather steadily downward. This means that the overall period of childbearing has been reduced, primarily because women are having fewer children. Similarly, the age of marriage of the last child is earlier, leaving a much longer *empty-nest* period (parents alone at home after children grow up and leave) for more recent birth cohorts. This period is primarily lengthened because of improvements in mor-

FIGURE 8.2 Median age of mothers at the beginning of selected stages of the family life cycle

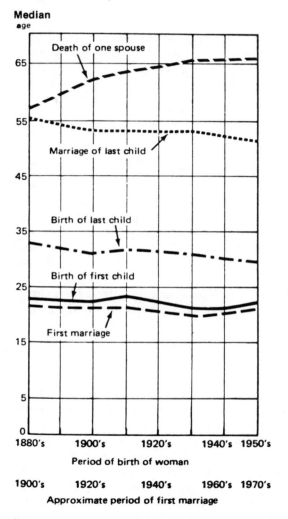

Source: Paul C. Glick, "Updating the Life Cycle of the Family," *Journal of Marriage and the Family,* 39 (February 1977), Figure 1, p. 7. Copyright 1977 by the National Council on Family Relations. Reprinted by permission.

tality rates, which have delayed the death of spouses. Thus parents can now expect to live together as a two-person family for nearly thirteen years, or about a third of their total married lives.

A recent analysis has also taken a life-cycle approach to the study of the impacts of changing death rates on families.[42] First, changing patterns of mortality since 1900 have important impacts on the childhood years. Because more children can be expected to live through their early years into adulthood, it is argued that parents have become more attached to them. The reasoning is that when childhood mortality was high, parents were more likely not to focus on children in order to cope better with the inevitable loss of some of them.

Secondly, changing patterns of mortality have meant that children have a greatly reduced probability of orphanhood. In 1900 there was a 24 percent chance that a child would lose at least one parent by death before reaching the age of fifteen. Currently that probability is only 0.5 percent. Similarly, survival of grandparents is much more likely. Almost two-thirds of all children now have all four grandparents living at their birth. In 1900 only one-fourth of all children born had four grandparents alive.

Changing mortality patterns also affect the period of young adulthood, both because there is a decline in early widowhood and because couples who can expect all their children to survive are better able to plan the size of their families. In middle age, more couples have parents still living who may need care, perhaps changing the character of the empty-nest period. Parents may become dependent on the marital couple, replacing the earlier dependence of children. Finally, in old age a larger proportion of couples are still married, but when widowhood occurs, there are more females alone than males.

Taken together, these life-cycle trends in fertility and mortality seem to portend greater family stability. Of course, high divorce rates produce instability of a different kind, making a net assessment of family well-being difficult.

Using this life-cycle approach, then, we can see how changing demographic patterns of birth and death influence the formation and composition of families. Since we have used data from the United States to examine these trends, it is important to note that these life-cycle patterns are quite different in many developing countries.

We have noted that in American families, the time between marriage and the birth of the first child is short, with a relatively short interval between children, a prolonged period of child rearing, and then an extended one without children in the home. In developing countries, these stages of the family life cycle are less distinct and overlap to a greater degree. Childbearing begins sooner, lasts longer, and overlaps with marriage of the children. Marriage of the last child may postdate the death of the parents. In short, in a society with high birth and death rates, the life-cycle patterns are quite different.

In any society there are several demographic events that can interrupt or change the usual processes of family formation. One of these is a phenomenon, discussed in Chapter 6, called the marriage squeeze. To repeat briefly, the term refers to a shortage of potential marriage partners. This situation may arise because of age, sex, or racial-ethnic imbalances in the population.

For example, in the United States it has been customary for females to marry males approximately two years older than themselves. But if in a two-year period the birthrate changes rather drastically, imbalances may occur. Suppose, for example, that men born in 1971 will be searching for potential brides among the women born in 1973. Since fertility was lower in 1973 than in 1971, there will not be enough females in the later cohort to provide brides for all these men, who are then said to be in a marriage squeeze. Likewise, women born in the first year of the post-World War II baby boom have been looking for husbands in a cohort of men born before the baby boom began, and therefore experience a shortage of potential marriage partners.

The solution to such age imbalance problems is to marry a person of the same age, to marry a person from an age cohort in which spouses are more plentiful, or to remain unmarried. Thus, fluctuations in the number of births may affect the number of families formed or the social definition of an acceptable marriage partner.

A recent analysis has even suggested that the marriage squeeze may be responsible in part for the recent attention to women's liberation and women's rights.[43] Because they could not find acceptable marriage partners during the 1970s, it is suggested, many women made plans for a career, and were more likely to graduate from college or from professional training schools. In other words, women's liberation may have been a momentary movement to help women reorient themselves to decreased opportunities for traditional roles as wives and mothers.

If this interpretation is correct, it has important implications for the future. The marriage squeeze for women is temporary, and during the 1980s will be replaced by a marriage squeeze for men that is predicted to be of some duration. Familistic values may again predominate among women, and gains won in the occupational sector during the 1970s may be lost.

Racial or ethnic imbalances, like gender imbalances, can also cause redefinition of an acceptable marriage partner. Members of groups immigrating to countries where there are not enough potential spouses from their own group must remain single or marry members of a race or religion ordinarily regarded as ineligible. Residential patterns of these groups have also been shown to affect intermarriage rates. In a study of marriage records from 1900 to 1950 in Connecticut, for example, one investigator found that intermarriage between ethnic groups was inversely related to the degree of residential segregation between them.[44] Jews and blacks were both the most segregated and the least likely to marry members of other groups.

Costs to Children and Parents

Still another way to view the impact of population processes on families is to examine the effect the number of siblings has on a child's growth, development, and success. Much research has been done on what happens to children who grow up in large or small families,[45] and it does not all reach the same conclusion.

Quite obviously, to sort out the direct influence of having many brothers and sisters, research must take into account the general economic status of the family. Since families with a low economic status have more children than those with a high one, differences in the developmental processes in large and small families may have more to do with economics than with size. Similarly, genetic differences could also play an important role in how children develop and must also be considered.[46]

Many studies that have addressed the relationship of number of siblings to other characteristics of children have not controlled for these or other factors. Whatever the underlying causes, one author has summarized the problems in large families in this way:

> The effects associated with family size on the well-being of individuals—primarily the children—in a family are varied, but serious: increased illness, including malnutrition, serious enough in younger children to increase mortality rates; less satisfactory growth and intellectual development. . . .[47]

In addition to economic and genetic explanations for these findings, some have postulated that the personal attention each child receives in large families is less. Certainly, however, a great deal of personal care and attention may be given to children in large families by mothers and fathers motivated to do so. The negative effects of having many brothers and sisters can thus be lessened, but it is not entirely clear that they can be eliminated.

Special research attention has also been given to only children. While it seems clear that the stereotypes of only children remain negative, research does not confirm many of the supposed negative characteristics among only children. Rather than being disadvantaged, only children are intellectually superior, achieve higher educational and occupational status, and are unlikely to be maladjusted or have special personality defects, according to recent findings.[48]

Of course, having additional children, or having children at all influences the opportunities and life-styles of parents as well. A recent estimate of the direct, out-of-pocket cost of having and raising a child is $85,000.[49] This figure includes having the child under the parent's roof until age eighteen, as well as four years at a public university. However, these are only the direct maintenance costs of a child, and they do not include the costs of opportunities foregone by mothers who reduce labor-force participation at the child's birth. When opportunity costs are added, the total for one child rises to $140,000 for middle-income families.

There has been much speculation and research on the impact of children on marital and parental satisfaction as well. While some have argued that the presence of children may keep marriages together, others have found that marital satisfaction goes down as the number of children goes up. Perhaps these effects are dependent upon the age of children, since the presence of preschool-age children seems to deter separation and divorce, while school-age children no longer seem to serve as a cause to continue a marriage.[50] One of the most recent analyses of these relationships suggests that neither the number nor spacing of children is related to marital satisfaction.[51] However, the number of children is related to satisfaction as a parent. Those with more children report feeling less parental satisfaction.

Further, the occurrence of a premarital pregnancy is negatively related to both marital and parental satisfaction among women. Along this same line, recent research has also found that parents who plan the birth of their children show greater marital stability than those who do not.[52]

In the preceding discussion, we have only touched on the myriad ways in which population processes can affect the formation, structure, and members of families. Suffice it to say that, while the family is usually the unit in which the birth of children takes place, and hence ultimately the location of many population-relevant decisions, it is in turn influenced by these very processes.

NOTES

1. Kingsley Davis, "Population and Power in the Free World," in *Population and World Politics*, ed. Philip M. Hauser (New York: Free Press, 1958), pp. 193–213.

2.   Gerry E. Hendershot, "Population Size, Military Power, and Antinatal Policy," *Demography*, 10, no. 4 (1973), 517–524.

3.   A. F. K. Organski, Bruce Bueno de Mesquita, and Alan Lamborn, "The Effective Population in International Politics," in *Governance and Population: The Governmental Implications of Population Change*. Research Report of the U.S. Commission on Population Growth and the American Future (Washington, D.C.: U.S. Government Printing Office, 1972) pp. 235–249.

4.   Hadi Soesastro, "The Population Factor in International Relations," *Indonesian Quarterly*, 7 (January 1979), 36–51.

5.   Roger H. Davidson, "Population Change and Representation Government," in *Governance and Population*, pp. 58–82.

6.   Daniel J. Elazar, "Population Growth and the Federal System," in *Governance and Population*, pp. 15–24.

7.   John G. Grumm, "Population Change and State Government Policy," in *Governance and Population*, pp. 125–140.

8.   Bryant Robey and Mary John, "The Political Future: The Demographics of Politics," *American Demographics*, 2 (October 1980), 15–21.

9.   Jeanne C. Biggar, "The Sunning of America, Migration to the Sunbelt," *Population Bulletin*, 34 (March 1979), 1–44; see also "1980 Census Final Population Count and Congressional Reapportionment," *Intercom*, 9 (January 1981), p. 5.

10.   Robey and John, "Political Future."

11.   Gordon Stavig and Larry Barnett, "Group Size and Societal Conflict," *Human Relations*, 30 (1977), 761–765.

12.   Stephen D. Mumford, "Population Growth and Global Security: Toward an American Strategic Commitment," *Humanist*, 41 (January–February 1981), 6–25; also William R. Kelly and Omer R. Galle, "Sociological Perspectives and Evidence on the Links Between Population and Conflict," Chapter 5 in Nazli Choucri, ed., *Population and Conflict* (New York: United Nations Fund for Population Activities, in press, 1982).

13.   Nick Eberstadt and Eric Breindel, "The Population Factor in the Middle East," *International Security*, 3 (1979), 190–196.

14.   A historical and more current analysis of this position can be found in Robert G. Weisbord, "Birth Control and the Black American: A Matter of Genocide?" *Demography*, 10 (November 1973), 571–590.

15.   Gerald C. Wright, Jr., "Racism and the Availability of Family Planning Services in the U.S.," *Social Forces*, 56, no. 4 (June 1978), 1,087–1,098.

16.   Quoted in Weisbord, "Birth Control," p. 580.

17.   Mary Treadwell, "Is Abortion Black Genocide?" *Family Planning Perspectives*, 4 (January 1972), 4.

18.   Reynolds Farley, *Growth of the Black Population*, (Chicago: Markham, 1970), p. 203.

19.   Michael Hout, "Age Structure, Unwanted Fertility, and the Association Between Racial Composition and Family Planning Programs: A Comment on Wright," *Social Forces*, 57, no. 4 (June 1979), 1,387–1,392.

20.   Farley, *Growth*, p. 49.

21. Themba Sono, "Demographic Trends, Growth, and Geographic Distribution of African Population as an Index of Political Conflict in South Africa: 1970–2000," *Journal of Southern African Affairs*, 3 (October 1978), 471–488.

22. Ibid.

23. Brian Silver, "The Impact of Urbanization and Geographical Dispersion on the Linguistic Russification of Soviet Nationalities," *Demography*, 2 (February 1974), 89–103.

24. George E. Johnson, Harold S. Himmelfarb, and Mordecai Waxman, "Zero Population Growth and the Jewish Community: A Symposium," *Analysis*, no. 60 (November–December 1976), 1–12.

25. For a fuller discussion of this process, see Gerhard Lenski, *The Religious Factor* (New York: Doubleday/Anchor, 1963), pp. 359–362.

26. Harvey Cox, *The Secular City: Secularization and Urbanization in Theological Perspective* (New York: Macmillan, 1965).

27. Lenski, *Religious Factor*, pp. 45–46.

28. Cox, *Secular City*, p. 54.

29. Robert Wuthnow and Kevin Christiano, "The Effects of Residential Migration on Church Attendance in the United States," in *The Religious Dimension*, ed. Robert Wuthnow (New York: Academic Press, 1979). pp. 257–276.

30. Francis X. Murphy, "Catholic Perspectives on Population Issues II," *Population Bulletin*, 35, no. 6 (February 1981).

31. Quoted in Murphy, "Catholic Perspectives."

32. A thorough discussion of events before and after the papal encyclical can be found in Leslie A. Westoff and Charles F. Westoff, *From Now to Zero* (Boston: Little, Brown, 1968). See especially Chapter 5.

33. Murphy, "Catholic Perspectives," pp. 37 and 39.

34. Peter C. W. Gutkind, "African Urbanism, Mobility and the Social Network," *International Journal of Comparative Sociology*, 6 (March 1965), 48–60.

35. Remi Clignet, "Urbanization and Family Structure in the Ivory Coast," *Comparative Studies in Society and History*, 8 (July 1966), 385–401.

36. Ming-Cheng Chang, Ronald Freedman, and Te-Hsiung Sun, "Trends in Fertility, Family Size Preferences, and Family Planning Practice: Taiwan, 1961–80," *Studies in Family Planning*, 12 (May 1981) 211–228.

37. Nilufer R. Ahmed, "Family Size and Sex Preferences Among Women in Rural Bangladesh," *Studies in Family Planning*, 12 (March 1981), 100–108.

38. Leonard Kasdan, "Family Structure, Migration and the Entrepreneur," *Comparative Studies in Society and History*, 7 (July 1965), 345–367.

39. Robert E. Kennedy, Jr., *The Irish* (Berkeley: University of California Press, 1973), pp. 195–196.

40. Paul C. Glick and Arthur J. Norton, "Marrying, Divorcing, and Living Together in the U.S. Today," *Population Bulletin*, 32 (October 1977), Table 17, pp. 1–39.

41. U.S. Bureau of the Census, "Population Profile of the United States: 1980," *Current Population Reports*, Series P-28, no. 363 (June 1981), Table 13.

42. Peter Uhlenberg, "Death and the Family," *Journal of Family History*, 5 (Fall 1980), 313–320.

43. David M. Heer and Amyra Grossbard-Schechtman, "The Impact of the Female Marriage Squeeze and the Contraceptive Revolution on Sex Roles and the Women's Liberation Movement in the United States, 1960 to 1974," *Journal of Marriage and the Family*, 43 (February 1981), 49–65.

44. Ceri Peach, "Ethnic Segregation and Intermarriage," *Annals of the Association of American Geographers*, 70 (September 1980), 371–381.

45. Summaries of this research can be found in John A. Clausen and Suzanne R. Clausen, "The Effects of Family Size on Parents and Children," in *Psychological Perspectives on Population*, ed. James T. Fawcett (New York: Basic Books, 1973), pp. 185–208; Joe D. Wray, "Population Pressure on Families: Family Size and Child Spacing," in *Rapid Population Growth: Consequences and Policy Implications*, (Baltimore: Johns Hopkins University Press, 1971); and Kenneth W. Terhune, *A Review of the Actual and Expected Consequences of Family Size*, DHEW Publication No. (NIH) 75-779 (Washington, D.C.: U.S. Public Health Service, 1974).

46. Sandra Scarr and Richard Weinberg, "Influence of 'Family Background' on Intellectual Attainment," *American Sociological Review*, 43, no. 5 (October 1978), 657–673.

47. Wray, "Population Pressure," p. 454.

48. Judith Blake, "The Only Child in America: Prejudice versus Performance," *Population and Development Review*, 7 (March 1981), 43–54.

49. Thomas J. Espenshade, "Raising a Child Can Now Cost $85,000," *Intercom*, 8 (September 1980), 1, 10–12.

50. Andrew Cherlin, "The Effect of Children on Marital Dissolution," *Demography*, 14, no. 3 (August 1977), 265–272.

51. Margaret M. Marini, "Effects of Number and Spacing of Children on Marital and Parental Satisfaction," *Demography*, 17 (August 1980), 225–242.

52. Frank C. Johnson and May R. Johnson, "Family Planning: Implications for Marital Stability," *Journal of Divorce*, 3 (Spring 1980), 273–281.

SUGGESTED ADDITIONAL READINGS

A collection of documents on Chinese population policy and its impact on many aspects of that society is:

TIEN, H. YUAN, ed. *Population Theory in China*, White Plains, N.Y.: M. E. Sharpe, 1980.

A discussion of how census data are used for congressional apportionment is found in:

POSTON, DUDLEY L., JR., AND MARION TOLBERT COLEMAN, "The Mechanics of Congressional Apportionment," *Intercom*, 1, no. 1 (January 1981).

The issues of population and birth control relative to the Roman Catholic Church are reviewed in:

MURPHY, FRANCIS X., *The Papacy Today*. New York: Macmillan, 1981.

Summaries of the interrelations of population processes and families, past and present, are offered in:

LEE, RONALD DEMOS, ed. *Population Patterns in the Past*. New York: Academic Press, 1977.

MASNICK, GEORGE, AND MARY JO BANE, *The Nation's Families: 1960–1990*. Boston: Auburn House, 1980.

Data on subgroup variation in timing of family life-cycle events are found in:

SPANIER, GRAHAM B., AND PAUL C. GLICK, "The Life Cycle of American Families: An Expanded Analysis," *Journal of Family History* (Spring 1980), 97–111.

TECHNICAL SUPPLEMENT NO. 8

How Is the Census Used for Apportionment?

The intent of the U.S. Constitution certainly seemed simple enough: "Representatives shall be apportioned among the several States according to their respective numbers . . ." And so, after each decennial census, the U.S. House of Representatives would be restructured, taking into account the population counts in each state. As it has turned out, it is not so simple after all. In fact, exactly *how* apportionment is to be accomplished has been the subject of much historical debate. The issue even caused the first presidential veto, by George Washington.

The basic problem of apportionment is the phrase, "according to their respective numbers." It would seem that the straightforward way to allocate seats in the House is to divide the total number of seats on the basis of each state's percentage of the total population. However, such a calculation creates remainders. For almost two hundred years, debate has been generated on what to do with those remainders.

The first system, proposed by Alexander Hamilton in 1790, specified that seats would be allocated by dividing the state populations by the number of seats to be apportioned. Each state was to receive the number of seats corresponding to the whole number in the division, and leftover seats were given to states with the largest remaining fractions. Washington subsequently vetoed this proposal, preferring instead a method devised by Thomas Jefferson. Jefferson's scheme used a single divisor of 33,000, in order to apportion representatives in each state at a ratio of one to every 33,000 residents. This method was used until 1850, and the divisor rose as the population increased. It was often criticized for favoring large states such as Thomas Jefferson's own, Virginia.

While argument over the method of apportionment continued during this period of time, it was not until 1850 that Congress reconsidered and adopted Hamilton's method. Nevertheless the method quickly appeared to be unsatisfactory, and various unofficial adjustments were made in the apportionment of seats, without a change in the law. In 1876 these adjustments resulted in the election of Hayes to the presidency by one vote in the electoral college even though Tilden had won the popular vote.

Real problems with Hamilton's method were apparent. Some states lost seats as the number of representatives increased because their remaining fractions became smaller than those of other states. Furthermore, this was a time when new states were added to the Union, throwing off the assignments in states that had not had changes in their population counts. Jefferson's method, on the other hand, clearly favored large states.

The debate continued until 1941, when Congress adopted the method used today. This is the method of equal proportions. Under this method, the first 50 seats in the House of Representatives are assigned, one to each state. Then a set of priority values are computed for each state for each of the remaining 385 seats. This is done by multiplying the population count in each state by the fraction:

$$\frac{1}{\sqrt{N(N-1)}}$$

where N = the number of the seat being claimed. For example, the proportion used to determine the claim to the second seat is:

$$\frac{1}{\sqrt{2(2-1)}} = \frac{1}{\sqrt{2(1)}} = \frac{1}{\sqrt{2}} = \frac{1}{1.41421356}$$

After multiplying these proportions by the population count in each state, the resulting priority values are then ranked in order to allocate the remaining seats. Sometimes the priority value of a state for a third seat will be higher than the priority value of another state for a second seat. Still, the next seat of the remaining 385 goes to the higher priority value of the first state.

As if this were not debatable and complicated enough, there have also been arguments about how to actually count the population of each state for purposes of apportionment. Recently there has been discussion of how to count overseas residents, members of the armed forces stationed out of the country, college students, and other categories for whom usual residence is not so clear. To deal with these situations, Congress has from time to time made special rules to facilitate counting. And, of course, states that lose population and hence representation are quite likely to complain that the counting methodologies used by the U.S. Bureau of the Census are inadequate.

It is likely that debate on the simple matter of apportionment of representatives "according to their respective numbers" in the population will reappear again and again.

Sources: Dudley L. Poston, Jr. and Marion Tolbert Coleman, "The Mechanics of Congressional Apportionment," *Intercom,* 9, no. 1 (January 1981), 8–10; Lynn Arthur Steen, "The Arithmetic of Apportionment," *Science News,* 121 (May 8, 1982), 317–318; Subcommittee on Census and Statistics of the Committee on Post Office and Civil Services, "The Decennial Population Census and Congressional Apportionment," Union Calendar No. 638, House Report No. 91-1314 (Washington, D.C.: U.S. Government Printing Office, 1970).

ISSUES SUPPLEMENT NO. 8

What Is Happening to the American Family?

Like the old gray mare, the American family is hardly what it used to be. In fact, the two-parent, two-child, family with the mother not working is no longer the average American family. While it is perhaps an overreaction to talk about the "death of the American family," there has clearly been a revolution in the numbers and types of arrangements that are now considered to be families. For example, a recent article on new family types (Sussman, 1979) listed the following:

nuclear families, intact, children present
nuclear family, no children at home or childless
nuclear family, remarried, children present
nuclear family, remarried, no children or childless
single parent family
kin networks, including several generations
single, divorced or widowed adults
communes
unmarried parents and children

These types may be further subdivided according to whether one or more adults in each family is employed.

What are some of the basic facts about the American family that are central to understanding such diversity? A few of these are listed here:

Marriage is being postponed.

Divorce ratios are still rising and are now up to 100 divorced persons per 1,000 married persons.

Among black children, 46 percent live with only one parent, and among all children, 20 percent live with only one parent.

Since 1970, the number of unmarried couples living together has tripled and is now about 1.5 million.

Nonfamily households comprise 25 percent of all households.

Childlessness has increased among women 25 to 29 years old to 26 percent.

Over 78 percent of married women aged 15 to 44 with husband present are employed and 45 percent of these women who have children under 6 years of age are employed.

These factors and others have brought great change to the American family.

What are the implications of these changes for understanding and supporting the families of today? In nearly every area of American life, these changes must be noted and adjustments made. Some of these adjustments may seem simple enough. For example, when so many children are living with only one parent, is it appropriate any longer to have father-son or mother-daughter activities at school? Since so many mothers work, how many children will have parents able to attend activities scheduled on weekdays between 9:00 A.M. and 5:00 P.M.? Some of the implications are more profound. In the many families where parents are remarried, who can give consent for the treatment of children in health-care settings, particularly emergency rooms? A stepparent bringing in a child with a broken leg hardly has time to seek consent for treatment from a biological parent who may live in another state.

Even the Census Bureau has adjusted somewhat to the variety apparent in families. The Bureau used to designate the husband as "head" of the household, regardless of who supported a family financially or made most of the decisions. It now uses the term "householder" for adults who own or rent houses, regardless of their sex.

Perhaps most important to families today is the recognition that they are not all made from one mold. Acceptance of alternative forms may be the first step to supporting the adults and children who live in these many different family arrangements.

Sources: Marvin B. Sussman, "Actions and Services for the New Family," in David Reiss and Howard A. Hoffman, ed., *The American Family: Dying or Developing.* (New York: Plenum Press, 1979), pp. 213–241. For facts on the American family today, see U.S. Bureau of the Census, "Household and Family Characteristics: March 1980," *Current Population Reports,* Series P-20, no. 366, September 1981.

CHAPTER NINE
INFLUENCING
DEMOGRAPHIC CHANGE

"Edgar! For God's sake! You can't just take population control into your own hands!"

Drawing by Ross: © 1972 *The New Yorker* Magazine, Inc.

The recognition that the size, growth rate, composition and distribution of the population have important implications for other aspects of society is not new. In the two preceding chapters we have already highlighted many of the current societal consequences of population change. There are also numerous historical examples of concern with population and of proposals to influence it in one way or another.

Plato, for example, believed that the ideal city-state should contain exactly 5,040 citizens. That number was large enough for self-sufficiency but small enough to have a workable government. Further, 5,040 happens to be evenly divisible by every number between 1 and 12 except 11. Thus, the population could easily be divided into even-size groups for accomplishing tasks. How appalled Plato might be today at both our tiny villages and the multimillions in metropolises!

If the recognition of the importance of population is not new, however, concerted efforts by nearly every nation of the world to carefully monitor population and influence it are. In this chapter we will try to understand what is meant by population policy, what the status of such policy is in the world today, and what issues surround attempts to control population processes. Then we will take a specific look at population policies in the United States, both present and future.

DEFINING POPULATION POLICY

Those who study, formulate, and write about population policy are not agreed on just what qualifies as policy.[1] While some say that any governmental action that influences population should be included, others argue that only those actions *intended* to influence population are truly policy.[2] Another potential confusion comes with attempts to distinguish "official" policies of various governments from other statements. Laws about population and its components, statements by public-health ministers, and even speeches by leaders might all be considered policy. If these sources conflict, sorting out the "real" population policy of a government may be difficult.

The legitimate scope of population policy is another dimension that must be considered. Since fertility, mortality, and migration are the components of population through which all change takes place, it is possible to limit policy inquiries to only those actions intended to influence these components directly. On the other hand, since it is possible that raising the general level of socioeconomic development of a nation or community may also reduce fertility, and in turn reduce population growth, perhaps development policies too should be included in a comprehensive definition of attempts to change population. Health policies that might influence mortality or employment policies that may stimulate immigration or internal migration are two other examples of this kind of policy.

Population policies may also be classified using other dimensions: the degree of commitment with which they are implemented, their strategies for producing change, their cost, who has responsibility for them, the degree to which they are monitored and ethical, and, of course, their effectiveness.

Some societies have no population policy at all. To have one requires both a recognition that population processes are important to an area and at least occasional dissatisfaction with them. Governments must judge their growth rates, their size, or some other characteristic of their population to be unsatisfactory in order to be motivated to attempt change. How many nations recognize population as an important factor to well-being today, and how many are doing something about it?

THE WORLD POPULATION CONFERENCE, 1974

The World Population Conference of 1974, sometimes called the Bucharest Conference because of its meeting place, is likely to be seen historically as a turning point in international recognition of the importance of population processes to societal well-being. Conventions of experts to discuss world population trends and their consequences have been held since 1927, but this conference occurred when greater attention was being given to population issues in the world than ever before. More and more nations were becoming aware of the role population growth was playing in the welfare of their citizens, and they were prepared to discuss the issues and their possible resolution. More than fifty countries, including the United States, had set up population commissions that would establish national positions and present them at the conference.[3]

The meeting actually consisted of two separate but related forums. The first was a conference of government delegates who were to consider and vote on the United Nations-sponsored World Population Plan of Action. The second was the Population Tribune, involving nongovernmental organizations and individuals. The two-week meeting often included lively debates on critical population issues. Some governments and individuals favored the original Plan of Action, which stressed the need for reducing population growth and suggested fertility control measures to bring that about. Others argued that economic assistance by developed countries was necessary *before* population limitation could become a reality.[4] Some nations (especially in Africa and Latin

America) took the position that further population growth would be beneficial, others preferred a laissez-faire attitude toward population change, and a great number of countries favored hastening the decline of population growth rates.

In the last analysis, the conference agreed upon a revised Plan of Action (with only the Vatican refraining from support), which incorporated some demographic recommendations and broader social and economic imperatives. Highlights of the accepted plan are presented on the following pages.

Highlights of the World Population Plan of Action as Agreed by the World Population Conference at Bucharest[5]

Population policies and programs are an integral part of economic and social development and should be directed toward the ultimate goal of improving the quality of life for all men, women, and children. To this end, the World Population Conference recommends that:

1. *Governments should develop national policies and programs relating to the growth and distribution of their populations, if they have not already done so, and the rate of population change should be taken into account in development programs.*
2. *Countries should aim at a balance between low rather than high death rates and birth rates.*
3. *Highest priority should be given to the reduction of high death rates. Expectation of life should exceed sixty-two years in 1985 and seventy-four years in 2000. Where infant mortality continues high, it should be brought down to at least 120 per thousand live births by the year 2000.*
4. *Because all couples and individuals have the basic human right to decide freely and responsibly the number and spacing of their children, countries should encourage appropriate education concerning responsible parenthood and make available to persons who so desire advice and means of achieving it.*
5. *Family planning and related services should aim at prevention of unwanted pregnancies as well as elimination of involuntary sterility or subfecundity to enable couples to achieve their desired number of children.*
6. *Where family planning programs exist they should be coor-*

dinated with health and other services designed to raise the quality of life.

7. Countries which consider their birth rates detrimental to their national purposes are invited to set quantitative goals and implement policies to achieve them by 1985.

8. Developed countries should develop appropriate policies in population, consumption, and investment, bearing in mind the need for fundamental improvement in international equity.

9. Because the family is the basic unit of society, governments should assist families as far as possible through appropriate legislation and services.

10. Governments should ensure full participation of women in the educational, economic, social, and political life of their countries on an equal basis with men.

11. Countries that wish to increase their rate of population growth should do so through low mortality rather than high fertility, and possibly immigration.

12. To achieve the projected declines in population growth and the projected increases in life expectancy, birth rates in the developing countries should decline from the present level of thirty-eight to thirty per thousand by 1985, which will require substantial national efforts and international assistance.

13. In addition to family planning, measures should be employed that affect such socioeconomic factors as reduction in infant and childhood mortality, increased education particularly for females, improvement in the status of women, land reform, and support in old age.

14. To assure needed information concerning population trends, population censuses should be taken at regular intervals and information concerning birth and deaths should be made available at least annually.

15. Policies should be developed to reduce the undesirable consequences of excessively rapid urbanization and to develop opportunities in rural areas and small towns, recognizing the right of individuals to move freely within their national boundaries.

16. International agreements should be concluded to regulate the migration of workers and to assure nondiscriminatory treatment and social services for these workers and their families.

17. *National efforts should be intensified through expanded research programs to develop knowledge concerning the social, economic, and political interrelationships with population trends; effective means of reducing infant and childhood mortality; new and improved methods of fertility regulation to meet the varied requirements of individuals and communities, including methods requiring no medical supervision; the interrelations of health, nutrition, and reproductive biology; and methods for improving the administration, delivery, and utilization of social services, including family planning services.*

18. *International, intergovernmental, and nongovernmental agencies and national governments should increase their assistance in the population field on request.*

19. *In exercising their sovereign right to determine their population policies and programs, governments should do so consistent with human rights and the effects of their national policies on the interests of other nations and of mankind.*

20. *The Plan of Action should be closely coordinated with the International Development Strategy for the Second United Nations Development Decade, reviewed in depth at five-year intervals, and modified as appropriate.*

Certainly the proposed Plan of Action was quite broad in scope, covering recommendations about not only fertility, mortality, and migration, but also families, employment of women, and health. In addition, the plan repeatedly stressed the right of each nation to formulate policy as it saw fit.

One of the provisions of the World Population Plan of Action is that the United Nations should provide frequent reports on the world population situation. In order to accomplish this task, the UN conducts surveys of governments asking for their perceptions, policies, and actions concerning population.

While it is too soon to have a historical perspective on the importance of the Bucharest Conference, it seems likely that it will be seen as having made at least two important contributions. It was a milestone in international recognition of the importance of population processes to development and well-being. The conference may also be credited with raising the consciousness of the developed nations about the needs of the developing ones. The leaders of the latter indicated that they would not look favorably on isolated attempts to influence population change without equal or greater attention to socioeconomic development.

IS POPULATION DEFINED AS A PROBLEM?

A 1980 report from the United Nations has indicated that virtually all developed and developing countries now believe that an understanding of population trends is vital for the future success of national development.[6] The problems recognized by these governments include the

TABLE 9.1 Perceptions of population processes in developed and developing nations

	Developed Countries	Developing Countries
	N = 42	N = 116
Natural increase	(percent)	(percent)
Higher rate desirable	31	20
Rate satisfactory	69	41
Lower rate desirable	—	39
Total	100	100
Expectation of life		
Acceptable	76	24
Unacceptable	24	76
Total	100	100
Level of fertility		
Too low	24	10
Rate satisfactory	74	46
Too high	2	44
Total	100	100
Spatial distribution		
Acceptable	31	5
Unacceptable	57	36
Highly unacceptable	12	59
Total	100	100
Level of immigration		
Too low	5	9
Satisfactory	90	85
Too high	5	6
Total	100	100
Level of emigration		
Too low	5	6
Satisfactory	76	79
Too high	19	15
Total	100	100

Source: United Nations Secretariat, "Concise Report on the Monitoring of Population Policies," *Population Bulletin of the United Nations,* no. 12 (New York: United Nations, 1980), pp. 23, 25, 27, 29, 32, 33.

overall growth of the population, fertility, mortality, and migration, and the distribution of population within national territories.

The degree to which these processes are perceived as problematic varies dramatically between developed and developing countries (see Table 9.1). While over two-thirds of those from developed nations think their rate of natural increase is satisfactory, the same proportion of those from developing nations see their rate of natural increase as unsatisfactory, being either too high or too low. Similarly, three-fourths of those from developed nations consider their average expectation of life to be acceptable, but only one-fourth of those from developing nations are happy with this average. On the issues of immigration and emigration, reports from the developed and developing nations are more similar, with majorities in each perceiving these rates as generally satisfactory.

Thus it is apparent that the leaders of many nations are now aware of the importance of population processes and have evaluated them and their immediate causes. What, then, are they doing about natural increase or decrease, fertility, mortality, and migration?

THE STATUS OF POPULATION POLICY

Many nations now have official policies to reduce the population growth rate. Others have policies supporting family-planning activities, although demographic change is not their stated goal for such a policy. However, many areas of Africa still lack both growth policies and family-planning programs. While most developed countries see their rate of natural increase as satisfactory, and none of them currently wants to lower it, a few consider a higher rate desirable.[7]

What do both developed and developing countries try to influence in order to achieve the growth rates they believe desirable? Table 9.2 shows that the demographic factor most often mentioned by these nations is spatial distribution of their populations. The population component least often manipulated deliberately is mortality. It is also interesting, however, that many nations indicate that socioeconomic restructuring is part of their attempt to change the rate of natural increase. This is an indication of the broad approach being taken to population growth in current policies.

It is also interesting to explore exactly what interventions nations attempt in terms of each population component. In regard to mortality, for example, virtually all nations have health policies, which, in turn, may affect the death rate. Some nations, particularly developing ones, set targets for future death-rate reductions. Recent health policies in

TABLE 9.2 Demographic and nondemographic variables most frequently chosen for intervention affecting the rate of natural increase

Countries	Mortality	Fertility	Spatial Distribution	International Migration	Socioeconomic Restructuring	No Problems Found to be Associated With the Rate of Natural Increase
Developed countries	9	14	19	19	24	12
Developing countries	26	58	98	62	104	10
Total	35	72	117	81	128	22

Source: United Nations Secretariat, "Concise Report on the Monitoring of Population Policies," *Population Bulletin of the United Nations*, no. 12 (New York: United Nations, 1980), Table 4, p. 24.

developing nations have emphasized distribution of technology to save lives, prevention of disease, improved health education, and general socioeconomic improvement in the level of living.[8] In the developed nations, on the other hand, health programs tend to be aimed at subgroups of the population that do not enjoy the normally low death rates. Developed nations, for example, are much more likely to concentrate on reducing mortality at older ages than are developing ones.

What about attempts to change fertility? What can governments do and what are they doing to change current birthrate levels? In Chapter 4 we discussed programs to influence fertility in some detail, but a review of them may be useful here. The options for changing fertility can be placed in five categories:

1. Change access to birth control, making it either more or less available.
2. Change the socioeconomic level of the population, including such influences on fertility as education, industrialization, and employment or status of women.
3. Use propaganda and restrict opposing views.
4. Use incentives or disincentives such as tax benefits, maternity leaves, child-assistance payments, and payment for being sterilized.
5. Use political pressure or direct sanctions such as minimum age at marriage or legal limits on family size.[9]

Table 9.3 indicates that in a few developed and developing countries, access to birth control is restricted. Even where it is not, this

TABLE 9.3 **Percentage distribution of governments' policies on access to modern methods of birth control**

	Developed Countries	Developing Countries
Access restricted	12	7
Access not restricted		
Not supported by government	9	20
Indirectly supported by government	17	11
Directly supported by government	62	62
Total	100	100

Source: United Nations Secretariat, "Concise Report on the Monitoring of Population Policies," *Population Bulletin of the United Nations,* no. 12 (New York: United Nations, 1980), Table 11, p. 28.

TABLE 9.4 Percentage distribution of governments' policies on spatial distribution and internal migration

	Maintain Migration	Reduce Migration	Reverse Flow	Accelerate Migration	Total Percent
Developing (N = 116)	20	66	12	2	100
Developed (N = 42)	26	60	14	0	100

Source: United Nations Secretariat, "Concise Report on the Monitoring of Population Policies," *Population Bulletin of the United Nations,* no. 12 (New York: United Nations, 1980). Table 13, p. 30.

policy is not always directly supported by the government. Further, even in countries where access is unrestricted, governments may have policies to increase fertility levels. Birth-control programs are then seen as being in the interest of well-being for individual families.

One of the most problematic population components for developed and developing nations is internal migration and the resultant distribution of the population into urban and rural areas. A look back at Table 9.1 reveals that only 31 percent of the developed nations and 5 percent of the developing ones consider the spatial distribution of their population to be acceptable. Table 9.4 shows that over 60 percent of both developed and developing nations have policies to reduce the flow of internal migration. In addition, 12 and 14 percent of developing and developed countries, respectively, have policies to reverse the flow of migration in their nations, either from urban to rural or vice versa. In some nations, industrialization has concentrated the population into crowded urban areas, emptying the countryside. In others, even without industrialization, the extreme poverty of the countryside has caused migration to urban areas. We noted earlier that in some developed countries, such as the United States, the traditional rural-to-urban population flow has recently been reversed, as more families move into small communities from central cities.

Finally, Table 9.5 summarizes current government policies on immigration and emigration. The majority of nations in both categories consider these processes to be either demographically unimportant or undesirable. In the developed nations, which receive most international migrants, about one-fourth have now instituted policies to slow the rate of immigration while maintaining the already established immigrant population.

Overall, then, it can be said that most nations of the world now recognize the importance of population processes to their national well-being. In an attempt to successfully control these processes, many nations now have population policies of one sort or another. As we

TABLE 9.5 **Percentage distribution of governments' policies on immigration and emigration in developed and developing nations**

	Developed Countries (N = 42)	Developing Countries (N = 116)
Immigration Policy Favors		
higher rate	5	7
maintain present rate but with strict control	5	12
slower rate but maintain already established immigrant population	26	4
immigration unimportant or not desirable	64	77
Total	100	100
Emigration Policy Favors		
higher rates	5	3
maintain present rates	2	20
slower rate	19	15
emigration unimportant or not desirable	74	62
Total	100	100

Source: United Nations Secretariat, "Concise Report on the Monitoring of Population Policies," *Population Bulletin of the United Nations,* no. 12 (New York: United Nations, 1980). Tables 15 and 17, pp. 32, 33.

have noted throughout the text, the concerns of developed and developing nations tend to differ, and their population policies reflect these differences.

POPULATION POLICY IN THE UNITED STATES

The United States does not currently have any overall population policy or goals. In fact, until recent decades, the nation has all but ignored population processes. National allegiance to such principles as maximum freedom for individuals and the right to privacy have often silenced those suggesting the need for government intervention into such matters as fertility or migration.

While it lacks a coherent and general population policy, the nation does have myriad laws and other policies that affect population processes. These cover such diverse subjects as advertising contraceptives on television and the prohibition of euthanasia. The nation regulates sterilization, abortion, sale and availability of contraceptives, rights of minors to obtain birth control, many aspects of health care, zoning, building permits, and numerous other areas that are only one step removed from actually regulating fertility, mortality, and residential mobility. And, of course, international migration is regulated both directly and indirectly.

This is not to say that population has not been the subject of official government concern in the United States. In 1969, for the first time in the history of the nation, the President and the Congress set up the U.S. Commission on Population Growth and the American Future.[10] The Commission was asked to examine the probable extent of population growth and internal migration in the United States until the end of the century. It was also asked to assess the impact that population change would have upon government services, the economy, and resources and the environment, and to make recommendations on how the nation could best cope with that impact.

The Commission spent two years conducting an extensive inquiry, during which it solicited research reports, heard numerous witnesses testify at public hearings and executive meetings, and prepared a series of reports surveying population conditions in the United States and giving numerous recommendations for influencing demographic change in the future. These recommendations were by no means arrived at unanimously. The group was composed of individuals from different walks of life—including minorities, youths and the elderly, women and men, rich and poor, governmental leaders and social scientists—and it was often difficult to achieve consensus on specific matters. In fact the Commission began its main report by citing three distinct approaches to dealing with population issues, apparently a reflection of the diversity of opinions on the Commission itself. The three views are still advocated by diverse groups today.

The first acknowledges the benefits to be gained by slowing growth but regards the population problem today primarily as a result of large numbers of people being unable to control an important part of their lives—the number of children they have. According to this view, freedom of choice and equality of access to the means of fertility control are recommended for achieving desired family size. This approach depends on education, research, and national debate to illuminate population issues that transcend individual welfare. It assumes that in this way the best collective decisions about population issues would be achieved. It also assumes that the situation will be reconsidered from time to time, with the expectation that new decisions might be forthcoming.

A second approach acknowledges the need for education and

knowledge but stresses that population is but one facet of the more general problem of denial of equal opportunity. Discrimination against ethnic minorities, women, the economically deprived, and other groups makes it difficult for them to act freely in matters relating to population. Permitting fuller access to social opportunities, it is reasoned, will result in modification of behavior relative to population.

The difference between these first two views should, by now, sound familiar. They are reminiscent of the arguments in developing countries over whether family planning alone is sufficient for fertility control or whether socioeconomic development is even more important.

Still a third viewpoint puts population in an ecological framework and calls for a far more fundamental shift in the operative values of modern society, stating that the need for more education and knowledge and elimination of poverty and racism, while important, is not all-important. The population problem is thought to be indicative of the imbalance between people and nature occasioned by the destructive effects of mass urban industrialism. To remedy the situation, a new set of values concerning nature, the economy, and human identity is needed, ones that will reject the growth ethic and promote realization of the highest potential of individual humanity.

Despite these disparities in basic positions, the Commission endorsed, with occasional dissenting opinions, a series of recommendations covering forty-seven areas of significance to population development. These recommendations, presented in the following pages, deal with population and sex education; child care, children born out of wedlock, and adoption; equal rights for women, racial minorities, and the poor; voluntary sterilization, abortion, other methods of fertility control, and fertility-related health services; the relation of contraception to the law and to minors; family planning and health training and services, for teenagers as well as adults; population stabilization; immigration, illegal aliens, population distribution, and migration policies; guiding urban expansion and assisting depressed rural areas; and a variety of research and government organizational steps that would facilitate the study of population trends and their consequences and permit government action, when and where needed.

Many of the recommendations involve actions that would be universally acceptable, provided the funds to implement them could be generated. Several recommendations, however, caused controversey when they were reported and may have drawn attention away from the numerous others in the Commission's report. The most controversial areas included provision of birth-control information and services for teenagers and the liberalization of abortion laws.

Highlights of the Recommendations of the U.S. Commission on Population Growth and the American Future

Population Education: The Commission recommends enactment of a Population Education Act to assist school systems in establishing well-planned population education programs and appropriation of federal funds for teacher training, for curriculum development and materials preparation, for research and evaluation, for the support of model programs, and for assisting state departments of education to develop competence and leadership in population education.

Sex Education: Sex education should be available to all, and should be presented through community organizations, the media, and especially the schools.

Child Care: The Commission recommends adequate child-care services, including health, nutritional, and educational components.

Children Born Out of Wedlock: The Commission recommends that all children, regardless of the circumstances of their birth, be accorded fair and equal status socially, morally, and legally.

Adoption: The Commission recommends encouraging adoption, subsidization of families qualified to adopt but unable to assume the full financial cost of a child's care, and review of current procedures that govern the adoptive process.

Equal Rights for Women: The Commission recommends approval of the Equal Rights Amendment.

Contraception and the Law: States should eliminate legal restrictions on access to contraceptive information, procedures, and supplies, and develop statutes affirming the desirability of access to contraceptive information, procedures, and supplies.

Contraception and Minors: The Commission recommends legislation to permit minors to receive contraceptive and prophylactic information and services.

Voluntary Sterilization: All administrative restrictions on access to voluntary contraceptive sterilization should be eliminated.

Abortion: With the admonition that abortion not be considered a primary means of fertility control, the Commission recommends that present laws be liberalized. Governments should make funds available to support abortion services in states with liberalized statutes, and abortion should be included in health-insurance benefits.

Methods of Fertility Control: The Commission recommends that this nation give the highest priority to research in reproductive biology and to the search for improved methods to control fertility.

Fertility-Related Health Services: The Commission recommends a national policy and voluntary program to reduce unwanted fertility, to improve the outcome of pregnancy, and to improve the health of children.

Population Stabilization: The Commission recommends that the nation welcome and plan for a stabilized population.

Illegal Aliens: The Commission recommends that Congress pass legislation that will impose civil and criminal sanctions on employers of aliens with an immigration status in which employment is not authorized.

Immigration: The Commission recommends that immigration levels not be increased and that immigration policy be reviewed periodically.

National Distribution and Migration Policies: The Commission recommends that the federal government develop a set of national population-distribution guidelines; the process of population movement be eased and guided in order to improve access or opportunities now restricted by physical remoteness, immobility, and inadequate skills, information, and experience.

Guiding Urban Expansion: The Commission recommends comprehensive land-use and public-facility planning.

Racial Minorities and the Poor: The Commission recommends vigorous and concerted steps to promote free choice of housing within metropolitan areas, the development of more extensive human-capital programs to equip black and other deprived minorities for fuller participation in economic life, and more suburban housing for low- and moderate-income families.

Depressed Rural Areas: The Commission recommends that programs for depressed rural areas emphasize human resource development, that programs enable an individual to relocate with a minimum of risk and disruption, and expansion of job opportunities in urban places located within or near declining areas.

Population Statistics and Research: The federal government should strengthen the basic statistics and research upon which all sound demographic, social, and economic policy must ultimately depend.

Organizational Changes: The Commission recommends that organizational changes be undertaken to improve the federal government's capacity to develop and implement population-related programs; and to evaluate the interaction between public policies, programs, and population trends.

The negative reaction of former President Nixon to the controversial recommendations, and his failure to endorse the Commission's work generally, muted the effect of the Commission's labors. The crucial recommendation that the nation welcome and plan for a stabilized population was presented to the Congress, the Administration, and the public at a time when the country's birthrate had already declined sharply and appeared to be dropping to a level consistent with a stable population. It may not be surprising, therefore, that many of the actions anticipated by the Commission following their report did not come to pass. But the Commission had informed the public about population conditions in the United States to perhaps a greater extent than ever before, and, should population trends be altered, there is much in the Commission's main report and research appendixes that can be instructive to lay people as well as to national, state, and community leaders.

A second official government inquiry into population matters was made by the Select Committee on Population, established by the House of Representatives in 1977. The Committee was set up to investigate

1. causes and consequences of population change in the world and in the United States;
2. characteristics of the population relative to demands on resources;
3. approaches to population planning;
4. means by which the United States might assist other nations in solving their population problems.

In 1978 the Committee issued a final report, containing the far-reaching recommendations included on the following pages. It includes not only recommendations about aspects of population processes in the United States, but suggestions on strategies for aid to other nations as well. Indeed, if governmental appropriations can be considered indicative of policy, the United States certainly has a policy of population assistance for other nations. In 1977 alone, the United States spent over $250 million for international population assistance. This is only about 2 percent of the entire governmental budget for all international assistance, however.

It is important to note that the Select Committee did not have any power of implementation, and was only charged with investigating population problems and making recommendations. Still, its existence perhaps indicates that the federal government at that time perceived the importance of population processes.

Also in 1978 several members of Congress sponsored a bill in the U.S. House of Representatives that recommended creation of a national Office of Population Policy and formulation of a population policy for the nation. No action was taken on the bill in that year, but it was reintroduced in 1979 and again in 1981. Perhaps these are preliminary signs that the nation is on the eve of such a national policy.

Highlights of the Recommendations of the Select Committee on Population, U.S. House of Representatives, 1978

DOMESTIC FERTILITY BEHAVIOR AND CONTRACEPTIVE SERVICES

The Department of Health, Education and Welfare (now Health and Human Services) should:

Make a more substantial commitment to providing infertility services.

Distribute public service messages concerning the availability of family planning and its medical and socioeconomic advantages, as well as the availability of infertility services.

Expand the training of nurse practitioners and encourage states to remove legal barriers to the effective utilization of such personnel.

Devote more resources to contraceptive services among rural women.

Increase provision of male contraceptive services, support outreach activities to attract males and involve men more actively in the family-planning decision-making process.

Evaluate the role of private physicians in the provision of family-planning services.

Determine the unmet demand for subsidized infertility services, voluntary sterilizations, and counseling in periodic abstinence methods.

Monitor the effect of sterilization regulations to ensure that these regulations do not hinder access to this procedure.

Increase funds for evaluation of family-planning programs.

ADOLESCENT FERTILITY

The following should be supported or expanded:

Comprehensive health and social programs for pregnant teenagers.

Efforts to strengthen teenage marriages.

Social science research on the causes and consequences of adolescent pregnancy and sexuality.

A program to collect data from existing studies, generate additional relevant data, and provide those data to all interested analysts and policymakers.

Studies to determine if oral contraceptive use is particularly hazardous for young teenage girls.

Development of contraceptives appropriate to the specific needs of adolescents.

Attention to the male role in the reproductive process.

Programs in family life and sex education including the entire range of social, emotional, psychological, moral, and ethical aspects of sexual behavior, as well as the use, risks, effectiveness, legal status, and social and emotional consequences of all contraceptive methods.

Programs to assist parents in educating their children and allowing parents to contribute to the development of school or community family life and sex-education courses.

Training programs for family-life and sex-education teachers.

Medical-school curricula, including courses on the physical and emotional aspects of sex and sexuality.

Social-science research in areas such as cognitive and psychological development of children, techniques for the measurement of knowledge, attitudes, and behavior among teenagers, the effects of family life and sex education on adolescents' knowledge and behavior.

Nontraditional approaches to providing family-planning services for adolescents.

CONTRACEPTION

Recommendations include:

The safety of American women and men as a first priority.

A broader range of acceptable methods of contraception for males.

More acceptable methods of fertility regulation for adolescent males and females, for postpartum women, and for women over 35 years of age.

More research on reversible voluntary-sterilization procedures.

Contraceptive methods that do not require assistance from physicians or nurses.

Increases in the acceptability of the current array of contraceptives, especially for teenagers.

Participation of the pharmaceutical industry and public-sector agencies in contraceptive research and development.

IMMIGRATION

The recommendations include:

A comprehensive review of the Immigration and Nationality Act of 1965.

Deportation of immigrants who, within five years of entry, receive welfare and other funds for conditions existing before entry.

No denial of educational opportunities and proper medical care to children of illegal immigrants.

Integration of students in bilingual education programs into the mainstream of American society.

Stricter U.S.-Mexico border enforcement.

Evaluation of Federal capacities in the area of immigration data and analysis.

Study of an expanded legal guest worker program.

An attack on the system of economic imbalance that now pervades the least-developed countries of the world, particularly those of the Caribbean Basin.

Efforts to help sending countries reach their fertility reduction goals and to achieve their family-planning and population objectives.

POPULATION AND DEVELOPMENTAL ASSISTANCE

Mechanisms should be developed to foster:

The systematic and continuous sharing of domestic and international contraceptive research and development results.

The transfer and adaptation of contraceptive technology from the more-developed world to the developing world.

DOMESTIC CONSEQUENCES OF POPULATION TRENDS

The recommendations include:

Investigation of the effects of the population size and growth rate on the well-being of our people.

Updating projections frequently to take into account possible fluctuations in fertility rates.

A wider range of assumptions in preparing long-range projections.

Study of demand for and supply of child-care facilities.

The institution of flex-time and part-time work schedules in all areas of public and private employment.

Utilization of school buildings for the educational needs of the entire population and the provision of other social services.

Programs to increase flexibility in the supply of teachers and to retrain excess teachers for alternative careers.

Improved forecasts of the labor force, particularly the female labor force.

Research on the relative well-being of the baby-boom generation, with a view to predicting the future mobility, earnings, needs, and social impacts of its members.

Investigation of home health care, personal care, and household help for the elderly; single-level housing; and congregate housing arrangements.

Expansion of the national data base concerning the elderly.

Debate on the best responses of the Social Security system to the future pressure of the baby-boom generation's retirement, and efforts to develop thoughtful policies and to prevent crisis-oriented, last-minute, and partial solutions.

Investigation of the impact of present laws and programs on the decisions of individuals and firms to locate or relocate within the United States.

Improvement in the economic outcome of migration by providing information on job opportunities, by developing training programs linked to such opportunities, and by providing transitional assistance to the unemployed who do move to take a job.

Research on the "management" of decline with a view to training administrators to anticipate and plan more efficiently for changes in population size, both upward and downward.[11]

POPULATION POLICY AT THE STATE AND LOCAL LEVEL

States and local communities in the United States also generally lack population policies, but, as we have discussed in several earlier chapters, population processes are often troublesome to local areas. Residential mobility has created particular challenges for local planners, while fertility fluctuations have been the subject of many a school-board meeting. Because of these concerns, some analysis has focused on what options local areas or state planners may have if they want to affect population growth, particularly through control of migration.

One such analysis led to the conclusion that governments have many options available, including at least those in Table 9.6.[12] These include both policies dealing with the allocation of goods and services, and procedural policies, imposing rules by which allocations will be made. For example, tax subsidies to industry, an allocative policy, might encourage more industrial development of an area, causing a net increase in the population from in-migration. On the other hand, procedural policies such as restrictive zoning or subdivision regulations may discourage growth of an area.

While such policies may be successful in local areas, they may not create regional redistribution of population unless they are coordinated with policies in nearby areas. Further, these policies may have other unintended effects, such as increasing housing costs in areas where developments are restricted.

TABLE 9.6   Alternatives for encouraging and discouraging migration at the state and local level

Allocative Policies	Procedural Policies
Tax subsidies to industry	State land use planning
Building infrastructure	Coastal zone management
Educational improvements	Pollution controls
Boosterism	Performance standards
Water allocation	Air and water quality standards
Flood control	Zoning
Land banking	Building and housing controls
Open space programs	Subdivision regulations
Tax ordinances	Growth management
Highway construction	Transfer development rights
	Development moratoria
	Planned unit development ordinances

Source: Adapted from R. Kenneth Godwin, "State Policy Options to Effect Demographic Change," in *Proceedings of the Symposium on Florida's Migration and Population Redistribution Patterns: Planning and Policy Implications,* 1980, p. 103.

POPULATION POLICY IN THE FUTURE

After two decades of increasing concern for population processes both in the United States and in the world as a whole, what is the future likely to hold for population policy? It seems likely that more and more nations will consider and adopt comprehensive demographic goals. The Bucharest Conference does indeed seem to mark a turning point in the nature of these policies as well. In a change from almost exclusive concern with family-planning programs, most nations have begun to incorporate and act on developmental goals as well, seeing these as a legitimate and even necessary part of a population policy.

A testimony to this more comprehensive strategy was the International Conference on Family Planning in the 1980s, held in Indonesia in 1981. While ostensibly a discussion of family-planning programs, and not population policy in general, the summary recommendations of the conference went well beyond the traditional aspects of a contraceptive-distribution program.[13] These recommendations are included on the following pages.

The Conference made recommendations concerning four different strategic approaches to family planning. These were:

1. Programs must do a better job of tailoring their services to the "user's perspective"; that is, they must be more cognizant of the needs and perspectives of the clients they serve.
2. Programs must actively engage local communities in the design and provision of family-planning services and information.
3. Programs should take an integrated approach to delivery of services, including where possible primary health care, or other services such as education, nutrition, or agricultural extension.
4. Programs must make every effort to improve the status and development of women and to get men to take a more active role in family-planning decision-making and practice.

While these recommendations do not, of course, include attention to migration, or even to population growth per se, they are not simply recommendations on how to run effective programs for the distribution of contraception. Rather, they underline the increasing tendency for population policies to be integrated with other kinds of policies in order to be most effective.

The concern with population policy as an integral part of other governmental policies also calls public attention to the fact that population dynamics are crucial aspects of social change and that public understanding of demographic determinants and consequences is therefore an especially meaningful undertaking.

Jakarta Statement

The following statement was approved by the participants and issued at the final plenary session of the International Conference on Family Planning in the 1980s.

During the last ten years a widespread popular demand for family planning information and services has been documented and many family planning programmes have been successfully implemented. One hundred and eighteen governments now support the provision of family planning information and services. However, on the average, less than 50 cents per capita per year is currently spent on family planning and population programmes in developing countries, and the demand for services far outstrips available funds.

Family planning is an essential component of any broad-based development strategy that seeks to improve the quality of life for both individuals and communities. The challenge of the 1980's is to secure the political commitment, financial and human resources to meet the family planning needs of 900 million couples of child-bearing age. The number of these couples in developing countries is projected to double by the year 2000. This challenge was dramatically stated by President Suharto in his opening address to the Conference when he declared, "Successful implementation of family planning programmes will be a key to the survival of the world in the future."

We believe that if the following steps are taken the lives of millions of mothers and children will be saved and the living conditions of individuals in a stabilised world population will be enhanced in the twenty-first century. Eighty million people are added to the global population each year and this annual growth is likely to reach 100 million by the end of the century. We believe that most serious changes may take place in the world environment and the fabric of society if our recommendations are not heeded.

The actions outlined below are of profound practical and moral importance for all mankind and deserve support by political leaders, religious groups, health professionals, development planners and all levels of society throughout the world:

1. *Family planning is a basic human right. Governments should be encouraged to translate this right into realistic policies and programmes which meet the needs of their people.*
2. *A wide range of fertility regulating methods should be made available to men and women, with information on their advantages and disadvantages. These should include reversible methods, and where legally accepted, voluntary male and female sterilisation. Since most currently available contraceptive methods fall short of providing complete protection against unwanted pregnancy, access to safe, modern abortion techniques should also be offered wherever laws permit. Where abortion is not legal, adequate medical care and contraceptive services should be available to those suffering from the consequences of badly performed abortions.*
3. *Family planning services are most effective when they are initiated, managed, evaluated and controlled by people of the community and when they are sensitive to the values, needs and problems of people. Mobilising community resources and generating local leadership will increase programme orientation towards people and self-reliance, therefore community participation in the planning and provision of family planning services must be ensured.*
4. *Family planning is an essential and integral part of economic and social development. Depending on local conditions, family planning can be linked with health, education, rural development, women and youth programmes. It may also be the lead component of a primary health care programme. Population education must be integrated into formal and non-formal educational systems to prepare future generations.*
5. *The non-governmental sector should be fully used to stimulate and complement government family planning programmes.*
6. *Women and men should be equal partners in social development. Programmes to encourage greater participation of women in community and national life will not only benefit women but also encourage smaller families. Family planning programmes should set an example by emphasising programme and policy responsibilities for women. The responsibilities of fatherhood should be emphasised for men.*
7. *Adequate supplies of contraceptives must be assured for all people. Because of rapidly expanding needs in the 1980's,*

planning and action to ensure continued availability of these commodities is necessary, and appropriate centres of manufacture should be established in the developing world.

8. Improved means of fertility regulation are urgently needed. The safety, acceptability and effectiveness of methods must be enhanced. Support for research to improve existing methods and to develop and test new technologies must be substantially increased.

9. There is an urgent need to increase current expenditure in developing countries from an estimated current $1 billion to approximately $3 billion annually in order to meet population and family planning programme needs. Countries providing development assistance should increase their support of population programmes from the current 2.1 per cent of development assistance outlays to at least five per cent. At the same time, the developing countries should substantially increase the proportion of their public expenditures which are allocated for family planning programmes.[14]

NOTES

1.   Steven Isaacs, *Population Law and Policy: Source Materials and Issues* (New York: Human Sciences Press, 1981).

2.   J. Mayone Stycos, "Population Policy and Development," *Population and Development Review*, 3, nos. 1 and 2 (March and June 1977), 103–112.

3.   The summary that follows is based partly on United Nations Fund for Population Activities, *World Population Year Bulletin*, no. 16 (September–October 1974), and partly on the special conference issue of *People*, 1, no. 5 (1974), published by the International Planned Parenthood Federation.

4.   For an enlightening presentation of typical views of the opposing camps, see the exchanges between Pierre Pradervand and R. T. Ravenholt in *Equilibrium*, 2 (April 1974), 12–17.

5.   Population Crisis Committee Circular, September 26, 1974.

6.   United Nations Secretariat, "Concise Report on the Monitoring of Population Policies," *Population Bulletin of the United Nations*, no. 12 (New York: United Nations, 1980).

7.   Ibid., Table 2, p. 23.

8.   Ibid., p. 26.

9.   Bernard Berelson and Jonathan Lieberson, "Government Efforts to Influence Fertility: The Ethical Issues," *Population and Development Review*, 5, no. 4 (December 1979), 581–613.

10. The discussion in this section is based on the Commission's principal report, *Population and the American Future* (Washington, D.C.: U.S. Government Printing Office, 1972).

11. Select Committee on Population, *Final Report* (Washington, D.C.: U.S. Government Printing Office, 1978).

12. R. Kenneth Godwin, "State Policy Options to Effect Demographic Change," in *Proceedings of the Symposium on Florida's Migration and Population Redistribution Patterns: Planning and Policy Implications,"* Florida State University, Tallahassee, 1980.

13. "Family Planning in the 1980s: Challenges and Opportunities," Recommendations of the International Conference on Family Planning, *Studies in Family Planning*, 12, nos. 6 and 7 (June–July 1981) 254–255.

14. *Studies in Family Planning*, 12, nos. 6 and 7 (June–July, 1981), pp. 254–255.

SUGGESTED ADDITIONAL READINGS

A discussion of needed research for the formulation of population policy is found in:

MIRO, CARMEN A. AND JOSEPH E. POTTER, *Population Policy: Research Priorities in the Developing World*. London: Frances Pinter, 1980.

A look back at the impact of the Bucharest Conference is found in:

URGUIDI, VICTOR L., "On Implementing the World Population Plan of Action," *Population and Development Review*, 2, no. 1 (March 1976), 91–99.

Interesting discussion of the morality of various population policies can be found in:

BAYLES, MICHAEL D., *Morality and Population Policy*. University, Ala.: University of Alabama Press, 1980.

MARINGOFF, MARQUE-LUISA, "The Impact of Population Policy upon Social Welfare," *Social Service Review*, 54, no. 3 (September 1980), 201–316.

TECHNICAL SUPPLEMENT NO. 9

Population Law*

Do individuals really have the right to have as many children as they want to? Can citizens really ask to be put to death with dignity if they have incurable diseases? Should individuals be allowed to move anyplace they want, even if those places are already overcrowded? These are the questions of population law, a new field that brings together those areas where law and population dynamics intersect. Neglected by both legal scholars and demographers, the emergence of population law as a legitimate field of inquiry perhaps signals the increased interest by society in regulating demographic processes.

Thus far in population law, fertility has received more attention than have mortality and migration. Population law has examined those laws that directly affect fertility, including contraception, sterilization, abortion, rights of minors to fertility-regulation services, marriage, and divorce. Laws that influence fertility indirectly are also the subject of study, including child welfare, taxation, maternity benefits, health care, women's employment and education, and socioeconomic development.

In the area of fertility regulation, it is easy to see a tension between the power of government to make laws to protect the safety, welfare, health, and morality of its citizenry and the right of individuals to make personal decisions such as those related to childbearing, free from governmental intrusion. Such issues as the U.S. Supreme Court's abortion decision, sterilization policies in India, and economic incentives to restrict childbearing can all be analyzed as a balancing of the competing interests of the states' "police power" and the individual's right to autonomy.

The laws relating to migration reflect both the legal aspects of migration from one country to another—with particular attention to refugees—and also governmental laws and policies concerned with internal migration of people from one area of a country to another. Population law experts might analyze how countries regulate this mobility and the impacts of such regulation on national well-being.

The legal aspects of mortality encompass those laws concerning health care, social welfare, protection of women and children, nutrition, and overall socioeconomic development. Particular attention is given to the right to die with dignity, an issue that is becoming more frequently litigated in the United States.

*Written for this text by Steven L. Isaacs, J. D., Columbia University.

Beyond the specifics of fertility, mortality, and migration, international conventions and national policies can attempt to cover population dynamics as a whole. The 1974 World Population Plan of Action and the Mexican National Population Law of 1976 are but two examples. Thus, the population-related policies of the United Nations, regional organizations, and governments are within the appropriate subject matter of population law.

The sources of population law are varied. They include court decisions, constitutions, legislation, executive orders, administrative regulations, treaties and international agreements, and, in some countries, religious structures. Population law is not concerned only with the laws as written. It also gives attention to the laws as applied. In some countries restrictive laws on the books are not enforced; in others permissive laws are not implemented. Abortion can be an example of either; in Latin America restrictive laws are not enforced, whereas in several European countries permissive laws are not implemented.

In sum, the study of laws influencing population is multidisciplinary, encompassing elements of constitutional law, family health, international law, and criminal law, and merges them with political science, sociology, and public health. It brings these diverse disciplines together into a coherent whole focused on the growth, distribution, and composition of population.

ISSUES SUPPLEMENT NO. 9

Do Nations Have the Right to Implement Population Policies?

Given that nations find that their rates of fertility, mortality, migration, or the size or growth rates of the population are unsatisfactory, do leaders really have the right to institute policies to interfere in these processes?

Some have asserted that it is not only the right of governments to make population policy but it is urgent that they do so. Others have denied that there are any population problems that justify governmental intervention into these most personal aspects of life. Even if population policy is justified, what policies are moral and which are not? Here we offer diverse opinions on whether or not there should be population policies, and if so, what kind.

First, there are the comments of the Ehrlichs, who are fearful of global ruin, and eager to embrace population policy to forestall disaster.

> *Population control is absolutely essential if the problems now facing mankind are to be solved. . . . Political pressure must be applied immediately to induce the United States government to assume its responsibility to halt the growth of the American population. Once growth is halted, the government should undertake to regulate the birthrate so that the population is reduced to an optimum size and maintained there.* (Paul R. Ehrlich and Anne H. Ehrlich, *Population, Resources and Environment.* San Francisco: W. H. Freeman & Company Publishers, 1970, p. 322.)

In a more moderate tone, others have reasoned that it seems to be the legitimate right of states to make population policies to protect the welfare of their citizens. Simone Veil writes:

> *The basic objective of the state is to promote the economic and social development of the country and to ensure the maximum well-being of its citizens. . . . The legitimacy of state concern in the demographic domain would seem to follow directly from that responsibility.* (Simone Veil, "Human Rights, Ideology, and Population Policy," *Population and Development Review,* 4, no. 2, June 1978, 314.)

But some are fearful of governmental intervention into demographic processes. Julian Simon argues:

The likeliest cause of distortion with respect to a "democratic" constitution is a population policy initiated and executed by bureaucrats who impose their own values upon the community while asserting that the rationale for the policy is the "scientific" finding that the policy in question is "provedly" better than noninterference and governmental neutrality with respect to parental decisions about family size. I believe that this danger is great because the officials or legislators may not recognize that their beliefs and values are values and beliefs and are not scientifically proven truths. (Julian Simon, *The Economics of Population Growth.* Princeton: Princeton University Press, 1977, p. 415.)

Another population policy skeptic is Howard Bahr, who has argued that the perception of population as a problem is incorrect and that the formulation of policies to "control" population is unnecessary and dangerous.

. . . many governments have or are preparing to embark on officially sponsored programs of population control. . . . pressures for both worldwide and national programs for population control are mounting. . . . The cry, "the problem is people—too many people," is a seductive one. It is easily understood: one need not admit the complex origins of our troubles; and with the identification of the problem comes a simple remedy—stop having children, and prevent others from having so many children. No matter that the invalid diagnosis may lead to wrong prescriptions. (Howard Bahr, "Values and Population Policy," in Howard Bahr, Bruce Chadwick, and Darwin Thomas, eds., *Population, Resources and the Future: Non-Malthusian Perspectives.* Provo, Utah: Brigham Young University Press, 1972, pp. 285–286.)

A completely different view is held by Michael Bayles, who makes a case for the immorality of *failure* to make population policy. At the end of a lengthy philosophical and moral analysis of population policy, he concludes:

Almost all countries should have a population policy. Some less developed countries may be justified in adopting coercive pol-

icies, at least policies using negative incentives. Developed countries should make substantial sacrifices to aid less developed ones. . . . By our present actions we are failing to fulfill completely our duties to members of the present generation in other countries and to members of future generations. We lack the concern, will, and foresight to meet our duties fully, but we have enough to avoid complete failure to meet them. Perhaps our ultimate commitment is to mediocrity. Unfortunately, mediocrity is not morality. (Michael Bayles, *Morality and Population Policy.* University, Ala.: The University of Alabama Press, 1980, pp. 101–102).

Should governments intervene in population processes? What actions by governments would you consider moral and justifiable?

APPENDIX A
1982 WORLD POPULATION DATA SHEET
OF THE
POPULATION REFERENCE
BUREAU, INC.

PREPARED BY CARL HAUB, DEMOGRAPHER,
POPULATION REFERENCE BUREAU

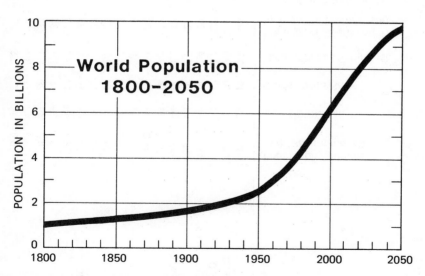

"---the present extended period of rapid population growth is unique when seen from a long-range perspective; it has never occurred before and is unlikely to occur again."
—Jonas and Jonathan Salk, in *World Population and Human Values, A New Reality*

Source: UN Population Division estimates and projections.

Region or Country[1]	Population Estimate, mid-1982 (millions)[2]	Crude Birth Rate[3]	Crude Death Rate[3]	Natural Increase (annual, %)[4]	Population "Doubling Time" in Years (at current rate)[5]	Population Estimate c. 1940 (millions)[2]	Population Projected to 2000 (millions)[6]	Population Projected to 2020 (millions)[6]	Infant Mortality Rate[7]	Total Fertility Rate[8]	Population < Age 15/65+ (%)	Life Expectancy at Birth (years)[9]	Urban Population (%)[10]	Labor Force Engaged in Agriculture (%)[11]	Per Capita GNP, 1980 (US$)[12]
WORLD	4,585	29	11	1.7	40	2,277	6,082	7,678	85	3.9	35/6	60	37	46	$2,620
MORE DEVELOPED	1,152	15	10	0.6	116	798	1,248	1,310	20	2.0	23/11	72	69	13	8,130
LESS DEVELOPED	3,434	33	12	2.1	33	1,479	4,835	6,368	96	4.6	39/4	57	26	60	680
LESS DEVEL. (Excl. China)	2,434	38	14	2.4	29	949	3,635	4,968	108	5.3	42/3	53	32	60	860
AFRICA	498	46	17	2.9	24	175	847	1,344	121	6.5	45/3	49	28	66	770
NORTHERN AFRICA	117	44	13	3.1	22	42	190	265	110	6.5	43/3	54	43	52	1,110
Algeria	20.1	46	14	3.2	22	7.7	36.3	56.8	118	7.4	47/4	56	61	51	1,920
Egypt	44.8	43	12	3.1	22	16.9	66.7	92.4	103	6.0	40/4	55	45	44	580
Libya	3.2	47	13	3.5	20	0.8	6.1	10.0	100	7.4	49/4	55	52	17	8,640
Morocco	22.3	45	14	3.2	22	7.6	37.5	56.5	107	6.9	46/3	55	41	52	860
Sudan	19.9	47	17	3.0	23	6.1	33.1	51.3	124	6.6	44/3	46	25	77	470
Tunisia	6.7	35	11	2.4	29	2.9	9.6	12.4	100	5.6	43/4	58	52	32	1,310
WESTERN AFRICA	150	49	19	3.0	23	47	265	449	140	6.8	46/3	47	22	64	750
Benin	3.7	49	19	3.0	23	1.3	6.6	12.0	154	6.7	46/4	46	14	46	300
Cape Verde	0.3	29	8	2.1	33	0.2	0.4	0.5	82	3.1	36/4	60	20	57	300
Gambia	0.6	49	28	2.1	33	0.2	1.0	1.8	198	6.4	42/2	41	19	78	250
Ghana	12.4	48	17	3.1	22	3.7	21.5	32.7	103	6.7	47/4	48	36	52	420
Guinea	5.3	46	21	2.5	27	2.1	8.8	15.0	165	6.2	43/3	44	19	81	290

Guinea-Bissau	0.8	40	21	1.9	36	0.4	1.2	1.8	149	5.4	38/4	41	24	83	160
Ivory Coast	8.8	48	18	2.9	24	2.5	15.1	25.0	127	6.7	45/2	46	38	80	1,150
Liberia	2.0	50	20	3.0	23	0.8	3.8	6.7	154	6.9	41/4	53	33	72	520
Mali	7.1	52	24	2.8	24	2.3	12.2	21.4	154	7.0	48/1	42	17	87	190
Mauritania	1.7	50	22	2.8	25	0.6	3.0	5.4	143	6.9	42/6	42	23	83	320
Niger	5.8	51	22	2.9	24	1.9	10.4	18.7	146	7.1	43/3	42	13	89	330
Nigeria	82.3	50	18	3.2	22	24.0	149.7	258.1	135	6.9	47/2	48	20	54	1,010
Senegal	5.9	48	22	2.6	27	2.3	9.7	15.3	147	7.1	44/3	42	33	75	450
Sierra Leone	3.7	46	19	2.6	26	1.6	6.1	9.8	208	6.2	41/5	46	25	66	270
Togo	2.8	48	19	2.9	24	1.0	4.8	8.0	109	6.5	50/4	46	17	68	410
Upper Volta	6.7	48	22	2.6	27	3.1	10.9	17.2	211	6.5	44/3	42	8	82	190
EASTERN AFRICA	**141**	**48**	**18**	**3.0**	**23**	**50**	**246**	**402**	**112**	**6.7**	**46/3**	**47**	**15**	**78**	**310**
Burundi	4.4	45	23	2.2	31	2.0	7.0	11.7	122	5.9	44/2	41	2	84	200
Comoros	0.4	44	14	3.0	23	0.1	0.6	0.9	93	6.2	43/3	46	19	64	300
Djibouti	0.5	49	22	2.6	26	0.1	0.7	1.0	—	—	—	—	74	—	480
Ethiopia	30.5	50	25	2.5	28	13.3	50.6	79.6	147	6.7	43/3	40	14	80	140
Kenya	17.9	53	14	3.9	18	4.8	35.4	59.3	87	8.1	50/4	54	14	78	420
Madagascar	9.2	45	18	2.7	26	3.6	15.2	24.2	71	6.4	44/4	46	18	84	350
Malawi	6.6	51	19	3.2	22	2.4	12.0	20.8	172	7.0	44/4	46	10	84	230
Mauritius	1.0	27	7	2.0	35	0.4	1.2	1.5	32.9	3.1	35/4	64	43	29	1,060
Mozambique	12.7	45	19	2.6	27	4.9	20.7	32.7	115	6.1	45/2	46	8	65	270
Reunion	0.5	25	7	1.8	38	0.2	0.7	0.8	20	3.1	35/4	65	41	29	3,830
Rwanda	5.4	50	19	3.0	23	1.7	9.5	15.5	107	7.0	51/2	46	4	90	200
Seychelles	0.1	28	7	2.1	34	(a)	0.1	0.1	26.6	4.2	38/6	65	25	18	1,770
Somalia	4.6	46	20	2.6	26	1.5	7.2	12.0	147	6.1	45/2	42	30	80	—
Tanzania	19.9	46	14	3.2	22	6.8	35.3	59.9	103	6.6	46/4	50	13	82	260
Uganda	13.7	48	16	3.2	22	4.3	23.9	39.0	97	6.2	45/3	52	7	81	280
Zambia	6.0	49	17	3.2	22	2.1	11.0	19.1	106	7.0	46/3	48	40	67	560
Zimbabwe	8.0	47	14	3.4	21	2.1	14.7	23.9	74	6.7	51/2	54	20	59	630

(continued)

Region or Country[1]	Population Estimate, mid-1982 (millions)[2]	Crude Birth Rate[3]	Crude Death Rate[3]	Natural Increase (annual, %)[4]	Population "Doubling Time" in Years (at current rate)[5]	Population Estimate c. 1940 (millions)[2]	Population Projected to 2000 (millions)[6]	Population Projected to 2020 (millions)[6]	Infant Mortality Rate[7]	Total Fertility Rate[8]	Population < Age 15/65+(%)	Life Expectancy at Birth (years)[9]	Urban Population (%)[10]	Labor Force Engaged in Agriculture (%)[11]	Per Capita GNP, 1980 (US$)[12]
MIDDLE AFRICA	**56**	**46**	**20**	**2.6**	**27**	**24**	**90**	**145**	**122**	**6.0**	**44/3**	**45**	**30**	**75**	**370**
Angola	6.8	48	23	2.4	28	3.7	11.3	19.2	154	6.4	44/3	41	21	58	470
Cameroon	8.9	45	20	2.5	28	4.3	13.8	20.9	109	5.7	43/4	46	35	81	670
Central African Republic	2.4	44	22	2.2	32	1.1	3.9	6.6	149	5.9	41/4	42	41	88	300
Chad	4.6	44	24	2.0	35	2.3	6.7	10.4	149	5.9	41/3	40	18	84	120
Congo	1.6	45	19	2.6	27	0.7	2.7	4.6	129	6.0	43/3	46	37	35	730
Equatorial Guinea	0.3	42	19	2.3	30	0.2	0.4	0.7	143	5.7	42/4	46	54	75	—
Gabon	0.7	34	22	1.2	58	0.4	0.9	1.2	117	4.7	34/6	44	36	77	3,680
Sao Tome and Principe	0.1	42	10	3.2	21	0.1	0.1	0.1	49.7	—	—	—	33	—	490
Zaire	30.3	46	19	2.8	25	10.7	50.5	81.3	112	6.1	44/3	46	30	75	220
SOUTHERN AFRICA	**34**	**37**	**12**	**2.5**	**28**	**12**	**55**	**82**	**98**	**5.2**	**42/4**	**59**	**47**	**35**	**2,120**
Botswana	0.9	51	18	3.3	21	0.4	1.6	3.0	83	6.5	46/5	48	29	81	910
Lesotho	1.4	40	16	2.4	29	0.7	2.2	3.3	115	5.9	40/4	50	4	84	390
Namibia	1.1	44	15	2.8	24	0.4	1.8	2.9	120	5.9	44/3	51	45	49	1,410
South Africa	30.0	36	12	2.4	28	10.3	48.9	71.5	96	5.1	42/4	60	50	29	2,290
Swaziland	0.6	48	19	2.8	24	0.2	1.0	1.7	135	6.5	48/3	46	9	74	680
ASIA	**2,671**	**30**	**11**	**1.9**	**37**	**1,245**	**3,528**	**4,368**	**91**	**4.2**	**36/4**	**58**	**23**	**59**	**920**

ASIA (Excl. China)	1,671	35	14	2.1	33	715	2,328	2,968	108	5.0	40/4	53	30	57	1,340
SOUTHWEST ASIA	106	39	12	2.7	26	36	171	250	102	5.6	43/4	58	52	48	3,520
Bahrain	0.4	37	8	2.8	24	0.1	0.7	1.0	53	7.4	41/3	66	78	3	5,560
Cyprus	0.6	22	9	1.2	55	0.4	0.7	0.8	18	2.3	25/10	72	53	35	3,560
Gaza	0.5	51	14	3.7	19	0.3	0.7	0.9	92	—	—	—	90	—	—
Iraq	14.0	47	13	3.4	20	4.0	24.2	37.4	78	7.0	49/4	55	72	30	3,020
Israel	4.1	24	7	1.7	40	1.5	5.6	7.1	14.1	3.5	33/8	73	89	5	4,500
Jordan	3.5	47	10	3.6	19	1.0	6.5	10.3	69	7.3	51/3	60	42	27	1,420
Kuwait	1.5	42	5	3.7	19	0.1	2.9	4.6	39.1	6.1	44/2	69	88	2	22,840
Lebanon	2.7	30	9	2.1	32	1.0	4.0	5.3	41	4.3	43/5	65	76	11	—
Oman	0.9	49	19	3.0	23	0.3	1.7	2.6	128	7.2	45/3	47	7	62	4,380
Qatar	0.3	37	10	2.8	25	(a)	0.4	0.6	53	6.8	45/3	57	86	—	26,080
Saudi Arabia	11.1	46	14	3.2	22	3.2	20.5	32.7	114	7.3	45/3	53	67	61	11,260
Syria	9.7	46	9	3.8	18	2.7	18.7	30.0	62	7.4	48/3	64	47	32	1,340
Turkey	47.7	33	10	2.2	31	17.8	70.7	95.2	123	4.3	40/4	60	44	56	1,460
United Arab Emirates	1.2	30	7	2.3	30	0.1	1.9	2.8	53	6.8	34/3	62	72	5	30,070
Yemen, North	5.5	49	24	2.4	28	2.5	8.8	13.5	162	6.8	45/3	41	10	75	460
Yemen, South	2.0	48	21	2.7	26	0.8	3.4	5.3	146	7.0	46/3	44	37	40	420
MIDDLE SOUTH ASIA	988	38	16	2.2	32	422	1,396	1,797	125	5.5	41/3	49	22	64	230
Afghanistan	15.1	48	23	2.5	27	7.0	26.5	39.3	205	6.9	45/3	40	11	78	—
Bangladesh	93.3	47	19	2.8	25	38.6	149.2	210.1	136	6.3	42/3	46	10	77	120
Bhutan	1.4	43	21	2.2	31	0.7	2.0	2.9	150	6.2	42/3	43	4	94	80
India	713.8	35	15	2.0	35	316.3	967.6	1,196.8	123	5.3	40/3	49	22	64	240
Iran	41.2	44	14	3.1	22	14.0	66.5	95.5	108	6.4	44/4	58	50	37	—
Maldives	0.2	47	14	3.1	22	0.1	0.3	0.4	120	—	45/2	—	11	—	260
Nepal	14.5	44	21	2.3	30	7.7	20.7	28.5	150	6.5	40/3	43	5	93	140
Pakistan	93.0	44	16	2.8	25	31.3	142.7	198.2	126	6.3	46/3	51	28	54	300
Sri Lanka	15.2	29	7	2.2	31	6.0	20.9	25.6	37.1	3.4	39/4	65	27	54	270

(continued)

Region or Country[1]	Population Estimate, mid-1982 (millions)[2]	Crude Birth Rate[3]	Crude Death Rate[3]	Natural Increase (annual, %)[4]	Population "Doubling Time" in Years (at current rate)[5]	Population Estimate c. 1940 (millions)[2]	Population Projected to 2000 (millions)[6]	Population Projected to 2020 (millions)[6]	Infant Mortality Rate[7]	Total Fertility Rate[8]	Population < Age 15/65+ (%)	Life Expectancy at Birth (years)[9]	Urban Population (%)[10]	Labor Force Engaged in Agriculture (%)[11]	Per Capita GNP, 1980 (US$)[12]
SOUTHEAST ASIA	**374**	**34**	**12**	**2.2**	**32**	**152**	**519**	**658**	**86**	**4.8**	**42/3**	**53**	**23**	**65**	**580**
Brunei	0.2	28	4	2.4	29	(a)	0.4	0.5	20.0	5.1	34/3	66	76	—	11,890
Burma	37.1	39	14	2.4	29	16.0	55.1	76.7	101	5.5	40/4	52	27	65	180
Democratic Kampuchea	6.1	38	19	1.9	36	3.0	9.2	11.7	212	—	—	37	14	74	—
East Timor	0.5	44	21	2.3	30	0.5	0.7	1.0	—	4.7	42/3	42	11	60	—
Indonesia	151.3	34	16	1.7	40	70.5	197.1	236.4	93	4.7	42/2	48	20	65	420
Laos	3.7	44	20	2.4	29	1.6	5.5	7.4	129	6.2	42/3	44	15	74	—
Malaysia	14.7	30	7	2.4	29	5.3	21.3	27.5	31	4.4	40/4	63	29	49	1,670
Philippines	51.6	34	8	2.6	26	16.5	77.3	102.8	55	5.0	43/3	61	36	49	720
Singapore	2.5	17	5	1.2	57	0.8	3.0	3.3	11.7	1.8	28/5	71	100	1	4,480
Thailand	49.8	28	7	2.1	33	15.3	69.9	88.0	55	3.7	42/3	61	14	73	670
Vietnam	56.6	37	9	2.8	25	23.0	80.0	102.3	100	5.3	41/4	53	19	71	—

EAST ASIA	1,204	21	7	1.4	50	635	1,441	1,663	41	2.7	31/6	66	22	54	1,330
China[13]	1,000	22	7	1.4	48	530	1,200	1,400	45	2.8	32/6	65	13	61	290
Hong Kong	5.0	17	5	1.2	59	1.8	6.6	7.4	13.4	2.4	27/6	76	90	1	4,210
Japan	118.6	14	8	0.8	92	72.5	126.4	129.0	7.4	1.8	24/9	76	76	9	9,890
Korea, North	18.7	32	8	2.4	29	8.0	27.3	35.8	34	4.5	40/4	62	33	47	—
Korea, South	41.1	19	5	1.4	50	15.5	52.8	62.2	34	2.6	38/4	66	55	34	1,520
Macao	0.3	28	8	2.0	35	0.4	0.4	0.5	—	—	38/5	—	98	—	2,020
Mongolia	1.8	38	9	2.9	24	0.8	2.7	3.7	55	5.4	43/3	62	50	50	—
Taiwan	18.5	23	5	1.8	38	6.0	24.6	29.6	24	2.7	33/4	71	66	30	—
NORTH AMERICA	**256**	**16**	**9**	**0.7**	**95**	**145**	**286**	**308**	**12**	**1.9**	**23/11**	**74**	**74**	**4**	**11,240**
Canada	24.4	16	7	0.8	82	11.7	26.9	33.4	10.9	1.8	24/9	74	76	5	10,130
United States	232.0	16	9	0.7	96	133.1	259.0	274.1	11.8	1.9	23/11	74	74	3	11,360
LATIN AMERICA	**378**	**32**	**8**	**2.3**	**30**	**129**	**549**	**769**	**67**	**4.4**	**40/4**	**63**	**63**	**40**	**$1,910**
MIDDLE AMERICA	**95**	**33**	**7**	**2.6**	**26**	**27**	**142**	**202**	**60**	**5.0**	**43/3**	**64**	**60**	**42**	**1,840**
Belize	0.2	40	12	2.8	25	0.1	0.3	0.3	—	—	49/4	—	49	29	1,080
Costa Rica	2.3	29	4	2.5	28	0.6	3.4	4.6	24.2	3.7	38/4	70	43	36	1,730
El Salvador	5.0	35	8	2.7	26	1.6	8.6	13.5	53.0	5.8	46/3	62	41	41	590
Guatemala	7.7	42	10	3.2	22	2.2	12.7	19.8	70.2	5.7	45/3	58	36	57	1,110
Honduras	4.0	47	12	3.5	20	1.1	7.0	12.0	88	7.1	48/3	57	36	61	560
Mexico	71.3	32	6	2.5	27	19.8	102.3	140.0	56	4.8	42/3	65	67	40	2,130
Nicaragua	2.6	47	12	3.4	20	0.8	4.6	7.9	90	6.6	48/2	55	53	42	720
Panama	1.9	27	6	2.1	33	0.6	2.7	3.6	34	4.1	43/4	70	51	51	1,730

(continued)

Region or Country[1]	Population Estimate, mid-1982 (millions)[2]	Crude Birth Rate[3]	Crude Death Rate[3]	Natural Increase (annual, %)[4]	Population "Doubling Time" in Years (at current rate)[5]	Population Estimate c. 1940 (millions)[2]	Population Projected to 2000 (millions)[6]	Population Projected to 2020 (millions)[6]	Infant Mortality Rate[7]	Total Fertility Rate[8]	Population < Age 15/65+ (%)	Life Expectancy at Birth (years)[9]	Urban Population (%)[10]	Labor Force Engaged in Agriculture (%)[11]	Per Capita GNP, 1980 (US$)[12]
CARIBBEAN	**30**	**27**	**7**	**1.8**	**38**	**14**	**41**	**53**	**62**	**3.7**	**38/6**	**66**	**52**	**39**	**1,540**
Antigua and Barbuda	0.1	16	6	1.1	64	(a)	0.1	0.2	31.5	2.6	—	—	34	—	1,270
Bahamas	0.2	22	5	1.7	41	0.1	0.3	0.4	31.9	3.5	44/4	69	54	—	3,300
Barbados	0.3	17	8	0.8	82	0.2	0.3	0.4	25.1	2.2	31/9	70	4	17	3,040
Cuba	9.8	14	6	0.8	85	4.6	12.3	14.0	19.3	1.9	35/11	73	65	24	—
Dominica	0.1	21	5	1.6	43	(a)	0.1	0.1	19.6	—	—	—	—	—	620
Dominican Republic	5.7	37	9	2.8	25	1.8	8.6	12.4	68	5.4	45/3	60	51	57	1,140
Grenada	0.1	24	7	1.8	39	0.1	0.1	0.2	15.4	—	—	70	—	—	690
Guadeloupe	0.3	19	6	1.3	54	0.2	0.3	0.4	25	2.9	32/6	69	43	18	3,870
Haiti	6.1	42	16	2.6	27	2.7	9.4	13.5	115	6.0	41/4	51	25	67	270
Jamaica	2.2	27	6	2.1	33	1.2	2.9	3.6	16.2	3.7	40/6	70	50	29	1,030
Martinique	0.3	23	7	1.6	43	0.2	0.3	0.4	22	2.9	32/6	69	66	16	4,640
Netherlands Antilles	0.2	29	7	2.2	32	0.1	0.3	0.4	25	—	38/5	—	90	1	4,290
Puerto Rico	3.3	23	6	1.7	41	1.9	4.1	4.9	20.4	2.8	31/7	74	70	6	3,010

St. Lucia	0.1	32	7	2.4	29	0.1	0.2	0.2	33.0	—	—	67	—	—	850
St. Vincent and the Grenadines	0.1	35	7	2.8	25	0.1	0.2	0.2	38.1	—	50/5	67	—	—	520
Trinidad and Tobago	1.1	25	6	1.9	37	0.5	1.4	1.6	26.4	2.7	—	69	49	12	4,370
TROPICAL SOUTH AMERICA	**209**	**33**	**9**	**2.4**	**28**	**67**	**313**	**452**	**74**	**4.5**	**37/4**	**62**	**62**	**37**	**1,890**
Bolivia	5.6	45	18	2.7	25	2.5	9.3	16.7	131	6.6	41/3	49	42	46	570
Brazil	127.7	32	9	2.4	29	41.2	186.7	267.2	77	4.4	42/4	62	63	39	2,050
Colombia	25.6	28	8	2.0	35	9.1	36.3	47.1	56	3.8	41/3	62	60	28	1,180
Ecuador	8.5	42	10	3.1	22	2.5	14.6	23.3	82	6.3	40/3	60	45	45	1,220
Guyana	0.9	28	7	2.1	33	0.3	1.2	1.5	44	3.9	45/4	69	30	22	690
Paraguay	3.3	34	7	2.6	26	1.1	5.4	7.9	47	4.9	44/4	64	40	44	1,340
Peru	18.6	38	11	2.8	25	6.5	30.7	50.2	88	5.3	45/3	57	67	40	930
Suriname	0.4	28	8	2.0	35	0.2	0.6	0.8	36	—	51/4	67	45	18	2,840
Venezuela	18.4	34	5	2.9	24	3.7	28.3	37.4	42	4.3	43/3	66	76	19	3,630
TEMPERATE SOUTH AMERICA	**43**	**24**	**8**	**1.5**	**45**	**21**	**53**	**61**	**40**	**2.9**	**29/7**	**68**	**82**	**14**	**2,360**
Argentina	28.6	25	9	1.6	43	14.2	34.3	39.3	45	2.9	27/8	69	82	13	2,390
Chile	11.5	22	7	1.5	47	5.1	14.9	18.1	37.9	3.0	34/5	66	81	16	2,160
Uruguay	3.0	19	11	0.8	87	2.0	3.4	4.0	37.4	2.8	27/10	70	84	16	2,820
EUROPE	**488**	**14**	**10**	**0.4**	**187**	**377**	**511**	**508**	**16**	**1.9**	**23/13**	**72**	**69**	**16**	**7,990**
NORTHERN EUROPE	**82**	**13**	**11**	**0.2**	**352**	**68**	**84**	**83**	**11**	**1.9**	**22/14**	**73**	**74**	**5**	**9,020**
Denmark	5.1	11	11	0.0	—	3.8	5.1	4.8	8.5	1.5	20/14	74	84	8	12,950
Finland	4.8	13	9	0.4	187	3.7	4.9	4.7	7.7	1.6	21/12	73	62	11	9,720
Iceland	0.2	20	7	1.4	50	0.1	0.3	0.3	5.4	2.5	29/10	76	88	12	11,330
Ireland	3.5	22	10	1.2	57	3.0	4.1	4.9	12.4	3.2	31/11	73	58	19	4,880
Norway	4.1	12	10	0.2	277	3.0	4.1	4.0	8.8	1.7	23/14	75	44	8	12,650
Sweden	8.3	12	11	0.1	990	6.4	8.0	7.4	6.7	1.7	20/16	75	83	6	13,520
United Kingdom	56.1	14	12	0.2	462	48.2	57.1	56.5	11.8	1.9	22/15	73	77	2	7,920

(continued)

Region or Country[1]	Population Estimate, mid-1982 (millions)[2]	Crude Birth Rate[3]	Crude Death Rate[3]	Natural Increase (annual, %)[4]	Population "Doubling Time" in Years (at current rate)[5]	Population Estimate c. 1940 (millions)[2]	Population Projected to 2000 (millions)[6]	Population Projected to 2020 (millions)[6]	Infant Mortality Rate[7]	Total Fertility Rate[8]	Population < Age 15/65+(%)	Life Expectancy at Birth (years)[9]	Urban Population (%)[10]	Labor Force Engaged in Agriculture (%)[11]	Per Capita GNP, 1980 (US$)[12]
WESTERN EUROPE	**154**	**12**	**11**	**0.2**	**423**	**113**	**155**	**142**	**11**	**1.7**	**21/14**	**73**	**81**	**7**	**12,600**
Austria	7.6	12	12	0.0	—	6.7	7.3	6.8	13.9	1.7	21/15	72	54	11	10,230
Belgium	9.9	13	12	0.1	630	8.3	9.9	9.3	11.0	1.7	21/14	73	95	3	12,180
France	54.2	15	10	0.5	147	41.3	56.4	56.6	10.0	2.0	22/14	74	78	8	11,730
Germany, West	61.7	10	12	0.2	—	43.0	59.9	49.3	12.6	1.5	20/15	72	85	6	13,590
Luxembourg	0.4	12	12	0.0	—	0.3	0.3	0.3	11.5	1.5	20/13	71	68	—	14,510
Netherlands	14.3	13	8	0.5	147	8.9	14.9	14.2	8.6	1.6	23/11	75	88	6	11,470
Switzerland	6.3	12	9	0.2	347	4.2	6.2	5.6	8.5	1.5	20/14	75	58	7	16,440
EASTERN EUROPE	**111**	**17**	**11**	**0.6**	**117**	**93**	**120**	**127**	**21**	**2.2**	**23/12**	**71**	**59**	**28**	**4,390**
Bulgaria	8.9	14	11	0.4	192	6.7	9.5	9.8	19.9	2.2	22/11	72	60	34	4,150

Czechoslovakia	15.4	16	12	0.4	169	12.7	16.6	17.9	16.6	2.1	24/12	71	67	11	5,820
Germany, East	16.7	15	14	0.0	—	16.8	16.8	15.3	12.1	1.9	20/16	72	76	10	7,180
Hungary	10.7	14	14	0.0	—	9.3	10.9	10.9	23.1	1.9	21/13	70	46	22	4,180
Poland	36.3	20	10	1.0	71	31.5	40.9	44.7	21.2	2.3	24/10	71	58	30	3,900
Romania	22.6	19	10	0.9	80	15.9	25.6	28.3	31.6	2.5	26/10	70	49	48	2,340
SOUTHERN EUROPE	**141**	**14**	**9**	**0.5**	**131**	**103**	**152**	**156**	**19**	**2.0**	**25/11**	**72**	**61**	**23**	**5,090**
Albania	2.8	29	7	2.2	32	1.1	3.9	4.8	47	4.2	38/5	69	37	61	—
Greece	9.8	16	9	0.7	96	7.4	10.6	11.3	18.7	2.3	23/13	73	65	38	4,520
Italy	57.4	11	10	0.2	462	43.8	57.4	54.1	14.3	1.7	22/12	73	69	14	6,480
Malta	0.4	15	9	0.6	110	0.3	0.4	0.4	15.5	2.0	24/8	71	83	6	3,470
Portugal	9.9	16	9	0.7	100	7.7	11.2	12.1	26.0	2.2	28/10	70	31	27	2,350
Spain	37.9	15	8	0.7	94	26.3	43.3	47.3	11.1	2.2	27/11	73	64	17	5,350
Yugoslavia	22.6	17	9	0.8	87	16.4	25.1	26.1	32.8	2.0	25/9	69	46	39	2,620
USSR	**270**	**18**	**10**	**0.8**	**88**	**195**	**302**	**346**	**36**	**2.3**	**24/10**	**69**	**62**	**17**	**4,550**
OCEANIA	**24**	**21**	**9**	**1.3**	**55**	**11**	**30**	**35**	**42**	**2.7**	**31/8**	**69**	**72**	**20**	**7,600**
Australia	15.0	15	7	0.8	87	7.1	18.0	19.9	11.0	1.9	27/9	73	86	6	9,820
Fiji	0.7	30	4	2.6	27	0.2	0.8	1.0	37	3.6	41/2	71	37	41	1,850
French Polynesia	0.2	30	7	2.3	30	0.1	0.2	0.3	—	—	45/2	—	39	—	6,780
New Zealand	3.1	17	8	0.9	80	1.6	3.8	4.3	12.6	2.1	28/9	73	82	10	7,090
Papua-New Guinea	3.3	44	16	208	25	1.1	5.2	7.5	104	6.3	44/4	50	13	83	780
Samoa, Western	0.2	37	7	3.0	23	0.1	0.2	0.2	40	5.8	48/3	65	20	61	—
Solomon Islands	0.2	44	9	3.5	20	0.1	0.4	0.7	78	6.2	48/3	—	11	—	460
Vanuatu	0.1	45	17	2.8	25	(a)	0.2	0.3	101	—	—	—	—	—	530

GENERAL NOTES

Copyright © 1982 Population Reference Bureau, Inc. Founded in 1929, the PRB is now in its 53rd year of gathering, interpreting, and disseminating information on the facts and implications of national and world population trends. A private, nonprofit organization, it is supported by grants and contracts, individual and corporate contributions, memberships, and sales of publications. It consults with other groups in the United States and abroad, issues publications, and operates information and library services. The PRB also assists the development of population education through formal and nonformal programs.

World Population Data Sheets of various years should not be used as a time series. Changes in data from year to year often reflect improved or revised estimates incorporated in successive editions, particularly in the case of the less developed countries (LDCs).

Figures for regions and the world: Population totals include small areas not listed separately; regional data have been independently rounded and rates and percentages are weighted averages.

Sources of data and estimates: Unless otherwise cited, basic data used come primarily from the following sources: United Nations (UN): *Demographic Yearbook,* and *Population and Vital Statistics Report* of the UN Statistical Office; periodic *Working Papers* and *Assessments* of world population of the UN Population Division. Other sources include: *World Population,* 1979 and 1981 editions, of the U.S. Bureau of the Census, published World Bank estimates and projections, Country Reports of the World Fertility Survey, official country publications, special studies, and direct communication with demographers and statisticians both in the U.S. and overseas. Thanks are expressed to staff members of the International Demographic Data Center and Foreign Demographic Analysis Division of the U.S. Bureau of the Census, the UN's Population Division and Statistical Office, the Office of Population of the U.S. Agency for International Development, and the World Bank for their assistance in obtaining some of the data and estimates. PRB demographer Cary Davis performed computer runs for the Data Sheet and intern Ken Kochanek gave valuable statistical assistance. The PRB assumes responsibility for all figures shown.

Meaning of symbols: Dashes (—) indicate that data or estimates are unavailable (a) indicates a population estimate less than 50,000 in 1940.

NOTES

1.   The *Data Sheet* lists all geopolitical entities with a population larger than 150,000 and all members of the United Nations. Classification of "more developed" and "less developed" regions follows UN practice, whereby "more developed" regions comprise all of Europe, and North America, plus Australia, Japan, New Zealand, and the USSR. All other regions and/or countries are classified as "less developed."

2.   Based upon data from a recent census or by incorporating estimates made by the UN, the U.S. Bureau of the Census, and official country publications.

The estimate for *circa* 1940 was obtained with primary consideration given to the UN *Demographic Yearbook,* 1959 and 1962 editions, the UN's 1963 *Assessment,* and special studies. Due to the many different geographic definitions of countries, boundary changes, and the presumably poorer quality of data in 1940, these estimates are not in all cases completely consistent with population figures given elsewhere on the *Data Sheet.*

3.   Annual number of births or deaths per 1,000 population. For more developed countries (MDCs) with complete registration of vital events, nearly all rates refer to 1979 or 1980. For LDCs, most of whom lack complete registration systems, estimates refer to some point in the late 1970s. "Crude" rates, particularly the crude death rate, can be affected by a population's age composition; thus, the higher death rates for MDCs are a reflection of the larger proportion of the older population in those countries (which is in turn caused by lower birth rates in MDCs).

4.   Birth rate minus the death rate; since the rates were based on the unrounded birth and death rate, they do not always exactly equal the difference between the rates shown on the *Data Sheet.*

5.   Based on the current *unrounded* rate of natural increase (RNI). This column is provided to provide some indication of the potential effect of different levels of the RNI and is *not intended* to forecast the actual doubling of any population. The columns on projected populations in 2000 and 2020 should be consulted for the change in population size actually anticipated under a reasonable set of assumptions regarding future birth and death rates.

6.   For most countries, projected by applying growth rates incorporated in projections prepared by the UN, the World Bank, or the U.S. Bureau of the Census. For many MDCs with low birth rates PRB projections incorporating an assumption of constant fertility were used. Projections to 2020 are, of course, subject to particularly wide margins of error.

7.   Annual number of deaths to infants under one year of age per 1,000 live births in a given year. For countries with data considered to be of good reliability by the UN (complete or nearly complete registration), nearly all data refer to 1979 or 1980 and are shown to one decimal place; these data are from UN *(Population and Vital Statistics . . .*). For countries with incomplete data, the estimates are shown in whole numbers and refer to 1980. They were derived by averaging the estimated rates for the periods 1975–1980 and 1980–1985 given in UN Population Division, *Infant Mortality Rates: Estimates and Projections By Country and Region, 1970–2000* (forthcoming). These estimates are the result of a new study by the Population Division, with financial assistance from UNICEF, which evaluated data from all available registration systems, surveys, and censuses. We thank the Population Division for their assistance.

8.   The total fertility rate (TFR) indicates the average number of children that would be born to each woman in a population if each were to live through her childbearing lifetime (usually considered ages 15–49) bearing children at the same rate as women of those ages actually did in a given year. A TFR of 2.1 to 2.5, depending upon mortality conditions, indicates "replacement level" fertility—the level at which a country's population would eventually stop growing (or declining), leaving migration out of account. Most TFRs shown here refer to the 1975–1980 period for less developed countries and are from the UN Population Division's *1980 Assessment . . .* or survey estimates such as those of the World Fertility Survey. For more developed countries, rates are the latest offi-

cially reported as shown in the sources noted above or from Alain Monnier, *L'Europe et les pay d'veloppés d'Outremer. Données statistiques, Population,* 36:4–5, Institut national d'études démographiques, Paris, 1981 and refer to 1980.

9.   Average years an infant can be expected to live under current mortality conditions. Estimates are primarily those of the UN Population Division or the *Demographic Yearbook* and refer to the mid to late 1970s.

10.   Percentage of total population living in areas termed urban by that country. Estimates refer to some point in the 1970s.

11.   Definition of agriculture also includes hunting, forestry, and fishing; data are from the UN Food and Agriculture Organization, *Production Yearbook,* 1979 or a recent census as given in International Labour Organization *Yearbooks.*

12.   Per capita Gross National Product estimates are *provisional* World Bank estimates, refer to 1980, and are from the *1981 World Bank Atlas.*

13.   Many unknowns regarding China's demography may be clarified when China conducts its first national census in some time during July 1982. Estimates given here represent a departure from previous *Data Sheets* and are largely based upon work done by Judith Bannister of the U.S. Bureau of the Census and in consultation with H. Yuan Tien, PRB's Visiting Scholar.

APPENDIX B
GLOSSARY

The following terms used in the text are listed here with brief definitions and/or explanations as a ready reference for understanding the dimensions of population status and change.

age A fundamental characteristic of population structure, usually expressed in years. For most demographic purposes, age is reckoned as of last birthday, but sometimes it refers to nearest birthday. According to the traditional Chinese method of counting age, a person is one year old at birth and becomes a year older at every Chinese New Year.

aged dependency The ratio of the older members in the population (usually taken to be those 65 and over) to those in the middle age groups (usually those aged 15 to 64).

age-sex pyramid A histogram, or vertical bar chart, that portrays the relative number of males and females in each age category of the population. Because of normal population processes, the chart often assumes the general shape of a pyramid (or triangle), but it can assume a variety of forms.

baby boom A rise in birth rates in the United States and other nations after World War II and including the years 1944 to about 1958.

baby bust A decline in birth rates in the United States and other nations throughout the 1960s.

birthrate (see **crude rate**)

cause of death The reported reason for death, such as a disease, condition, or misfortune. Frequently multiple or joint causes of death are given, and a distinction may be made between immediate and underlying causes.

census Typically a complete canvass of the population of a given area that lists the people and some of their characteristics.

census tract A small area of enumeration in a city or county, usually defined by natural boundaries such as rivers, railroads, or major highways.

cohort fertility The number of births experienced over time by a group of women or men who were born at about the same time (a birth cohort) or married at about the same time (a marriage cohort). (see **period fertility** for a contrasting measure.)

circular migration Repeated movements between home and a distant area, usually for work reasons.

color (see **race**)

components of population change The basic processes of mortality, fertility, and residential mobility, which account for all variations in population size over time.

contraception The prevention of conception; it may involve mechanical, chemical, or surgical means, or the regulation of intercourse to avoid the ovulation stage of the menstrual cycle.

crude rate A ratio of the number of events (births or deaths) reported in an area during a year to the total population of that area.

demographic gap The second stage of the demographic transition, characterized by a high birthrate and a declining or low death rate.

demographic transition A historical transformation of birth and death rates from high to low levels; the decline in mortality precedes the decline in fertility, thus leading to substantial population increase.

demography The scientific study of human populations, including their size, composition, distribution, and characteristics, and the causes and consequences of changes in these factors.

dependency ratio The ratio of the older and/or younger segments of the population to those in the middle age groups. It assumes that the latter generally provide support for the former, and hence the measure is an approximation of the economic burden carried by those in prime working ages. (See also **aged dependency** and **youth dependency**.)

desired family size The number of own children a woman would like to have, irrespective of other considerations (sometimes called **preferred family size**).

development Refers to the process of economic and social change. Developed areas have reached later stages of that process, whereas developing areas are at earlier stages even though they may be progressing.

doubling time The amount of time required for a population to increase to twice its current size.

ecology Adaptation of organisms to an environment. Where humans are the organisms, the term **human ecology** is generally used.

educational attainment The total number of years of formal schooling obtained by an individual.

emigration The departure of persons from a country for places outside the country's borders.

employment status Whether or not an individual is working full-time or part-time (employed) or without a job but looking for work (unemployed) during a specific period of time.

ethnic status Classification of an individual on the basis of race, color, nationality, religion, or other factors in the cultural background.

expected family size The number of own children a woman anticipates having, with due consideration for fecundity or possible inability to control childbearing in conformity with her desires.

family Two or more persons living in the same housing unit who are related by blood, marriage, or adoption. (Related persons who live elsewhere are not part of a family, demographically speaking, although they are often reported in the social-science literature as members of an extended family.) Family units may be further differentiated according to internal relationships (for instance, there may be two or more marital sets within one family).

fecundity The physiological capacity of a woman, man, or couple to produce a living child. Lack of fecundity may be due to physical or biological impairments, prolonged psychological inhibitions, or a surgical operation (sterilization). The term **subfecundity** is used to indicate that the capacity is below normal for any of the foregoing reasons but may not be a permanent condition.

fertility Actual reproductive performance, or the bearing of a live child by a woman.

fertility ratio The number of children under age 5 in a population divided by the number of women aged 15–44 and multiplied by 100.

fetal death A spontaneous abortion, miscarriage, or other development that terminates the life of a fetus (or pregnancy) before birth.

geographic mobility The physical movement of people across space. Can be separated into **residential mobility** (including local mobility and migration) and **temporary mobility.**

gross reproduction rate The average number of live daughters that would be born to each member of a female birth cohort that completes the reproductive cycle, subject to current age-specific fertility rates (that is, those prevailing in the population at the time). The measure is thus a hypothetical one that illustrates the reproductive consequences of a given fertility schedule.

household A group of persons who occupy a housing unit. A household may consist of one person living alone, two or more unrelated individuals, one or more families, or a combination of families and unrelated individuals. In addition to some household members who are not family members, there are some persons (such as military personnel in barracks or residents of homes for the aged) who are not (private) household members.

ideal family size The number of own children a person regards as most suitable for members of a group to have.

immigration   The entry of people into a country from places outside the country's borders. While attempts are made to record all such movements, there are frequent illegal entries that go unrecorded.

infant mortality rate   The ratio of deaths of children under one year of age in a given year to the total number of live births registered in the same year. Often this rate is broken down into deaths during the first month of life (neonatal deaths) and deaths during the remainder of the year (post-neonatal deaths).

in-migration   Movement into a political unit (such as a county) from some place outside the unit.

institutions   The set of behavior patterns and physical settings that characterize basic segments of societal and communal life (for instance, economy, education, polity).

intermediate variables   The factors immediately preceding fertility that affect exposure to intercourse and to conception, and affect gestation and birth.

internal migration   The movement of people within nations intending to change residence and crossing some political boundary, such as a county line.

international migration   The movement of people between nations with an intent to change residence.

labor force   The total number of persons currently employed (at work) and unemployed (not at work but seeking a job). Persons in neither category (such as some housewives, students, and retired persons) are regarded as not in the labor force.

life expectancy   The average number of years of life remaining to each of a group of persons reaching a particular age. At age zero (or birth), this measure, which is derived from a life table, is heavily influenced by survival rates during infancy.

life-span   The maximum possible number of years of life one could expect to live.

life table   A statistical table that converts age-specific mortality information into measures of survival and life expectancy at given ages.

literacy   The ability to read and write in some language.

local movers   Persons who change their permanent residence but do not move across a critical boundary (such as a county boundary in the United States).

logistic curve   A mathematical function that describes fairly well the long-term growth of world (and many national) populations. The curve first rises at an increasing rate, then continues at a decreasing rate, and ultimately approaches an upper asymptote (or levels off).

macro influences   Factors such as economic cycles or wars that operate at global levels, such as regions or societies, that have an impact on population processes.

marital status   Matrimonial condition, typically broken down into single (never married), currently married, divorced, separated, and widowed. Among the currently married, legal and consensual marriages are sometimes differentiated.

marriage squeeze   A relative scarcity in the availability of marital partners for some group produced by demographic processes such as changing birth rates or migration.

medial influences   Group-level influences on population processes, such as those exerted by families or churches.

megalopolis   A group of large metropolitan areas clustered together.

menarche   The onset of menstruation, or bleeding, among women, caused by the (usually) monthly shedding of the uterine lining.

menopause   The cessation of menstruation.

metropolitan area   A central city plus an adjacent area that is socially and economically integrated with the central city. In the United States the standard metropolitan statistical area is composed of one or more contiguous counties, at least one of which has a city of 50,000 or more on which all the counties depend for economic activity.

micro influences   Individual-level impacts on population change, such as biological makeup or decision making.

migrant   A person who changes permanent residence and in the process crosses a critical boundary (for instance, a county boundary in the United States).

migration   Movement of people across a critical boundary (for example, a county boundary in the United States) for the purpose of establishing a new permanent residence.

mobility   (see **geographic mobility**)

modernization   A process involving change away from traditional social, economic, political, and cultural practices of a society or group of people.

mortality   Death of members of a population.

movers   People who change their permanent residence, regardless of the distance or direction of the move; this includes both migrants and local movers.

nationality   A characteristic of individuals based on their country of origin, or sometimes their country of citizenship.

nativity   Place of birth, usually categorized as foreign-born or native to a nation.

natural decrease   An excess of deaths over births in a population during a given period of time.

natural increase   An excess of births over deaths in a population during a given period of time.

neonatal deaths   Deaths that occur during the first month (or four weeks) of life after birth.

net reproduction rate   The average number of live daughters that would be born to each member of a female birth cohort that completes the reproductive cycle, subject to current age-specific fertility and mortality rates. It differs from the gross reproduction rate in that allowance is made for mortality of some of the women before they complete the reproductive cycle.

optimum population The number of people in an area that would best facilitate a balance of people and goods. The goods may be measured in terms of various resources or other economic or social criteria. Overpopulation exists when the population is considered too large for the allocation of goods, and underpopulation means the population is below the optimum balance.

out-migration Movement out of a political unit (such as a county in the United States) to some other place.

period fertility The current reproductive performance of a group of women or men, or their fertility during a particular period of time. (see **cohort fertility** for a contrasting measure.)

population The number of people in a given area at a specified point in time.

population change Alteration in population size, which may be positive (an increase), or negative (a decrease), or a change in population composition or distribution.

population characteristics Items of information that distinguish certain people (such as their education, occupation, and religion).

population composition Classification of people according to basic demographic attributes (for instance, age, race, sex).

population density The total number of people in an area in relation to the size of the area (e.g., the number of persons per square kilometer).

population distribution The geographical spread or arrangement of people over units of land area (for example, between urban and rural areas or among places of different size).

population education The teaching and learning of the dynamics of population change and its causes and consequences. Such education may occur at any level of formal schooling (from primary grades through the university) or in out-of-school situations (through adult education or the mass media).

population equation The formula that indicates that population change in an area between two points in time equals births during the time interval minus deaths during the interval plus or minus the net movement into and out of the area. This formula is sometimes referred to as the **balancing equation of population.**

population estimate An indirect determination of the size or other aspects of a population, usually when direct information is lacking. The calculated number may relate to past, present, or future status.

population explosion A term used in the popular literature to refer to a period of rapid population increase. It is most often used to describe the stage of the demographic transition where the gap between birth and death rates is the greatest.

population growth An increment to the size of a population resulting from the balance of births, deaths, and residential movements (the basic components of population change).

population growth rate A measure of the average annual increase in size of a population over a period of time; for example, in recent years, the world's population growth rate was about 1.7 percent per year.

population mobility (see **geographic mobility**)

population policy Stipulated and understood means by which a government (or other formal organization) intends to influence population change.

population projections Estimates of future numbers of people based on certain assumptions regarding fertility, mortality, and residential mobility.

population redistribution The geographical relocation of people over a period of time as a result of the basic population processes of fertility, mortality, and residential mobility.

population register A continuous registration system in which a card or listing on every member of the population is maintained and updated by local registration officers. A person's record is transferred when the person changes residence.

population size The number of people enumerated or estimated to be in a given area at a specified time.

race A group of persons with certain common physical characteristics that are hereditarily transmissible.

residential mobility The process of movement of people for the purpose of establishing a new residence. It is one of the three basic components of population change.

rural population The number of people living in communities smaller than a given size (for instance, 2,500 in the United States) or in areas not classified as urban; it is often broken down into the number of people living on farms and in rural nonfarm areas.

sample household survey A data-collection mechanism; information is collected from a sampling of households in an area through interviews or questionnaires. Such surveys may be taken periodically and used to provide data during the interval of time between censuses.

school enrollment The number of people enrolled in formal school programs.

sex ratio The number of males per 100 females in a population.

socialization The process whereby persons learn about, and integrate, the norms and behaviors of a group.

sociocultural Refers to the social institutions and other learned behavior, as well as products, of a particular group of people.

socioeconomic status A classification of people or groups on the basis of such social and economic variables as their education level, occupation, income, and place of residence.

stable population A population with constant birth and death rates such that the proportion of persons at each age interval remains constant.

stillbirth A type of fetal death in which the delivery of a child from its mother results in a dead rather than a live birth.

subfecundity (see **fecundity**)

temporary mobility The movement of people which does not result in a change of (permanent) residence. Such mobility includes commuting, vacation trips, shopping trips, business trips, and the like.

total fertility rate The same type of measure as the gross reproduction rate, except that both sons and daughters are included in the numerator of the rate; it therefore provides a good approximation to the average number of children in a population subject to a given set of age-specific birth rates.

unemployment   The situation in which an individual does not have a job but is looking for work during a specified period of time.

urban population   The number of people living in communities larger than a given size (for instance, in the United States, more than 2,500) or in areas closely integrated with such places.

urbanization   Growth in the number of urban places and/or in the size of populations in such places.

urbanized area   A central city of 50,000 or more people and the contiguous densely settled area. It differs from a metropolitan area in that it is composed not of county units but of census enumeration districts. Hence an urbanized area incorporates only urban population, while a metropolitan area may include rural population within the county boundary.

vital registration   A system of recording vital events in a population (typically births, deaths, marriages, and divorces).

youth dependency   The ratio of the younger members of the population (usually those aged 14 or younger) to those in the middle age groups (usually those 15 to 64).

INDEX

NAME INDEX

Robinson, Warren C., 55, 255
Rodgers, G. B., 96
Rosenberg, Harry, 68–69, 95, 157
Rosenberg, Morris, 58
Rosenman, Ray H., 98
Rosenwaike, Ira, 95
Ross, John A., 161
Rossi, Peter H., 202
Rothenberg, Jerome, 202
Ryder, Norman B., 160

Salas, Rafael, 28
Salk, Jonas, 353
Salk, Jonathan, 353
Sanger, Margaret, 163
Sauli, Hannele, 97
Sax, Karl, 122, 158
Scarr, Sandra, 313
Schnore, Leo F., 244–45
Schrier, Arnold, 198
Schultz, Theodore W., 54
Schultz, T. Paul, 55
Schulz, Richard, 98
Select Committee on Population (U.S. House of Representatives), 337–38, 347
Selvik, Arne, 280
Sembajwe, I., 161
Seminatore, Kenneth F., 201
Shapiro, David, 268
Shaw, R. Paul, 200, 202
Sheps, Mindel C., 163
Shorter, Edward, 159
Shryock, Henry S., 28, 199, 248
Sicron, Moshe, 199
Siegel, Jacob S., 28, 95, 248
Sigit, Hananto, 202
Silver, Brian, 295, 312
Silver, Morris, 160
Silverman, Lester P., 246
Simmons, Alan, 200–202
Simon, Julian L., 32, 278, 351
Singer, Paul Israel, 278
Sly, David F., 54, 199, 245–46, 248
Smith, James P., 279
Smith, T. E., 156
Smith, T. Lynn, 22
Soedarmadk, M., 162
Soesastro, Hadi, 311
Solzhenitsyn, Aleksander, 201
Sono, Themba, 312
Spanier, Graham B., 314
Speare, Alden, Jr., 201
Spengler, J. J. 54, 161, 200
Spiegelman, Mortimer, 95, 97–99

ssui-ying, Yang, 279
Stavig, Gordon, 311
Steen, Lynn Arthur, 316
Stewart, John Q., 200
Stilkind, Jerry, 245, 250
Stockwell, Edward, 28, 97
Stoeckel, John, 160
Stolnitz, George J., 54, 96, 98
Stouffer, Samuel A., 199
Strehler, Bernard L., 95
Stycos, J. M., 158, 346
Suchman, Edward, A., 97
Sumbung, Peter Patta, 162
Summers, Gene F., 280
Sun, Te-Hsiung, 312
Surjaningrat, Suwardjono, 162
Sussman, Marvin B., 318–19
Svala, Gertrude, 161
Sweet, J. A., 159
Sweezy, Alan R., 279
Sykes, Zenas, 161

Taeuber, Conrad, 177, 198
Taeuber, Irene B., 22, 54, 177, 198
Tapinos, Georges, 202
Taylor, Carl E., 159
Tayman, Jeffrey, 54, 245
Terhune, Kenneth W., 313
Terry, Geraldine B., 159
Tesfaghiorghis, Habtemariam, 199
Thomas, Brinley, 200
Thomas, Darwin, 351
Thomas, Robert N., 280
Thompson, Warren S., 42, 44, 54
Thornton, Arland, 158, 160
Tien, H. Yuan, 162, 279, 313, 366
Tietze, Christopher, 163
Tisdale, Hope, 244
Todaro, Michael P., 96, 201, 245, 249–50
Treadwell, Mary, 311
Tsui, Amy Ong, 167
Turner, Eba S., 125, 159
Tyler, Carl W., 157

Udry, J. Richard, 157
Uhlenberg, Peter, 313
Unhanand, Manasui, 277
United Nations, 27–28, 53, 55, 67, 71, 77, 89, 95–96, 99, 109, 113–15, 156–57, 201, 229, 231, 245, 247–48, 323, 326–27, 329–32, 346, 364–66
United Nations Food and Agriculture Organization, 366

SUBJECT INDEX